INTERNATIONAL BUSINESS

Wiley Series in Management

INTERNATIONAL BUSINESS

SECOND EDITION

R. Hal Mason
UNIVERSITY OF CALIFORNIA AT LOS ANGELES

Robert R. Miller
UNIVERSITY OF TEXAS AT DALLAS

Dale R. Weigel
INTERNATIONAL FINANCE CORPORATION

JOHN WILEY & SONS, INC.
New York Chichester Brisbane Toronto

Library of Congress Cataloging in Publication Data
Mason, Robert Hal.
  International business.

  (Wiley series in management)
  First ed. published in 1975 under title: The economics of international business.
  Includes index.
    1. International business enterprises—Management.
2. International economic relations. I. Miller,
Robert R., 1929– joint author. II. Weigel, Dale R.,
1938– joint author. III. Title.
HD62.4.M37   1981b   658′.049   80-23483
ISBN 0-471-06217-0

Printed in the United States of America
10 9 8 7 6 5 4 3 2 1

Preface

While preparing this book, a revision of our earlier *The Economics of International Business*, we recognized the many environmental and analytical changes that have occurred since 1975. Accordingly, we substantially revised many chapters, consolidated others, and incorporated some entirely new ones. Although more noneconomic topics are treated here than in the earlier version, the book retains its economics flavor. It is our belief that basic economics tools best serve to explicate and describe both the international environment and the operations of firms participating within it.

The book also retains its three-part division. Part I discusses the international economic environment, beginning with a presentation of the theory of comparative advantage in Chapter 2. The question of different bases for trade between countries is examined and placed in the context of the decision maker within the firm. Chapter 3 discusses balance of payments accounting and how the balance of payments should be interpreted for business purposes. Foreign exchange markets are the subject of Chapter 4, particularly stressing certain aspects of interest to managers, for example, forward market hedging. Chapter 5 describes the institutional structure of the international monetary system and discusses methods of financing balance-of-payments disequilibria. Then, the development of international capital markets is reviewed in Chapter 6 along with a thorough analysis of the important Eurocurrency markets. The book's first major section closes with Chapters 7 and 8, providing an overview of the relationship of national economic policies to international trade and finance and reviewing changes in the international economy plus their implications for business. In Part I, Chapters 6 and 8 are completely new, and major updating characterizes other chapters.

Part II examines decision-making activities in firms with international operations, and it includes chapters on selection of methods of entry into international business, decisions on technology, and the financing and organizing of international businesses. Chapters 9 and 10 are companion pieces, providing perspective on the methods and vehicles firms can use to

v

undertake business abroad. These include exportation and importation of goods and services, licensing of patents and trademarks, and the sale of technological and managerial know-how through technical aid and management contracts. Chapter 10 concentrates on direct investment, the *sine qua non* of the multinational corporation, and examines what motivates managements to engage in investment abroad. Chapter 11 deals with the selection of technology by international firms and also examines the influence of host-country policies in this selection. Methods of evaluating foreign projects are the topic of Chapter 12. Here cost–benefit analysis is described from the viewpoints of both corporation managements and host-country governments.

Part II continues with the discussion in Chapter 13 of methods of financing foreign investments and of sources of financial resources in the world economy. Chapter 14, a new chapter, concentrates on problems of managing the financial assets and liabilities of the multinational company, particularly those problems related to foreign exchange exposure. Organizational interdependence and the choice of organization structure in the multinational firm are treated in Chapter 15, making evident the problems of decentralized control. Part II ends with another new chapter, 16, which reviews staffing and management methods in the multinational corporation.

The book's final section, Part III, explores the interface between the firm's international activities and nation-states, especially those conflicts continually arising. In Chapter 17, many of the criticisms of direct foreign investment and emergent issues surrounding the large international firm are aired. Chapter 18 summarizes the book's discussion and also speculates about the future of multinational enterprises.

The book in its earlier form has been used in a variety of academic settings. Some professors have taught courses with such titles as "Introduction to International Business" and found the book to be a more analytical approach to the subject than is available in other textbooks. Other instructors have been involved in courses related to business policy, especially in international business, while still others have used the book successfully in international economics courses emphasizing the multinational enterprise. The earlier edition was used at both undergraduate and graduate levels, generally with supplementation for graduate students, from reading lists following each chapter. Usually, these citations are a little more advanced than the text material and give users an opportunity to broaden their background in the subject area.

We hope this book transmits some of the excitement we have found in the study of international business, for of all the topics normally taught in a business school, none is more dynamic and important than the study of international management. We have attempted to transmit the basic intellectual notions and practical facts in an interesting fashion, hoping to stimulate students to seek further knowledge through more specialized study in other internationally related business courses.

Again, we have received generous assistance from a variety of individuals. Detailed reviews were provided by Professor F. Glenn Boseman, Temple University; Professor L. Jacque, University of Pennsylvania; and Professor Joseph C. Miller, Indiana University. Their efforts were scrutinized carefully and are greatly appreciated. Dr. Janice J. Miller served faithfully and patiently as the author's demanding editorial reviewer. Later, after the manuscript was submitted, Joseph Marcelle, our editor, forced us back to the typewriter with a series of suggestions for improving the exposition and organization of the text. His instincts were unerring. Finally, typing chores were performed diligently and accurately by Mrs. Ellie Magnuson at the University of Texas at Dallas, by Carol Pincus at the University of California at Los Angeles, and by Olivia Dyhouse at the International Finance Corporation in Washington, D.C. All are to be commended for doing truly excellent work on a tight schedule.

R. Hal Mason
Robert R. Miller
Dale R. Weigel

Contents

CHAPTER 1

Introduction to International Business

Almost everyone is affected, directly or indirectly, by the functioning of the international economy. Most people consume imports, while some work for firms that export to other countries. Some actually are engaged in one or another aspect of international business, such as writing bills of lading, banker's acceptances, or forward contracts for foreign exchange; yet few people view such transactions in the perspective of an integrated international economy that connects economic agents in one country with those in other countries. It is the purpose of this book to provide that perspective, not only for those who actually make such decisions, but for others as well.

One need not be engaged directly in international business to appreciate how it affects everyday life: without it, each of us would be worse off. Many Americans would find it disconcerting, if not a downright hardship, to be denied access to fine French wines, Scotch whiskey, English bicycles, German and Japanese automobiles, Italian and Spanish shoes, Brazilian and Colombian coffees, Central American bananas, Philippine plywood, Indian cashew nuts, Swiss watches, Hong Kong textiles, Ceylonese tea, Jamaican bauxite, Venezuelan oil, and a host of other items we obtain only through international trade. It is through our own exports of goods and services, moreover, that we earn the foreign currencies needed to buy the imported goods and services we desire. Few persons see this connection, but it is a basic truth that will be stated and restated in various contexts throughout this book.

1

International business has been expanding at a rapid rate. Exports of goods and services increased from only 5 percent of U.S. domestic production in 1960 to 8 percent in 1977. An even more rapid increase in the share of production taken by exports occurred in the other advanced industrial countries (from 12 percent to 18 percent). International investment likewise increased rapidly (see Chapter 6). As a result, international business now accounts for over half of the profits of several of the largest New York banks, and U.S. industrial corporations count on international business for an important share of their sales and profits. It is clear that any student of business should have a basic understanding of how the international economy functions and how business decisions may be made within the world economy.

That world is full of diversity. Just as there are no two individuals who are identical, so, too, there are no two countries that are identical. They differ in many ways. Among other features, they differ in size and age composition of population, in language, income levels, extent of urbanization, currencies, climate, resource availabilities, trade and investment regulations, tax laws, and the structure of consumption. Out of this great diversity, opportunities arise for trade and investment by business firms. However, there is also order in this diversity, providing patterns of development, trade, and investment that can be used in the analysis of business decisions.

The following sections of this chapter provide a brief tour of the world economy, stopping to examine the economic characteristics of countries, world trade, and international investment. The chapter concludes with a brief preview of the remainder of the book.

DISTRIBUTION OF WORLD INCOME

A world traveler would know from first-hand experience that income and wealth are not evenly distributed among the nations of the world. There are a relatively few advanced countries whose citizens are substantially better off than the vast majority of the world population. Table 1–1 shows that the world now contains over 4 billion people. The industrialized countries (which include the United States, Canada, Western European countries, Australia, New Zealand, and Japan) contain only about 15 percent of the world's population but produce (and consume) about 65 percent of its goods and services. Projections of the World Bank indicate that this relative imbalance is not likely to change much by 1990. Per capita incomes in the industrial countries are 40 times the per capita income in the very poor countries of Africa and Asia (including such countries as India, with a population of over 600 million and an average per capita income of $150

Table 1–1 Structure of Population, Production, and Exports

	Population (millions) 1976	GNP Per Capita (U.S. $) 1976	Percentage Share in World Total					
			Population		Gross Domestic Product		Exports	
			1976	1990	1976	1990	1976	1990
Industrial countries	661	6,414	16.2	13.6	64.6	62.5	63.9	65.8
Capital surplus oil exporters	12	6,691	0.3	0.4	1.1	1.4	5.7	3.0
Centrally planned economies	1,276	1,061	31.3	29.2	19.0	15.9	7.8	7.0
Developing countries	2,129	538	52.2	56.8	15.3	20.2	22.6	23.2
Low income	1,193	157	29.3	31.6	2.5	3.1	1.9	1.7
Africa	156	158	3.9	4.4	0.3	0.3	0.4	0.4
Asia	1,037	157	25.4	27.2	2.1	2.7	1.5	1.3
Middle income	936	1,022	22.9	25.2	12.8	17.1	20.6	21.5
East Asia/Pacific	162	671	4.0	4.1	1.4	2.7	4.3	6.3
Latin America	320	1,159	7.8	8.7	5.0	6.6	5.7	5.7
Middle East/North Africa	142	989	3.5	4.0	1.8	2.2	4.4	3.7
Sub-Sahara Africa	190	523	4.6	5.6	1.5	1.6	2.9	2.0
Southern Europe	122	1,948	3.0	2.8	3.2	4.0	3.3	3.8
Total	4,078	1,673	100.0	100.0	100.0	100.0	100.0	100.0

Source: World Bank, *World Development Report 1979* (Washington, D.C.: World Bank, August 1979), Table 12, page 12.

per person per year, and Kenya in Africa with a population of 15 million and a per capita income of $270 per year). The countries of Latin America (such as Brazil and Mexico) are considerably better off than the low-income countries just mentioned, with average annual per capita incomes of over $1,000. The countries of Southern Europe (including Greece and Spain) are at the upper end of the developing-country spectrum and are about to move into the ranks of the advanced industrial countries.

It is difficult to conceive how life could be sustained at the average annual income of the poorest developing countries. If we think what $160 would have bought in the United States in 1976 (the data in Table 1–1 are in 1976 dollars), it is clear that it would not have been possible to live on such a low income. Yet, not only is life sustained in these low-income countries, but, in fact, populations have been expanding at a rapid rate.

This seeming paradox exists because income per person is not a sound indicator either of relative well-being or of the goods and services that individuals are able to command. Relative well-being may differ between countries having the same income per capita because the amount of income required to obtain a given level of consumption differs. For example, in a tropical climate, housing is less costly than in a frigid climate. Simply put, in a colder climate more insulation and more heat are required for human comfort. Also, in countries at low levels of per capita income, services are relatively less costly than in countries at high levels of per capita income. If per capita income of the poor countries is adjusted for this last factor, it is seen in Table 1–2 that the per capita income of India is 7 percent of the per capita income of the United States, rather than only the 2 percent obtained by converting the per capita income of India, expressed in rupees, to dollars at the existing exchange rate. The adjusted incomes of all the countries shown in Table 1–2 are closer to the U.S. income than would be suspected by simply converting their per capita national product to dollars at the exchange rate in effect at the time (1970).

Even with these adjustments, it is still difficult to conceive of living on an income that is only 7 to 10 percent of that obtained by the average person in the United States. The problem is compounded by the fact that the distribution of income is more uneven in many developing countries than is the case in the advanced industrial countries. Table 1–3 shows that in the Philippines, Peru, Turkey, Mexico, and Brazil, the poorest fifth of the population gets less than 5 percent of the national income of the country. Unfortunately, that is also true in the United States, where average incomes are, of course, much higher. Nevertheless, on average, the distribution of income is much more even in the advanced industrial countries, including the United States, than in the poor countries. In the advanced countries, the 20 percent of the population with the highest incomes usually takes less

Table 1–2 Comparisons of Per Capita Gross Domestic Product: 1970

Indices	Kenya	India	Colombia	Hungary	Italy	U.K.	Japan	Germany	France	U.S.
Per capita product converted to dollars at exchange rates (U.S. $ = 100)	3.00	2.04	6.85	21.6	35.4	44.6	41.7	64.2	60.4	100.0
Per capita product valued at international prices (U.S. $ = 100)	5.72	7.12	15.9	40.3	45.8	60.3	61.5	74.7	75.0	100.0

Source: Irving Kravis, et al., *A System of International Comparisons of Gross Product and Purchasing Power* (Baltimore: Johns Hopkins, 1975), Table 1, page 8.

Table 1–3 Percentage Shares of Household Income, by Percentile Groups of Households

Country	Year	Lowest 20%	2nd 20%	3rd 20%	4th 20%	Highest 20%	Highest 10%
India	1964–65	6.7	10.5	14.3	19.6	48.9	35.2
Sri Lanka	1969–70	7.5	11.7	15.7	21.7	43.4	28.2
Philippines	1970–71	3.7	8.2	13.2	21.0	53.9	N.A.
Korea	1976	5.7	11.2	15.4	22.4	45.3	27.5
Peru	1972	1.9	5.1	11.0	21.0	61.0	42.9
Turkey	1973	3.4	8.0	12.5	19.5	56.5	40.7
Mexico	1977	2.9	7.4	13.2	22.0	54.4	36.7
Taiwan	1971	8.7	13.2	16.6	22.3	39.2	24.7
Brazil	1972	2.0	5.0	9.4	17.0	66.6	50.6
Yugoslavia	1973	6.5	11.9	17.6	24.0	40.0	22.5
United Kingdom	1973	6.3	12.6	18.4	23.9	38.8	23.5
Germany	1973	6.5	10.3	15.0	22.0	46.2	30.3·
United States	1972	4.5	10.7	17.3	24.7	42.8	26.6
Sweden	1972	6.6	13.1	18.5	24.8	37.0	21.3

Source: World Bank, *World Development Report 1979* (Washington, D.C.: World Bank, August 1979), Annex Table 24.

than 45 percent of total income, whereas in many poor countries, the highest-income segment of the population often takes 55 percent of total income.

There are some exceptions to this general pattern, however: Korea, Taiwan, and Yugoslavia, among market-oriented developing countries, have combined rapid economic growth with a distribution of income that is as even as that of the more advanced countries. They have done so by pursuing a development strategy that started with a redistribution of assets: both Korea and Taiwan carried out major redistribution of land in the early 1950s, and Yugoslavia, of course, underwent a socialist revolution before adopting a system of market socialism. The three countries followed redistribution of assets with a major effort to increase education, particularly universal primary education. By doing so, they have achieved high levels of adult literacy and have produced a relatively well-educated labor force. Korea and Taiwan then pursued a development strategy that emphasized expansion of labor-intensive industries, thus creating widespread employment opportunities. High levels of employment led to relatively high incomes in even the lowest-income segments of the population.

Other poor countries, including India and Sri Lanka, also have achieved relatively even income distribution; nevertheless, low average incomes and uneven distribution of that income have combined to condemn a large portion of the population of the world to a life of absolute poverty. The World Bank has estimated that 40 percent of the population of the developing world, or 800 million people, live in a state of absolute poverty: "a condition of life so characterized by malnutrition, illiteracy, disease, squalid surroundings, high infant mortality and low life expectancy as to be beneath any reasonable definition of human decency."[1]

Even under a relatively optimistic scenario of growth in the gross domestic product of developing countries of 5.5 percent per year, it is projected that 600 million people will still live in absolute poverty in the developing countries in the year 2000. This is a scenario that can be altered only by more rapid growth and by a massive effort to bring the benefits of growth to the poorest of the poor.

This is not impossible, for there has been a measure of success in the development effort in the second half of the 1960s and the 1970s that previously had not been thought possible. Middle-income developing countries such as Brazil, Turkey, and Korea realized growth in their domestic production of almost 7 percent per year between 1965 and 1974. While balance-of-payments difficulties have restrained growth of these countries after 1974, they still are achieving 5 percent annual increases in production. The low-income countries, meanwhile, did not match the high growth rates of middle-income countries, and fell further behind. Recently, however, their growth has accelerated, particularly with improved performance in India.

The economic growth of nations has been associated with far-reaching changes in their social and economic structure that, when viewed as a whole, have tended to follow some broad patterns. As pointed out by the World Bank, "The central feature is the increase in the share of industry in total output, and the decline in the share of primary production (agriculture and mining) as countries develop. The poor countries of Asia and Africa are in the early part of the transformation, followed by the middle income nations of Latin America, East Asia, and the Mediterranean region, while in the industrialized countries, where income per capita is highest, the rising share of services in the economy is accommodated by stabilization and eventual decline in the share of industry."[2] This pattern arises because of the accumulation of capital and skills and changes in the composition of

[1]Robert S. McNamara in the Foreword to the World Bank, *World Development Report 1978* (Washington, D.C.: World Bank, 1978).

[2]World Bank, *World Development Report 1979* (Washington, D.C.: World Bank, 1979), page 44.

demand. For example, food consumption falls from 40 percent of aggregate demand in an economy at $150 per capita to less than 20 percent of the total at $3,000 per capita, and this decline helps explain the falling share of primary production. The evolving composition of production is reflected in the sectoral employment of the labor force—as the share of labor employed in agriculture falls—with a lag. The complete transformation of the agricultural sector to modern commercial agriculture takes a very long time, and only now is being completed in Western Europe.

The pattern of transforming poor agricultural societies into modern industrial economies will vary with the size and resource endowment of the country. The process will be slower in small countries and in those that have abundant natural resources. Resource-rich countries may achieve growth by exploiting their resources and are under less pressure to pursue a rapid industrial transformation.

There are also many patterns in the commodities a country is likely to export and import, as well as in the countries with which it is most likely to trade. A country's international trade is largely a reflection of its industrial structure and, in turn, its level of development. Countries at low levels of development tend to be heavily dependent for their export trade on primary commodities and intermediate goods. Their imports, on the other hand, are heavily oriented toward finished manufactured goods. Countries that are industrially advanced tend to export advanced manufactured goods and sophisticated services such as financing, insurance, and transportation. Their imports tend to be heavily oriented toward fuels, minerals, raw materials, and a diversity of manufactured goods.

There are also patterns in the growth and development of institutions to be found in various countries, although organization of financial, goods, and labor markets is also a function of cultural variables and even historical accident. It does tend to be true, however, that institutions, their functions, and their diversity are closely related to level of economic development, composition of output, level of urbanization, and size of market. The many-layered structure of financial institutions found in the United States is the exception rather than the rule. Much the same can be said of the available marketing institutions and distribution channels. For example, the chain-store system so common in the United States is a recent development in Europe. In developing countries, one seldom if ever finds this form of marketing and distribution. In the field of finance, the United States has many different types of specialized institutions. For instance, many savings institutions receive deposits (or premiums in the case of life insurance) that can be invested in long-term commitments. Thus, the United States has developed a highly diversified market for equity issues, bonds, mutual fund shares, and the like. This is not so much the case in Europe, and, in developing countries, long-term markets are even less in evidence. Differences in financial institutions found in various country groups are discussed in more detail in Chapter 14.

Development of highly diversified financial and marketing systems calls for, among other things, a large market, high levels of economic activity, and highly developed systems of communication. It might be expected that the enlarged European Common Market, with a population of nearly 350 million and a gross national product on the order of $660 billion, would begin to look increasingly like the United States with respect to institutional structure, as integration of financial and other markets takes palce.

WORLD TRADE

The value of world trade currently is over $1,300 billion per year and has been growing at a nominal rate of almost 20 percent per year. The rapid growth in the dollar value of the world trade has been due to a combination of real growth, inflation, and depreciation of the dollar relative to other currencies. In 1978 it is estimated that the nominal value of trade grew by 15 percent and that approximately one-third of that growth was due to an increase in the volume of trade. Another one-third was due to price inflation, and the final one-third was due to the depreciation of the dollar relative to other currencies: the dollar value of trade that actually was denominated in German marks and Japanese yen increased in dollar terms simply because a given quantity of marks and yen were worth more dollars in 1978 than previously.

International trade continues to be dominated by the advanced industrial countries. Looking back at Table 1–1, it can be seen that these nations account for about 65 percent of world exports, which is similar to their share of world product. Table 1–4 provides some information regarding the direction of international trade among several major trading areas. The advanced market economies account for 70 percent or more of the trade in most instances. This merely means that the developed industrial countries are the major customers for virtually everything that is traded internationally.

Proximity is important in determining who a country's major trading partners are to be. Approximately 51 percent of exports of the members of the European community is with other members. About 59 percent of Germany's trade takes place with the United Kingdom, Switzerland, France, Sweden, the Netherlands, Italy, Denmark, Belgium, and Austria. All of these countries are virtually contiguous with Germany's borders. Much the same can be said of France. The United States took 68 percent of Canadian exports and supplied the same percentage of Canadian imports

Table 1–4 Distribution of World Trade (1973–1978 Average)

Exports from:	Amount (billions U.S. $)	Exports (in percent) to: World	Developed	Developing	Latin America	Africa	Middle East	Other Asia	Centrally Planned
Developed countries	630.7	100	71.6	22.6	5.9	5.2	5.4	6.0	5.3
Developing countries	231.8	100	71.9	22.6	8.0	2.5	3.4	8.6	4.2
Latin America	50.4	100	67.6	23.6	19.5	2.0	1.1	1.0	7.8
Africa	39.1	100	82.5	12.0	5.3	4.4	1.3	1.0	4.8
Middle East	84.0	100	72.5	22.8	6.5	1.7	4.9	9.5	2.4
Other Asia	57.1	100	66.9	29.4	2.2	2.7	4.9	19.2	3.1
Centrally planned economies	89.7	100	28.4	16.3	3.1	2.4	3.5	3.9	54.7

Source: World Bank, *1979 Annual Report* (Washington, D.C.: World Bank, 1979), Statistical Annex Table 2.

in 1978. The pattern is similar but less pronounced for Mexico, which also shares a border with the United States. While geographic proximity is important, it must be supported by efficient transportation and communications systems. It is notable that Latin American countries, despite geographic proximity to one another, do not trade substantially with one another because they are not closely linked by land-transport systems.

A few countries account for most of the exports of the world. The United States and Germany each exported between 115 and 120 billion dollars of goods in 1977, which was in each case about 12 percent of total world exports. The 10 largest exporters accounted for 65 percent of total world exports, as is shown in Table 1–5. The dominance of international trade by such a small group of exporters has been a major concern among countries not in this exclusive club; however, the dominance of the largest exporters has declined since 1970, when the 10 largest exporters were responsible for over 70 percent of world exports. A new country moved into the top 10 in the 1970s: with the increase in oil prices, Saudi Arabia became the eighth largest exporter. Other developing countries also became major exporters: Brazil, Spain, Nigeria, Iran, Indonesia, and Korea, all with exports in excess of $10 billion.

Table 1–5   The Largest Exporters in 1977

	Merchandise Exports (billions U.S. $)	Exports of Goods & Services as Percentage of GDP	Percentage of World Trade
United States	119.0	8	11.7
Germany	117.9	26	11.6
Japan	80.5	14	7.9
France	63.6	20	6.2
United Kingdom	57.5	31	5.6
USSR	45.2	N.A.[a]	4.4
Italy	45.1	26	4.4
Netherlands	43.7	54	4.3
Saudi Arabia	43.5	78	4.3
Canada	41.4	24	4.1
World Total	1,017.4	——	100.0

[a]N.A. = Not available.
Source: World Bank, *World Development Report 1979* (Washington, D.C.: World Bank, 1979), Annex Tables 5, 8; and U.N., *Monthly Bulletin of Statistics* (New York: United Nations, May 1979), Table 52.

Oil became the single most important commodity traded in the world in late 1973, due to the increase in oil prices. Table 1–6 shows that fuels constituted almost 20 percent of world trade in 1977, up from 11 percent in 1973, and less than 10 percent in 1969. It was possible for the OPEC countries to raise the price of oil so dramatically in 1973 because the long-term growth of consumption of energy had outstripped production, especially in the advanced industrial countries but also in the oil-importing developing countries. Table 1–7 shows that consumption of energy had grown by 4.1 percent per year between 1960 and 1976 in the advanced industrial countries, while energy production of all types had grown by only 2.6 percent per year; consequently, these countries had a deficit of 23.3 million barrels of oil equivalent per day in 1976, and that deficit was projected to grow to 39 million barrels equivalent per day by 1990.

Even though oil is the single most important traded commodity, 60 percent of world trade is still manufactured products, a share that is down only slightly from 1973. The declining share of manufactured products has been in the more simple products such as textiles, while machinery and transport equipment have maintained their share at over 28 percent of the total. The share of food and raw materials has also fallen and amounted to less than 20 percent of the total in 1977. Thus, about 20 percent of world trade is now in oil and other fuels, another 20 percent is in food and other raw materials, and 60 percent is in manufactured products.

These trends in the commodity composition of world trade would tend

Table 1–6   Commodity Composition of Trade

	1973		1977	
	Amount (billions U.S. $)	*Percentage*	*Amount (billions U.S. $)*	*Percentage*
Total	574	100.0	1,124	100.0
Food, beverages, tobacco	78	13.6	126	11.2
Crude materials except fuels	58	10.1	85	7.6
Fuels	63	11.0	221	19.7
Chemicals	40	7.0	78	6.9
Machinery and transport equipment	164	28.6	318	28.3
Other manufactured goods	159	27.7	276	24.6
Textiles	23	4.0	34	3.0
Clothing	12	2.1	24	2.1
Iron and steel	28	4.9	47	4.2
Other goods	12	2.1	20	1.8

Source: U.N., *Monthly Bulletin of Statistics* (New York: United Nations, May 1979), Special Table D.

Table 1–7   Energy Balances: 1976 (million barrels a day of oil equivalent) [a]

	Production	Consumption	Annual Growth Rate 1960–1976 Production	Consumption
Developing countries	26.5	16.8	6.7	6.7
Net oil exporters	20.0	4.2	7.2	6.9
Net oil importers	6.5	12.6	5.2	6.7
Capital surplus oil exporters	16.1	0.8	10.7	13.9
Industrialized countries	46.5	69.8	2.6	4.1
Centrally planned economies	37.9	34.4	4.4	4.3
Others	N.A.[b]	5.3	____	____
Total	127.0	127.1	4.5	4.5

[a]Includes coal, lignite, crude petroleum, natural gas, hydro and nuclear electricity expressed in barrels per day of oil equivalent.
[b]N.A. = Not available.
Source: World Bank, *World Development Report 1979* (Washington, D.C.: World Bank, 1979), Table 24.

to hurt the oil-importing developing countries, which have in the past relied on exports of food and raw materials to finance imports of fuel and manufactured products. In fact, these countries *have* been hurt by the massive real increases in the price of oil that occurred in the 1970s; nevertheless, their problem has been alleviated somewhat by a new phenomenon—the developing countries are emerging as exporters of manufac-

Table 1–8   Exports of Manufactured Products from Developing Market Economies (billions U.S. $)

	1973	1977	Percentage Increase
Chemicals	1.8	4.0	222
Machinery and transport equipment	4.6	11.9	259
Other manufactured goods	20.4	37.9	180
Textiles	4.2	6.4	150
Clothing	3.8	8.7	229
Iron and steel	1.0	2.0	200
Non-ferrous metals	4.4	5.7	129
Other metal products	0.5	1.4	280
Total exports, non-OPEC Developing countries	68.0	137.7	202

Source: U.N., *Monthly Bulletin of Statistics* (New York: United Nations, May 1979), Special Table D.

tured products! These manufactured products now provide almost 40
percent of total exports of the developing countries that are not oil exporters
(see Table 1–8). Their manufactured exports have been concentrated in
simple items such as textiles, but the most rapid growth has taken place in
exports of garments and in products classified as machinery and transport
equipment. In reality, most of these latter products are electronic subassemblies and finished electronic products that are classified as electrical machinery in the international trade statistics. Textile exports from developing
countries have not kept up with the growth of other manufactured products,
perhaps as a result of import restrictions applied by the advanced industrial
countries.

Everyone has seen shirts from Korea or Colombia, calculators from
Taiwan or Thailand, and shoes from Uruguay and Brazil. Manufactured
products offer promise of future export growth that is not present in the
case of most raw materials; we may see automobiles as well as shirts from
developing countries. Whether this growth is achieved will depend on the
policies of both the exporting and the importing countries. Later chapters
will deal with the effect of government policies on the quantity and
composition of world trade.

INTERNATIONAL INVESTMENT

International trade and international investment are the principal means by
which international business is conducted. International investment occurs
when an individual, a firm or other institution, or a government in one
country acquires an asset in another country. Chapter 6 contains a detailed
description of the forms international investment takes and the magnitudes
involved.

International investment has a long history stretching back to ancient
times. In the nineteenth century the United Kingdom was the main source
of international investment, and the *stock* of assets held by citizens in the
United Kingdom and other investing countries reached $44 billion by 1913.
The stock continued to grow during the 1920s, when the United States
emerged as a major international investor, but declined in the first part of
the 1930s in the face of worldwide depression and resulting loan defaults.
Investment recovered only toward the end of the decade, to reach $55
billion in 1939, a net growth of only $11 billion from 1913. The gross value
of long-term international investment outstanding then fell during the
Second World War, to $35 or $40 billion, as the main creditor nations (the
United States and United Kingdom) used their foreign assets to support the
war effort.

After the war, international investment increased rapidly, but in so many different forms that it is difficult to compile a comprehensive total for all investing countries. By the end of 1978, U.S. citizens, firms, and Government held assets valued at $450 billion in foreign countries. At the same time, foreign investors held assets of almost $375 billion in the United States.

The different forms that foreign investment may take are seen in Table 1–9. (International investments may be classified in a number of different ways and will be discussed in more detail in Chapter 6.) In Table 1–9, foreign assets held by the U.S. Government are distinguished from those held by private citizens and firms. U.S. Government reserve assets (line 2a) are those that can be used to support the value of the dollar on foreign exchange markets and include Government holdings of gold, foreign currencies, and assets in the International Monetary Fund, convertible to foreign currencies if necessary. Other Government assets (line 2b) include long-term loans made to foreign governments, such as loans made under the foreign aid program. Assets held abroad by private citizens (line 2c) include direct investments (line 2ci), holdings of stocks and bonds issued in foreign countries (line 2cii), and loans made by U.S. banks to foreigners (line 2civ). The amount of direct investment (line 2ci) is of particular interest to students of international business because it measures invest-

Table 1–9   International Investment Position of the United States (billions U.S. $)

		1974	1976	1978
1.	Net U.S. assets abroad	58.8	82.6	76.7
2.	U.S. assets abroad	255.7	347.2	450.0
	(a) U.S. official reserve assets	15.9	18.7	18.6
	(b) Other government assets	38.4	46.0	54.2
	(c) Private assets	201.5	282.4	377.2
	(i) Direct investment	110.1	136.8	168.1
	(ii) Foreign securities	28.2	44.2	53.4
	(iii) Other claims by non-banks	17.0	20.3	26.1
	(iv) Claims by banks	46.2	81.1	129.6
3.	Foreign assets in the United States	196.9	264.6	373.3
	(a) Foreign official assets	79.8	105.5	175.1
	(b) Other foreign assets	117.1	159.0	198.2
	(i) Direct investment	25.1	30.8	40.8
	(ii) U.S. securities	34.9	54.8	55.4
	(iii) U.S. liabilities of non-banks	13.6	13.0	15.1
	(iv) Liabilities reported by banks	43.5	60.5	86.9

Source: U.S. Department of Commerce, *Survey of Current Business* (Washington, D.C.: U.S. Government Printing Office, August 1979), Table 3, page 56.

ments made by U.S. firms in foreign subsidiaries. Assets held by foreigners in the United States are classified in a similar way in lines 3a and 3b.

There are several interesting features of the data in Table 1–9. First, they show that the United States has been a net lender to the rest of the world on balance through 1978, as foreign assets held by U.S. citizens and the Government ($450 billion) exceeded liabilities to foreigners ($373 billion). The U.S. net asset position has fallen since 1976, however, indicating that the United States was a net borrower from the rest of the world in 1977 and 1978. Direct investment is the largest single type of foreign asset, but its share in the total has been falling (down to 37 percent of the total in 1978), while loans by U.S. banks to foreigners have become increasingly important. Direct investment by the United States abroad is much larger than direct investment by foreign countries in the United States, and the gap is widening.[3] The major source of growth of U.S. liabilities to foreigners has been the accumulation of assets held by foreign governments in the United States (line 3a). These assets reflect the fact that the dollar is held widely as a reserve asset by governments around the world, and that foreign governments have been accumulating dollar assets rapidly in recent years because of large-scale U.S. balance-of-payments deficits.

Governments hold foreign reserve assets for many reasons, but mainly to be used to cushion adjustments made necessary by changing circumstances in the local economy as well as in the world economy. Reserves were more important in the international monetary system when exchange rate fluctuations were limited prior to 1972. With the adoption of a system of more flexible exchange rates, an increasing share of the adjustment burden has been borne by exchange-rate changes; however, most countries still wish to cushion exchange-rate changes and therefore maintain foreign reserve assets so that the adjustments required in the economy can be phased in over time.

Holdings of international reserves by governments, in fact, have expanded rapidly since flexible exchange rates were adopted, *de facto,* in 1972. The total increased from $93 billion in 1970 to $364 billion at the end of 1978. Even though the growth in reserves was rapid, it only just kept up with the growth in world trade, so that the ratio of world reserves to world imports in 1978 was the same as in 1970.

Most of the growth came in foreign exchange holdings, which were valued at $288 billion at the end of 1978. Table 1–9 (line 3a) shows that

---

[3]Both the value of U.S. investment and foreign direct investment in the U.S. probably are understated because they are recorded at historical cost, less depreciation, plus retained earnings, and do not include the effect of inflation on the value of the underlying assets.

$175 billion in foreign exchange reserves, or 60 percent was held in dollars in the United States. Germany alone held reserves of $54 billion, or 15 percent, of world reserve assets at the end of 1978. Together, Germany, Japan, and Switzerland had 30 percent of world reserves as a result of their massive balance-of-payments surpluses in the 1970s. Most of these assets were invested in dollar assets in the United States; consequently, as Table 1–10 reveals, Europe and Japan were both net lenders to the United States at the end of 1978. That is, Japan and the European countries have been helping to finance U.S. investments in Canada and the other, mostly poorer, countries of the world.

Canada is the largest single recipient of U.S. direct investment, and Western Europe contains the largest concentration of U.S. direct investment. European firms, in turn, are the largest direct investors in the United States, although U.S. direct investment in Europe exceeds European investment in the United States by a wide margin. While the United States is still the largest source of direct investment, its position of dominance has eroded over time, as seen in Table 1–11. German, Japanese, and Swiss firms have increased their investments in foreign operations substantially since 1967. In 1976, U.S. direct investors had $137 billion in assets in foreign countries, while firms in all other countries had foreign investments worth about $150 billion. Of that total, about 20 percent were in the United States, leaving $120 billion in other countries.

It appears that international direct investment, like trade, is concentrated among the advanced industrial countries. This is true of U.S. direct investments, as shown in Table 1–12. Of the total stock of direct investment outstanding in the mid-1970s, three-quarters were located in advanced industrial countries, with only about one-quarter in the developing countries

Table 1–10 Distribution of U.S. Assets and Liabilities in 1978 (billions U.S. $)

	Total			Direct Investment		
	Assets	Liabilities	Net	Assets	Liabilities	Net
Western Europe	130.2	205.2	−75.0	69.7	27.9	41.8
Canada	80.4	21.9	58.4	37.3	6.2	31.1
Japan	23.1	40.4	−17.2	5.0	2.7	2.3
Latin America	112.2	42.2	70.0	32.5	3.4	29.1
Other countries	74.3	56.4	18.0	16.8	0.7	16.1
International organization	29.8	7.3	22.5	6.9	——	6.9
Total	450.0	373.3	76.7	168.1	40.8	127.3

Source: U.S. Department of Commerce, *Survey of Current Business* (Washington, D.C: U.S. Government Printing Office, August 1979), Table 3, page 56.

Table 1–11   Stock of Direct Investment Abroad of Major Investing Countries (billions U.S. $)

	1967	%	1976	%
United States	56.6	53.8	136.8	47.5
United Kingdom	17.5	16.6	32.1	11.2
Germany	3.0	2.8	19.9	6.9
Japan	1.5	1.4	19.4	6.7
Switzerland	5.0	4.7	18.6	6.5
France	6.0	5.7	11.9	4.1
Canada	3.7	3.5	11.1	3.9
Netherlands	2.2	2.1	9.8	3.4
Sweden	1.7	1.6	5.0	1.7
Belgium	2.0	1.9	3.6	1.2
Italy	2.1	2.0	2.9	1.0
Other	4.0	3.8	16.8	5.8
Total	105.3	100.0	287.9	100.0

Source: U.N., *Transnational Corporations in World Development, A Re-Examination* (New York: U.N., March 1978), Table III–32, page 236.

Table 1–12   Stock of Direct Investment in Host Countries

	1967	1975
Host countries Total stock (billions U.S. $)	105	259
Distribution (percentage) Developed market economies	69	74
Canada	18	15
United States	9	11
United Kingdom	8	9
Germany	3	6
Other	30	33
Developing countries	31	26
OPEC countries	9	6
Other	22	20

Source: U.N., *Transnational Corporations in World Development: A Re-Examination* (New York: U.N., March 1978), Table III–33, page 237.

of the world. This concentration is not surprising because firms from the advanced industrial countries find the best opportunities in other advanced countries. It might be expected, moreover, that there will be even greater interpenetration of advanced countries in the future as Japanese and German firms, in particular, take advantage of the strong currencies of their home countries to establish producing facilities in other nations.

Summary

It should be clear from this survey of world income, trade, and investment that, although there is great diversity in the world, there are also regularities to be found in the international economy. The study of these patterns allows us to predict the composition and direction of intercountry trade. The level of development and population of a country are highly critical factors determining industrial structure and, in turn, the composition of its exports. A few highly industrialized countries dominate world trade. They also undertake virtually all of the international investing and own the lion's share of international reserves. In the following chapters we will attempt to show how the international economy functions (Part 1), show how crucial business decisions can be made in the context of the international economy (Part II), and review conflict in international business, with some view of the future, (Part III).

SELECTED READINGS

U.N. Commission of Transnational Corporations, *Transnational Corporations in World Development* (New York: U.N., 1978).

World Bank, *World Development Report 1978* (Washington D.C.: World Bank, 1978).

World Bank, *World Development Report 1979* (Washington D.C.: World Bank, 1979).

One

THE ECONOMIC ENVIRONMENT OF INTERNATIONAL BUSINESS

Business operations, whether international or purely domestic, are affected profoundly by current events within the global economy. For this reason, and because the international environment imposes limitations and provides opportunities not found at home, all professional managers now must have a basic understanding of events occurring elsewhere in the world. While this statement may seem trivially apparent for multinational corporate managers, few such managers have had explicit training by their companies in international economic affairs. Fewer still, even in today's sophisticated management schools, learn about these matters while attending colleges or universities.

Knowledge of the international economic environment is vital not only for multinational company executives but also for those from smaller firms interested mostly in domestic markets. Ask the presidents of Brown Shoe or Magnavox (TV) or J. P. Stevens (textiles), all dependent predominantly on

domestic sales, how global competition has impacted
upon their companies. Foreign firms now have
captured major shares of the markets of each
company.

In Part I we will discuss basic concepts related
to the international economic environment,
addressing such questions as:

1. Why do nations trade?
2. What are the effects of trade barriers?
3. What are the financial links between countries?
4. What is the balance of payments and how is it interpreted?
5. How are exchange rates determined?
6. What is the Eurodollar market and why does it exist?

The approach in Part I, therefore, is general,
directed to the economic world within which all
business firms function.

2

The Theory of Comparative Advantage

INTRODUCTION

Trade, almost inevitably, precedes direct foreign investment, which, in turn, is the hallmark of the multinational firm. Most firms now involved in international operations first developed their foreign interests through foreign trade. Even very large multinational corporations, such as General Electric or IBM, began manufacturing overseas to service better those markets previously supplied by exports from the United States. In some instances, the international division of a company started because the firm desired closer control of a foreign source of supply for raw materials or semiprocessed manufactures.

A clear understanding, therefore, of the basis for trade and of the factors influencing changing patterns of trade is essential to an understanding of international business. Such an understanding provides the manager or decision maker with considerable insight regarding the decisions involved with an ongoing multinational enterprise. This chapter briefly discusses the economic theory of comparative advantage, as it might interest a business executive, and focuses on the operational implications of the theory for decision making.

THE BASIS FOR TRADE

The Basic Model

We begin by assuming a world made up of only two countries, Agraria and Metropole. Initially there is no trade between them. Agraria has an abundance of fertile, sparsely populated agricultural land. Metropole is more heavily populated. Its people live and work mainly in urban centers. These differences are noted in Table 2–1. Both countries produce similar sets of agricultural and manufactured products, although output quantities and relative prices are dissimilar. Agraria's production capabilities are considerably larger than those of Metropole in the sense that, for any specified level of production for one type of commodity, Agraria can produce more of the other type than can Metropole. It follows that the people of Agraria are more prosperous, although it should not be inferred that Metropole is necessarily a "poor" country.

Table 2–2 depicts three production combinations that are possible in each country. These selections are arbitrary, and many other intermediate combinations also would be possible. The figures given in the table are derived from a graphical device frequently used in economics called a "production possiblities diagram." The diagrams pertaining to Agraria and Metropole are depicted in Figure 2–1, where the bold lines represent possible maximum production combinations in fully employed economies. Agraria, for example, could produce 150 units of agricultural goods if all productive factors were devoted to farming and none to industrial pursuits, or, by shifting resources to manufacturing, it could produce the various

Table 2–1   Resource Endowments

	Agraria	Metropole
Arable land (sq. miles $\times$ 10^6)	1	0.3
Workers ($\times$ 10^6)	25	45.0

Table 2–2   Possible Production Combinations (composite units $\times$ 10^9)

Agraria		Metropole	
Agricultural	Manufactured	Agricultural	Manufactured
145	20	36	20
120	45	27	45
80	70	15	70

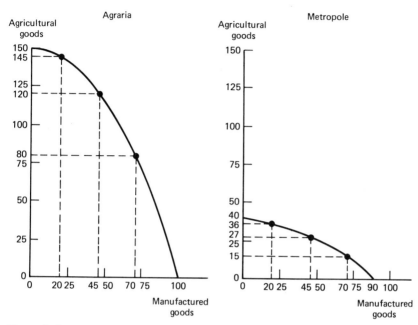

Figure 2–1.

combinations represented by its curve. The figures given in Table 2–2 correspond to the three points shown on each curve in Figure 2–1.

Since both countries are assumed to be fully employed, increasing production of one type of output necessitates reducing output in the other product category in either country. Economies of scale, therefore, are ruled out in this example; in fact, increasing costs for both products are implicit in a concave curve. Two points should be mentioned about the table and figure. First, the units of measurement for agricultural and industrial product sets are in each case some composite of the actual units of output for the various products in the sets. In a "real world" situation, the use of such measures would cause many problems, but for our purposes here the units are intended only to roughly suggest relative production possiblities. The other point to be noted is that Agraria is the more prosperous country with respect to possible consumption levels per person. More sparsely populated Agraria can produce (consume) for any given level of industrial production considerably more agricultural output.

The two questions to be answered in this fictional example are:

1. Would trade between the countries be worthwhile?
2. Which set of products would be exported by each country?

To answer these questions, additional information is needed. The posibility of trade depends on products being more attractively priced abroad than at home, as yet, prices have not been considered. To facilitate the discussion, we introduce currency (monetary) units in each country; rurits and urbans in Agraria and Metropole, respectively.[1] Prices in the two countries before trade are expressed in local currencies, and, because no economic relationship exists between the countries, there exists no established exchange rate between the two currencies.

Intuitively, it might be expected that agricultural product prices relative to industrial prices would be higher in Metropole than in Agraria—this simply because Metropole has little arable land. With anything like a "normal" pattern of consumer demand, this intuition would be correct and is reflected in the prices given in Table 2–3.

The price relationships in Table 2–3 also indicate the opportunity costs of producing items in each country, given the assumed levels of production. In Agraria, the opportunity cost of having an additional unit of agricultural products would require the giving up of one-half unit of industrial product. In Metropole, the opportunity cost would be $2\frac{1}{2}$ units of industrial product. Thus, in terms of productive opportunities, Agraria is comparatively the more efficient country in agricultural goods. Obviously, by similar reasoning, Metropole has an opportunity cost advantage in industrial products, compared with Agraria.[2]

It should be recognized that higher or lower opportunity costs are simply a restatement, in somewhat revised form, of the fact that relative prices of the products differ in the two countries. The opportunity cost concept, however, does bring trade opportunities more clearly into focus because it points out that a marginal unit of agricultural production is less costly, in terms of foregone industrial output, in Agraria than in Metropole.

Table 2–3 Product Prices Before Trade (per Composite Unit)

	Agraria (rurits)	Metropole (urbans)
Agricultural products	2	5
Industrial products	4	2

[1]Currency units are convenient in the analysis but are by no means necessary for it. The whole discussion could be carried through without introducing currencies.

[2]The complete graphic analysis would incorporate both the product price lines and consumer preferences in Figure 1–1. Interested readers are encouraged to become familiar with this analysis, which is given in the international economic references following this chapter.

Conversely, increased industrial production has a lower opportunity cost in Metropole. If trade were made possible between the two countries, each could gain by expanding output in its least-cost product and trading to obtain desired amounts of the other type of product. The gain does *not* depend on the relative efficiency of total output between countries, as measured on some basis of consumed resources per unit of production. Indeed, Agraria is technically more efficient in the production of *both* types of products. The possibility of gain through trade depends, instead, on comparative differences in the relative costs of output between products in each of the two countries. Agraria gains if it can obtain industrial products abroad with a lower expenditure of agricultural products than it can at home, with the converse being true for Metropole.

Although derived from an abstract model of the real world, this conclusion can be used in rejecting many commonly held misconceptions. For example, one reads continually of the danger to our economy of allowing "cheap labor" imports from Korea, Hong Kong, or Taiwan. In some industries, it is claimed, U.S. labor productivity is higher than in the competing foreign country, and yet, because of drastically lower wages, imports are "unfairly" cheaper than domestically made products. The argument usually concludes that such imports should be prohibited or at least regulated. Another similar position is taken frequently in cases where an American company undertakes a foreign manufacturing investment for the purpose of exporting back to the United States. Here the investment is said to be "exporting jobs" to a foreign country to the detriment of American workers; hence, it ought to be prevented.

Although arguments of this kind are, in fact, considerably more complex than that indicated, use of emotional language can and does obscure the underlying forces operating in the world economy. In both instances, a strong *prima facie* case can be made that imports result in lower real prices to American consumers and not only should be allowed but encouraged. The products involved in these arguments evidently are at the low end of the U.S. efficiency spectrum, even though U.S. labor productivity, as measured by unit output per labor hour, is higher than in the foreign country. Resources being absorbed in the production of such items would be better utilized in more efficient industries that, not surprisingly, often would be exporters. Stopping imports raises prices in the comparatively inefficient sectors of the economy and discourages the allocation of resources to their most productive uses. As subsequent chapters show, however, the world is more complicated than we have thus far admitted, and factors such as oligopoly, military security, and difficulties in resource reallocation can alter our conclusions. Nonetheless, today the burden of proof should fall on those who would interfere with the free flow of trade.

Establishing a World Price through the Exchange Rate

It is clear in the example just given that both Agraria and Metropole stand to gain by trading. Each can produce one of the product composites at a lower opportunity cost than the other. The question remaining is whether or not observed prices in the world would lead both countries to trade. This question requires us to specify an exchange rate between the two national currencies: we need a price of one currency in terms of the other. Suppose the exchange rate were one rurit per urban ($R1 = U1$). Thus, referring to Table 2–3, a resident of Metropole could obtain a unit of agricultural product for five urbans at home, but by exchanging his urbans for rurits: he could obtain the same product unit for only two urbans. Similarly, in Agraria, industrial products would be available overseas for only half their domestic price. Under these circumstances, trade clearly would begin, assuming only that consumers purchase in the market with the lowest price and transportation costs are ignored. It can be shown easily that total world output increases as a result of trade.

Agraria, as a result of its trading, expands its output of agricultural products while reducing industrial production and purchasing an increasing proportion of its industrial product needs from Metropole. Conversely, Metropole shifts resources from its agricultural sector to manufacturing. This process, however, affects the relative costs of production and, hence, the price structure of both countries.[3] The manner in which relative costs are changed depends on one's assumptions about the overall production process. If it is assumed that as the production of a commodity is increased, the new resources required are less well suited to that production than are resources already being utilized, then average costs of production will rise as output increases. This constitutes diminishing returns, as is implied by the curves in Figure 1–1. Moreover, it might be assumed that industries which are reducing output will remove from production first those facilities that are least efficient. This action would lower average costs of production for contracting industries. The two assumptions taken together would tend to raise the price of each country's export product relative to its imported good.

Many observers find these assumptions about cost behavior to be somewhat foreign to their intuition or experience. This feeling is particularly apparent when we consider an expansion of production, where increasing or, perhaps, constant returns to scale (decreasing or constant average costs) are perceived to be more typical of actual business operations. Certainly

---

[3]Changing the consumption possibilities open to consumers might also alter their demand characteristics. This effect is ignored here.

the evidence for individual firms tends to support this view;[4] however, when viewed from the perspective of a whole industry or, as in this case, a total national economy, it seems reasonable to assert that the increasing cost assumption generally tends to be true. The competitive position of the least efficient enterprise in an industry improves in a period of output expansion and deteriorates first in a contraction. This outcome is consistent both with the assumption used here and with the real-world observation that many firms can individually expand or contract at essentially constant average costs of production.

There is yet another reason, however, to expect cost behavior to be approximately as postulated in our example. Returning to our example, assume that Agraria experiences a lower relative cost of production for farm products because of its comparative abundance of arable land. When agricultural production increases, resources must be taken from the shrinking industrial sector; but the two factors of production, land and labor, are used in different proportions in the two industries. Land is employed more intensively in farming and labor is employed more intensively in manufacturing. The rising demand for agricultural products after trade commences tends to increase the demand for both land and labor but, with respect to the Agrarian economy as a whole, proportionately more for land. Likewise, diminishing demand for domestically produced manufactured goods releases both land and labor. The supply of labor, however, rises proportionately more than land because of the labor-intensive nature of the industry. These two effects, relatively increasing demand for land and increasing supply of labor, combine in clearing their respective markets to raise the price of land in relation to labor. Since agricultural production mostly requires land and manufacturing mostly requires labor, farm products tend to rise in price compared with industrial outputs. Exactly the reverse process occurs in Metropole, where manufactures become higher in price in relation to the pretrade level.

This pattern of price changes resulting from trade will continue as long as it is advantageous for purchasers to import goods; that is, as long as an international price differential exists. We have now seen, however, that trade tends to bring closer together relative prices of the two goods in each country. Indeed, if both countries continued to produce both goods as trade expanded, relative prices between agricultural and manufactured goods in both countries eventually would become equal. This situation is depicted in Table 2–4, which incorporates the somewhat unlikely assumption that the exchange rate remains unchanged. Thus we see that agricultural products

---

[4]J. Johnson, *Statistical Cost Analysis* (New York: McGraw-Hill, 1960).

Table 2–4   Product Prices after Trade (per composite unit)

	Agraria (rurits)	Metropole (urbans)
Agricultural products	3.5	3.5
Industrial products	3	3
(Exchange rate: $R1 = U1$)		

become more expensive in Agraria ($R3.5$ compared with $R2$), but industrial goods are cheaper ($R3$ compared with $R4$) than before trade commenced. In Metropole, the reverse is true, with agricultural prices lower ($U3.5$ compared with $U5$) and industrial prices higher ($U3$ compared with $U2$). Both countries, however, can consume more of both goods than before trade began, and therein lies the persuasive argument of free-trade advocates.

EXPANDING THE BASIC MODEL

The model from which our conclusions have been drawn is considerably simpler than the real world; however, certain complexities can be introduced without substantially altering the results. Adding more countries or more products to the model increases only the mathematical complexity; it does not fundamentally change the analysis. The conclusions discussed previously also remain the same when additional factors of production are introduced, although some ramifications of the complete economic analysis of comparative advantage, not treated here, can become ambiguous under these circumstances. The model is thus quite flexible and provides considerable insight into the more practical policy questions of the real world.

In our discussion thus far, we have skirted at least one issue that frequently causes governmental consternation. The exchange rate arbitrarily chosen in our two-country example will result in equating price ratios in each country, assuming only that both nations continue to produce both goods. It is not necessarily true, however, that this exchange rate will yield balanced trade between the countries; that is, exports might not exactly offset imports for either country. In the simple world postulated here, such trade imbalances would be synonymous with a balance-of-payments deficit for one country and a surplus for the other. This topic is discussed more fully in Chapter 3. For our purposes, it is sufficient to note that these imbalances must be corrected eventually and that an excahange rate adjustment is one mechanism by which the correction can be made.

The Effect of Price Inflation

The phenomenon of imbalance can be demonstrated easily using our numerical example. We begin our brief analysis by assuming that the specified exchange rate ($R1 = U1$) equates export and import values in both countries and the resulting prices are as stated in Table 2–4. Suppose, then, that Metropole experiences a period of price inflation while in Agraria price levels are initially stable. The source of Metropole's inflation is not particularly important, except as it might differentially affect the existing cost and price structure in that country. It might be assumed here that all prices are increased by precisely the same amount. What, if any, are the trade effects of such a unilateral inflation?

Obviously, with free trade between the two regions and an exchange rate of $R1 = U1$, prices in Metropole cannot increase without in some way affecting Agraria. Because the two markets are linked, prices in the two countries must be identical, except for differences caused by transportation and marketing costs. How does the equalization take place? It occurs in either of two ways. The first and most apparent way is through an adjustment of the exchange rate; urbans can be devalued relative to rurits. If, for example, a 10 percent Metropole general inflation is matched by a 10 percent decline in the number of rurits obtainable for one urban, then the trade relationship between the two countries would be unchanged. This situation is depicted in Table 2–5. Clearly, the value of exports and imports for each nation, measured in its own currency, again would be equal, and the quantity of trade would be identical with the preinflation amount. The price inflation in Metropole, under these circumstances, has not affected at all the underlying "real" relationship between the two countries.

If, however, the exchange rate cannot be changed for some reason, then the equalization of prices must be maintained through trade. As prices begin to rise in Metropole, Agraria would tend to purchase fewer industrial imports and to further expand agricultural exports. This movement would have the effect of increasing the price of agricultural products and, because of the decline in Metropole's industrial output for export, of lowering the

Table 2–5 Product Prices after Trade and Inflation in Metropole with Devaluation (per composite unit)

	Agraria (rurits)	Metropole (urbans)
Agricultural prices	3.5	3.85
Industrial prices:	3.0	3.3
(Exchange rate: $R1.0 = U1.1$)		

price of manufactured goods. Both of these effects, of course, depend on our assumption of diseconomies of scale in each producing sector. The resulting price structure might take the form given in Table 2–6.

Notice that international equalization of prices still occurs, but that Metropole experiences a trade deficit. The inflating country has "priced itself out of world markets" or has become "noncompetitive." Both of these terms appear frequently in business and press statements to describe such situations. It is important to understand, however, that nothing in our changing example has altered the basic structure of comparative advantage in the two-country world. No unilateral shifts have occurred in productive efficiency; no new resources have been uncovered in either country. The "noncompetitiveness" is strictly a phenomenon that arises because of the inability of the exchange rate to adjust to the changing relative value of the currency units. More generally, a world monetary system in which various currencies are linked through fixed or infrequently changed exchange rates will be characterized by deficits and surpluses that result from differential rates of price inflation between countries.

In the particular case, in our example, Metropole's deficit must be eliminated eventually, if not through an exchange-rate adjustment, then by some alternative means. Agraria's trade receipts would exceed its expenditures, which means either an increase in holding of urbans or an increase in short-term loans to Metropole's residents. The possible effects of these increases depend on the disposition of the financial assets made by Agrarians, which is a subject too involved to discuss at this point. It seems clear, however, that since the root of the Metropole deficit is its overvalued currency, it is not likely that Agrarians would be willing to accumulate urban-assets for very long.

The Effect of a Change in Production Possibilities

Another interesting and often pertinent variation in our model involves a change in available resources in one or both countries. Such a change might

Table 2–6 **Product Prices after Trade and Inflation in Metropole without Devaluation (per composite unit)**

	Agraria (rurits)	Metropole (urbans)
Agricultural prices	3.2	3.2
Industrial prices	2.9	2.9
(Exchange rate $R1.0 = U1.0$)		

be caused by a variety of factors, but for the purpose of illustration we focus here on a single but not unusual circumstance. Suppose that in Metropole some technological innovation makes labor more productive in an industrial process; that is, the amount of manufactured output per applied labor hour increases.[5] This gain in labor productivity would be equilvalent to an expansion of the labor supply and would affect the pattern of production and trade in both countries. The price of manufactured goods would tend to fall relative to agricultural output, and production of manufactured items would rise, both for domestic consumption and export. Assuming retention of balanced trade between the two countries, higher labor productivity in Metropole's export sector will result in further production specialization in both countries and increased international trade.[6]

EMPIRICAL INVESTIGATIONS OF COMPARATIVE ADVANTAGE

Numerous other possible conclusions can be derived from the basic model of comparative advantage. One only has to alter one or more of the underlying assumptions. The time has come, however, to consider whether or not the model has any real-world validity. Does the theory actually explain observed trade patterns? As one might expect, the answer to this question turns out to be ambiguous; sometimes the theory is verified, sometimes it is not. For the brief review here, a few well-known studies are selected from the many available works in the field.

Support for the Theory

One of the earliest studies testing the theory of comparative costs, done by British economist G. MacDougall, contrasted the pattern of exports of the United States and the United Kingdom.[7] MacDougall hypothesized that a country should export the products in which it is relatively most efficient in production and that this relative efficiency could be measured by between-country comparisons of output per worker in various industries.

---

[5]The assumption also is made here that the technical change does not alter the relative capital intensity of the manufacturing process, although in this simplified example capital is not explicitly a factor of production.

[6]The actual result of increased incomes in Metropole resulting from the productivity increase depends on the use made of that income. A highly income elastic demand for imports in Metropole could combine with an inelastic demand for manufactured goods to lower the quantity of trade, but this result is unlikely.

[7]G. D. A. MacDougall, "British and American Exports: A Study Suggested by the Theory of Comparative Costs, Part 1," *Economic Journal*, 61:244, 1951, pp. 697–724.

Using pre-World War II data adjusted for currency differences. MacDougall found that American workers on average earned approximately twice the amount of their British counterparts; therefore, the United States should have tended to export products of industries where labor productivity of American workers was more than twice that of the British workers. The United Kingdom, on the other hand, should have exported products where productivity differences were less than this amount.

MacDougall's results, which related labor productivity to export performance, are summarized in Table 2–7. Clearly, his simple rule explains with considerable accuracy which country would predominate in exports to

Table 2–7 United States and United Kingdom Prewar Output per Worker and Quantity of Exports in 1937

United States outputs per worker more than twice United Kingdom			
Wireless sets and valves	U.S. exports	8	times U.K. exports
Pig Iron	U.S. exports	5	times U.K. exports
Motor cars	U.S. exports	4	times U.K. exports
Glass containers	U.S. exports	3½	times U.K. exports
Tin cans	U.S. exports	3	times U.K. exports
Machinery	U.S. exports	1½	times U.K. exports
Paper	U.S. exports	1	times U.K. exports
United States output per worker 1.4 to 2.0 times the United Kingdom			
Cigarettes	U.K. exports	2	times U.S. exports
Linoleum, oilcloth, etc.	U.K. exports	3	times U.S. exports
Hosiery	U.K. exports	3	times U.S. exports
Leather footwear	U.K. exports	3	times U.S. exports
Coke	U.K. exports	5	times U.S. exports
Rayon weaving	U.K. exports	5	times U.S. exports
Cotton goods	U.K. exports	9	times U.S. exports
Rayon making	U.K. exports	11	times U.S. exports
Beer	U.K. exports	18	times U.S. exports
United States output per worker less than 1.4 times United Kingdom			
Cement	U.K. exports	11	times U.S. exports
Men's/boys' outer wool clothing	U.K. exports	23	times U.S. exports
Margarine	U.K. exports	32	times U.S. exports
Woolen and worsted	U.K. exports	250	times U.S. exports

Exceptions (U.S. output per worker more than twice the British, but U.K. exports exceed U.S. exports)
Electric lamps, rubber tires, soap, biscuits, watches

Source: G. MacDougall, "British and American Exports: A Study Suggested by the Theory of Comparative Costs," reprinted in Caves and Johnson (eds.), *Readings in International Economics* (Homewood, Ill.: R. D. Irwin, Inc.), 1968, p. 554.

the rest of the world. Furthermore, the export supremacy of a country tended to increase as its relative labor efficiency increased. Again, it should be made clear that MacDougall's relative efficiency measure had some shortcomings for testing the theory because it concentrated on a single factor of production, labor. Land, capital, and other factors were assumed to be sufficiently well incorporated into the labor productivity variable that they could be ignored. In addition, the exchange rate was assumed to reflect accurately the relative value of the two currencies. Even so, MacDougall's results have been corroborated since by R. M. Stern data for the years 1950 and 1959.[8]

Both studies lend quite remarkable support to the theory of comparative advantage, especially considering the limitations both in the data and methodology utilized by the researchers. For example, no allowance was made for production or distribution costs other than direct labor and, in most instances, such costs were significant. In addition, the studies took no account of product differentiation between the industries of each country. In some industries, such as the automobile industry, the products of the national industries were markedly different. Other shortcomings could be cited, but the point should be clear: by having information only on labor productivity, it was possible to determine quite closely which country, the United States or the United Kingdom, would predominate in the export for a particular industry.

The Leontief Paradox

Not all studies, however, have been as supportive of the theory as MacDougall's and Stern's work. Professor W. W. Leontief surprised the international economics community in 1953 by publishing his finding that, contrary to theoretical expectations, the United States tended to export products that were labor intensive in their production and to import capital-intensive items.[9] This determination resulted from Leontief's large input-output analysis on the 1947 structure of the American economy and therefore was based on U.S. production technology.

[8]R. M. Stern, "British and American Productivity and Comparative Costs in International Trade," *Oxford Economic Papers,* New Series, 4:3 1962, pp. 275–296.

[9]W. W. Leontief, "Domestic Production and Foreign Trade: The American Capital Position Re-examined," *Economia Internationale,* 7:1, 1958, pp. 3–32, reprinted in part in American Economic Association, R. Cave and H. Johnson (eds), *Readings in International Economics,* (Homewood, Ill: Richard D. Irwin, Inc. 1968), pp. 503–527. See also W. W. Leontief, "Factor Proportions and the Structure of American Trade: Further Theoretical and Empirical Analysis," *Review of Economics and Statistics,* 38, November 1956, pp. 386–407.

The findings of Leontief's study are summarized in Table 2–8. As Leontief stated," . . . an average million dollars' worth of our exports embodies considerably less capital and somewhat more labor than would be required to replace from domestic production an equivalent amount of our competitive imports."[10] Because the United States was considered to be a comparatively capital-abundant country, this finding was exactly contrary to theoretical expectations and became known as "Leontief's paradox." His work precipitated extensive research to explain his seemingly perverse result. A sampling of this research is briefly reviewed below.

Factor Intensity Reversal Rationale. Numerous explanations have been advanced in recent years. Some of these efforts have concentrated on Leontief's underlying assumption that the relative factor intensity of production methods used in the United States to duplicate imports is actually found in countries exporting to this country.[11] There is a presumption in Leontief's work that goods which are produced by capital-intensive techniques in the United States also are made by comparatively capital-intensive methods in other countries. His assumption, however, does *not* state that foreign countries use production means that are more capital intensive than in the United States for similar products, but rather that foreign-country production of such items is capital intensive relative to other types of output in that country; in other words, that industries across countries tend

Table 2–8 Domestic Capital and Labor Requirements per Million Dollars of United States Exports and of Competitive Import Replacements (of average 1947 composition)

	Exports	Imported Replacements
Capital (dollars, in 1947 prices)	2,550,780	3,091,339
Labor (man-years)	182.313	170.004

Source: W. W. Leontief, "Domestic Production and Foreign Trade: The American Position Re-examined," in R. Cave and H. G. Johnson (eds.) *Readings in International Economics,* (Homewood, Ill.: R. D. Irwin, Inc., 1968); p. 522.

[10]W. W. Leontief, *op. cit.,* p. 522.
[11]See especially P. T. Ellsworth, "The Structure of American Foreign Trade: A New View Examined," *Review of Economics and Statistics,* 36, August, 1954, 279–285; and B. S. Minhas, "The Homophypallagic Production Function, Factor Intensity Reversals and the Hecksher-Ohlin Theorem," *Journal of Political Economy,* 70, April, 1962, pp. 138–156. Leontief's response to Minhas is also of interest; see W. W. Leontief, "International Factor Costs and Factor Use," *American Economic Review,* 54:4, 1964, pp. 335–345.

to maintain the same ordering when ranked by the amount of capital used per worker. Under this assumption, Leontief's use of only American data is perfectly justifiable.

Those who express criticisms, however, notice that if various nations really do have markedly different factor endowments, then the relative costs of labor and capital also could diverge widely. In fact, this expectation accords closely with observations in the world; the relative cost of labor in the United States is much higher than, say, in the Philippine Islands. With this being the case, is it not possible, indeed probable, that in the Philippines a type of manufacturing that is relatively labor intensive at one stage of development (or at one set of factor prices) could become capital intensive at a later stage (or at another set of factor prices)? If such factor intensity reversals do occur, then the Leontief result is inconclusive. United States imports might be relatively capital intensive by American standards but labor intensive in terms of foreign-country techniques of production.

This argument can be illustrated quite easily by specifying the production relationships for two industries, textiles and nonferrous metals.[12] Suppose that the amount of capital equipment used, in proportion to labor, is functionally related to the comparative wage rate in the following way:

$$\log(K/L) = a + b \log(w/r)$$

where K = capital used
     L = labor used a and b are parameters that
     W = real wage rate   vary depending on the
     r = real cost of capital   particular industry

For the two industries chosen, the equations are:

Textiles $\log(K/L)_t = 0.16 + 0.8 \log(w/r)_t$
Nonferrous metals $\log(K/L)_m = 0.10 + 1.0 \log(w/r)_m$

(Subscripts t and m refer to textiles and metals, respectively.) The log-linear equations state that for both industries a rise in relative wages will result in substitution of capital for labor, as one might expect; however, the rates of substitution differ between industries. The equations are graphed in Figure 2–2, which shows that at comparatively low wage rates, perhaps resulting

[12]The parameters are taken from Minhas, *op. cit.* The equation is derived from a generalized constant elasticity of substitution production function.

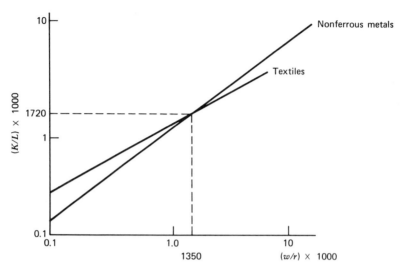

Figure 2–2. An example of factor intensity reversal as relative wages rise. *(Note:* scales are logarithmic.) *K/L* = capital–labor ratio; *w/r* = wage rate/cost of capital.

from an abundance of labor, the production of textiles is capital intensive compared with nonferrous metals. For *w/r* ratios larger than 1350, however, textile output becomes relatively labor intensive; that is, factor intensities are reversed.

One can visualize easily the conditions that could lead to such a reversal in the industries chosen. Textiles production might require a fairly large capital investment to achieve any output, regardless of the availability of low-cost labor, whereas nonferrous metals, might be produced, under these conditions, in small batches with relatively little need for sophisticated equipment. As wage rates rise, however, the possibilities of substituting capital for labor in nonferrous metals becomes far greater than in textile manufacturing. In any case, it is clear that Leontief's study could err in its conclusions because the orderings of industries by capital intensity are different for the United States and other countries, especially countries where the relative cost of labor is substantially less than for the United States.[13]

---

[13]Leontief questions whether factor intensity reversals are particularly important in trade. See W.W. Leontief, "An International Comparison of Factor Costs and Factor Use," *American Economic Review,* 54:4, 1964, pp. 335–345. His view seems to be supported today by most economists; see G. Hufbauer, "The Impact of National Characteristics and Technology on the Commodity Composition of Trade in Manufactured Goods," in R. Vernon ed., *The Technology Factor in International Trade* New York: National Bureau for Economic Research, 1970).

The Composition of Trade Rationale. There are several other reasons why American exports are comparatively labor intensive and American imports are capital intensive. Some of the more interesting explanations focus more closely than did Leontief on the nature of particular products entering U.S. trade with the rest of the world. For example, a fairly large proportion of American imports is made up of raw materials, such as iron ore and petroleum. Often the location and development of the foreign sources for these materials is undertaken by subsidiaries of American corporations, and, in a sense, these operations can be considered as extensions of the corporations' domestic activities. In most instances, the exploitation of natural resources, whether or not carried out by U.S. firms, does tend to be a heavily capital-intensive activity. This holds true even when processes in developing countries are compared with other processes in developing countries are compared with other processes in well-developed countries such as Australia or Canada.[14] In those less developed countries where it exists, the extractive sector of the economy is likely to be characterized by heavy use of capital equipment, despite the fact that other sectors remain fairly primitive. Under these circumstances, the exports of such countries obviously would exhibit a substantial bias toward more capital-intensive production methods.

The tendency exists for American overseas corporate subsidiaries to use familiar techniques of production in manufacturing as well as in raw materials industries.[15] Where this occurs, it is possible for the American firm in the foreign country to have a higher capital-to-labor ratio than local manufacturers in the same industry. The subsidiary again functions more as an extension of its U.S. parent than as a foreign company. Since many of these subsidiaries now export substantial quantities of products to the United States and the production methods used closely approximate those used in this country, these U.S. imports appear to be comparatively capital intensive.

This line of reasoning implies that the American subsidiary somehow enjoys lower costs than its foreign counterpart because it uses more efficient methods. Presumably, the local firm could improve its relative position simply by emulating the subsidiary's technology. There is cause to believe, however, that the two firms are not in equivalent positions. First, the American firm probably experiences a lower cost of capital than its foreign

[14]On this point, see J. Vanek, *The National Resource Content of United States Foreign Trade,* 1870–1955 Cambridge, Eng: Cambridge University Press, 1963), pp. 132–135.

[15]Wayne Yeoman, "Selection of Production Processes for the Manufacturing Subsidiaries of U.S.-Based Multinational Corporations," unpublished doctoral dissertation Graduate School of Business Administration, Harvard University, Boston, 1968.

competitor; therefore, substituting capital equipment for labor is more attractive. Moreover, if the equipment itself is obsolete compared with the prevailing technology in the United States, then the cost to the subsidiary (but not to a local competitor) of such machinery might be very small, particularly in the absence of a viable used-machinery market. Finally, even in cases where the subsidiary's use of more capital-intensive production methods does not yield lower relative costs, the subsidiary, through its parental connection, can have an advantage in exporting to the United States or in importing components from the parent at low prices. For example, it might have easier access to distribution channels at home — distribution channels that would be expensive, if not impossible, for its foreign competitors to duplicate.

The Product Cycle Rationale.   Clearly, there are numerous possible explanations for the surprisingly heavy capital content of U.S. imports; there are also some reasons to expect that our exports might be labor intensive, which is the other half of the Leontief paradox. One such explanation, first set forth by Professor Vernon, suggests that for many products the U.S. pattern of trade is strongly dependent upon unique characteristics found in the American economy.[16] His analysis begins with the observation that the number of new products first introduced in the United States, when compared with other developed countries, is disproportionately large. Apparently new-product development, as contrasted to basic scientific research, occurs comparatively early in this country. Why should this be true?

Vernon believes that, in part, the explanation lies in the considerably larger economic size and relative homogeneity of the American market. Relative to other developed nations, the U.S. market contains vastly more potential purchasers; therefore, the likelihood of being able to develop a viable market in a short time period for almost any new product tends to be higher in the United States than elsewhere in the world. Because of this characteristic, an American entrepreneur enjoys a higher probability of success in a new venture, even if consumer preferences are everywhere similar. His rich market is his making, and yet it is not obvious that market size alone is adequate to explain U.S. predominance in new-product development. Foreign companies, after all, can develop and sell their own new items, both in their own and in the American markets, thereby eliminating the U.S. producer's advantage. The fact that they historically

[16]Raymond Vernon, "International Investment and International Trade in the Product Cycle," *Quarterly Journal of Economics,* May 1966, pp. 190–207.

have not done so suggests that other factors peculiar to the American economy also must be operating.

Vernon points out that one such factor might be related to American consumers themselves. Consumption patterns in the United States are likely to diverge from other areas simply because Americans have considerably more discretionary income to spend on leisure-time products and items that in another economy would be considered luxurious. Many such products come to mind: color television, stereo sound systems, air conditioners, automatic heating controls, and outdoor carpeting. United States firms, being in close proximity to their consumers, have developed, produced and marketed these types of products long before their use has become common in the rest of the world. This phenomenon is not limited to individual consumers but can be seen in business purchases as well, especially those connected with increased leisure time; witness products such as artificial turf or sophisticated communications equipment.

The obvious corollary to high income is the cost of labor, which is also high and is rooted in the advanced level of human skills. Vernon suggests that efforts to reduce these costs through research and development have been the source of many other new products in the United States. The probability of developing labor-saving products first is undoubtedly greater in the locale where these costs are most important. Clearly this is the case in the United States. There seems little doubt that developments intended to lower unit labor costs have been even more important than the consumption pattern effects discussed previously. Again, there is virtually an inexhaustible list of examples where innovations have appeared earliest in this country. In business, electric typewriters, automation equipment, and even commercial jet aircraft were first developed in the United States primarily to decrease the number of man-hours required to accomplish various tasks. Labor-saving products, of course, are by no means confined to business; in the home, there are automatic dishwashers, clothes dryers, and other types of equipment that are purchased partly to reduce effort but partly also to save time.

What does all of this have to do with international trade and especially with the U.S. propensity to export labor-intensive products? Vernon believes that manufacturers normally will choose to produce new items in plants located fairly close to their anticipated primary market and that the production techniques selected usually, at least at the outset, will be labor intensive. The introduction of new products is an uncertain business, with the failure rate being on the order of five to one. Under these circumstances, early producers are not likely to commit themselves to long production runs involving heavy expenditures on capital equipment. Instead, the firms hedge their bets by using more costly, but less risky, labor-intensive methods of production. This stage can continue for some length of time.

Vernon suggests that a substantial amount of U.S. exports are products innovated here, for the reasons set forth previously, and are not available soon from local manufacturers overseas. Compared with other manufactures of the United States, these exports are likely to be made by labor-intensive means of production. If true, this observation could, in part, account for Leontief's findings. As production becomes more established, of course, a tendency would develop both for the United States to adopt more capital-intensive techniques of manufacture and for production to be initiated overseas. This tendency, as succeeding chapters show, can be helpful in explaining the pattern of foreign direct investment by U.S. companies.

How well has Vernon's hypothesis been verified? The empirical research conducted thus far confirms quite strongly that research- and development-oriented industries in the United States are also the largest exporters.[17] More specifically, industries employing a large proportion of engineers and scientists tend to be more important in exporting than industries with a lower proportion. In a more detailed study, Baldwin has found that not only are scientists and engineers more characteristic of exporters, but so also are craftsmen, skilled laborers, and persons with higher levels of education generally.[18] Table 2–9 reproduces some of Baldwin's data on both capital intensity and labor skills incorporated in U.S. exports and imports. The figures relate to bilateral trade patterns between this country and several other areas.

Several interesting points emerge in Table 2–9. First of all, the net capital–labor ratio is higher for U.S. import industries in trade with both Canada and the less-developed countries, a finding that would accord with Leontief's determination. Both of these areas, however, exported large amounts of raw materials to this country, and we have already seen that production of this type tends to be relatively capital intensive. On the other hand, engineers and scientists were more important in U.S. export industries, as to a lesser extent were professional employees and craftsmen. Thus, while none of these studies demonstrates conclusively that Vernon's hypothesis is correct in its entirety, they do lend support to the proposition

---

[17]See especially W. H. Gruber, D. Mehta, and R. Vernon, "The R. and D. Factor in International Trade and International Investment of U.S. Industry," *Journal of Political Economy,* February 1967, pp. 20–37. Also see D. Keesing, "The Impact of Research and Development on U.S. Trade," *Journal of Political Economy,* February 1967, pp. 38–45.

[18]R. E. Baldwin, "Determinants of the Commodity Structure of U.S. Trade," *American Economic Review,* 61:7, 1971, pp. 126–146; and D. Keesing, "Labor Skills and the Structure of Trade in Manufactures," in P. Kenen and R. Lawrence (eds.), *The Open Economy: Essays on International Trade and Finance,* New York: Columbia University Press, 1968), pp. 3–18.

Table 2–9 Factor-Content Ratios for United States Trade with Selected Regions, 1962

Economic Characteristic	Import/Export Ratios			
	Canada	Western Europe[a]	Japan[a]	Less Developed Countries
Net capital–labor ratio	1.41	0.93	0.84	1.78
Average years of education	0.99	0.98	0.95	0.98
Proportion of engineers and scientists	0.82	0.74	0.64	0.75
Skill groups:				
Professional and technical	0.96	0.87	0.77	0.93
Craftsmen and foremen	0.91	0.92	0.81	0.83

[a]Excludes natural resource industries.
Source: R. E. Baldwin, "Determinants of the Commodity Structure of U.S. Trade," *American Economic Review*, 61:1, 1971, p. 140.

that technology and innovation are important determinants of U.S. export strength.

Interestingly, there is considerable evidence that manufacturers in other countries now sense opportunities, foregone earlier, in the U.S. market. As mentioned previously, such a possibility always has existed. Foreign manufacturers now are developing products specifically aimed at capturing a share of the large American market, in many cases with no expectation of selling at home. This is demonstrated graphically by Japanese production of innovational electronic products for consumer markets in this country. In several countries of the world, average incomes already exceed American levels, and it can be anticipated that market structures in industrialized regions will increasingly approximate the U.S. pattern; thus, one might expect that even more innovational activity having application in this country will be undertaken by firms abroad.

COMPARATIVE ADVANTAGE AND DECISION MAKING

The theory of comparative advantage was formulated by economists seeking to explain the basis for trade flows between countries. Essentially macroscopic in its perspective, the theory considers neither lower-level effects on individual businesses nor larger impacts upon whole industries. Furthermore, it is essentially static and hence not directly applicable to the more dynamic decision problems of the international businessman. This is not to say that knowledge of the principles of comparative advantage has been of no interest to business managers. At least *ex post facto,* a greater understanding of one's economic environment is certainly helpful in perceiving the underlying reasons for the occurrence of particular types of trade movements. Similarly, the historical justification for governmental advocacy of free-trade policies has been rooted in the theory of comparative cost, and the business executive seeking relief through federal agencies from import pressures obviously should comprehend the rationale for such policies.

We consider here, however, possible ways in which theoretical and empirical concepts might be brought to bear upon business decisions. For example, if gross movements of goods and factors between countries are predicated on discernible differences among factor endowments and relative prices, as the theory suggests, then it ought to be possible to predict the effects of anticipated future movements on the relative positon of a firm or industry with respect to its foreign competitors. Moreover, companies might be able to approximate better at an early date the appropriate timing of an overseas manufacturing investment. Or, as another example, analysis of the effects of particular types of technological change on international trade relationships should be possible.

As it happens, "real-world" analysis having to do with shifts in the patterns of comparative advantage is not a simple task. Changes in relative factor prices, for example, can have varying impacts depending upon how easily factor substitutions are possible. If a firm is limited in its ability to substitute capital for labor in its production processes as relative wages rise, then clearly it can anticipate that its own costs will increase faster than costs in the economy as a whole. Instances of this phenomenon abound, most conspicuously in service areas, such as education, where technical substitution of one factor for another is difficult. In traded goods, one might assert that the textile industry's past competitive problems are tied, at least in part, to the lack of increasingly capital-intensive forms of technology in some phases of production.

To demonstrate, however, that the analysis is complex, it is not necessarily true that rising relative costs at home for an industry also mean a deteriorating competitive position with respect to similar industries elsewhere in the world. Costs in such industries would be relatively increasing everywhere, and the trade effects hinge on the comparative rates of growth of relative wages in the various producing countries. For example, the international competitive position of a labor-intensive U.S. industry with few capital-substitution possibilities would deteriorate if relative wages were rising at a faster rate in this country than abroad. If the rate of change were higher overseas, however, the American industry might actually improve its position vis-à-vis its foreign competition.[19]

[19]These results assume common production functions of the Cobb–Douglass type.

Most managements would have great difficulty undertaking such an analysis without utilizing a simplifying method. As one possibility, consider the work of MacDougall and Stern discussed earlier. Their research implies that total production and distribution costs for many industries are correlated closely with a single important element of these costs; the cost of labor. In fact, some indication of future international competitive conditions can be gleaned from looking only at productivity trends in the United States. Industries with a relatively declining productivity of labor, measured in terms of physical output, tend to experience a worsening in their international competitive position. It appears to be approximately true that industries for which labor productivity gains are consistently less than the average gain for the economy can expect, sooner or later, to confront increased foreign competition, perhaps first in export markets and later at home. Thus an analysis of trends in labor productivity can give company managers an early warning of the competitive problems ahead.

This tendency can be identified clearly in Table 2–10, which gives trends in productivity for all manufacturing firms in the United States and for selected industries. The relative decline in labor productivity is readily apparent in several industries, most notably footwear, steel, and glass containers. In each of these industries, imports have increased markedly, both in absolute terms and in relation to the total U.S. market for the products. For example, footwear imports have more than doubled since 1960, as the domestic industry's relative productivity has fallen off. The long-term competitive difficulties of the U.S. steel industry are well known,

Table 2–10 Indexes of Labor Productivity for Selected Industries (Physical output per employee-hour, 1967 = 100)

	1967	1969	1971	1973	1975	1976
All United States Manufacturing	100	105.0	110.2	117.8	116.3	124.2
Paper, paperboard, pulp	100	110.5	119.9	135.4	128.4	138.6
Tires	100	103.3	114.0	117.1	115.7	131.8
Footwear	100	96.7	105.9	102.0	104.3	107.6
Steel	100	104.0	104.9	123.6	108.6	116.5
Radio, TV	100	102.8	111.6	128.4	124.6	132.2
Motor vehicles	100	106.4	119.0	126.6	129.3	141.1
Glass containers	100	108.5	107.8	112.5	119.8	N.A.[a]

[a]N.A. = Not available.
Source: 1967–1973: *Handbook of Labor Statistics,* U.S. Department of Labor, Bureau of Labor Statistics, 1977. 1975–1976: *Statistical Abstract of the Unites States,* U.S. Government Printing Office, Washington, D.C., 1978.

but the table suggests that at least a part of the problem can be attributed to the industry's inability to raise productivity as rapidly as the manufacturing sector as a whole.

Relative improvement in labor productivity obviously is not independent of an industry's capital intensity. With the exception of productivity gains resulting from qualitative improvement in the labor force itself (i.e., through education and training), most increases in output per man-hour stem from the employment of more capital equipment per person employed. Much labor-saving technology is embodied in new types of machinery. For this reason, rising labor productivity generally is synonymous with increasing capital intensity; as the amount of labor needed for a particular product declines, capital inputs increase.[20] Labor productivity, therefore, tends to improve faster in industries where better process technologies have developed more rapidly.

It should be noted that productivity indexes are notoriously susceptible to distortion in situations where firms or industries are operating well below capacity. Manufacturing operations require some minimum work force in place before any production is possible; consequently, for this reason alone, decreases in production usually are not matched by proportionate decreases in the work force required. In addition, firms experiencing a decline in business are likely to view it as a temporary phenomenon and, anticipating an upturn, typically will not reduce employment as much as the current level of orders might indicate. For these reasons, labor productivity tends to be understated in firms and industries operating significantly below capacity levels. Therefore, companies experiencing a recession or perhaps strong foreign competition might demonstrate relatively declining levels of labor productivity from that cause alone. Needless to say, productivity data should be used with discretion.

The general approach just outlined does enable companies to at least concentrate attention on the more important factors affecting their position relative to other firms in their own country. All other things being equal, one generally might expect that relatively capital-intensive industries in the United States or industries with a wide range of capital substitution possibilities will be, in the long run, better insulated from prospective foreign competition than other industries or firms. The problem is that other things are seldom equal, but at least companies with relatively declining capital intensities might be able to identify aspects of their own operations that may differentiate them from firms in prospective difficulty. For example,

[20]This conclusion is by no means necessary. New capital equipment might be "factor neutral" in conserving both labor and capital equally.

a company might employ a disproportionate amount of highly specialized manpower, whose training might be considered a form of capital input and therefore less susceptible to duplication by foreign competitors. The point of the matter is that firms can gain some amount of additional knowledge about their international competitive postion by comparing themselves with a composite of other U.S. firms engaged in businesses quite different from their own.

The typical business firm, both in this country and abroad, also faces a world in which possible production methods to be used in converting raw materials to finished goods are changing continuously. Businessmen not only must find ways to keep abreast of this technological movement, perhaps through their own research and development departments, but they also require means to assess the impact of change on their firm's normal activities. Such analyses, while clearly of great importance, are extremely difficult. In part, this difficulty stems from having to deal with the uncertainty of future technical developments, but it also is caused by the problem of determining the effects of such developments on the firms' operations.

One difficulty of projecting the effects of technological change on trade patterns is that the analysis must account for several types of technical innovation. Then, too, the possible effects depend not only on the technological change itself but also on whether the industry experiencing the change is an export- or import-competing industry. Even if we could assume that relative factor prices are unaffected by a particular technological movement, product prices and, through them, demand conditions are certain to be influenced.

To begin our discussion, three types of technological changes should be defined: *neutral, labor-saving,* and *capital-saving.* Some innovations enable the firm to produce its output both with less labor and less capital. When, for a given output, both factors are diminished by exactly the same proportion with the capital–labor ratio therefore remaining unchanged, the innovation is said to be *neutral.* The basic oxygen furnace for steel making is said to represent a "neutral" improvement compared with open-hearth methods. Clearly, a neutral technological change would reduce average production costs by conserving capital and labor. Another change, however, might lower labor more than capital inputs, in which case the capital–labor ratio would increase. This type of change, not surprisingly, is called *labor-saving* because it has the immediate effect of increasing the supply of labor. Most automation equipment would fit into this category. Finally, when the new technology decreases the proportionate amount of capital required for production, it is a *capital-saving* form of innovation. In the United States research and development might be expected to concentrate on labor-saving technology, since the relative cost of labor is high; however, in many other parts of the world, where labor is more abundant, innovations have been directed toward reducing capital inputs.

It will suffice to present here a single hypothetical case that serves both as an illustration of a possible general approach to such problems and as a vehicle for discussion of some implications that technological change may have for a firm's international competitive position. Consider a vertically integrated company producing both final consumption goods and intermediate products. We have in mind a fully integrated steel firm, but the example could apply as well to various other types of companies. Such a firm might operate several plants or divisions in which the product of one plant becomes the input of the next stage of production, which for illustrative purposes takes place in a different division of the company. To simplify, we disallow external sales or purchases of intermediate products in this example (although this exclusion would not affect materially the outcome of the analysis); that is, semiprocessed material flows from division to division. Each division increases the value added of the product, with the last division selling the final product to consumers.

Now, suppose that an important technological change occurs in the production methods available to a single division within the company and that no other division is affected directly by the innovation. The nature of the change is important, as is the particular division in which it takes place. Here we assume that the innovation results in a neutral improvement in productivity. By this we mean that the technology is both capital- and labor-saving in equal proportions. For example, in the steel industry, the basic oxygen process is believed to have doubled productivity with respect both to capital and labor.[21] We assume further that the division in which the improvement becomes available is more capital intensive than all other divisions in the company. In other words, a neutral technical change in production methods is assumed to have occurred in the relatively capital-intensive division. The purpose here is to trace the effect of this change on the international competitiveness of the firm, assuming that the technology is freely available in the world.

It is helpful to express this example in a simple numerical form. Let Division 1 be the plant in which the new equipment is utilized. Other divisions are numbered 2 to n. Then, let:

$$K_i = \text{capital used per unit of output in Division } i, \, i \neq 1$$

$$K_1 = \text{capital used per unit of output in Division 1}$$

[21]United Nations, Economic Commission for Europe, *Comparison of Steel Making Processes* (New York: United Nations, 1962), Table 30.

L_i = labor used per unit of output in Division i, $i \neq 1$
L_1 = labor used per unit of output in Division 1
X = output rate

Then, capital intensity, R, can be defined in the following manner:

$$R_l = \frac{XK_l}{XL_l} = \frac{K_l}{L_l} R_i = \frac{\sum\limits_{i=l}^{n} XK_i}{\sum\limits_{i=l}^{n} XL_i} = \frac{\Sigma K_i}{\Sigma L_i}$$

and for the total company:

$$R = \frac{XK_1 + \sum\limits_{i=2}^{n} XK_i}{XL_1 + \sum\limits_{i=2}^{n} XL_i} = \frac{k_1 + \sum\limits_{i=2}^{n} k_i}{L_1 + \sum\limits_{i=2}^{n} L_i}$$

As stated previously, we assume that Division 1 is more capital intensive than the remainder of the company, which for illustration can be expressed as follows:

$$K_l = 3, \sum\limits_{i=2}^{n} K_i = 6$$

$$L_l = 1, \sum\limits_{i=2}^{n} L_i = 3$$

$$K_l/L_l = 3, \frac{\sum\limits_{i=2}^{n} K_i}{\sum\limits_{i=2}^{n} L_i} = 2$$

From these data, it can be determined that the capital intensity of the firm as a whole, before the introduction of the new technology, is:

$$R_B = \frac{3+6}{1+3} = 2.25$$

The introduction of new equipment results in a reduction of unit output requirements for both capital and labor. Again, we assume that input requirements in Division 1 are halved. Then, after the equipment installation:

$$R_A = \frac{.5(3) + 6}{.5(1) + 3} = 2.15$$

Notice that the introduction of a neutral technological change in the most capital-intensive division of the company reduces the overall capital intensity of the firm. In other words, the innovation, from the standpoint of the company as a whole, is relatively capital-saving despite the fact that it is neutral with respect to the single division. If the neutral change had taken place in a division of the company that was more labor intensive than the average, the result would have been an increase in total capital intensity of the company. Clearly, the effect on a firm's capital–labor ratio of an innovation depends on (1) the specific nature of the technology change itself, and (2) the type of production techniques used in an operation before the change is introduced. Together, these two factors determine the overall effects on the firm.

The implications of this example for international business can be seen most easily by continuing the steel industry example mentioned previously. If steel making is the most capital-intensive activity undertaken by an integrated steel firm and if the basic oxygen process is both labor- and capital-saving in equal degree, as seems to be true, then the use of this new process lowers the capital intensity of the steel industry. In other words, the basic oxygen process was more capital-saving than labor-saving for the industry as a whole. If it is assumed that the technology also was adopted abroad, it is possible that the basic oxygen process increased the advantage of overseas producers relative to steel makers in this country; that is, the process reduced the international competitiveness of the American industry because it increased the labor–capital proportion incorporated in the industry's product output.

This possibility certainly does not mean that U.S. producers should have avoided the new technology. The very large improvement in overall efficiency resulting from the use of this process forced the technology on American companies, as it did on industries throughout the world. The example here suggests at least the possibility, however, that the oxygen process was more beneficial in less capital-intensive countries than in the United States. Clearly, American production costs declined, but foreign costs might have been reduced even more through the application of new technology.

More generally, the numerical example given previously suggests an approximate method by which the impact of future changes in production techniques on the international competitive position of the firm can be assessed. The company must have fairly detailed technical information on the characteristics of any innovation, particularly the effects of the new technology on productivity with respect to various factors of production. Moreover, because the new method is to be compared with existing means of production, similar data are required for the current technology. With this information, it is possible to estimate the longer-run trade effects of a given change in production method.

Summary

The theory of comparative advantage has evolved to explain two fundamental questions:

1. What goods will be traded and at what prices?
2. What do nations stand to gain from trade?

Understanding the theory is useful to business executives because they respond to prices and profitable investment opportunities that frequently are determined in the vast interplay of international economic forces described by the theory. To be sure, many business decisions also are affected by other factors that are not the subject of comparative cost analysis. One thinks of personnel acquisition, training and legal problems, or the development of new technology. At best, a thorough understanding of theory can provide some comprehension of the large, systematic elements that shape the international environment.

There are possible ways in which techniques suggested by the theory of comparative cost analysis might be applied to decision problems. In some instances, companies might be powerless to influence events that will affect the firm's competitive environment. Trends in labor productivity might illustrate such a situation. In other instances, companies might be forced to adopt methods that will cause adverse shifts in their prices relative to their international competitors. The steel industry's investment in new steel-making technology might be such a case; yet, even in these situations, it is precisely this kind of foreknowledge that allows firms to adapt their long-range plans to meet the expected realities of the future, and therein lies one of the values of understanding the nature of one's competitive environment.

Any system of trade is supported by a financing arrangement or method of payment. In Chapter 3 we will discuss this system, which involves accounting principles of a sort. We call this system "balance-of-payments accounts.'' Once the balance of payments has been explored, Chapter 4 on foreign exchange markets will provide the connecting link between trade and financial flows as expressed by the balance-of-payments accounting system.

SELECTED READINGS

Bhagwati, J., "The Pure Theory of International Trade," *Economic Journal,* March 1964.

Caves, R.E., & R. W. Jones, *World Trade and Payments* (Boston: Little, Brown, 1973).

Chacholiades, M., *International Trade Theory and Policy* (New York: McGraw-Hill, 1978). This is a more advanced textual treatment.

Ellsworth, P. T., "The Structure of American Foreign Trade: A New View Examined," *Review of Economics and Statistics,* August 1954.

Harkness, J., & J. Kyle, "Factors Influencing United States Comparative Advantage," *Journal of International Economics,* 5, 1975.

Harrod, Roy F., *International Economics,* Fifth Edition (Cambridge, Eng., Cambridge Economic Handbooks, Cambridge University Press, 1973).

Kilpatrick, J., & R. Miller, "Determinants of the Commodity Composition of U.S. Trade: A Discriminant Analysis Approach," *Journal of International Business Studies,* Spring 1978.

Kindleberger, C. P., *International Economics,* Fifth Edition (Homewood, Ill: R. D. Irwin, 1973).

Kravis, Irving, "Availability and Other Influences on the Commodity Composition of Trade," *Journal of Political Economy,* April 1956.

Linder, S. B., *An Essay On Trade and Transformation* (Stockholm: Almquist and Wiksell, 1961).

Stern, R.M., "Testing Trade Theories," in Peter B. Kenen (ed.), *International Trade and Finance: Frontiers for Research* (Cambridge, Eng.: Cambridge University Press, 1975).

3

International Transactions: The Balance of Payments

INTRODUCTION

International economic events have dominated the news almost continuously for 30 years. Although it seems almost impossible to imagine today, news stories of the 1950s discussed the acute problem of dollar shortages in the world. Also covered in detail during that decade was the potential impact on American business of the formation of the European Economic Community. In the news articles of the 1960s, concern centered on the Kennedy round of tariff negotiations, the emergence of the Eurodollar market, and the now-apparent problem of a world dollar glut. In the 1970s, events included chronic deficits in the American balance of payments and, most significantly, the immense financial dislocations occurring as a consequence of large oil price increases. The events described in these news items alter the economic relationships between countries and, therefore, the environment within which international businesses operate. For this reason, managers must be able to analyze the likely effects of such changes on their own organizations. Typically, the analysis begins with data on international economic transactions, which are recorded and organized in the balance-of-payments accounts of the various countries. These accounts are the subject of this chapter.

All countries of the world systematically collect economic data pertaining to the international sector. In fact, for most nations, international transactions figures have been among the first economic statistics to be derived, simply because the levying of customs duties on trade was one of the earliest, if not the first, form of gathering tax revenues. Although the data can be categorized in several ways, depending on the purposes to be served, we consider here two basic types of transactions: (1) those involving trade in goods and services, or so-called "real" transactions, and (2) those involving transfers of purchasing power, or financial transactions.[1] In principle, any business interchange between residents of two countries is defined as an international transaction by both nations. In addition, a variety of other types of intergovernmental dealings are recorded.

TYPES OF INTERNATIONAL TRANSACTIONS

For the United States, commercial imports and exports of movable goods constitute, by far, the largest real transactions component. For example, shipments of this kind amount to more than two-thirds of the total U.S. foreign transactions in goods and services. The remaining one-third consists of a diverse assortment of interchanges between residents of this country and the rest of the world. Included are such transactions as travel expenditures by citizens of one country in another country, the purchase of transportation services in shipping merchandise, and the transfer from one country to another of fees, royalties, and profits, all of which are considered to be compensation for services rendered by the owner. For instance, dividends paid by a subsidiary firm to its foreign parent measure the returns from a previous capital investment or, in other words, the payment for services provided to the subsidiary at some earlier time by the parent. Because they do not entail the transfer of real goods, all of these latter transactions represent trade in services that are sometimes called "invisible" exports or imports.

Trade transactions in goods and services also involve a method of payment, or, stated differently, a matching financial obligation. In the early days of collecting international economic data, the recording of these liquid claims was the financial mirror image of the underlying trade patterns. These flows were said to reflect the "financing" of foreign trade. Today, however, international finance has become far more complex, and the types of transactions now recorded are commensurately more diversified. For example, a change in ownership of a bank deposit in the United States might result from the simple payment for an import shipment; however, it might also take place as a consequence of a rise in Eurodollar interest rates

---

[1]Detailed definitions of international transactions, as compiled by the U.S. Department of Commerce, are given in the appendix to this chapter.

(a subject to be discussed in subsequent chapters). In addition, financial flows of a longer-term nature have become an extremely important part of most countries' international transactions, and these transactions have little to do directly with trade in goods and services. These relationships will be discussed further when the balance of payments is explained later.

Capital movements are recorded largely in two categories: (1) movements involving short-term financial investments (i.e., those having a contractual maturity of a year or less) and (2) movements involving long-term investments and other forms of longer-duration investments. Short-term private claims are comprised mostly of demand and time deposits, various governmental obligations (such as U.S. Treasury bills), commercial or financial claims, and several other forms of short-term obligations. Also classified in this category are somewhat less liquid claims, such as trade acceptances,[2] business loans between countries, and various outstanding collectibles. Frequently, short-term claims result from the financing of foreign trade, but many transactions that occur using such instruments are entirely unrelated to trade. For example, movements of short-term funds in response to international interest-rate differentials, so-called "hot" money flows, usually would be carried out through deposit transfers. So also would international capital shifts due to speculation on exchange-rate changes. In fact, the hallmark of transactions in this category is the expected volatility of the funds moving between countries in response to any number of causes.

The U.S. Government, like its counterparts elsewhere in the world, also engages in a variety of transactions involving short-term credit instruments. Perhaps most importantly, the government, through the Federal Reserve Bank of New York, purchases and sells monetary and other assets for the purpose of maintaining currency exchange rates with other countries. With a pegged (or infrequently adjusted) exchange-rate system, as existed between 1958 and 1971, governments enter foreign exchange markets to force the supply or demand for their currencies to be consistent with the selected rate. Even with rates more flexible, the Federal Reserve enters international financial markets to offset exchange-rate changes that are, for one reason or another, considered inappropriate.

Information on flows of long-term capital has become very important for the United States. American investments abroad have been a major balance-of-payments item for many years, and in more recent times foreign long-term investments in the United States have been expanding rapidly as well. Two broad types of investments are designated in the U.S. accounts,

---

[2]A trade acceptance is a short-term financial instrument used in trade. Generally, it is an obligation of a commercial bank.

although in practice distinguishing between the two is frequently difficult and always arbitrary. On the one hand, there are *portfolio* transactions involving international purchase or sale of equity and debt securities, where the transaction's purpose is *not* control of the foreign enterprise. Thus, the purchase of 100 shares of Royal Dutch Shell common stock by an American would be a long-term portfolio transaction in the United States payments accounts. On the other hand, the purchase of controlling interest in a foreign corporation by an American firm, possibly through common-stock acquisition, is called a *direct investment*. The difference between the two types of long-term transactions is supposed to be simply the presence or absence of the control element.

This definitional distinction, of course, raises an immediate measurement problem: how large a purchase represents controlling interest? Is 51 percent required? Or, because of the pattern of distribution of equity shares, is 30 percent of the outstanding shares adequate? The answer obviously must be arbitrary in many cases. In the American balance-of-payments accounts, 10 percent ownership of a company's voting securities is sufficient to be termed direct investment. Where such ownership already has been established in previous transactions, further capital flows also are classified as direct investment. The 10 percent demarcation figure between portfolio and direct investment applies both to U.S. acquisitions abroad and to foreign investments in this country.

Direct investment figures today also include an entry for the reinvested earnings of controlled affiliates abroad. Recording such nonrepatriated earnings in the direct investment category represents a relatively recent change in U.S. balance-of-payments policy. In earlier years, foreign affiliates were considered to be residents of their country of location, and if affiliate earnings did not result in an international financial flow, nothing was recorded in the balance-of-payments accounts. The recent move to report nonrepatriated earnings as direct investment recognizes the fact that the decision to leave funds abroad typically is made at corporate headquarters in the parent firm's country. Such earnings, therefore, are assumed implicitly to have been repatriated and then reinvested abroad, even though the two intermediate transactions actually never took place. Without this type of treatment, a major source of funds for corporate expansion abroad would be ignored for balance-of-payments purposes.

There are numerous other forms of long-term capital transactions made across international borders that involve nonequity securities. These instruments carry a contractual maturity exceeding one year or, in some cases, no stated maturity at all. Typical of securities in this category are corporate bonds of various types and longer-term government bonds. Finally, long-term loans, not represented by marketable securities, also are included in this classification.

It should be clear by now that international commercial and financial interactions result in a wide variety of reported transactions. Before considering the complex subject of how these data are combined into balance-of-payments accounts, we must mention one or two features of the transactions themselves. We have learned that the distinction between short- and long-term transactions is based on the *contractual* maturity of the particular issue. No account is taken of the remaining time to maturity. An international transaction involving a 20-year corporate bond maturing in 6 months is treated in the U.S. data as a long-term capital movement. Perhaps more important is the arbitrary division between short- and long-term securities, which is meant to reflect the relative liquidity of such claims. Short-term securities supposedly can be bought and sold quickly with little danger of capital loss; in fact, however, many long-term securities, such as corporate stocks, are traded on well-established securities exchanges and are themselves quite liquid. Such distinctions are therefore somewhat artificial. The importance of this observation will become more apparent in the following section on the balance of payments, where other similar problems are pointed out.

THE BALANCE-OF-PAYMENTS ACCOUNTS

Types of Entries

Possibly because of their exposure to accounting concepts, students of business administration usually have little difficulty comprehending the basic structure of the balance-of-payments accounting system. This system, with minor differences, is constructed and published for most countries of the world and, at least in rough outline, is familiar to anyone reading a daily newspaper. Yet, the simplicity of the accounts' organization is lost quickly when the balance of payments for some period of time is used as the basis for economic analysis leading to international policy decisions. Then the interpretation of events portrayed in the accounts becomes exceedingly difficult, and, as we shall see, rather fundamental and seemingly irreconcilable differences of belief arise.

The balance-of-payments accounts for a country are simply an elaborate double-entry system most closely akin, but not identical to, a corporation's income statement. More particularly, the balance of payments measures *flows* of real assets and various debt instruments across national frontiers. The major difference between this system and an income statement is in the fact that some transactions, most notably the exchange of different types of real or financial assets, are included in the balance of payments but are not included in an income statement. Also, the structure of the accounts themselves as well as the timing of entries are dissimilar.

While debit and credit entries are made simultaneously in corporate accounts, the two sides of the ledger are often picked up independently in the international accounts. Thus fairly substantial time lags are inherent in the balance of payments, and this fact alone necessitates the inclusion of a residual account, appropriately called a "statistical discrepancy," which does not appear in a corporation's statements. Like any financial statement, however, the balance-of-payments debits and credits, in principle, should offset each other; that is, the payments accounts form an identity in which total debits equal total credits.

Debit items in the balance of payments include entries that increase funds in foreign hands, or, conversely, that result in increased use of funds by domestic residents. Credit entries, on the other hand, increase domestic holdings of funds or reduce foreign holdings. Examples of debit entries would include imports of goods and services, loans to other countries or residents of other countries (or repayments of loans previously made by foreigners), gifts to foreign residents, overseas tourist expenditures, or foreign investments by domestic business firms. Obviously, credit entries are the opposing flows, such as exports, loans and investments by foreigners, nonresident tourist outlays in this country, and the like.

The similarity of these entries to corresponding entries for an individual corporation should be readily apparent, but a few numerical examples are helpful. Consider the following transactions.

1. Ford of Canada, a wholly owned subsidiary of Ford Motor Company (U.S.), transfers subassemblies worth $5 million to the parent firm.
2. Ford (U.S.) invests $10 million to expand its Canadian facility.
3. Ford (Canada) sells $5 million of U.S. Treasury bills and reinvests in Canadian government short-term bills.
4. Ford (Canada) publishes its income statement showing net income (after taxes) of $3 million. No dividend is declared.

These transactions would result in the corporate ledger and balance of payments entries shown in Table 3–1. Transaction #4, for example, demonstrates the recording of reinvested earnings already discussed. Before 1978, no entry would have appeared in the balance of payments of the United States. Other transactions are straightforward, but entry #3 deserves additional comment. The subsidiary's exchange of U.S. for Canadian short-term assets clearly would not affect the financial position of the American parent from an income viewpoint; consequently, no entries are required on the U.S. firm's books. However, the switch does affect the liquidity position of the U.S. government, because its short-term liability now is to the Canadian government, an official reserve-holding agency. As

Table 3–1   Accounting Entries

Corporate Ledger Accounts (× 10⁶): Ford Motor Company (U.S.)			
Debit (U.S. $)		*Credit (U.S. $)*	
1. Merchandise: Inventory subassembly	5	1. Intercompany accounts payable	5
2. Investment: subsidiary	10	2. Cash	10
3. No entry		3. No entry	
4. Investment: subsidiary	3	4. Subsidiary income	3
U.S. Balance-of-Payments Accounts (× 10⁶)			
1. Merchandise imports	5	1. U.S. short-term nonliquid liabilities	5
2. Direct investment by U.S.	10	2. U.S. liquid liabilities	10
3. United States liquid liabilities	5	3. U.S. liquid liabilities to foreign official agencies	5
4. Direct investment by U.S.	3	4. Reinvested earnings of foreign affiliates	3

we further explain somewhat later in the chapter, this liability is considered to be quickly convertible and therefore is treated somewhat differently in balance-of-payments analysis. But it is worth recognizing that Ford of Canada's holding of U.S. Treasury bills also can be translatable easily into an official claim, as the example demonstrates.

The inclusion of various exchanges of assets in the balance-of-payments accounts, but not in a corporate income statement, is perhaps the most notable difference between the types of transactions incorporated into the two statements. This difference, of course, is traceable directly to the different purposes of the documents. Balance-of-payments statistics do provide the basic data for measuring the international economic performance of a country over some time period, which is similar to the purposes of an income statement. The criteria of performance are not the same, however. For a nation, interest focuses partly on the flow of real goods and services and partly on changes in the country's financial liquidity position; whereas, for a corporation, major interest centers on changes in the owner's equity accounts. Balance-of-payments statistics are used to conduct analyses related to a country's international trade and financial policies and to reach decisions on internal monetary and fiscal policy. The difference in purpose between corporate and balance-of-payments financial summaries is exemplified not only in the transactions deemed relevant but also, as we shall see, in the manner in which accounts are assembled for analysis. In fact, the balance-of-payments accounts most closely approximate a consolidation of a national income statement with changes in the structure of the country's existing international assets and liabilities.

The System of Accounts

The arrangement of international transactions into the balance-of-payments format is given in Table 3–2, using somewhat hypothetical figures. In practice, many of the pairs of depicted accounts might be shown netted out, with only a single net figure reported. For example, travel and transportation might be reported as a net debit of $3 billion ($19 billion minus $16 billion). Also, for simplicity, several smaller accounts that provide additional detail in published summaries have been omitted from this table.[3]

Table 3–2   Abbreviated Annual Balance-of-Payments Accounts (billions of dollars)[a]

Debits		*Credits*	
Current account:			
Merchandise imports	176	Merchandise exports	141
Travel and transportation expenditures	19	Travel and transportation receipts	16
Income paid on investments of foreigners	16	Income received from foreign investments	34
Remittances to foreigners	2	Remittances from foreigners	1
Government grants given	13	Government receipts	2
Total Current Account:	226		194
Capital account:			
Direct investment abroad	15	Direct investment by foreigners	6
Foreign securities bought	3	Securities bought by foreigners	5
Increased claims on foreigners: non-bank	2	Increased liabilities to foreigners: non-bank	2
Increased claims on foreigners: banks	34	Increased liabilities to foreigners: banks	17
Reserve assets		Reserve assets	
Gold	1	Government securities	25
Foreign currencies	5	Other government liabilities	3
Total Capital Account:	60		58
		Statistical discrepancy:	34
Total debits:	286	Total credits:	286

[a]Figures are rough approximations of U.S. data for the year 1978.

[3]U.S. balance-of-payments accounts for the year 1978 are given later in Table 3–3. (The statement is published quarterly in the Department of Commerce's *Survey of Current Business*.)

The two major subdivisions of the balance of payments are clearly depicted in Table 3–2: the current and the capital accounts. The first of these account groupings aggregates expenditures on goods and services, including earnings on private investments and governmental services. The net balance of the current account measures the amount of net foreign investment by a country. For example, the net current account debit balance of $32 billion shown in Table 3–2 must be matched by a net credit of the same amount in the capital account. Offsetting credit and debit items are an obviously necessary condition for the totals to be equal. The net credit in the capital account, however, represents an increase in domestic financial liabilities to foreign residents (or, of course, a decrease in foreign liabilities). This increase is equivalent to an expansion of net investment by foreigners in the country whose accounts are depicted.

It is helpful in understanding this point to consider the current account as consisting only of merchandise imports and exports; then a credit balance simply means an excess or surplus of exports over imports for the time period. This surplus might be regarded as the purchase of a single large foreign importer who, in turn, might pay for the shipment in any number of ways. For our purposes here, however, it is sufficient to represent the method of payment simply as a check drawn on his local commercial bank and payable to a resident of the exporting country. The check's recipient would then hold a liability of a foreign bank, and it could be used for various purposes. For example, the check might be deposited in a foreign bank in anticipation of some future need there. The deposit plainly increases short-term financial assets in another nation and therefore is a foreign investment. The important point to remember, however, is that even if the exporter had deposited the check in a local bank the claim on the foreign bank would continue to exist as a foreign asset of some domestic banking institution. The export surplus results in an increase of foreign investment, as the offsetting debit would imply.

One of the problems in recording transactions of this type, however, is that the two sides, debit and credit, generally are not picked up at the same time. Exports and imports are recorded as the goods pass through port customs inspection, but the corresponding financial transaction might require several weeks to appear. The financial entry also would never appear explicitly identified with a particular shipment; instead, it might show up as a small part of recorded international bank clearings or of some other financial category. As a result, it is virtually impossible to precisely delimit increases and decreases in various capital accounts as depending on specific trade surpluses or deficits. All that can be said is that the current account balance for a period indicates the overall change in foreign investment for a nation, but the exact form of that investment is influenced by a wide variety of circumstances other than trade alone.

Investment flows, the mirror image of the current account, are set forth in the capital account. In a more detailed set of balance-of-payments data, financial claims and liabilities would be further broken down into long-term and short-term components. In addition, as Table 3–2 demonstrates, exchanges of reserve assets are listed separately among financial transactions on both debit and credit sides. Changes in ownership of these assets are considered to be especially noteworthy, since they are believed by many economists to indicate the degree to which a currency is subject to exchange market "pressure." This topic is discussed in detail in Chapter 4.

Capital account figures, it should be noted, significantly understatte the total financial flows occurring during a particular time period. Each of the listed accounts is netted. For example, the $3 billion figure given for foreign security purchases actually represents the net difference between purchases and sales. Total purchases and sales would be very much larger. In fact, Wilson Schmidt has claimed that a *single* American security dealer might transact over $200 million in business on a good day.[4] Turnover in international financial markets can be 40 times the amount booked in foreign trade, clearly a very substantial figure.

Deficits and Surpluses

Before 1976, the Department of Commerce published the balance of payments accounts in a markedly different format than appears in Table 3–3, that summarizing current data. Along with the numerical presentation, the government also set forth a series of "balances" by which deficits and surpluses were defined. These balances were computed by taking the net difference between credits and debits in specified account aggregates. Clearly, the calculated difference in each case could be either positive (credits exceeding debits) or negative (vice versa). When negative, the balance was defined to be in deficit; conversely, when positive, a surplus was said to exist. Whether or not a country's balance-of-payments accounts were in deficit or surplus depended entirely upon which balance one was viewing for a particular time period. Some balances for the period could be in surplus at the same time that others were in deficit. Needless to say, such possibilities precipitated considerable confusion in popular discussions of our own balance-of-payments developments.

As an example, consider the now defunct balance on current account and long-term capital, sometimes called the "basic" balance. To arrive at

---

[4]Wilson E. Schmidt, *The United States Balance of Payments and the Sinking Dollar* (New York: New York University Press, International Center for Economic Policy Studies, 1979), p. 12.

Table 3–3   The United States Balance-of-Payments Summary (billions of dollars)

Line		1961	1975	1976	1977	1978
1	Exports of goods & services	29.9	155.7	171.3	183.2	218.0
2	Merchandise (excl. military)	20.1	107.1	114.7	120.6	141.8
3	Military transfers	1.9	6.1	5.6	7.3	8.0
4	Travel & transportation	2.8	11.7	13.7	14.5	16.4
5	Fees, royalties, services	1.5	7.2	7.9	8.7	9.9
6	U.S. government services	.2	.4	.5	.5	.6
	Income on assets abroad:					
7	direct investment	3.8	16.6	19.0	19.9	24.0
8	Interest & dividends	2.8	8.5	11.3	12.6	13.3
9	Reinvested earnings	1.0	8.1	7.7	7.3	10.7
10	Other private receipts	.8	7.6	9.0	10.9	15.9
11	U.S. government receipts	.4	1.1	1.3	1.4	1.5
12	Imports of goods & services	− 23.6	− 132.6	− 161.9	− 193.7	− 228.9
13	Merchandise (excl. military)	− 14.5	− 98.0	− 124.0	− 151.6	− 176.0
14	Defense expenditures	− 3.0	− 4.8	− 4.9	− 5.7	− 7.2
15	Travel & transportation	− 3.7	− 14.2	− 16.0	− 17.6	− 19.6
16	Fees, royalties, services	− .7	− 2.0	− 2.4	− 2.8	− 3.0
17	U.S. government payments	− .7	− 5.6	− 5.8	− 6.9	− 10.2
	Income on foreign-held assets:					
18	direct investment	− .4	− 2.2	− 3.1	− 2.8	− 3.7
19	Interest & dividends	− .2	− 1.0	− 1.5	− 1.3	− 1.6
20	Reinvested earnings	− .2	− 1.2	− 1.6	− 1.5	− 2.1
21	Other private payments	− .5	− 5.8	− 5.8	− 6.2	− 9.2
22	U.S. military grants	− 1.5	− 2.2	− .4	− .2	− .3
23	Unilateral transfers	− 2.5	− 4.6	− 5.0	− 4.7	− 5.1
24	U.S. assets abroad [net outflow (−)]	− 5.5	− 39.4	− 34.7	− 58.7	
25	U.S. official reserve assets	− .6	− .6	− 2.5	− .2	− .9
26	Other government assets	− .9	− 3.5	− 4.2	− 3.7	− 4.7
27	U.S. private assets	− 5.2	− 35.4	− 43.9	− 30.7	− 55.0
28	Direct investment (including reinvested earnings)	− 2.7	− 14.2	− 11.6	− 12.2	− 15.4
29	Foreign securities	− .8	− 6.2	− 8.9	− 5.4	− 3.4
	Private non-bank claims:					
30	Long-term	− .1	− .4	———	———	———
31	Short-term	− .4	− 1.0	− 2.0	− 1.7	− 2.3
	Private claims by banks:					
32	Long-term	− .1	− 2.4	− 2.4	− .8	− .3
33	Short-term	− 1.1	− 11.2	− 19.0	− 10.7	− 33.6
34	Foreign assets in U.S. [net inflow (+)]	2.7	15.6	37.0	50.9	63.3
35	Foreign official assets in U.S.	.8	6.9	18.1	37.1	34.0
36	Other foreign assets in U.S.	1.9	8.6	18.9	13.7	29.3
37	Direct investment (including reinvested earnings)	.3	2.6	4.3	3.3	5.6
38	U.S. government securities	.5	5.1	4.1	3.4	5.2
	U.S. private non-bank liabilities:					
39	Long-term	———	.4	− 1.0	− .6	———
40	Short-term	.2	− .1	.5	.9	1.7
	U.S. private bank liabilities					
41	Long-term	———	− .3	.2	.4	.2
42	Short-term	− 1.0	.9	10.8	6.3	16.6
43	Statistical discrepancy	− 1.0	5.4	9.3	− 1.0	11.4

Note: Details may not add precisely to totals due to rounding.
Source: U.S. Department of Commerce, *Survey of Current Business*, U.S. Government Printing Office, Washington, D.C., various issues.

this figure, export and import values were added to long-term capital movements, taking into account the appropriate algebraic sign. All of these accounts were believed to be autonomously determined, in the sense that the business decisions reflected in the accounts were made on the basis of existing world prices or investment opportunities. Contrasting with these transactions were so-called "accommodating" transactions, for the most part consisting of liquid capital transfers. These transfers were believed to be the financial counterparts of the autonomous transactions "above the line." Thus, a deficit in the American basic balance would signify that autonomous expenditures abroad exceeded foreign outlays in the United States, with a concomitant increase in short-term (liquid) U.S. debts to foreigners. Such a deficit, it was thought, could not continue long because eventually foreigners would refuse to accumulate more short-term, dollar-denominated financial assets in the United States. Some type of "basic" readjustment would be necessary.

The fact is, however, that the United States has continued to run basic balance deficits for many years. Even today, with rather flexible exchange rates, the figures would reveal persistent deficits. Obviously, something is deficient in the previous interpretation of the basc balance measurement, and, since the balance figure has been dropped, it will be useful to investigate some of the problems.

The most obvious problem is with the attempted distinction between autonomous and accomodating transactions; it is not a simple matter to say which is which or, indeed, if the distinction is meaningful at all. For example, a U.S. import results in an increase in foreign-held bank deposits in New York, which might, in turn, be used to finance the purchase of American export goods. Was the "autonomously" determined U.S. import "accommodated" by the short-term capital flow, or did the capital flow make possible the U.S. export? One could argue either way. Similarly, if temporarily idle funds of a foreign exporter are invested in the U.S. stock market, the transaction would involve a below-the-line debit and an above-the-line credit. The result would be a decrease in a reported basic balance deficit (or an increase in any surplus); yet, the long-range impact of the foreign exporter's choice of a place to hold idle funds is presumably unchanged. He might consider an efficient securities market for equities to be equivalent to maintaining his funds in some other shorter-term form. The balance of payments, however, treats his investment as a long-term commitment, unlikely to have rapid impact on the nation's international liquidity position.

A number of other similar problems related to data collection should be mentioned at least in passing. For example, a transfer of funds from the U.S. parent of an international company to its overseas subsidiary usually is treated as an increase in American direct investment, even if such a transfer is made for the purpose of temporarily increasing the subsidiary's working capital. Another problem involves the distinction between long- and short-term investment flows. Any long-term investment eventually becomes short-term as the maturity date draws closer; however, only the initial maturity is considered in recording transactions. Thus, a fair proportion of security holdings classified as long-term may, in fact, belong in the "below-the-line" category for the purpose of computing the basic balance.

The most serious problem with using the basic balance as an analytical measurement, however, is concerned with the dollar's special position as an international currency. This subject is treated in detail in Chapter 5. It should be readily apparent, even without the particulars, that the desire of other peoples of the world to use the dollar as, say, a medium of exchange for their own international transactions directly affects the basic balannce figure. Increased foreign holdings of liquid dollar assets, to be used for international dealings not necessarily involving the United States, generally would raise the deficit; yet, the motivation for increasing such holdings is clearly their usefulness in conducting business and not their potential interest earnings. While it is true that foreign-held U.S. bank balances are potentially convertible to other currencies, the probability of a large proportion of these funds being so used is surely quite small.

RECENT DEVELOPMENTS IN THE U.S. BALANCE OF PAYMENTS

As Tables 3–3 and 3–4 indicate, the basic balance measure is no longer reported in the United States, despite the fact that until the mid-1970s it was a center of international attention. Why should this be so? Partly, the reason is related to difficulties in measurement, as suggested previously,

Table 3–4 Balances Now Reported as Memoranda in U.S. Balance of Payments (billions of dollars)

	1961	1975	1976	1977	1978
Balance on merchandise trade (line 2 minus line 13)	5.6	9.0	−9.4	−31.1	−34.1
Balance on goods & services (line 1 minus line 12)	6.3	23.1	9.4	−10.5	−10.9
Balance on current account (line 1 minus line 12 minus line 23)	3.8	18.4	4.3	−15.2	−16.0

Note: Since debits are defined as being negative, balances are actually arithmetic summations.

but more important was the ascendance of the view that for the United States, the basic balance figure, as well as other reported balance measures, was severely misleading and as a consequence was an inappropriate figure upon which to build balance-of-payments policy. To see the crux of the opposing views, which eventually led to the new payments format of Table 3–3, we now will briefly review the argument of the late 1960s and early 1970s.

The "traditional" approach to balance-of-payments analysis argues for strong measures to correct continual U.S. deficits. Using the basic balance for illustration here, this approach would hold that nations cannot indefinitely run deficits, for two interrelated reasons. First, deficits mean that in terms of "autonomously" determined transactions, debits exceed credits. In a very rough sense, this fact indicates that a combination of import purchases and long-term overseas commitments, whether private or governmental, surpass a nation's ability to finance internationally such obligations through earnings on exports and reverse flows of investment funds from overseas. If the basic balance included only trade flows (i.e., abstracting from autonomous capital flows), deficits would mean that a country was absorbing more real resources than it was producing. In this view, such an excess represents a fundamental disequilibrium that was made possible only by short-term loans from foreigners; accordingly, it should not be allowed to continue indefinitely.

The second reason relates to the effect on the foreign exchange market of the short-term inflows themselves. These flows can take many forms, such as increases in private foreign-held bank deposits in the deficit country or, perhaps, short-term government obligations purchased by a foreign central bank. Regardless of the manner of holding, such debts constitute a potential claim on the deficit nation's monetary reserves that are made up predominantly of exhaustible supplies of convertible currencies and gold. As long as these reserves are sufficient to cover likely claims on them, no problem arises, but as short-term debt to foreigners grows from persistent deficits, the possibility of large-scale conversions presumably also grows. Assuming no correction of the underlying balance-of-payments problem, the ultimate consequence would be a "crisis of confidence" and possibly a run on the deficit country's currency, much akin to a run on a commercial bank. This action would preciptiate a devaluation and a departure from a fixed exchange-rate system.

Generally, economists would accept the traditional analysis of deficits for most countries of the world under a fixed exchange-rate system. To be sure, some might argue that the burden of adjustment to a balance-of-payments disequilibrium should fall partly on nations experiencing a surplus. Except for inconsistencies in the accounting data, deficits in one country or group of countries clearly must be matched by surpluses elsewhere. This difference in viewpoint, however, need not detain us here, since both sides of the argument would agree that deficits should not be allowed to become chronic.

Many economists assert, however, that even under fixed rates the traditional view of balance-of-payments deficits is not particularly relevant in analyzing the situation in the United States. Although the complete rationale for this somewhat more sanguine view of American deficits is rather complex, the basic idea is simple enough. For various reasons, the dollar has been accepted as the predominant vehicle for international transactions. For example, if a Japanese importer purchases bauxite in Australia, there is a strong likelihood that the transaction will be carried out in neither country's currency, but instead in U.S. dollars. Moreover, when a foreign central bank enters the foreign exchange market to stabilize its currency value or when it conducts periodic financial settlements with another central bank, the instrument used probably will be dollars. In brief, therefore, the dollar has become the major international currency, and because of this fact, traders and bankers throughout the world find the need to maintain dollar balances. As international commerce expands, so also does the need for additional dollar balances. The source of these rising balances necessarily is the continued inflow of short-term capital to the United States.

The deficit of a country like the United States in this view is of an entirely different nature from deficits that might occur in other countries. The origin of the U.S. deficit is not an excess of autonomous expenditures over receipts but is, instead, the simple desire of peoples throughout the world to use the dollar for their own financial purposes. If they wish to expand their dollar balances in the United States, then a deficit will be the result. In short, the source of the deficit, in this view, is largely external and perhaps even beyond the effective reach of standard internal correctional remedies. Under these circumstances, the optimal balance-of-payments policy for the Americans is one of "benign neglect"; that is, letting externally derived deficits be adjusted externally by the foreign countries themselves if they feel the need.

Moreover, under the type of quasi-flexible exchange rate system that has existed since 1973, the argument for adopting strong economic measures to correct deficits is even less convincing. The foreign exchange market, a subject discussed in detail in Chapter 4, should adjust the dollar's value relative to other currencies in accordance with its international need and availability. If basic balance deficits are precipitated by foreigners' desires to increase liquid dollar holdings, for whatever reason, then the dollar's relative value should be maintained. On the other hand, if the deficits indicate excess U.S. expenditures in the world, then the dollar's value should fall, with attendant impacts upon trade and financial flows. The point is that reporting quarterly or annual deficits, with the negative connotation implied, serves little purpose today and may, in fact, be grossly misleading. In any case, few balances now are reported in the United States, and even those are relegated to memorandum mention as a footnote to the balance-of-payments statistics (see Table 3–4).

BALANCE-OF-PAYMENTS FORECASTING

The most important part of a business executive's professional responsibilities consists of decision making, and this activity carries with it the obvious need to predict future events that presumably will affect the outcomes of those decisions. Whenever a business manager selects an investment project, sets a price for a product, or makes any of a myriad of possible business decisions, implicitly or explicitly taken into account are beliefs about the future. Thus far in this chapter, we have considered the usefulness to international businessmen and to government policy makers of understanding something about the balance-of-payments accounting system. Yet, when it comes to decision making in the international environment, it is clearly not sufficient to know only the structure of accounts or the definition of deficits and surpluses. Even some comprehension of the complex interplay of economic forces producing a payments position is not enough for one involved in forming decisions. What obviously is needed in such cases is information about *future* changes in balance-of-payments data.

Because predictive information is so important to both public and private agencies, considerable effort has been expended to devise methods to forecast balance-of-payments developments. The results of this work have been mixed, partly because payments forecasts are extremely difficult to render and as a consequence, are highly speculative. Uncertainty, of course, characterizes any economic forecast, but the problems are magnified in predictions about the international environment. Our purpose in this section is simply to discuss in an abbreviated way some of the requirements of a forecast and to point out the resultant problems for the analyst. The U.S. situation is cited not because it is particularly unique but because the context is more familiar.

Major (but not sole) interest in any balance-of-payments forecast for the United States typically would center on whether or not foreigners continued to build up liquid dollar balances. The reason for this emphasis is not hard to understand. Many international business decisions are affected by potential exchange-rate movements of the type that have occurred since 1971. Future changes, in turn, are based on the prospects for an additional increase in foreign-held dollar assets. Such increases might signal further deterioration of the dollar's relative value or, short of that, might be a harbinger of restrictions on capital flows, which can have an obvious effect on profitability calculations.

Balance-of-payments figures, however, typically are net balances, computed by taking the difference between two numbers that are comparatively large and frequently of approximately equal magnitude. Small changes (or, in a forecast, small errors) in either or both of these figures can result in very large movements in the difference. For example, the large U.S. trade deficit in 1978 ($10.9 billion) was less than 5 percent of the value of the nation's exports ($218 billion) and about 4.8 percent of imports ($228.9 billion) in that year. A 1 percent change (or forecast error) in either exports or imports would shift the residual figure by more than 20 percent. Obviously, the deficit or surplus projections are extremely sensitive to small changes in forecasts of the component figures, the basic items in the analysis.

Consider also the difficulties involved in a line-by-line forecast of major balance-of-payments accounts. For purposes of illustration, by no means unique, exports are convenient. Even abstracting from the future effects on export shipments of recent exchange-rate changes, which clearly could not be ignored in practice, a forecast would necessarily involve assumptions or explicit predictions about:

1. Rates of economic growth in major customer countries, because growth typically raises the demand for imports.
2. The pattern of economic growth overseas, because expansion typically increases the demand for some products more than others and because this pattern can shift as a consequence of progressing through various stages of growth.
3. Price levels for export goods in foreign countries, which tend to be a function not only of productivity changes and factor costs but also of overall demand conditions in each country.
4. Price levels for export goods in the United States, reflecting, together with overseas prices, the ability of American exporters to compete.

Somehow, also, the relation of each of these forecasts to U.S. exports would have to be derived, which would involve assumptions about the responsiveness of our exports to income and to relative price changes both here and abroad.

As if these matters were not enough to be concerned about, other problems arise in forecasting an aggregated figure like exports. First

complex interrelationships exist in the world economy, which should not
be ignored. For example, an increase in European or Japanese economic
activity affects not only U.S. exports to those areas but also to other
regions as well. This occurs because third-country exports to these areas
are raised, increasing the capacity of the country to buy more imports,
some of which originate in the United States. Also, vigorous economic
activity in, say, Europe tends to make European exports less readily
available elsewhere, which has the effect of opening futher export opportunities to U.S. producers. Such interrelationships are quite intricate and
probably not stable from one time period to another, yet any forecast of
our exports, just one item in the balance of payments, obviously would
have to take the effects into account.

     Another problem that must be tackled in forecasting balance-of-pay-
ments figures is the reciprocal relationship that exists between the account
categories. A commonly cited example of this phenomenon is the connection between exports and direct investment. Usually an increase in exports
would be interpreted as contributing to a surplus in the basic balance.
Suppose, however, that the increase were due to an American corporation's
adding to its investment in an overseas subsidiary by shipping machinery.
Then the machinery export would be exactly offset by an increase in direct
investment outflows, with no effect on the basic balance. Another similar
example would be enlarged commodity exports resulting from a governmental assistance program. The point is that changes in exports might not
have their origin in changes in foreign economic conditions but, instead,
might be based on decisions made in this country.

     Another example of the interrelationship between account categories,
involves only the two trade items, exports and imports. Frequenty, for less
developed countries, the ability to purchase goods in the world is constrained by a lack of the means for payment, or so-called "hard" currencies,
including the dollar. Even though a demand might exist for American goods
in the country, it is stifled by shortages of foreign exchange. In these
instances, an increase in the value of U.S. imports from the region, for any
of several possible reasons, improves the foreign exchange position of the
country, which, in turn, enables it to purchase additional goods from the
United States. In a very real sense, in other words, exports depend on the
level of imports.

     There are literally hundreds of such interrelationships between the
various balance-of-payments accounts. Some are important; some are not;
some might be important in one time period but not in another. Clearly, it
is up to the forecaster to appreciate these subtleties in analysis. To some
extent, analysts will be helped by the fact that account relationships tend
to be both positive and negative; therefore, errors in one direction might be

compensated for by errors in the opposite direction. However, under any circumstances the forecaster's life is not an easy one; as with many types of business information, the more its potential value, the greater the difficulty in obtaining it. When the usual complex situation is complicated further by fluctuating exchange rates between national currencies, as we have witnessed recently, the forecaster's job becomes commensurately harder and more uncertain. Nonetheless, it bears repeating that virtually any business decision requires, as input, information about future conditions. For international firms, where future balance-of-payments figures are important, a forecast that is little more than an informed guess is better than no information at all.

Summary

This chapter describes in some detail the balance-of-payments accounting system of the United States. The basic structure of the accounts has been shown to be a relatively straightforward double-entry system, recording for any period of time the flow of real assets and financial obligations into and out of the country. Obviously, in a system of this kind, total debits offset total credits and the net difference is zero. Because of difficulties in collecting data, however, many transactions go unrecorded, typically leaving a positive or negative residual called a statistical discrepancy. The specific classification scheme for entries into the balance of payments is outlined in the chapter appendix.

The particular groupings of accounts for analytical purposes have changed in recent years, largely because of misinterpretation caused by earlier formats. In the U.S. balance-of-payments, only three balances now are reported regularly. These can be described and briefly summarized symbolically in the following schema:
Let:

X = merchandise exports
M = merchandise imports
S = travel, transportation, service expenditures, and investment earnings
R = unilateral transfers
C = capital flows

Balance on Merchandise Trade

$$X + M = R + S + C$$

Balance on Goods and Services

$$X + M + S = R + C$$

Balance on Current Account

$$X + M + S + R = C$$

These identities demonstrate clearly that the various balances merely involve different categories of transactions. Each balance is intended to measure, from somewhat dissimilar perspectives, changes in the economic position of the United States in relation to other countries. More detailed accounts are published quarterly for various regions of the world.

Future changes in the balance of payments, like those of the recent past, are extremely important to business managers involved in international trade or investment. Clearly, major shifts in the foreign economic policies of important countries directly affect the operating environment of international and multinational businesses. The aim of this chapter has been to provide a better understanding of the major data source for analyzing international economic movements, that is, the balance-of-payments accounts. Although the format for collecting data differs from country to country, the basic elements and structure of the accounts are quite similar everywhere; therefore, attention to such information should provide clues to the probable future direction of economic policies and should allow aware international businessmen to adjust operations accordingly.

The next two chapters provide additional background for some of the concepts already introduced. These chapters give specific attention to foreign exchange markets and to the international monetary system. The first, on exchange markets, seeks answers to such a question as, "Under what circumstances, if any, will a revaluation of exchange rates provide a remedy for chronic balance-of-trade deficits for a country?" Chapter 5 expands the analysis to a consideration of official and nonofficial monetary relationships between nations and shows how these relationships are undergoing change. In these chapters, frequent reference is made to the balance-of-payments adjustment problems briefly discussed in this chapter.

SELECTED READINGS

Cohen, Benjamin J., *Balance of Payments Policy,* (Baltimore: Penguin Books, 1969)
    The economics of balance of payments issues can be found in this book.
Johnson, Harry G., *Money, Balance of Payments Theory and the International Monetary Problem* (Princeton, N.J.: Princeton University Press, 1977).

Krueger, Anne, "Balance of Payments Theory," *Journal of Economic Literature*, March 1969.

Meade, J.E., *The Balance of Payments* (New York: Oxford University Press, 1951).

Schmidt, Wilson E. *The U.S. Balance of Payments and the Sinking Dollar*, International Center for Economic Policy Studies (New York: New York University Press, 1979) The newly revised accounts structure discussed in this chapter also is covered in Schmidt's book.

Stern, R. M., *The Balance of Payments: Theory and Economic Policy* (Chicago: Aldine Publishing, 1973).

Stern, R. M., et al., "The Presentation of the U.S. Balance of Payments: A Symposium," Essays in International Finance, #123 (Princeton, N.J.: Princeton University, 1977).

Appendix: Definition of Classifications in the United States Balance of Payments

This appendix provides a more detailed definition of account categories used by the Department of Commerce in compiling the U.S. statistics. These definitions conform to the revisions described in the *Survey of Current Business* of June 1978, and are not necessarily consistent with previous definitions; however, the classification system outlined here accords with the discussion in the preceding chapter. Some account definitions relating to quite small amounts have been ignored in the following definitions.

Merchandise Exports Includes all movable goods transferred from the United States to foreign ownerships, valued usually FAS (free alongside ship) at the port of exit. This value reflects selling price plus packaging, inland freight, and insurance costs. Not included are certain governmental transfers, largely military, covered in the following definitions.

Military Transfers Includes deliveries of goods and services by U.S. military agencies under foreign military sales program contracts. Also included are sales of excess property of military installations abroad and logistical support provided to allies and U.N. emergency forces.

Travel and Transportation Credits include expenditures by foreign travelers (non-government) in the United States and foreign payments to U. S. transportation firms for passengers and freight. Debits include equivalent U.S. payments to foreigners.

Fees, Royalties, Services Credits include U.S. receipts in a variety of transactions, such as payments for use of intangible property (patents, etc.); management services; international communications operations; and construction, engineering, and consulting contracts. Debits cover similar payments by U.S. residents to foreigners.

U.S. Government Services Includes receipts for goods and services delivered to foreigners by nonmilitary U.S. government agencies.

Direct Investment Interest and Dividends Credits include interest and dividend payments to U.S. direct investors. Debits are similar U.S. payments to foreign direct investors here.

Direct Investment Reinvested Earnings Credits measure U.S. direct investors' shares in the earnings of incorporated foreign affilitates, less dividends paid to U.S. investors and less withholding taxes on dividends. Debits reflect similar reinvested earnings of foreign direct investors in the United States.

Other Private Receipts or Payments Credits include interest and dividend receipts by U.S. nondirect investors abroad. Debits are similar payments to foreign investors in the United States.

Unilateral Transfers Includes U.S. Government grants and pensions (excluding military grants of goods and services), as well as private unilateral transfers between U.S. and foreign residents.

U. S. Official Reserve Assets Includes transfers of gold between U.S. government agencies and foreign governments and international agencies, changes in U.S. holdings of Special Drawing Rights at the International Monetary Fund, changes in U.S. reserve position at the Fund, and changes in holdings of foreign currencies.

Other U.S. Government Assets Includes U.S. government loans and other credits to foreigners requiring repayment over a period of years, repayments of U.S. loans, and foreign currency holdings derived from various government programs.

Direct Investment Debits (credits) include increases (decreases) in U.S. equity holdings and intracompany accounts where the U.S. investor holds 10 percent or more of the incorporated foreign enterprise's voting securities (including reinvested earnings). Credits (debits) are increases (decreases) in foreign direct investment in the United States.

Foreign Securities Includes U.S. purchase of foreign equity and debt securities with maturities of more than one year.

Private U.S. Nonbank Claims: Short-Term Includes loans to finance exports, demand and time deposits held abroad, and other short-term foreign obligations.

Private U.S. Claims by Banks: Short-term Includes changes in claims on foreigners reported by U. S. banks for their own accounts and for the custody accounts of customers.

Foreign Official Assets in the United States Includes foreign official agency net purchases of U. S. Treasury securities, other government securities, bank liabilities, and equity and debt securities of U.S. corporations.

U. S. Private Nonbank Liabilities: Short-term Measures changes in such short-term liabilities as notes, bills, drafts, and advance payments.

U. S. Private Bank Liabilities: Short-term Includes changes in such U.S. bank liabilities as demand and time deposits, certificates of deposit, etc.

Statistical Discrepancy · A residual item equal to the algebraic sum of all other lines in the international accounts, with the sign reversed.

CHAPTER 4

The Market for Foreign Exchange

INTRODUCTION

Perhaps the major feature distinguishing international from purely domestic business operations is the need for managers to deal in several distinct currency areas. For traders, the problems caused by having receipt or payment streams denominated in a foreign currency are relatively straightforward. Even here, however, the decision to accept an order or to purchase imported goods must take into account the possibility of a change in currency values. When business firms locate manufacturing or other facilities overseas, financial issues become both more important and much more complex. Long-term commitment of resources is not reversed easily, and the investor becomes, in effect, a hostage to unanticipated changes in international relations. Operating a business in a foreign environment necessitates close monitoring of international financial events by businessmen to assure that corporate interests are protected. For example, executives who are thoroughly familiar with the reasons behind exchange-rate movements frequently can make sizable profits on the propitious shifting of corporate liquid funds from one currency regime to another. In other cases, potential restrictions on capital flows from a particular country, brought on possibly by chronic balance-of-payments deficits, can spell the difference between a profitable and an unprofitable new foreign investment.

The pervasive influence of international financial events on corporate activities makes it imperative that businessmen today understand the workings of the foreign exchange market and the world's monetary system. These topics are the subject of this and the next chapter. The present chapter begins by briefly summarizing the nature of formal economic linkages between various countries. In a sense, some of these connections already have been implied in Chapter 3, on the balance-of-payments accounts. There, much of the discussion involved accounting for the financing of trade and for other types of international capital movements. Here relationships between the market for foreign exchange and so-called "real" transactions will be sketched. In the next chapter, international monetary developments will be described. The role of the International Monetary Fund in a reformed world financial system will receive special attention at that time.

ECONOMIC LINKAGES BETWEEN COUNTRIES

The necessity of exchanging one currency for another represents the most obvious connection between economies of the world. When an American imports Italian wine, he expects to pay for it in dollars. At the same time, the Italian exporter ultimately desires lira to finance purchases at home. Clearly, for each to be satisfied, a currency transaction must be involved at some time. Either partner in the wine sale might be the one required to purchase one currency with the other. For example, the whole wine transaction might have been carried out in dollars, in which case the exporter's receipt would be a dollar-denominated debt instrument. For simplicity, we can assume that the receipt is a check drawn on an American commercial bank. The Italian exporter probably would deposit this check in a local bank which, in turn, would credit the exporter's lira account. The Italian bank would base its calculation of the lira credit on the prevailing price of lira in terms of dollars.[1] This price is called an *exchange rate*. The bank, of course, now holds the dollar check; what it does with the check is a matter that we shall discuss shortly.

The exchange rate obviously can be expressed either in terms of dollars or lira (i.e., lira/dollars or dollars/lira). Thus, an American, for convenience, thinks in terms of the dollar price of lira, while an Italian thinks of the lira price of dollars. In the analysis of exchange rates, this fact is a source of some confusion among observers accustomed to viewing prices in only one way. Typically, for example, one thinks of buying a product, say books, with dollars; but it is equally valid to say that the bookstore purchases dollars with books; it is all a matter of viewpoint.

---

[1] This abstracts from the bank's service charge for making the currency exchange.

The need to acquire foreign currencies or, in other words, to purchase foreign exchange, can arise from a vast array of possible international transactions other than trade. The purchase of foreign securities, overseas travel expenditures, and business investments or purchases are just a few of the myriad other possibilities. Virtually any economic interchange between residents of two countries *might* result in a foreign exchange transaction. The term "might" is important here, because many international dealings occur without the exchange of one currency for another. For instance, the loan of Eurodollars[2] by a British bank to a German importer does not involve a foreign exchange trasaction. Even so, the point here is that the demand and supply of various currencies, and therefore their equilibrium prices relative to one another, depend on the interplay of a wide range of underlying international economic events.

In fact, it is misleading to view the foreign exchange market strictly in terms of currency transfers. Actual movement of currencies is a trivial part of the market's total activities. By far the larger proportion of transactions involves interbank adjustments in various types of deposits. We use our earlier wine export example to illustrate. The check on the U.S. bank has ended temporarily in the possession of an Italian commercial bank. Thus far no foreign exchange transaction has occurred, since the check merely has been shifted from one Italian resident to another. The Italian bank, however, now has a number of alternatives, one of which might be simply to return the check to the American bank and accept in return an increase in its dollar deposits in the United States. Again, no foreign exchange transaction would be involved. On the other hand, the check might be sent to the Italian bank's foreign exchange department which, together with similar units in large banks throughout the world, "makes" the market for currencies. This department would locate a counterpart bank interested in obtaining a dollar deposit for lira at a rate negotiated between the two. Clearly, both banks would be aware of alternative exchange possiblities, and both, therefore, would be seeking to close the transaction on the best terms available. Depending on the demand and supply of various national monies, the rate at which the deal is consummated might be higher, lower, or the same as the established par value. In any case, the foreign exchange transaction involves interbank movements in the ownership of deposits at a price (exchange rate) determined in the money market.

An important point to remember in this example is that the export of Italian wine to the United States had the ultimate effect of increasing the demand for lira in the foreign exchange market. Obviously, an Italian import would have had the opposite effect by increasing the supply of lira being

---

[2] A full description of the Eurodollar market is reserved for Chapter 6.

exchanged for other currencies. It follows that a surplus in a country's balance-of-trade tends to increase the demand for its money. Admitting various capital movements into the scheme complicates matters considerably, but, in general, capital inflows increase the demand for a country's money and outflows increase the supply. Thus, if residents and banks of one nation were unwilling to hold balances in another currency, a trade surplus combined with capital inflows would tend to raise the demand for a country's money. The result would be to increase the exchange rate as expressed in foreign currency units (in our example, the dollar price of lira would increase). In the absence of central bank intervention, therefore, international money markets might be expected to operate similarly to more familiar commodity markets.

THE FOREIGN EXCHANGE MARKET AND TRADE

We have just learned that in the absence of government intervention or speculation, or both, the demand for foreign exchange derives from underlying trade and investment decisions. We have learned further that if world prices are constant, then an increased desire by U.S. residents for imported goods would tend to lower the value of the dollar with respect to other currencies. In foreign exchange market terms, this result takes place because a higher U.S. demand for imports has the effect of increasing the demand for foreign currencies needed to pay for the goods. The move in exchange rates, however, also has a reciprocal effect on import–export markets. When the exchange rate between two national currencies changes, the previously existing price relationships for traded goods obviously change, too. Again, assuming world prices to be fixed, raising the dollar price of foreign currencies would tend to make imports more costly for Americans and, in foreign currency units, to make U.S. exports cheaper in other countries. One might expect that this shift in relative prices would increase the volume of U.S. export shipments and would extinguish some of the American fervor for imported goods. Eventually, the value of exports might exactly offset the value of imports, evaluated in both currencies, and both product and exchange markets would return to equilibrium at the new set of prices.

Allowing Exchange Rates to Change

The process through which these adjustments take place is, as one might anticipate, not as simple as that just outlined. A further explanation will prove helpful. Suppose at a given point in time that the demand and supply for Italian lira in terms of dollars could be presented by the solid curves given in Figure 4–1. Here lira are being used as a proxy for all other currencies and the exchange rate, r, is expressed as dollars/lira. Again, we assume the price of Italian export goods to be fixed in Italy and the price of U.S. export goods to be fixed in the United States. For simplicity, it also is assumed that autonomous capital flows not related to trade are ruled out. Under these circumstances, the demand for lira, derived from U.S. importers desiring to purchase lira to pay for Italian goods, would be downward sloping because as the price of lira falls, Italian goods become less and less costly in terms of dollar purchases. Italian importers (U.S. exporters) account for the supply of lira being offered on the exchange market, and, as r rises, United States products are cheaper in Italy. Therefore, the S-curve rises as the exchange rate increases.

Two important points should be noted before we proceed. The first concerns the shape of both demand and supply curves. Whether or not the demand curve falls as the exchange rate declines (or the supply curve rises with a rising r), as has been asserted previously, clearly depends on the response of U.S. importers to lower prices for Italian goods (or, on the supply side, the Italian response to lower-priced U.S. goods). If the reactions of consumers are sufficiently price-elastic, then the curves would be correct as graphed. For any specific change in exchange rate, however, an elastic response is by no means assured, and it is possible, say, for a lower exchange rate to *reduce* the demand for lira, exactly the converse of the graphical display. The effect of both demand and supply elasticities on

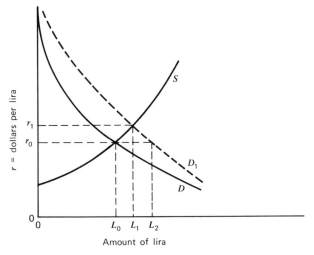

Figure 4–1. S = supply curve for lira, expressed in dollars; D = demand curve for lira, expressed in dollars; r = dollar price of lira.

the foreign exchange market will be discussed in more detail later. For now, it is sufficient to assert that, under normal circumstances, an exchange-rate change can be found for which a relatively elastic purchase reaction would be anticipated.

The other important point was implicit in the discussion of the source of supply of lira, that is, Italian importers. It should be noted that the supply curve for lira and the demand curve for dollars are, in effect, the same, except that normally the latter curve would be expressed in terms of the lira price of dollars. That is, to determine the demand curve for dollars, we need only to find the amounts of lira supplied at various rates of exchange, r, then to multiply these amounts by r to express them in dollars, and finally to plot them against the reciprocal of r (or $1/r$). Similarly, the supply of dollars and demand for lira are also reciprocal relationships. Evidently, therefore, if we assume a two-country world, equilibrium in the lira market implies equilibrium in the market for dollars, and vice versa, which should not be a surprising conclusion.

Returning to Figure 4–1, a freely fluctuating exchange rate would equilibrate the demand and supply of lira at L_0 with the rate r_0. Notice that in the simple world portrayed here, this equilibrium implies balanced trade in both countries. Suppose now, as previously, that U.S. residents suddenly change their preferences in favor of Italian goods. Such a shift might occur, for example, if Fiat automobiles received high acclaim in U.S. road tests. However, the source of the change in demand in Italian goods is not important here. The preference change would increase the demand for Italian goods in the United States and, therefore, would shift te demand for lira upward, as is portrayed in Figure 4–1 by D_1. At the existing exchange rate, r_0, the shift in demamd for lira would result in an excess demand for lira of L_0L_2. With the rate free to adjust, the dollar price of lira would move upward, precipitating two changes. First, Italian goods would become more costly to Americans, so they would tend to purchase fewer imports, an adjustment represented by a move upward along D_1. Second, Italians would purchase more of the now-cheaper U.S. goods, thereby supplying more lira. The new equilibrium rate would be r_1 with OL_1 lira being exchanged. Again, imports offset exports in both countries, and, with the assumptions made, the equilibrium is stable.

The analysis could be complicated by allowing more countries into the system, but the essential conclusions would remain the same. Given the demand and supply conditions for exports and imports just hypothesized, an arrangement of freely floating exchange rates between all countries would automatically result in the value of exports exactly offsetting imports in each country. Any movement away from this condition would bring into play exchange-rate adjustments that would return the country (and its trading partners) to balanced trade. Because of this remarkable property, many economists have strongly advocated such an arrangement as a solution to the world's persistent monetary and balance-of-payments problems.

It should be pointed out, however, that not all experts are convinced that flexible exchange rates are a complete answer. Some would assert that exchange-rate movements have secondary effects that cannot be ignored. For example, constant internal price levels cannot be assumed, especially in the devaluing currency's country. There, the lowering of relative currency value will raise not only import prices but also prices of export goods and, eventually, product prices generally. In fact, these economists believe that price levels would adjust to reestablish the previously existing international relationships.

One might ask why the opposite phenomenon would not take place in the other country; that is, if prices rise in one nation, why shouldn't they fall in the other? The usual argument against such a trend materializing is the observation that downward adjustments in price rarely occur in highly developed countries because of industry structural characteristics. We need not delve into these arguments here, but, if true, the consequences for the world economy clearly would be unpleasant. Flexible exchange rates would inevitably lead to inflation in devaluing countries with no commensurate and opposing effects in the appreciating nations. Since countries in such a system typically would swing back and forth between devaluation and appreciation, prices would tend to ratchet upward everywhere over time.

It is probably fair to say that the position just outlined remains a minority one. Most economists believe that prices of many products, especially commodities, are more adjustable than would be implied by this view. Moreover, the majority group would state that an overall price inflation is not a necessary consequence of a downward change in a country's exchange rate; it all depends upon the monetary policies pursued by the government. To be sure, if governments do not follow policies conducive to more stable prices, then the worst outcome could happen . If it does, however, the fault lies with the policies, not with the exchange rates.

Pegging Exchange Rates

Although the conclusions of the last section are generally accurate, a number of factors enter the picture to disrupt its appealing simplicity. One of them is the fact that for most of the period since World War II, exchange rates generally have not been permitted to adjust to the equilibrium levels established in a free international money market. By international agreement, until 1973 governments were obliged to take steps to assure that their currency values remained close to an infrequently adjusted per value. If, for example, the Italian lira increased in value, the Italian government would be obligated to supply additional amounts of lira to the foreign exchange market. The purpose of this move would be to offset the rising demand for lira that caused the rate to increase. Alternatively, if the lira value were increasing relative to dollars, the U.S. Federal Reserve System might have entered the market to purchase dollars with lira from its own reserves of convertible currencies. If the price of lira fell to its lower acceptable bound, then lira would have to be purchased with other convertible currencies. It was possible, of course, that a government might not have had sufficient reserves to support the value of its own monetary unit. In that case, two alternatives existed. First, the government could have borrowed the necessary currencies from another country, or, as will be pointed out in the next chapter, from the International Monetary Fund. Second, if all else failed, the government could have re-pegged its currency at a new and presumably lower level.

Clearly, in the absence of the automatic equilibrating mechanism provided by flexible exchange rates, it behooves each country's government to maintain a supply of foreign currencies simply to furnish a cushion of liquidity with which to defend the agreed-upon world price of its own currency. The need for this supply of international reserves on the part of all countries and the method of providing this liquidity have been the focal points around which recent discussions on the world's monetary system have centered.

We defer elaboration of these discussions until Chapter 5; however, one further element of a pegged rate system deserves attention here, because it is related to previous comments on the floating rate. Suppose that a trade-deficit country, having exhausted its alternative remedies, decided to re-peg its exchange rate at a new, lower level. Would such an action automatically lead to the required corrective movements in trade patterns? That is, would the devaluation correct the deficit? The answer is "not necessarily," as might have been suspected from the earlier discussion.

To see why a devaluation would not necessarily correct the deficit, we return to the two-country world of the U.S. and Italy but discard the requirement that product prices are fixed in the country of origin. Also, a previously pegged exchange rate now is revalued downward for the United States; that is, lira are now more expensive. Figure 4–2 depicts the consequences of this change for the United States, with panel *a* showing the supply–demand relationship for American exports and panel *b* showing the relationship for U.S. imports. The revaluation has the effect of increas-

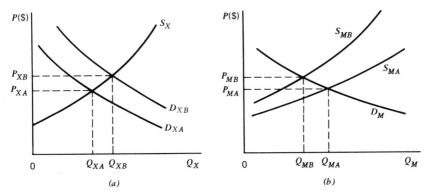

Figure 4–2. *(a)* United States exports. *(b)* United States imports.

ing the demand for U.S. exports valued in dollars, as we have seen previously. This change is shown as a shift in the export demand curve from D_{XA} to D_{XB} in panel *a,* resulting in an increase in the quantity of export $(Q_{XA}$ to $Q_{XB})$ at a higher dollar price P_{XA} to P_{XB}. It is possible, of course that the Italians might not respond to the lower lira prices for U.S. exports, which would imply a vertical demand curve with an elasticity of zero. With any increase in the quantity of U.S. exports sold, however, the dollar value of these shipments must rise, representing a positive contribution in closing the deficit.

The import side, however, is not as straightforward. Here, as is depicted in panel *b,* the devaluation makes imports more costly in dollar terms, raising the effective import supply curve (again expressed in dollars). One might anticipate fewer import purchases at a higher dollar price, as is shown by the move from Q_{MA} to Q_{MB} and P_{MA} to P_{MB}. Here, however, the overall effect on the dollar value of imports is ambiguous and depends on the relative size of the changes in quantity and price. If imports decline proportionately more than import prices rise, that is, if the elasticity of demand exceeds unity, then the dollar value of imports will decline. If, on the other hand, the demand elasticity for imports is less than unity, then total expenditures rise even though the quantity of imports is less than before the devaluation.

Enough has been stated to indicate that a devaluation might not correct a country's trade deficit and therefore might not renew equilibrium in the foreign exchange market. If the elasticities of demand for a country's exports abroad and its imports at home are sufficiently high, an improvement will occur. Or, if one elasticity is low but the other is much higher, then, again, the deficits should be reduced. But if both are low, it is entirely possible that a devaluation would worsen the deficit.[3] A frequently cited example is the less-developed country exporting one or a few agricultural commodities and importing mainly the necessities of consumption. In these circumstances neither export nor import quantities are necessarily responsive to price changes and domestic expenditures, for imports could rise without an offsetting gain in export earnings.

The very simple model depicted in Figure 4–2 is deficient in several respects in its ability to represent real-world foreign exchange situations. A few problems should be mentioned before we continue. First, the analysis concentrated on demand elasticities without mentioning possible responses on the supply side. Generally, the more elastic the supply of both exports and imports, the greater is the likelihood of a devaluation correcting a deficit.[4] Moreover, the analysis focused solely on price effects, but ignored the effects of changes in national income. Without going into the details of income analysis, it might be observed that expanding exports as a consequence of a devaluation is an income-generating activity in the domestic economy since export demand is a part of total demand. When total demand goes up, total economic activity expands or total income flows expand. Part of the additional income normally would be spent on imports, adding to the deficit burden. The converse might be expected in the foreign economy, where exports to the United States have declined, extinguishing some of the capacity to purchase imports (U.S. exports). Thus the income effects of a devaluation generally increase the job to be done by the price changes. Finally, the analysis ignores monetary effects of devaluations, particularly the impact of the resulting inflation on holdings of money balances. This topic is discussed in more detail in the next chapter.

Many other important elements of foreign exchange market operation also were eliminated in the analysis in order to concentrate on product-price movements. For example, foreign exchange markets are affected not only by international trade requirements but also by capital movements not related to trade. Especially important in this regard are short-term capital transfers made for speculative purposes, and they can be (and have been) very large. Suppose, for illustration, that we return to our two-country world of Italy and the United States and assume that exchange rates are free to fluctuate as supply and demand conditions in the exchange market dictate. Now, suppose a rise in the dollar price of lira takes place as a result of an increased U.S. demand for Italian merchandise. Speculators

---

[3]The Marshall–Lerner relationship in economics states that the sum of the two elasticities must exceed unity for a devaluation to help. For more detailed discussion, see any of the international economics texts cited at the end of Chapter 5.

[4]Readers may want to return to Figure 4–2 to work out the reasoning.

might react to this exchange-rate change in either of two ways. If they believe the change to be temporary, they will wish to take advantage of a return movement in the rate. How? By converting lira financial assets to dollar assets at the higher dollar/lira exchange rate and then waiting for the anticipated downward rate move. This activity increases the supply of lira (or the demand for dollars), having the effect of dampening the earlier upward change in the exchange rate. For this reason it is called "stabilizing" speculation. However, if a further upward change in rate had been expected, exactly the reverse speculative strategy would have been undertaken with exactly the opposite effect. Speculators would increase the demand for lira-denominated assets, driving the rate still higher. This form of speculation is termed "destabilizing" for obvious reasons. More will be said on speculative capital flows later in the chapter.

THE FORWARD MARKET FOR FOREIGN EXCHANGE

The foreign exchange market serves functions other than the clearing process outlined previously. One important function, which is of great interest to businessmen, is the provision of credit, particularly for financing trade. The extension of credit is a necessary ingredient of any trade relationship, because trade involves time in the production and shipping of goods. Frequently, credit is offered over even longer periods of time. Most U.S. trade is financed either by letters of credit or, less often, by dollar or foreign-currency drafts. A letter of credit, issued by the importer's bank, authorizes the bank to pay the exporter for goods to be forwarded. The bank usually is better known than the importer, and the risk of default to the exporter is minimized with such a letter. Generally, the bank is authorized to forward funds (usually dollars in U.S. trade) on the receipt of various shipping documents. Therefore, the seller accepts responsibility for the goods until delivery to a common carrier, at which time the seller is immediately compensated. The exporter finances the trade with this instrument, and the foreign exchange transaction is left to the option of the bank issuing the letter of credit.

Currency drafts, on the other hand, can be either sight or time drafts. These instruments are similar to normal bank checks except that they are drawn by the exporter on the importing firm or its bank. As an example, suppose that a U.S. firm exports $1,000 worth of computer parts to a purchaser in France. The exporter might have agreed to extend credit for a period of 90 days, in which case the company (or its bank) would draft a note to this effect. The note, drawn either on the importing firm or its bank, instructs the recipient to pay the exporter (or bank) the amount of $1,000 (plus interest) in 90 days. At 12 percent per annum, the total face amount to be paid would be $1,030. When the importer signs the document, it becomes an acceptance and is returned to the exporter, who, in turn, might either hold or sell it to a bank at a suitable discount rate. Although no foreign exchange transaction has occurred, the French importer is obligated to pay $1,030 in 90 days; that is, the importer eventually must convert francs to dollars to meet the obligation.

The French importer now is in a position where future liabilities in dollars would appear to exceed dollar assets. It is possible that within the 90-day period, exchange rates could change in such a way that the franc obligation would be larger than originally contemplated; that is, the franc could be devalued vis-à-vis the dollar. Because of this possibility, if no further action is taken, the French importer is essentially accepting the risk of an exchange-rate shift; in short, the importer is speculating. Since most choose *not* to speculate on currency movements, we might ask whether or not a method exists that would enable the importer to eliminate the "short" position. The answer is affirmative, and the foreign exchange market provides one means.

The obvious way for the French importer to be extricated from the "short" position is by finding a dollar-denominated asset to offset the liability. One alternative simply would be to acquire dollars today and hold them against the future obligation. This arrangement might be accomplished by establishing a dollar deposit in, say, a New York bank. Suppose, however, that the importer's lack of familiarity with foreign banks prevented this possibility. In that case, the importer could arrange through a local bank to purchase the required amount of dollars for delivery in 90 days at a stipulated price. This contract is known as a "forward" purchase of dollars (sale of francs), as contrasted to a "spot" purchase involving an immediate exchange of funds. It should be emphasized that forward contracts involve promises to buy (or sell) currencies in the *future* at a price known *today*. With such a contract, the French importer acquires the desired dollar asset, and the currency position is eliminated. Clearly, a "long" position could be cancelled by an exactly opposite strategy.

The purchase of forward dollars by the French importer is called "hedging" and is common in international financing to avoid foreign exchange risk. The implication of having thousands of such transactions is that essentially two foreign exchange markets must exist, one for day-to-day, or spot, transfers and one for forward contracts. In fact, forward exchange rates are quoted regularly in major financial periodicals for a number of currencies, for 30-, 90-, and 180-day contracts (see Table 4–1). Beyond these quotations, forward exchange transactions are usually possible in most currencies of important trading countries.

Despite the existence of these quoted rates, however, forward exchange

Table 4–1 Spot and Forward Exchange Rates for Major Currencies, January 15, 1980

Currency	Spot Rate	30-Day Forward Rate	90-Day Forward Rate
British pound	$2.2845	$2.2793	$2.2720
Canadian dollar	.8584	.8583	.8588
French franc	.2473	.2478	.2479
Japanese yen	.004168	.004194	.004231
Swiss franc	.6280	.6335	.6420
West German mark	.5792	.5825	.5878

Source: The Wall Street Journal, January 16, 1980.

markets are merely an extension of the spot markets, and exchange rates in the two, although usually different, are not independent of one another. This relationship can be seen most readily through a hypothetical case example. Suppose that the spot rate for British pounds is $2.30, the 90-day forward rate is $2.40, and the short-term interest rates in New York and London are 12 percent and 8 percent per annum, respectively. Could these four rates exist simultaneously? Clearly not, because a foreign exchange dealer in a New York bank could buy spot pounds, invest them in London and enter into a contract to sell pounds forward at the prevailing rate. If the initial outlay amounted to $2.3 million and if transactions costs could be ignored, then the dealer would receive $2.4 million on the forward contract in three months, a difference of $100,000. The transaction, however, does involve an opportunity cost, since funds left in New York would have earned a higher rate of return (12 percent for a quarter year) than those invested in London (6 percent). The amount of this cost is: $2,300,000 (1.03 − 1.02) = $23,000. The net profit on a 3-month transaction would be $77,000 (or $100,000 − $23,000), which on an annual basis would be a rate of return of 13.4 percent. It is important to note that the bank is fully hedged, because its pound investment is exactly offset by its forward sale, and it is left with no risk of exchange-rate changes that might affect the bank adversely.

When the bank enters into this type of transaction, it is engaging in "arbitrage" between the spot and forward markets. Notice that its actions increase the demand for spot pounds and the supply of forward pounds, which, in turn, tends to bring the rates closer together. As long as the arbitrage operation is profitable, it might be expected to continue, but the difference in short-term rates on each side of the Atlantic assures that the spot and forward rates would not be equated. When the opportunity costs (foregone interest) of entering the transaction balance the gain from the forward contract, further arbitrage would cease. In our case, the 90-day forward rate would be approximately \$2.323.[5] Divergences on either side of this rate would reflect other bank transaction charges or, in some instances, exchange restrictions that prevent interest arbitrage from taking place. In this latter case, the differential can be very large and hedging can become commensurately more expensive.

Arbitrage operations can be undertaken between various spot markets or between forward exchange markets, and the arbitrage might involve several financial centers simultaneously. Suppose, for instance, that the West German mark at a particular time was selling for \$0.58 in Frankfurt and in New York. At the same time, the French franc could be converted to marks in both Paris and Frankfurt at a rate of 2.5 francs per mark, and the dollar price of francs was \$0.25. Note that no profitable arbitrage is possible between any two markets in isolation; however, a quick calculation will reveal that a profit can be made by purchasing marks with dollars in either New York or Frankfurt, converting the marks to francs in either Frankfurt or Paris, and finally repurchasing dollars with francs in either Paris or New York. Thus, \$1,000 buys 1724 marks in New York or Frankfurt; 1724 marks buys 4310 francs in Frankfurt or Paris; and 4310 francs buys \$1,078 in Paris or New York. Arbitrage among three or more points keeps exchange rates mutually consistent between financial centers and serves to unify these centers into one large foreign exchange market. Speculative activities can involve forward as well as spot exchange markets. If, for example, an upward movement in a country's exchange rate is anticipated by speculators to be a harbinger of further rate increases, then their reaction might be either to buy the country's currency in the spot market or to buy it forward. The consequence might be that both rates would be driven higher.

THEORIES OF EXCHANGE-RATE DETERMINATION

The move away from fixed exchange rates toward a system generally characterized by more flexibility has stimulated considerable research as to how exchange rates are determined. It is an extremely important question for international business executives because many decisions depend substantively upon the state of future exchange rates. Fortunately, as a consequence of this recent work, some conclusions can be described. This section briefly reviews these conclusions.

To begin with, it is a readily observable fact that money markets in

---

[5]The computation involves adding the opportunity cost of entering the transaction to the spot exchange rate, or \$2.30 + 0.01 (2.30) = \$2.323.

various countries, and particularly industrialized ones, are linked together. Funds flow between nations in response to trade financing needs, investment opportunities, and, finally, expectations with respect to future exchange-rate changes. Such funds transfers do not take place perfectly freely, to be sure. Governments frequently restrict capital movements both into and out of some countries. Investors, moreover, probably show a marked preference for placing funds at home because of their far greater familiarity with domestic money markets and investment opportunities. And yet, economic events in one part of the world today impact almost immediately upon financial markets everywhere.

Still, despite these international financial links, interest rates on equivalent securities often diverge substantially from one country to another. If funds flows are relatively unimpeded, why doesn't arbitrage occur, to equate interest rates everywhere? The answer to that question involves an understanding of the relationship between changes in exchange rates, interest rates, and product prices. In order to take advantage of higher interest rates in another country, an investor must convert funds into that country's currency. This move implies that the investor also must be concerned with coming back to his or her currency when the investment matures. It is this presumed necessity that accounts for the interest-rate differentials observed among countries of the world.

Suppose, for example, that three-month Italian treasury bill yields (denominated in lira) were 15 percent per annum, while yields in like bills in the United States were 10 percent. Clearly, there would appear to be a motivation for Americans to convert to lira, invest in Italian treasury bills, and, in three months, take the proceeds and convert bank to dollars. This pleasant outcome, however, would hold true only if the relative value of the two currencies, dollars and lira, did not change sufficiently for the gains to be wiped out. In this case, if lira depreciated by 5 percent against the dollar, gains over and above a U.S. investment would be offset by exchange losses occurring as a consequence of the lira depreciation.

Thus, interest-rate differences can continue with no arbitrage incentive as long as investors anticipate exchange-rate movements adverse to their potential interest profits. In fact, if international financial markets were frictionless, interest-rate differences in various currencies would have to be equal to anticipated exchange-rate changes between the currencies. Otherwise, arbitraging financial transfers would take place to eliminate the difference, and we have seen already that arbitrage assures that *forward* exchange rates are consistent both with spot rates and with expected interest yields. The point to remember is that in perfect, or even reasonably efficient, international financial markets, country interest rates and exchange rates, both spot and forward, are inextricably linked. All are determined by market participants who act on the basis of expectations about the future.

What about interest rate changes themselves? What determines them? Monetarists can show substantial support for the proposition that interest rates are related closely to expected price movements, and that, in turn, price movements are caused basically by changes in the money supply. The latter link is not important for our purposes here, except to state that varying price-level changes in different countries can be caused by varying rates of monetary expansion. The vital point here is the impact of antici- pated price changes on interest rates; on this point, any elementary finance course covers the "Fisher effect," which states that lenders always will demand an interest return that reflects inflationary expectations over the period of the loan. Interest rates, in other words, incorporate two elements: (1) a time-value component necessary to reward lenders for foregoing consumption and (2) an anti-inflationary element to assure lenders that their interest return does not erode in terms of purchasing power. Money markets generally assure that interest rates will be related directly to price-level expectations on the part of market participants.

It is also true that inflationary expectations are linked to rates of change in exchange rates. This relationship is described in the purchasing- power parity theorem, long a standard part of economic theory. The notion begins with the observation that, in the absence of transportation costs or trade restrictions, prices of goods that are traded internationally must be equal everywhere. If this were not the case, commodity arbitrage would take place between those countries in which prices were unequal. Inflation- ary expectations in one of the countries can be shown to have an equal, but opposite, effect on the exchange rate. For example, relative inflationary anticipations of 10 percent in one country for a given year would be expected to precipitate a decline in the value of that country's currency by approximately 10 percent.

In summary, if relatively free international commodity and capital markets can be assumed, then price-level expectations and interest rates in each country, as well as exchange rates between national currencies, are all interrelated. Inflationary anticipations impact directly upon both interest rates and exchange rates through the Fisher effect and purchasing-power parity, respectively. We have also seen, however, that interest rates and exchange rates are linked directly by international arbitrageurs investing and disinvesting in various currencies, depending upon their expectations about future exchange-rate changes. Moreover, forward rates are main- tained in close relationship to spot exchange rates through the interest arbitrage activities of market participants. With efficient national and international capital markets, therefore, the entire interrelated system of variables functions on the basis of market anticipations about future price levels and exchange-rate movements.

One might ask what the evidence demonstrates about international financial market efficiency. It turns out that this is a complex question, because the anticipations upon which financial decisions are based cannot be observed directly. Still, the data that can be analyzed are consistent with results to be expected from efficient markets, at least for the major industrialized nations of the world. For example, while information about spot exchange rates and interest rates does not provide a perfect prediction for the forward rates to be expected from an interest arbitrage calculation, such a calculation gives at least a better prediction than other possible methods. Similarly, forward exchange rates are a "best" predictor of future spot rates, as would be anticipated from the perfect market model. The point is that no better models have emerged for describing international financial market behavior, at least for the larger countries.

Some additional conclusions based on the notion of efficient markets will be discussed in Chapter 15, which is concerned with financial management problems. There we shall see that the type of strategic decisions chosen within a multinational corporation depend closely upon management's ideas about precisely how exchange rates are determined.

Summary

Foreign exchange transactions involve the exchange of one country's money for another. The market in which these purchases and sales takes place is a worldwide network of interconnected financial centers. Trade and investment flows ultimately are reflected in foreign exchange transactions. For this reason, the economic conditions summarized in a nation's balance-of-payments accounts generally are mirrored in the price of the country's currency in terms of other currencies, or its system of exchange rates. If exchange rates were perfectly free to adjust to the supply and demand for the currency, then balance-of-payments deficits would create an excess supply of the currency, pushing the rate downward, and *vice versa* for a surplus. An exchange-rate change, however, also affects relative prices for traded goods; that is, while exchange rates change in response to international trade movements, trade patterns shift because of rate changes. Therefore, with freely determined rates the adjustment process simultaneously involves changes in trade, investment, and exchange rates until a new equilibrium is established.

In fact, exchange rates themselves are merely another set of prices linking financial markets worldwide. In an efficient international capital market, they are determined simultaneously with interest rates and product prices in all countries. They cannot diverge for long from levels consistent with other prices in the system without arbitrage taking place to reestablish the linkages.

To be sure, many countries establish controls over arbitraging capital flows, in order to accomplish particular national goals. In such cases, of course, the foreign exchange market can become divorced from other markets in the system and exchange rates can be maintained at nonequilibrium levels. In fact, until 1973 governments were required to peg their exchange rates relative to other rates and, except in unusual circumstances, hold their exchange rates within very narrow bounds. Thus, under these "rules of the game," some exchange rates could depart significantly from equilibrium levels. The international monetary system, in other words, did not allow exchange rates to be part of the equilibrating mechanism, as other prices were.

This formal and informal institutional framework for the international monetary system is the subject of the next chapter. Although these arrangements have undergone rather fundamental review in recent years, suggested reforms that might occur should be understood in the context of the system's development. Impending changes should have important ramifications for all firms engaged in international operations.

SELECTED READINGS

Aliber, Robert Z., *Exchange Risk and Corporate International Finance* (London: MacMillan, 1978).

Aliber, Robert Z., "The Interest Rate Parity Theorem: A Reinterpretation," *Journal of Political Economy,* December 1973.

Baron, David, "Flexible Exchange Rates, Forward Markets, and the Level of Trade," *American Economic Review,* June 1976.

Chacholiades, Miltiades, *International Monetary Theory and Policy* (New York: McGraw-Hill, 1978).

Dornbusch, R., "Expectatious and Exchange Rate Dynamics," *Journal of Political Economy,* December 1976.

Einzig, Paul, & Brian Scott, *The Eurodollar System: Practice and Theory of International Interest Rates,* 6th Edition (New York: St. Martins Press, 1977).

Friedman, Milton, "The Case for Flexible Exchange Rates," in *Essays in Positive Economics* (Chicago: University of Chicago Press, 1953).

Giddy, Ian, "An Integrated Theory of Exchange Rate Equilibrium," *Journal of Financial and Quantitative Analysis,* December 1976.

Giddy, Ian, & Gunter Dufey, "The Random Behavior of Flexible Exchange Rates," *Journal of International Business Studies,* Spring 1975.

Holmes, A.R., & F.H. Schott, *The New York Foreign Exchange Market* (New York: Federal Reserve Bank of New York, 1965).

Kohlhagen, Steven, "The Performance of Foreign Exchange Markets: 1971–1974," *Journal of International Business Studies,* Fall 1975.

McKinnon, R.I., *Money in International Exchange: The Convertible Currency System,* (New York: Oxford University Press, 1979).

Officer, L., "The Purchasing-Power-Parity Theory of Exchange Rates: A Review Article," *IMF Staff Papers,* March 1976.

5

The International
Monetary System

INTRODUCTION

The preceding discussion on foreign exchange markets implies that many
feasible arrangements might be envisioned under which international financial transactions could be carried out. Possibilities could be arrayed along
a spectrum. At one end would be an arrangement in which all the world's
currencies were joined by a structure of exchange rates left perfectly free
to fluctuate as conditions dictated. Governmental interference with the
rates would be disallowed, and official attention would be restricted to
internal problems such as full employment and economic growth. At the
other extreme would be a system in which the value of each country's
money was inextricably linked to other currency values through an arrangement of absolutely fixed exchange rates. Governments would be expected
to enter the foreign exchange market constantly, on either the demand or
supply side, keeping the rate within very narrow bounds. Domestic economic policies would be subordinated to maintaining external balance, even
when unemployment might be a consequence. Between the two extreme
points on the spectrum would be a wide assortment of other possibilities
combining features, sometimes the worst ones, of each polar system.

This chapter opens with a brief description of the international monetary system as it evolved after World War II. Next is a discussion of the
very rapid and significant changes that have occurred in international

monetary dealings since about 1971. Likely consequences of current negotiations among country governments also are outlined, along with their implications for multinationally interested business executives.

THE INSTITUTIONAL SETTING

The International Monetary Fund

The basic structure of the pre-1971 International Monetary Fund was established by the 1944 United Nations Monetary and Financial Conference at Bretton Woods, New Hampshire. The conference created two important financial institutions: the International Monetary Fund (IMF or Fund) and the International Bank for Reconstruction and Development (IBRD or World Bank). We are interested here principally in the IMF and its role in the functioning of the world monetary system.

Membership in the Fund, originally 40 nations, had grown to 138 in late 1979 and comprised virtually all of the important non-Communist countries in the world. Each of the Fund's member countries originally agreed to establish a par value for its currency, either against the U.S. dollar or against gold. The dollar itself also was to be pegged to gold at a specific price. Because maintaining absolutely precise rates against the dollar would be impossible, the agreement stipulated that countries would keep their currency values within a narrow band around the established par. The Bretton Woods conferees were aware that parity adjustments would be needed from time to time, but such changes were to be made only after prior consultation and approval of the IMF. Thus, the 1944 agreement formalized a system based on fixed, or infrequently adjusted, exchange rates.

The IMF was to fill other roles as well. Perhaps most important to the fixed-exchange-rate system were currency-loan provisions to assist countries having balance-of-payments difficulties. In this role, the Fund functions as a reservoir of currencies, with each member country contributing a preestablished quota, paid partly in its own currency and partly in gold (see Table 5–1). Governments then were permitted to borrow needed currencies to support their currencies' par values. Such borrowings, part of which were to be automatically available, normally were expected to be repaid within a three-to-five-year period.

The Bretton Woods agreement made formal an international monetary system in which each currency unit had a parity value established in terms of a given weight in gold. Currencies were to be convertible into gold on demand, at least for settlements between central banks. Thus, the arrange-

Table 5–1   Members' Fund Quotas, International Monetary Fund—1979 (millions of United States dollars)

United States	10,926
United Kingdom	3,803
Germany	2,803
France	2,495
Japan	2,157
Canada	1,764
Italy	1,612
Netherlands	1,232
Australia	1,157
Belgium	1,027
All others	9,426
Total	50,714

Source: International Monetary Fund, *International Financial Statistics*, 32:10, 1979.

ment was known as a "gold exchange" system. Also, since rates were not to be fixed unalterably, it was called an "adjustable peg" system.

Much has occurred in international monetary affairs since the formation and early development of the IMF. The Fund itself has become somewhat peripheral in the system's operation, and fixed exchange rates recently have been replaced by a set of rates that fluctuate in response to world economic forces. Perhaps naturally, the United States became dominant in international monetary affairs. The series of events that led to each of these outcomes now will be described in some detail.

The Dollar as International Money

While the Bretton Woods agreement did recreate a quasi-fixed exchange-rate system, it did not provide for all of the needs of a viable international monetary system. For example, the IMF arrangement did not specify explicitly just what was to serve as international money. Is, in fact, a separate international money necessary, given that readily exchangeable national monies exist? The answer is both complex and debatable, and the following discussion represents only a consensus of views. Where major disagreement occurs, the outline of the argument also is mentioned.

Textbooks on money and banking generally enumerate three classical requirements for money: it must serve as a numeraire, a medium of exchange, and a store of value. These needs are no less true in the international economy than they are within a single currency jurisdiction. Looking at the first requirement, we already have discussed how other currencies originally were pegged to the dollar under the rules of the IMF. To be sure, each currency, through the dollar, was tied to gold, but, in practice, the dollar link has been by far the more important and only partly because of the dollar's fixed gold value. In addition, most central banks have held their international financial reserves predominantly in gold or foreign exchange. Of the amount held in foreign exchange, the U. S. dollar is by far the most important currency held. When governments have intervened in foreign exchange markets to stabilize their currency values, the dollar almost always has been the vehicle for carrying out the transaction. Thus, the dollar for many years clearly seemed to fulfill the numeraire requirement of international money. Even today, with more flexible exchange rates being the rule, central bank reserves and intervention transactions still typically are denominated in dollars.

The dollar also has been the unit of account most frequently used by international traders and private bankers in carrying out their transactions, even where the United States was not one of the parties. In a typical year foreigners might hold $30 to $35 billion in deposits in this country, in addition to Euro-deposits, for use in trade and financial transactions. For over 30 years, the dollar overwhelmingly has been the chief medium of exchange in the world.

Finally, as a store of value, interest focuses on a currency's command over an assortment of real goods during a time period. In general, more stable prices and a claim to a wider assortment of goods lead to a greater store of value. Table 5–2 depicts price-level trends in various major countries during a time when the U.S. inflation rate was unusually high. Only Germany's prices rose more slowly than the U.S. rate. The picture

Table 5–2   Consumer Prices in Industrial Countries (1967 = 100)

Unit	1963	1967	1970	1973	1976	1977
United States	91.6	100	116.3	133.1	170.5	181.5
United Kingdom	86.7	100	117.4	150.3	252.4	292.4
France	89.5	100	117.1	140.7	196.1	214.4
Germany	89.8	100	107.0	127.1	150.5	156.5
Italy	85.2	100	109.2	134.2	218.3	257.6
Japan	82.1	100	119.3	148.5	223.7	241.9

Source: U.S. Department of Commerce *Statistical Abstract of the United States* (Washington, D.C.: U.S. Government Printing Office, 1978), for years 1967–1977 and IMF, *International Financial Statistics* (June 1972) for 1963 (base year changed).

changes somewhat when exchange-rate changes are taken into account, but the general conclusion remains unaltered. Table 5–3, which does consider exchange-rate movements in its derivation, shows that U.S. relative price increases have been outdistanced by the United Kingdom, Germany, and Japan, while prices have risen only slightly less rapidly in France and Italy. The period covered in the Table 5–3 was one of fairly rapid inflation everywhere as a reaction to oil price hikes by the oil-exporting countries. Of the possibly available currencies, therefore, the dollar historically has offered the most secure store of value. There appears to be no argument among economists that international money does exist and that the U.S. dollar has occupied this role.

How did the dollar come to this preeminent position among the world's currencies, and why does it retain this position despite the adoption of relatively flexible exchange rates? The answers are, in part, historical. For several years following World War II, the major national currencies, especially those of Western Europe, were not convertible. Holders of these currencies could not exchange them either for other currencies or for gold. Needless to say, if international trade had depended on the ability to carry out currency transactions, a world of inconvertible currencies most certainly would have presented a formidable barrier. Two factors combined to ease this situation. First was the willingness of the United States to exchange dollars for gold at a fixed dollar price per ounce; for a period of more than 13 years following the close of World War II, the dollar was the only currency thus maintained. Because of this convertibility feature, traders could confidently undertake transactions in which the dollar was used as denominator. However, the dollar was in extremely short supply internationally, which meant that even though traders might be willing to use it, they had no dollar resources on which to draw.

To ease this dilemma and to assist in efforts at reconstruction, the United States initiated a massive program of grants and credits to wartorn countries. This program constituted the second factor, to expand the supply

Table 5–3 Relative Wholesale Prices (1975 = 100)

Unit	1973	1974	1975	1976	1977	1978
United States	98.0	99.8	100.0	103.1	100.9	93.9
United Kingdom	96.5	96.8	100.0	93.9	100.5	105.0
France	96.8	88.5	100.0	95.8	90.2	92.6
Germany	102.4	103.0	100.0	101.6	103.7	104.9
Italy	98.9	98.6	100.0	92.6	93.5	92.2
Japan	111.1	113.7	100.0	103.8	107.3	119.7

Source: IMF, *International Financial Statistics*, October 1979.

of available dollars. As Table 5–4 indicates, these financial flows were truly immense and enabled many industrial countries to import needed equipment, mostly from the United States, for rebuilding war-ravaged factories. In less than five years, more than $25 billion was made available for reconstruction and development purposes. Even though most of these funds were expended in the United States and therefore did not substantially enlarge dollar availability for normal trade, they enabled the European countries and Japan to begin redevelopment of their normal export trade patterns. These exports, together with continued U.S. assistance (see Table 5–5), provided sufficient dollar reserves that European convertibility could be restored late in 1958.

Table 5–4 United States Foreign Grants and Credits in the Immediate Postwar Period, June 1945 to December 1949 (millions of dollars)

Group	Grants[a]	Credits	Total
1. Western Europe, Japan, and other developed countries	11,509	9,097	20,606
2. Less-developed countries	2,291	776	3,067
3. Eastern Europe	1,090	348	1,438
4. International organizations	530	23	553
5. Unallocated	298	——	298
Total	15,718	10,244	25,962

[a]Grants are essentially gifts, while credits are loans.
Source: U.S. Department of Commerce, *U.S. Statistical Abstract,* 1950 (Washington, D.C.: U.S. Government Printing Office, 1951).

Table 5–5 United States Foreign Grants and Credits, 1945–1968 (millions of dollars)

Area of Receipts	Military	Other	Total
Western Europe	16,554	23,900	40,544
Eastern Europe	——	1,602	1,602
Near East and South Asia	6,804	19,480	26,284
Africa	271	3,251	3,522
Far East and Pacific	13,302	17,543	30,845
Western Hemisphere	1,149	7,806	8,955
Other	410	3,007	3,417
Total	38,490	76,679	115,169

Source: U.S. Statistical Abstract, 1969 (Washington, D.C.: GPO 1970).

Thus, for many years after World War II, the U.S. dollar was the *only* world currency acceptable as an international medium of exchange. Nations accumulated dollars, at least in part, as reserves, and the dollar was used later both as an intervention currency for exchange-rate stabilization and as the unit of account for international settlements. Traders and bankers held dollar balances for financing international commerce and investment. These uses for the dollar have continued until the present time, although there are indications that changes will be occurring in future years.

We might ask why the dollar maintained its importance as international money after the restoration of other major currencies to convertibility. With conversion possible, any major currency presumably could be exchanged for any other, and an important reason for utilizing a single money unit thereby was removed. Alexander Swoboda has analyzed this question and has provided at least a partial answer.[1] Swoboda believes that in the absence of concern about possible exchange-rate changes, traders will desire to hold balances in foreign currencies to meet their day-to-day needs. Alternatively, traders could maintain balances only in their own money and could utilize the foreign exchange market as required, but this strategy would involve continual costs of converting. Therefore, assuming interest earnings to be equal on foreign and domestic balances, traders will choose to avoid these transactions costs by maintaining foreign-currency balances in amounts that are roughly proportional to the business being done with a particular currency domain.

The demand for foreign balances, however, also concentrates on one or a few currencies, called "vehicle" currencies. Swoboda's economic rationale for this is that reducing the foreign exchange component of working balances from many currencies to one enables traders to lower the costs of keeping such balances. The argument is similar to the familiar inventory notion that a specified amount of business in a single, stocked item requires fewer inventories than would the same amount of business comprised of many items. In financial inventories, the larger the number of separate currency needs that can be consolidated into one currency, the greater are the savings to be made.

There are varied reasons for choosing the dollar as the vehicle currency. One is the expectation that necessary exchange costs will be lowest in the best-developed capital market. New York is far and away the deepest and broadest financial market of the world. Another reason for choosing the dollar has been the smaller risk of exchange loss associated with it. Since 1971, however, holders of dollar balances have experienced significant

---

[1]Alexander Swoboda, "The Euro-dollar Market: An Interpretation," *Essays in International Finance*, No. 64. Princeton, N.J.: Princeton University, February 1968.

exchange losses as the currency has been devalued successively, and one might anticipate some substitution of other currency units for the dollar in future transactions use. Nonetheless, until very recently, nonspeculative holders of foreign balances tended to prefer the currency with the smallest likely fluctuation, the dollar, against the domestic monetary unit. Finally, Swoboda points out that once a currency becomes the major vehicle for international transactions, the tendency for it to continue to be used is self-reinforcing. As the currency's use widens, so also do the related financial markets. As their size and efficiency increase, the markets provide services at lower cost, leading more traders to concentrate in the currency.

THE INTERNATIONAL MONETARY SYSTEM: PROBLEMS AND SOLUTIONS

The framers of the international monetary system at Bretton Woods envisioned a world in which each country's currency would be maintained at a fixed (or, at least, infrequently changed) parity with other currencies and, in particular, with the U.S. dollar. The value of the dollar, in turn, would be pegged to a specific quantity of gold. The ultimate monetary asset on which the system's viability was believed to depend was gold. When individual countries ran prolonged balance-of-payments deficits that exhausted their supply of gold and convertible currencies, they were to take appropriate measures to correct the imbalance, in general without adjusting their exchange rates. Only when a "fundamental disequilibrium"[2] was believed to exist, in the judgment of the IMF's Board of Governors, were exchange rates to be altered.

We have discussed already some ways in which this arrangement evolved into something perhaps not anticipated by its designers. Most important was the dollar's evolution as a key international currency and as the system's primary reserve asset. This development had two effects. First, it changed the basic operational characteristics of the system, because the expansion of international liquidity was dependent on the international availability of dollars. Second, the rise in the importance of the dollar was matched by a crescendo of protest by those who disliked the preeminent position in international monetary affairs occupied by the United States and its dollar. In some instances these protests have been mainly emotional, but in others, as we shall see, the objections were founded on the belief that a dollar-based system enabled the United States to benefit at the cost of other countries. Under any circumstances, the solutions suggested for

---

[2]A deficit or a surplus had become chronic.

the two important problems in the system, the need for an adequate adjustment mechanism and the need for stability, are closely dependent on one's view about exactly how the system *should* function.

One of the major functions of any international monetary arrangement, and one foreseen by the Bretton Woods conferees, is the provision of sufficient credit to allow countries to correct or adjust balance-of-payments disequilibria. Within the framework of the IMF, this need was recognized in the Fund's provision for loans, some of which were to be automatically available to member countries experiencing payments difficulties. When a nation found itself with inadequate supplies of convertible currencies (or gold) to support its exchange rate, then the IMF simply stepped in with loaned currencies, within specified limitations based on individual country quotas. As economic growth ensued, so also did the amount of assigned quotas, which in turn meant that larger loans were possible. If a borrowing nation were to exhaust its available IMF drawings without finding internal policy measures sufficient to adjust the deficit, presumably a devaluation would be its last recourse under the system.

Clearly, the burden for adjustment under the IMF arrangements fell on the deficit, not the surplus, countries. Because of this asymmetry and the fact that devaluation is considered to be undesirable, central banks around the world attempted to accumulate reserves to allow themselves as much cushion as possible for the protection of their exchange rates. Aside from the opportunity costs associated with reserve holding, there were no penalties in the system for countries expanding their reserves. Surplus countries under this setup were under no pressure to enlarge imports, while deficit nations were pressured to reduce them; in fact, countries that accumulated surpluses were considered to be somehow more virtuous than countries incurring deficits. Demands for remedial action in the face of balance-of-payments disequilibria inevitably went from surplus to deficit nations, seldom, until recently, in the reverse direction.

There is no necessity for this incongruity to have existed. A system could be envisaged whereby surplus countries would be penalized for "excess" holdings of reserves. Moreover, upward revaluations of exchange parities conceivably could become as acceptable in the system as devaluations historically were. As we point out in later discussion, both of these possibilities have emerged as part of a revitalized monetary arrangement. First, however, the problems forcing the changes should be outlined.

From a balance-of-payments adjustment viewpoint, the major problem that arose concerned the adequacy of reserve expansion through the IMF. Most new reserves entering the system were in the form of convertible currencies, and most of these had been dollar balances. Nearly two-thirds of international reserve holdings consisted of currencies, and nearly 40 percent were dollars. For many countries, even this growth was inadequate to finance their deficits for the required amount of time. The French experience between 1968 and 1969 provided an example of how rapidly a country's reserves could be depleted. Between the end of 1967 and mid-1969, France lost $3.3 billion or nearly one-half of her total reserves, which most observers would have believed sufficient beforehand.

Part of the reason for reserve inadequacy was the apparent unwillingness of countries to adopt internal economic policies in times of deficit that were consistent with adjustment. When faced with a choice, many governments would not subordinate employment and price policies to the requirements of external balance. For example, correcting a deficit might have called for restrictive monetary steps that could have resulted in higher levels of unemployment. Typically, countries chose instead to maximize employment, even when continued balance-of-payments deficits resulted. Under these circumstances, the need for reserves became greatly magnified, and governments responded to this need in two ways. First, various ad hoc measures were developed through international cooperation to increase the level of reserves. Second, when even these devices proved inadequate, governments resorted to deliberate methods of controlling international payments flows.

An example of the informal arrangements that were instituted to effectively enlarge reserves was the Basel agreement of 1961. This agreement, worked out through the Bank for International Settlements, called for the major central banks of Europe to purchase currencies being sold in excessively large amounts on the foreign exchange market. In the situation precipitating the agreement, Great Britain was experiencing payments difficulties, and private holders of pounds sterling were dumping the currency to acquire other, hopefully more stable, currencies. The central banks simply agreed to absorb sterling until the "run" subsided. Obviously, no speculative movement from one currency to others could succeed if all central banks stood ready to purchase it at the prevailing exchange rate. Since that time, numerous automatic "swap," or loan, arrangements have been consummated among central banks of the large industrial countries, and frequent meetings are held among major executives of these institutions. Perhaps significantly, these agreements did not involve the IMF, but they did achieve the objective of increasing international liquidity, thus providing countries more flexibility in handling their monetary affairs.

To avoid the inevitable devaluation that accompanies exhausting the supply of international reserves, governments resorted to various methods of controlling the payments accounts themselves. One obvious way was to limit imports through tariffs, quotas, or some other more subtle means. Conversely, export subsidies of one kind or another frequently were provided, either directly through tax rebates or indirectly through low-cost export financing. In addition to influencing trade flows, governments regulated the availability of foreign currencies to private users. Rationing of foreign exchange has been particularly prevalent in less-developed countries, where balance-of-payments deficits have been a chronic problem and foreign exchange has been scarce. To assure that these currencies were used for purposes that contributed to development, governments required that exporters and other recipients of foreign exchange sell it to the central bank at an established exchange rate. The bank, in turn, determined who among the potential users had first access to the available supply of foreign currencies. Such exchange control programs often incorporated multiple exchange rates as one method of rationing. Under this system, high-priority needs received lower exchange rates, whereas less desirable users required much larger, sometimes prohibitive, outlays of domestic funds. All of these methods are discussed in more detail in Chapter 7, on economic policies.

The utilization of dollars as the primary source of international reserve expansion led to both problems and advantages for the United States. From our discussion of the balance-of-payments accounts in Chapter 3, it should be clear that an increase in foreign short-term claims on this country implies that the U.S. balance on current account and long-term capital must be in deficit. Since dollar reserves take the form of short-term claims, an enlargement of such reserves could occur only if the United States ran deficits. This fact, together with the added use of the dollar as an international transactions currency, meant at the very least that the usual assessment of the balance-of-payments adjustment process should be altered when applied to the reserve-currency country. In such a case, continuing deficits might not reflect a fundamental disequilibrium in a nation's external economic relations at all but, instead, reflect the ordinary desire of foreign governments, banks, and individuals to expand their holdings of liquid assets denominated in that nation's currency. The difficult judgmental question is in assessing the degree to which U.S. deficits were a response to international liquidity needs or, on the other hand, an indication of changes taking place in the underlying structure of trade and financial relationships.

Many economists, advocates of a dollar-based system, believe that in terms of U.S. policy the question really did not matter. If the dollar, in fact, has been the international monetary standard, then the United States might be viewed as the world's banker. In this role, the country would hold long-term assets and issue short-term liabilities, as would any bank. The readily observable fact is that until quite recently the U.S. balance-of-payments typically exhibited a trade surplus and long-term outflows exceeding short-term inflows, consistent with the banker role. The dollar system proponents, however, would go further. When asked how the U.S. Government should have responded to increasing gold outflows, reflecting adjustments in foreign reserve portfolios, they would reply that these claims should have been honored so long as the gold supplies lasted, but that under no circumstances should the United States have repurchased the gold at the set price. After that, foreign accumulation of unwanted dollar assets would have had to be remedied by policy measures taken in those countries, not in the United States. This was the essence of the "benign neglect" point of view, which included that the United States should not have maintained any policies directed specifically to balance-of-payments adjustment.

The problem with this viewpoint was that its viability depended on international acceptance of the dollar as the monetary standard and of the United States as the major supplier of increased world liquidity. Neither was universally achieved. One of the important objections was that the United States stood to profit from being the key currency country. This was the so-called "seigniorage" issue. The word seigniorage is defined as the difference between the circulating value of a money and the cost of producing or minting it. In the international context, seigniorage implies that the United STates, issuing international money through its short-term borrowings held as reserves in other central banks, could employ these funds at a rate of return higher than the interest cost of the loan. Moreover, because dollar balances also are used privately for financing trade, the seigniorage gains are even larger than the reserve status of the dollar would have implied. At the risk of oversimplifying, seigniorage gains mean that the reserve-currency nation could create credit at very low cost, which it then used to purchase real goods and services from the rest of the world. Needless to say, governments of non-key-currency countries disliked the notion of transferring real goods to the world's richest nation to obtain additional international liquidity. The solution, they suggested, was to distribute seigniorage profits more widely by transferring reserve creation to some international agency.

Actual seigniorage accruing to the center country, however, has been considerably overstated in much discussion of the issue. Foreign holders of dollar balances need not be content with interest earnings from the United States but, instead, could increase rates of return greatly by activating these deposits through the Eurodollar market. This very important market is discussed in detail in Chapter 6. Sophisticated and highly competitive international capital markets provide the means for foreign banks to have bid away much of the potential seigniorage gains that might otherwise have gravitated to the reserve-currency country. While it may be true that central bankers for various reasons might have felt constrained in their ability to expand earnings on dollar assets, there was certainly little reason to expect private dollar holders to react similarly. Private dollar balances presumably are maintained only because these assets generate some measure of utility for their owners. In fact, even central banks placed funds in the Eurodollar markets and negotiated with the American government for higher-yield dollar instruments. Such moves, of course, reduced the potential gains to the United States from seigniorage.

Other observers who might have been willing to accept the idea of a single key currency believed that the Americans did not act responsibly in their role of overseers of the international money. Most particularly, vociferous discontent was registered against the price-inflationary trend in the United States. The domestic economic policies that led to this inflation had two closely interrelated direct effects on other countries, in this view. First, the lack of a restrictive monetary policy in the United States precipitated a large short-term inflow of funds to other countries. Movement of these funds undercut the monetary policies of these countries, making it extremely difficult for authorities to prevent the "export" of the U.S. inflation to their own countries. Second, efforts to negate the inflationary effects of these flows forced the central banks to absorb large amounts of liquid dollar assets, thereby substantially altering the portfolio composition of their reserves. The central banks became involuntary holders of dollars that could not be translated into other forms of assets without undermining the international monetary system. It was minor consolation to these bankers that any system free of controls over capital movements could have resulted in the same phenomenon.

The upshot of this argument from the standpoint of balance-of-payments policy was the widespread belief, even in this country, that the United States should have taken steps to remedy its persistent deficits. That is, the view that the American deficit was mainly determined by portfolio preferences elsewhere in the world was not accepted generally by monetary authorities. This led to the demand that the United States subject itself to the same balance-of-payments discipline expected of others in a fixed exchange-rate system. Obviously, this position implied that an alternative source of acceptable international reserves had to be developed.

TRANSITION IN THE INTERNATIONAL MONETARY SYSTEM

In recent years, a rapid succession of international financial crises occurred that shook confidence in the continued viability of existing monetary arrangements. These dramatic events precipitated widespread rethinking about the underlying structure of the system. Even today, in late 1980, international monetary affairs remain in a state of flux, adding considerable uncertainty to world business operations. In this section, we attempt to bring some order to the existing chaos by tracing briefly the events leading to the crisis and by outlining likely future directions for international economic policy.

In 1968, during a deep French currency crisis, enormous speculative purchases of gold drove the gold price upward. The obvious expectation of gold purchasers was that currency parities against gold, including that of the dollar, were to be raised. This anticipation apparently was based on the belief that the ratio of gold to foreign exchange (mostly dollars) in expanding international reserves was too low. In the absence of larger supplies of gold entering the system, one way to make the available gold go further is simply to increase its value. To counter the speculation and to support gold's pegged value, central banks were required to sell gold from their own reserves. The run persisted, however, and it soon became evident that unless very large quantities of gold were exchanged for currencies, the speculation would continue. Instead, central banks jointly decided to suspend their support of the gold price, and official trading was discontinued.

The suspension of gold sales and purchases by the central banks, of course, had the effect of cutting loose the private market for gold. The price of gold (in money terms) was then free to find a level determined by the demands of speculators and private users and by whatever supplies might reach the market. Speculators no longer were assured of being able to dump gold back with the central banks at a fixed price, and therefore the risks of speculation were increased. The expectation was that, without a floor provided by central banks, gold prices would ultimately decline. This expectation, however, reckoned neither with continued monetary instability, which led people to hedge against an uncertain future by holding gold, nor with generally rising commodity prices, one of which was the price of gold. Despite the central banks' action, gold prices soared to over $500 per ounce in 1980 (compared with $35 in 1968) and have remained high.

The decision not to intervene in private gold markets, however, still left the question of how gold would be treated by the central banks in its role as a component of international reserves. Would reserve holdings be valued at the fluctuating free-market price? And how would international settlements involving gold be carried out, if at all? These problems led to the establishment of a "two-tier system" for the gold market. Under this arrangement, the major central banks of the world agreed neither to buy nor to sell gold in the free market; however, gold transactions among the central banks themselves were to be continued at the previously pegged rates of exchange. Essentially two markets (tiers) were to exist, one for private transactions and the other for official intergovernmental dealings.

Needless to say, this agreement effectively diminished the importance of gold in the system and was the first of a series of steps that have tended to demonetize the metal internationally.

This tendency to "put out fires" as problems arose in the system was evident in other spheres as well. One such area was the provision of international liquidity, an area of need recognized explicitly in the quotas established by the International Monetary Fund. Even so, the IMF has been a distinctly peripheral institution, both in providing liquidity and as a source of monetary stability. Part of the Fund's impotence has been due to its inadequate financing, even with successive enlargement of quotas over the years; part has stemmed from the disinclination of the important industrial nations to subordinate their own freedom of action in monetary affairs to the requirements of the international agency. Moreover, the development of Eurocurrency markets greatly expanded the magnitude of actual and potential short-term capital flows responding both to high interest rates and to speculative motives. As periodic problems have arisen, solutions have been largely ad hoc in nature and involved only the major countries operating outside the IMF structure.

One example was the formation in late 1961 of a group of central-bank officials from the large industrial countries.[3] This group has become known as the "Group of Ten." Since its organization, the Group of Ten has met regularly to consider developing international financial problems and, where possible, to derive solutions. Out of its early deliberations came a series of bilateral loan arrangements, called "swaps," in which countries agreed to lend their currencies to any other country in the group that was experiencing unusual pressure on its exchange rate. These swap agreements, of course, substantially increased a nation's ability to cope with currency crises, and thereby effectively added to the world supply of liquidity. The arrangements, however, were not intended by most countries to be a long-range solution to the problem of expanding international reserves but, instead, as a stop-gap series of measures to provide additional monetary flexibility until a more permanent solution could be found. The major difficulty, as might be expected, was to uncover a reserve-expansion mechanism on which all countries could agree.

Perhaps the most significant event of recent years in the rapidly shifting scenario of world finance was the 1967 annual meeting of the IMF Board of Governors in Rio de Janeiro. This meeting, culminating a long series of formal and informal preparatory sessions, laid the foundation for creating a new reserve asset called the Special Drawing Right (SDR). Participating

---

[3]The countries involved were Belgium, Canada, France, Germany, Italy, Japan, The Netherlands, Sweden, United Kingdom, and United States.

countries, who must be members of the Fund, periodically receive credit balances in a new IMF account, appropriately called the Special Drawing Account. The total size of this account would grow over time, and each participant would acquire additional credits on the basis of a predetermined system of allocations. The new rights could be used by countries only to acquire an equivalent amount of convertible currencies from other countries. Today, SDR units are valued in terms of a "marketbasket" (weighted average) of major world currency values, thus avoiding problems associated with the unit being tied to a single currency (dollars) or to a commodity (gold).

Participants are required to accept SDRs within specified limits in exchange for their own currencies. In general, then, SDRs can be used by countries to supplement existing reserves of gold and convertible currencies in supporting their exchange rates. The flows of SDRs would tend to be from countries having balance-of-payments deficits to those having surpluses. The first allocation of SDRs was made on January 1, 1970, with additional distributions in later years now totalling over 12 billion units.

Although the Special Drawing Account is maintained by the IMF and new allocations are decided by the governors, SDRs are not a liability of the Fund or of any particular government. SDRs owe their acceptability as international money not to some ultimate claim on a specific official agency but, rather, simply to the willingness of central banks to accept them in exchange for their own currencies. They are, therefore, a creation of an international agreement and, like gold, represent claims to generalized purchasing power over real goods. SDRs are acceptable only because the using agencies (central banks) have committed themselves to their acceptance within defined limitations. Because SDRs are to be utilized as international reserve money, but are not claims on the IMF, they have been likened to gold, which has similar properties, and the term "paper gold" is seen frequently in press accounts describing their role.

The creative and cooperative international effort resulting in SDRs, however, was unfortunately not enough to prevent monetary crises from arising. Most significantly, 1970 and early 1971 were times of great uncertainty in the exchange markets, manifested, insofar as the United States was concerned, by a very rapid increase in liquid liabilities to foreign central banks. In the 18 months of that period, these liabilities more than doubled, totaling $34 billion by June 1971. Moreover, the transfer of privately-held short-term dollar assets to foreign central banks, caused by the desire to achieve positions in those currencies, precipitated monetary expansions in those countries that became increasingly difficult for the central banks to neutralize. In the United States, the Federal Reserve, not surprisingly, was faced with a relatively heavy foreign official demand for gold and other reserve assets and, with the rapidly enlarging official reserve transactions deficit, was confronted with the real possibility of massive conversions of liquid dollar assets. The long-feared liquidity crisis involving the dollar appeared to be developing and with it the potential of collapse of the international monetary structure.

Several events occurred in mid-1971 that emphasized the severity of the crisis. In May, the German mark and Dutch guilder were allowed to float freely in the foreign exchange market. In August, the United States, without prior consultation, formally announced the suspension of dollar convertibility into gold and set forth a series of unilateral measures designed to improve its balance-of-payments deficit. Among these steps was a uniform surcharge, or tax, on imports, to be removed only if other industrial countries agreed to "realign" their exchange rates in a manner favorable to this country; that is, an appreciation against the dollar, which obviously is equivalent to a dollar devaluation. Without convertibility, foreign central banks were faced with the dilemma of either accepting additional dollars or finding methods to stave the flow. The decision for most countries was immediate: to withdraw from supporting their exchange rates and, therefore, to allow the rates to be determined by market forces. Generally, rates rose against the dollar in the last half of the year as dollar conversions continued. By the end of 1971, U.S. liquid liabilities to foreign central banks had increased to more than $50 billion.

The August crisis precipitated multilateral negotiations by the major countries on a new structure of exchange rates. These meetings, of course, were among the objectives of the U.S. Government in its mid-year actions. The outcome of these negotiations at the Smithsonian Institution in Washington, D.C., were announced in December 1971, and virtually all of the world's major currencies individually were revalued upward against the dollar. The net results of the realignment of exchange rates was an implicit devaluation of the dollar by approximately 9 percent, on the average.

The hopes of the Smithsonian accord were apparent. The Americans saw the possibility of resolving their balance-of-payments deficit, which had reached the staggering figure of nearly $30 billion in 1971 (official reserve transactions balance), by correcting for a chronically overvalued exchange rate relative to major trading partners. Europeans saw the opportunity to now reduce unwanted dollar reserves, albeit at a lower rate, and to prevent further currency speculation. All participants, American and European alike, wished to see the U.S. role in monetary affairs reduced by diminishing the importance attached to the dollar.

In 1972, however, world financial conditions continued to be very unsettled. Important currency values hovered near their upper limit, two percentage points above par, and gold prices on the free London market ranged above $60 an ounce. By midyear, the British government floated the pound sterling and renewed speculation against the dollar ensued. The Federal Reserve activated "swap" arrangements with both the Belgian and German governments, selling foreign exchange for dollars. All indications were that speculators did not believe that the Smithsonian currency realignments were sufficient.

Developments continued to occur rapidly in late 1972 and early 1973. Early in the year, the Italian government established its own version of a two-tier system by supporting a fixed exchange rate for current account transactions but allowing the rate for capital transactions to float. The intention of this decision was to make speculative moves into lira more costly, thus reducing the unwanted accumulation of dollars by the Italian central bank. The move, however, only transferred speculative pressure to other countries, as might have been expected, and the sequence of responses took place quickly. The Swiss almost immediately removed support for the franc and allowed it to float upward. Finally, on March 12, major European countries decided on a plan to maintain relatively fixed exchange rates internally but to conduct a "joint float" against the dollar and other dollar-tied currencies.[4] As part of this agreement, Germany revalued the mark upward by an additional 3 percent. Japan joined Great Britain and Italy in individual floats of their respective currencies.

Major world currency values continue to float against one another. Early efforts to return to a system characterized by more stable exchange rates were stifled in the aftermath of the oil-importing countries' joint decision to raise petroleum prices dramatically. This single move created continuous and massive capital movements as oil-using countries paid for imports and oil exporters readjusted their expenditure and reserve-holding patterns. As one indication of the magnitue of these new capital flows, oil-exporting countries' reserve holdings alone increased from $9 billion in 1972 to nearly $64 billion in mid-1979. No system of fixed exchange rates could survive the financial chaos created by such capital movements and by the world price inflation at least partially engendered by the oil price increases.

The impact of the continuation of flexible exchange rates on the dollar's value can be seen in both Table 5–6 and Figure 5–1. With the exception of the British pound rate, the dollar has declined significantly against all major industrial-nation currencies since 1972. Despite this exchange-rate deterioration, however, the dollar remains the world's major trading and financing currency. Even so, business managers have had to become accustomed to

---

[4]Included were West Germany, France, Norway, Belgium, Luxembourg, Denmark, The Netherlands, and Sweden.

Table 5–6   Recent Exchange-Rate Movements (local currency units/U.S. dollar)

	1972	1973	1974	1975	1976	1977	1978	(Aug.) 1979
Germany	3.202	2.703	2.409	2.622	2.362	2.105	1.828	1.828
Japan	302.0	280.0	300.9	305.1	292.8	240.0	194.6	220.0
France	5.125	4.708	4.444	4.485	4.970	4.705	4.180	4.262
United Kingdom	2.348	2.323	2.348	2.023	1.702	1.906	2.034	2.251
Switzerland	3.774	3.244	2.540	2.620	2.451	2.000	1.620	1.656

Source: IMF, *International Financial Statistics,* October 1979.

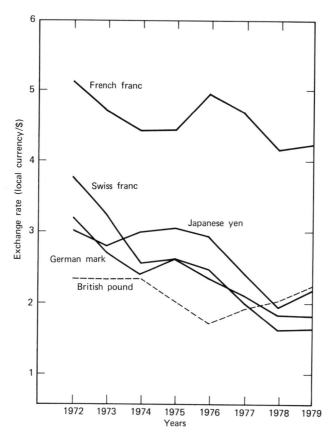

Figure 5–1. Recent Exchange-Rate Movements (*Note:* For Japanese yen, multiply scale figures by 100). *Source:* IMF, *International Financial Statistics,* October 1979.

dealing with day-to-day currency adjustments and, judging from the dearth of public commentary, apparently have not been affected adversely.

In spite of the current experience with more flexible exchange rates, efforts continue among central bankers to reestablish an international monetary system with rates that are more stable. The likely shape of this emerging system deserves elaboration. Before doing so, however, it will be useful to review some of the possibilities for organizing an international financial system and to point out commonly cited potential difficulties.

ALTERNATIVE MONETARY ARRANGEMENTS

Flexible Exchange Rates

Of all the various plans that have been suggested to remedy the problems of the current monetary system, perhaps none has the very attractive simplicity of an arrangement of freely flexible exchange rates. Under such a plan, national governments would be relieved once and for all from having to pay explicit attention to their balances of payments. Moreover, in theory at least, reserves would not be required, since the primary need for them, defending exchange rates, would be removed. When monetary payments deficits or surpluses occurred, the exchange rate would change automatically in the desired direction, and renewed payments equilibrium would be assured. Largely because of its simplicity and its reliance on accommodating price movements, the flexible-exchange-rate idea has long been supported by most international economists; yet, until very recently, the system has found little favor in either governmental or commercial circles, and, although always a topic of discussion, it has not received much consideration as a serious alternative in places where it counts. Why should this be true?

Perhaps the most frequently cited reason is the widely held belief that flexible exchange rates would introduce an unacceptable level of uncertainty to international business operations. As a result, both trade and investment activities would dwindle. The argument is based upon the fact that financial returns denominated in a foreign currency would be subject to greater variability with the introduction of fluctuating rates. International traders might eliminate this risk by engaging in the usual hedging operation, but opponents of flexible exchange rates assert that the costs of hedging are bound to increase as rates become unrestrained. Forward exchange rates, in this view, would have to incorporate the greater probability of short-run rate changes; moreover, there are numerous business situations where hedging becomes very difficult, if not impossible. Long-term commitments of capital through foreign direct investment would be an example. In this case, a stream of earnings denominated in a foreign currency might be anticipated; even if hedging were conceptually possible, it would be prohibitively expensive. Thus, the opponents conclude, flexible exchange rates would eliminate previously marginal trade and investment with commensurate costs in terms of economic welfare.

There are other opposition arguments in addition. One focuses on the possibility of destabilizing speculation that causes wide gyrations in rates, which would exacerbate the problems brought out in the previous paragraph. Another asserts that elimination of the need for a government to worry about its balance-of-payments condition would lead to a more rapid rate of price inflation. In this view the major reason governments now fight inflation is the realization that eventually relative increases in price level will be reflected in payments deficits. Finally, the last important argument against flexible rates is concerned with the disposition of the very large reserves that already exist in the system. What does the central bank of a country like Germany or Japan do with $30 to $40 billion worth of gold and convertible currencies? Permanent continuation of a flexible rate system almost certainly would depress the prices of the major reserve elements (gold and dollars), resulting in a marked capital loss for the current large reserve holders. Such countries hardly can be expected to approve a move to fluctuating rates unless some provision is made to handle this problem realistically.

Advocates of flexible exchange rates are not completely swamped by such arguments, and their main defenses can be summarized briefly. First, many economists simply reject the notion that flexible rates increase uncertainty. They note the readily observable fact that exchange rates under the Bretton Woods scheme were not fixed. The difference is that rate adjustments were made precipitously when all other alternatives had been exhausted. In this opinion, such fluctuations are far more difficult for businessmen to deal with than are rates free to drift. Even if more uncertainty were introduced, however, these economists believe the costs would be overwhelmed by the potential benefits. What benefits? Substantial gains would be possible from the dismantling of trade barriers, exchange controls, and investment regulations, many of which were effected for balance-of-payments reasons. Moreover, these advocates find no reason to anticipate that speculation should be destabilizing. Other types of markets appear not to be prone to instability; currency markets with vast numbers of participants should be even less susceptible. Similarly, inflation should not be encouraged by a flexible rate system, since most countries have ample motivation to control rising prices without reference to the balance of payments. Indeed, fixed rates make the spread of inflation between nations more difficult to control because of the greater likelihood of short-term international capital flows.

Fixed Exchange Rates

Practically nobody today would endorse a monetary system based on unalterably fixed exchange rates, yet such an arrangement offers a convenient point of departure for evaluating other schemes. The essential workings of a fixed-rate system are fairly straightforward, provided that all national governments subscribe to the principles on which it is based. The simplest way to describe the system is by abstracting from various long-term capital movements so that balance-of-payments accounts become synonymous with the trade balance. We follow this convention here. Generally, a fixed-rate system is founded on an accepted reserve asset, such as gold, to which the value of each currency is linked. International reserves consist of holdings of this asset; thus, other types of reserves made up of financial assets, like currencies, do not exist. International debts are converted quickly to transfers of the reserve asset. In addition, gold serves a second function as the reserve unit for each nation's money; gold losses are tantamount to a shrinkage of the country's money supply.

Suppose, under such a system, that the United States were to fall into deficit; that is, imports exceeded exports. The short-term debts to foreigners that resulted from the deficit would be converted rapidly through the banking system to claims on the U.S. gold reserves. The drain on reserves, in turn, would force a reduction in U.S. money supply, and prices would fall (and possible employment as well). Exactly the opposite process would occur in the rest of the world, where rising prices would result. The combination of falling U.S. prices and rising prices elsewhere might be expected to expand American exports and to reduce imports, driving the balance-of-payments deficit back toward the zero point. As long as all countries adjusted their internal economic conditions to suit the needs of external balance in a fixed-rate system, automatic balance-of-payment equilibration would be achieved. The essential difference between this arrangement and a flexible-rate system is in the method of adjustment. In a fixed-rate situation, internal prices and income fluctuate and the exchange rate is stable; in a flexible-rate system, internal prices and incomes can remain unaltered (in money terms) because the exchange rate is free to adjust.

The obvious problem of the pure fixed-exchange-rate system is that countries simply are not willing to behave as the rules of the gold standard would dictate. With a commitment to maintain full employment and reasonable growth, governments persistently refuse to subordinate these goals to achieving external balance. Gold usually is not a major determinant of a nation's money supply, and where it is, it is removed quickly when a reduction in available gold would indicate that the money supply should be shrunk. Moreover, as we have seen, central banks and businesses frequently are willing to accumulate foreign financial assets, either because such assets are more useful than gold or because they yield a higher rate of return. For all of these reasons and several others, the appealing automaticity of the fixed-rate system is destroyed when applied to the real world.

Actually, the quasi-fixed-rate, gold-exchange system that evolved from Bretton Woods is more closely similar to the pure fixed-rate system than to the flexible-rate system. Some observers, in fact, would claim that it combines the worst features of both arrangements. Exchange rates do change but always by abrupt shifts, where the effects are difficult to foresee; yet, because rate changes are believed to be a last resort, some nations, most notably the United States, have followed economic policies that were not optimal from the viewpoint of internal needs. Evidence exists, however, that changes in viewpoints are occurring that will have major impact on any future arrangements.

CURRENT AND FUTURE TRENDS

The international monetary system in recent years has settled into a lengthy period of flexible, if frequently managed, exchange rates. Rates have been managed in several ways to achieve varying purposes. In some cases, governments have decided to maintain their currency values on a fixed par with some reference currency. Usually the currency chosen has been that of the large nation most important in the smaller country's trading relationships. In other cases, groups of countries have attempted to maintain relatively fixed rates among themselves, while the whole structure of rates floated against outside currencies. The European "snake" arrangement is the most prominent example. Finally, even in cases where governments have been willing to allow their exchange rates to be determined by fundamental market forces, their banking authorities have intervened in the market from time to time to stem what they perceive to be undesirable speculative activities.

Thus, the international monetary system since the early years of the 1970s decade has functioned in a markedly differenct manner than the system originally envisioned at Bretton Woods. Whether or not the more flexible exchange rates have been desirable, however, is a matter that continues to be debated. Few today would argue against the view that rapid exchange-rate adjustability has allowed the international financial system to absorb the severe shocks emanating from the price actions of the oil-exporting cartel. Within a very short time during 1973, petroleum prices quadrupled. This single move radically altered balance-of-payments positions of virtually all nations and stimulated massive financial flows to the oil exporters. Under such circumstances, and particularly considering the varying national rates of price inflation that have occurred, a Bretton Woods-style fixed exchange-rate system would have been impossible to maintain. Most observers would agree, therefore, that the world has been reasonably well served in the 1970s by a system based upon exchange rates that could change by small amounts almost continuously.

Despite this apparently successful record over a rather chaotic time period, flexible exchange rates have not been enthusiastically endorsed by central bankers or by many economists. On the other hand, there is certainly no unanimity of opinion on possible alternative monetary arrangements that might be derived for the future. Why should this be so? In part, the reason is tied in with the observation that one's notions about the future depend heavily on one's beliefs about the true relationships existing in the past. Governments simply do not agree in their definitions of international monetary problems, much less in their responses to these problems.

This observation is well illustrated by reference to the potential impact of Special Drawing Rights on the monetary system of the future. Among advocates of a fixed-rate system, some believe that SDRs represent a fundamental change in the method of reserve creation and therefore give renewed life to the now-peripheral International Monetary Fund. Such opinions probably would view SDRs as a definite eventual replacement for reserve currencies and for gold. With a new form of internationally controlled and expandable reserves, the system of fixed, or at least quasi-fixed, exchange rates originally envisioned at Bretton Woods could continue to serve the world for years to come. Occasional currency crises might arise, but without reserve currencies to worry about, the added liquidity in the system should allow for rational adjustment of such problems.

Others, representing a variety of viewpoints, are far less sanguine about the system's future. Some would maintain that since SDRs are to be transferred only between central banks and are never to become private instruments, they cannot become international money in the usual sense. Some widely acceptable national monetary unit, probably the U.S. dollar, still would be required for private transactions; thus, the role of the dollar as an official reserve and international settlements currency would be reduced, but it would continue to be important both in private use and as an intervention currency in maintaining monetary values within the prescribed bands. In fact, it is quite possible that countries may eschew holding SDRs beyond the agreed minimum because they prefer the dollar, with all its defects. Since dollar reserves typically carry a higher interest rate than SDRs, and since the dollar has superior liquidity properties, many nations might desire logically to retain at least part of the dollar-based system, even for purely official transactions. Indeed, some economists would maintain that the willingness of countries to hold SDRs at all must be based on the ready convertibility of SDRs into real purchasing power through the dollar or other currencies. In any case, the conclusion of this general viewpoint is that the use of SDRs gradually will expand and that the dollar, although somewhat diminished in importance, will continue to be the primary international monetary unit. This conclusion probably will hold even though it is unlikely that the dollar ever will be restored to full convertibility with gold; therefore SDRs probably will substitute more for gold than for dollars, or become "paper gold" in international reserves, in this view.

Basic disagreements among nations also occur in other areas. For example, in recent negotiations between governments on possible ways to reform the international monetary system, Europeans tended to differ with the Americans on two issues. First, the Europeans were far more adamant about a return to a stable rate structure at the earliest possible date. Americans, on the other hand, who had been subjected to constant pressure to correct persistent balance-of-payments deficits under the pre-1971 fixed-rate schema, were more receptive to plans allowing for relatively easy exchange-rate adjustment. Probably also underlying the difference in viewpoints was the Europeans' general belief in tighter control of economic activity.

The second area of disagreement has centered on the manner in which balance-of-payments adjustment would take place. In this case, the U.S. government has been particularly insistent that remedying balance-of-payments disequilibria should not be the burden of deficit countries alone. In practice, this would mean that surplus nations would be penalized in some fashion for holding "excess" reserves. The obvious point that the Americans have attempted to make is that payments disequilibria are necessarily symmetrical—deficits always offset surpluses for the world—and adjustments in a fixed exchange-rate system logically should involve both sets of countries. Needless to say, other industrialized nations, which have been net accumulators of liquid dollar assets through their surpluses, would have much preferred a system where deficit countries retained their singular responsibility for correction of deficits.

In any case, the precise structure of the emerging international monetary system is thus far indefinite. It is clear that some governments desire a return to a modified Bretton Woods-type arrangement, with relatively established par rates of exchange. Even were such a system to evolve, however, there would be some notable differences. For example, and as suggested earlier, SDRs would assume the role of primary reserve asset, hopefully replacing both gold and dollars. Gold already is essentially demonetized, because no government has reestablished convertibility between its currency and gold at a fixed price. In addition, new SDRs once again are being issued and distributed, an activity that had been halted in 1972 for seven years. Moreover, the rate of return on SDR holdings has been keyed to prevailing market interest rates to increase the instrument's attractiveness as a reserve unit. All of these changes anticipate the eventual return to some form of stable, if adjustable, exchange-rate system.

Mostly at the behest of the United States, however, the IMF Executive Directors in 1976 proposed amendments to the articles of agreements that essentially would legitimize flexible rates. Under the changes, nations could choose the exchange arrangements that would apply to their currencies. Some might choose to have their currency values market determined, while others might opt to peg their exchange rates to other currencies or groups of currencies. This amendment, of course, merely recognized the established fact that most major currencies had been floating in greater or lesser degree for some time. It could come to pass that at some future date most national governments would choose once again to peg their currencies to the dollar. Given the continuing uncertainties in the world's financial affairs, such an outcome seems neither likely nor particularly desirable.

Insofar as multinational businesses are concerned, the adjustment to a system of rapidly fluctuating exchange rates has been far less traumatic than would have been predicted a decade ago. Business executives, it is fair to say, have become rather accustomed to continuous rate movements and have adopted financial procedures that make international dealings quite straightforward. (We shall have more to say on this important topic in Chapter 14.) In fact, most knowledgeable managers probably welcome greater exchange-rate flexibility because it enables them to make more rational decisions in a long-term context and forces them to consider constantly the shifting international economic conditions. The additional uncertainty introduced by frequent exchange-rate movement is more than compensated for by the ability to avoid the large readjustments emanating from less frequent but precipitous rate changes of the past. With the experience of floating rates since 1972 behind them, managers are far more receptive to the advantages of a more flexible system.

Summary

This chapter provides an outline of the international monetary system and of recent developments that promise to yield substantial future changes in that system. As originally envisioned at Bretton Woods following World War II, the monetary arrangement was to be a fixed exchange-rate system, with each currency carrying an established value in terms of a specified quantity of gold. Valuation changes were to be admitted, but only in the case of "fundamental" disequilibrium in a nation's balance of payments. In subsequent developments, a "key" currency system evolved, based predominantly on the American dollar. Dissatisfaction with certain elements of these arrangements, especially with the role of the United States, led to the introduction in 1969 of IMF Special Drawing Rights, a new form of reserve unit. More recently, a series of financial crises, beginning in 1971, resulted in the establishment of new par values for most currencies— generally devaluing the dollar in terms of other important currency units— and in the introduction of wider allowable exchange-rate bands for each currency. At the same time, the United States unilaterally suspended the dollar's convertibility with gold, reinforcing a downplaying of gold in the system begun earlier with the introduction of the two-tier gold market. Subsequent developments led to a lengthy period of floating exchange rates and a further implicit devaluation of the dollar. Current discussions within the IMF indicate some residual preference for a more stable exchange-rate regime, but, under any likely circumstances, future rates will be far more flexible than under the pre-1971 system.

SELECTED READINGS

Aliber, R.Z., *The International Money Game* (New York: Basic Books, 1973).

Cohen, B.J., "International Reserves and Liquidity," in P.B. Kenen (ed.), *International Trade and Finance* (Cambridge, England: Cambridge University Press, 1975).

Horsefield, J.K. *The International Monetary Fund, 1945–1965* (Washington, D.C.: IMF, 1969).

Machlup, Fritz, *Remaking the International Monetary System: The Rio Agreement and Beyond* (Baltimore: Johns Hopkins University Press, 1968).

McKinnon, R.I., *Money in International Exchange: The Convertible Currency System* (New York: Oxford University Press, 1979).

McKinnon, R.I., "Private and Official International Money: The Case For the Dollar," Essays in International Finance, No. 74, Princeton University, Princeton, N. J., April 1969.

Solomon, R., *The International Monetary System, 1945–1976: An Insider's View* (New York: Harper & Row, 1976).

de Uries, M., *The International Monetary Fund, 1966–1971* (Washington, D.C.: IMF, 1976).

Wallich, H.C., "The International Monetary System in the Seventies and Beyond," in *The International Monetary System in Transition,* A Symposium at the Federal Reserve Bank of Chicago, March 16–17, 1972.

Yeager, L.B., *International Monetary Relations,* 2nd Edition (New York: Harper & Row, 1976).

CHAPTER 6

International Capital Markets

INTRODUCTION

Capital has moved across national borders through all of recorded history and probably even before records were kept, but the rapid evolution of international money and capital markets in recent years has transformed international economic relations and international business. This chapter describes the evolution and resulting characteristics of international capital markets. It begins with a description of the forms that international capital flows take and the ways in which they are classified in balance-of-payment statistics. A short history of the evolution of international capital movements then follows. The remainder of the chapter is devoted to an analysis of the development of Eurocurrency markets in recent years.

FORMS OF INTERNATIONAL CAPITAL FLOWS

An international capital *flow* occurs when an individual or institution in one country changes its holdings of assets in another country. Capital is said to flow into country *A*, for example, when an institution in country *B* increases its assets in *A*. On the other hand, capital flows out of *A* when the foreign institution reduces its assets in *A* by, say, selling stock it has purchased in *A*'s stock market. Likewise, capital flows out of *A* (and into *B*) when institutions or individuals in *A* increase their holdings in *B*. If, on the other hand, the institutions or individuals in A reduce their holdings in B, there is said to be a capital flow from B into A. Thus, international capital flows between countries A and B can be due to actions of institutions or individuals in either A or B, and the actions can be either to increase or to decrease asset holdings in the foreign country.

It is important to understand these distinctions between the actor and the type of action when explaining international capital flows in a country's balance of payments. For example, a capital outflow from the United States may occur either because U.S. citizens and institutions are increasing their assets abroad or because foreigners are reducing their holdings in the United States. A U.S. exporter may be extending trade credit to importers in Japan (an increase in an asset), while European investors are reducing their holdings in the U.S. stock market (a reduction in a liability). Both actions constitute an outflow of capital from the United States.

International capital flows are classified in balance-of-payments statistics in terms of one or more dimensions: (1) characteristics of individuals or institutions holding assets (provider of funds), (2) characteristics of those using funds, and (3) characteristics of the assets held. The supplier of funds may be either a government, a private individual or an institution. Likewise, the user may be a government, government-related institution, or a private individual or corporation. The asset itself can be described in a variety of ways:

One can examine the terms on which funds are provided. Is their legal status that of a loan or equity investment, and would their maturity be classified as short or long term? Then one should examine the control exercised by the fund provider. Is it direct investment, involving direct control, or portfolio, with no direct control? One also should consider the proposed use of the funds, for this also contributes to a description of the asset, alone or in combination with any or all of the preceding characteristics.

The system used by the International Monetary Fund illustrates at least one way in which international capital flows may be classified. Capital flows of the United States, by IMF classification, are shown in Table 6–1. First, the IMF distinguishes between assets and liabilities of private individuals and institutions on the one hand (private sector), and the U.S. Government (public sector) on the other. Within the private sector, assets and liabilities of banks (which are private in the United States but publicly owned in some other countries) are separated from those of other private individuals and corporations. Next, direct investment in subsidiaries of U.S. firms abroad and foreign firms in the U.S. is distinguished from other security transactions. The U.S. banking-sector transactions are classified by maturities of the assets and liabilities. Capital flows involving the U.S.

Table 6–1   Classificaton of U.S. International Capital Flows in 1977 by IMF (millions of SDR)

			Flows in 1977[a]
Private	Non-bank sector	Direct investment by foreigners in the U.S.	2,867
		Direct investment by the U.S. private sector abroad	−10,467
		—reinvested earnings	−6,269
		—new investment	−4,198
		Other long-term liabilities	1,928
		—stocks	1,131
		—bonds	1,327
		—commercial credit	−530
		Other long-term assets	−4,602
		—foreign securities	−4,628
		—other assets	26
	Banking sector	Long-term	−326
		—liabilities	320
		—assets	−646
		Short-term	−3,640
		—liabilities to foreign banks	4,395
		—liabilities to other foreigners	986
		—assets	−9,021
Government		Long-term liabilities of general government	3,537
		Long-term assets of general government	−3,636
		—disbursement of loans	−4,753
		—loan repayments	2,299
		—subscriptions and contributions	−1,182
		Short-term liabilities of general government	−1,201

[a] Remember that a *flow* is a *change* in an asset or liability. A negative number indicates an increase in asset or decrease in liability of the United States.
Source: International Monetary Fund, *Balance of Payments Yearbook, Vol. 29* (Washington, D.C.: IMF, December 1978), Table 3, pp. 656–659.

Government also are classified by maturity, whether the flow involves a change in U.S. Government foreign assets, or in U.S. Government liabilities to foreigners.

Table 6–1 shows that in 1977 U.S. Government assets held abroad increased by SDR 3,636 million, a capital outflow. The net increase in assets was composed of loan disbursements of SDR 4,753 million and subscriptions and contributions to international organizations like the World Bank of SDR 1,182 million. These outflows were offset in part by loan repayments (reduction in assets) of SDR 2,299 million. Similarly, the short-term capital outflow of the banking sector was due mainly to an increase in foreign assets of SDR 9,021 million (an outflow) and an increase in liabilities to both foreign banks of SDR 4,395 million, and to other foreigners of SDR 986 million (inflows). It also is interesting to note that the increase of SDR 10,467 million in the direct investment by U.S. corporations in subsidiaries abroad was due mainly to reinvested earnings (SDR 6,269 million) rather than to new capital provided from the United States (SDR 4,198).

There is thus a wide variety of forms that international capital flows can take. The following section outlines the historical development of international capital flows over the last 100 years as the basis for later discussion of the present state of international capital markets.

CAPITAL FLOWS DURING THE NINETEENTH AND TWENTIETH CENTURIES

International flows of capital across political borders date back to at least the ancient civilizations around the Mediterranean. European kings borrowed from German and Italian bankers during the Middle Ages to finance both consumption and investment, and international flows grew in the sixteenth and seventeenth centuries with the development of institutions able to handle such transactions.

Capital Flows before 1920

The period between the end of the Civil War in the United States and the beginning of World War I saw an unprecedented expansion in the world economy. The industrialization of Europe and the United States along with the opening up of new temperate agricultural lands, the commercialization of tropical agriculture, and the discovery of new mineral resources stimulated international trade and migration from Europe, China, and the Indian subcontinent. Greatly increased levels of international capital flows helped to finance these developments, so that outstanding international loans grew from $4 billion in 1870 to $44 billion in 1913.[1]

The United Kingdom and France were the most important exporters of capital during this period, with the U.K. accounting for 40 percent of the loans outstanding in 1913. French foreign lending reached 4.5 percent of

[1]Helen Hughes, "Debt and Development: The Role of Foreign Capital in economic Growth," *World Development,* Vol. 7, February 1979, pp. 95–112.

national income prior to the First World War, while British foreign investment was 8.5 percent of national income in 1913.[2] London was by far the
most important center of international capital in the nineteenth and early
twentieth centuries.

Countries in Europe were the main borrowers as well as lenders during
the nineteenth century. Latin America was a larger net borrower than the
United States, which accounted for only 15 percent of total foreign debt
outstanding in 1913. Nevertheless, foreign capital was quite important in
financing the economic growth of the United States after the Civil War.
The United States was a consistent net capital importer through most of
the nineteenth century, when it was not unusual for net foreign capital
inflows to exceed 2 percent of *net* national product.[3] Foreign investors
purchased Union bonds during the Civil War and provided an important
part of the funds needed to finance construction of U.S. railroads. It was
only after 1897 that the United States began to emerge as a net capital
exporter to the rest of the world. Of course, foreign investment continued
to flow in, but U.S. investment abroad began to exceed the inflows by
increasing margins.

Most British investment abroad during the nineteenth and early twentieth centuries was made through the purchase of foreign bonds by private
individuals and financial institutions. The borrowers themselves were usually private firms financing major infrastructure investments, such as railroads and electric utilities. Of total British loans outstanding in 1913, 40
percent financed railroads, while loans to governments (both national and
municipal) accounted for 30 percent. Mining and other projects exploiting
raw materials had received another 10 percent of the outstanding loans.

Capital Flows after 1920

The character of international lending changed dramatically with the start
of the First World War. Transfers of capital between governments became
increasingly important during the war, as loans by the United States
supported the European war effort. The United States became the single
largest international lender during the war.

Public capital flows continued after the war in the form of humanitarian
assistance and war reparations. The United States continued as the single

[2]Charles Kindleberger, *Economic Growth in France and Britain, 1851–1950* (New York:
Simon & Schuster, 1964), p. 13.

[3]Milton Friedman & Anna Schwartz, *A Monetary History of the United States, 1897–1960*.
(New York: National Bureau of Economic Research, 1973), Appendix A, Table A–4, pp.
771–796.

most important source of international capital during the 1920s. Although Great Britain continued to be an international lender, the volume of British capital exports declined during the 1920s. France lost over half of her foreign assets during the war, and Germany nearly all of hers. Germany became the largest international borrower in the 1920s, obtaining funds mostly from the United States. In all, the United States supplied about two-thirds of all international investment during the 1920s.

The environment for international investment was different during the 1920s than had been the case prior to World War I. In the earlier period, British lending, at least, was accompanied by substantial imports of the products produced by the borrowing countries. Moreover, the loans themselves usually were used for productive purposes that ultimately led to increased exports, which helped to service the loans. Investments in U.S. railroads, for example, facilitated wheat exports that then could be used to pay the foreign exchange cost of interest and principal on the foreign loans. Some of the U.S. loans abroad in the 1920s, however, were not used for productive purposes, but to maintain consumption in the borrowing countries. Moreover, the United States was a poor market for the exports of borrowing countries such as Germany, whose exports were competitive with products produced in the United States. These factors, together with the collapse of raw-material prices, reduced the ability of the borrowing countries to service their debts and undermined the stability of capital markets as a whole.

Difficulty in servicing foreign debts incurred during the 1920s was one factor contributing to the world economic collapse of the early 1930s. The collapse of the international economy in turn led to major reductions in savings, investment, and international trade; to restrictions on currency convertibility; and to the rise of protectionism, which virtually eliminated international lending during the 1930s. Eastern European borrowers defaulted on 90 percent of government bonds that had been issued in the U.S. in 1920s, and there were defaults on 80 percent of loans to Latin American governments. Direct investment proved to be more resilient in the 1930s than lending, but as a result of defaults, U.S. overseas investments of all types were worth $3.8 billion less in 1938 than in 1930. At the beginning of the hostilities in Europe in 1939, therefore, international investment outstanding was only about $55 billion. The United Kingdom remained as the most important investor, followed by the United States. Latin America was the largest borrower, accounting for 20 percent of outstanding investments.

Capital Flows after World War II

The Second World War drastically altered the investment position of the main creditor countries. Both the United States and the United Kingdom had to draw down their foreign assets and increase their foreign liabilities to finance the war effort. Many former debtor countries, particularly those in the British Commonwealth and in Latin America, were able to reduce their debts by expanding exports of raw materials to the belligerents. The debtor position of the Commonwealth was reduced by $12.5 billion, while Latin American debts were reduced by $6 billion. Gross debt outstanding fell during the war from $55 billion in 1938 to $35 or $40 billion after.

There was a remarkable resurgence of international investment after the war, but again with some important changes reflecting changed economic circumstances. The United States emerged from the war as by far the most important economic power. Consequently, the United States accounted for almost 70 percent of net foreign investment during the postwar period through the 1960s. Britain continued to invest abroad, but by 1960 was replaced by Germany and Japan as the second and third largest capital exporters. *Net* investment increased from about $4 billion per year in the early 1950s to $8 billion per year in the first half of the 1960s.

The most striking feature of postwar international investment was the dominance, at least through the mid-1960s, of government loans. Public aid to Europe under the Marshall Plan and other measures to assist European (and British) reconstruction amounted to $40 billion. The aid was mostly made available as grants, which did not increase the level of international indebtedness. Through the mid-1960s at least, most international capital flows to developing countries also were in the form of government-to-government loans or grants (foreign aid) or loans through multilateral agencies such as the World Bank. Altogether, about 50 percent of net capital exports of the developed countries were bilateral government loans, while 40 percent were private investments and around 10 percent were made through international financial agencies. Most private international investment went to developed countries, while most of the investments by governments went to developing countries. International aid to poor countries was a new factor that marked and set apart the postwar economic scene.

The other striking feature of the postwar era through the mid-1960s was the emergence of direct investment as by far the most important form of private international investment. Firms in the industrial countries had for many years been establishing subsidiaries abroad, but such capital flows had been relatively insignificant in the years prior to World War II, compared with private investment in foreign bonds and other securities. However, with improvements in transportation and communication after the war, the establishment of the European Economic Community, and the rapid expansion of the industrial economies, private firms rushed to establish operations in the most rapidly growing markets. At the same time, memories of bond defaults in the 1930s dampened enthusiasm for international bond sales, so that direct investment accounted for perhaps 80 percent of private international capital flows during the postwar period through the mid-1960s.[4]

With the increasing interdependence of the world economy that was the result of growing direct investment and trade, conditions for a resurgence of international lending began to emerge again in the mid-1960s. The private lending that began to grow and develop was different from the international lending of the nineteenth and early twentieth centuries. In the earlier era, borrowers sold bonds denominated in the currency of the lending country directly to savers, with perhaps the intermediation of an underwriter. For example, a U.S. railroad needing to raise capital sold bonds denominated in sterling in London to private individuals. In the 1960s, on the other hand, loans were made increasingly through intermediaries, such as commercial banks. The loans, moreover, usually were not made in the currency of the country where the lending institution was located, but in dollars or some other "international" currency. A bank in London, for example, would make a dollar loan to a Japanese firm.

Because larger amounts of international private lending are made now through intermediaries, it is increasingly difficult to trace the amounts and origins of such lending. Table 6–2 shows publicized private lending beginning in 1970 in three categories: (1) Eurocurrency credits, (2) international bonds, and (3) foreign bonds. Eurocurrency credits are loans made by financial intermediaries, usually commercial banks, in a currency other than that used in the country where the intermediary is located. Foreign bonds are the traditional form of international lending and are denominated in the currency of the country in which they are sold (e.g., sterling bonds sold in London). International bonds, by way of contrast, usually are denominated in currencies other than those of the country or countries where they are

Table 6–2   Publicized Private International Lending 1970–1978 (billions U.S. $)

	1970	1971	1972	1973	1974	1975	1976	1977	1978
International bonds	3.0	4.2	6.9	4.7	4.5	10.5	15.4	19.5	15.9
Foreign bonds	1.5	3.6	4.3	5.3	7.8	12.3	18.9	16.6	20.8
Eurocurrency credits	4.7	4.0	6.6	20.8	28.5	20.6	28.8	34.2	72.0
Total	9.2	11.8	17.8	30.8	40.8	43.4	63.1	70.3	108.7

Source: World Bank, Borrowing in International Capital Markets, (Washington: World Bank), various issues.

[4]Much of the data on postwar investment through the mid-1960s is taken from John Dunning, Studies in International Investment (London: Allen & Unwin, 1970).

sold. For example, foreign bonds often are denominated in dollars but sold in Europe.

The data in Table 6–2 by no means cover all private international lending, but only those loans that have been made public. It is clear, nevertheless, that there has been a remarkable upsurge in private lending, beginning in the late 1960s and accelerating in the 1970s, led first by international bonds and later by loans through intermediaries. Traditional lending through the purchase of foreign bonds accelerated after controls on foreign investment were lifted by the United States in 1974.

A more complete picture of international private lending for recent years is shown in Table 6–3, which illustrates that publicized lending by financial intermediaries has been only part of their total lending volume. The table also shows that such lending by intermediaries is now by far the dominant form of private international lending, accounting for 85 percent of the total.

The growth of private lending was so rapid in the 1970s that it has become the most important source of medium- and long-term capital for developing countries. As seen in Table 6–4, private investors (both lenders and direct investors) provided almost 65 percent of net foreign medium- and long-term capital flows to developing countries, while the share of official grants and loans fell to around 35 percent. The share of direct investment in private capital flows to developing countries has fallen from

Table 6–3 International Banking and Bond Finance (billions U.S. $)

	1974	1975	1976	1977	1978
Net new international bank lending	50	40	70	75	110
Net new international bond lending	10	20	30	31	30
New international bond issues	11	23	34	36	37
Less: redemption and repurchases	1	3	4	5	7
Total new bank and bond financing	60	60	100	105	140
Less: double-counting	2	2	4	5	8
Total net new bank and bond financing	58	58	96	100	132

Source: International Monetary Fund, "IMF Survey," September 3, 1979, *Supplement on International Lending,* (Washington, D.C.: IMF), p. 271.

Table 6–4 Developing Countries: Medium- and Long-Term Debt Outstanding at Year End (billions U.S. $)

		1970	1977	Change: 1970–1977
To:	private creditors	32	155	123
	low-income countries	2	10	8
	middle-income countries	30	145	115
To:	official creditors	37	104	67
	low-income countries	15	39	24
	middle-income countries	21	66	45
Total[a]		68	258	190

[a]Totals may not add due to rounding.
Source: World Bank, *World Development Report, 1979* (Washington, D.C.: World Bank, August 1979), Table 22, page 29.

75 percent of the total in 1970 to 30 percent in 1977.[5] Private lending has increased commensurately and now has replaced official loans as the single most important source of foreign capital for developing countries.

As the form of international investment changed in the 1970s, so did the main sources of investment. The United States became a net capital importer in some years, while Germany and Japan became large capital exporters, as reflected in their large current account surpluses. The oil-exporting countries also became large capital exporters after oil prices were quadrupled in 1974, but their capital exports declined progressively through 1978 as their current account surpluses narrowed. With renewed-oil price increases in 1979, however, it is expected that these countries again will be large capital exporters (see Chapter 8).

In a sense, the world has come full circle to an era when international private lending is again a major force in world economic development. The mechanisms of lending are completely different from those of the nineteenth century, however. The Eurocurrency market, in particular, is a new phenomenon that must be understood by a student of international business. Consequently, the remainder of the chapter is devoted to a description of this market.

INTERNATIONAL CAPITAL MARKETS

The Eurocurrency market is formed by commercial banks that accept deposits in currencies other than the currency of the country where the bank is located. The deposit may be made by any holder of the currency in question. For example, a bank in London may accept dollar deposits from

[5]OECD *International Cooperation Review, annual, issues for 1970–1978 (Paris: OECD).*

U.S. citizens, British citizens, or from anyone else who happens to have dollars. Likewise, a bank in Luxembourg may accept deposits in German marks from anyone, including residents of Germany.

How the Eurocurrency Market Operates

It may be useful to examine the mechanics of a Eurocurrency transaction. Suppose a German firm has exported $1 million worth of goods to the United States and has received payment in dollars. Instead of converting the payment to marks, the firm deposits the dollars in a London bank. The London bank has thus gained a deposit liability of $1 million, a Eurocurrency deposit, and an equal dollar asset held in a U.S. bank. These changes would be registered on the balance sheet of the London bank in the following way:

Bank L

Assets	Liabilities
+$1,000,000 deposit with U.S. bank	+$1,000,000 deposit of exporter

Now suppose that the subsidiary of a U.S. firm in France wants to import $500,000 worth of goods from the United States. The subsidiary could finance the import by borrowing from the London bank, whose balance sheet would change in the following way:

Bank L

Assets	Liabilities
+$500,000 loans	+$500,000 deposit of subsidiary

The subsidiary could transfer its borrowed funds to a U.S. bank. In that case, both the London bank's assets and liabilities would be reduced, as follows:

Bank L

Assets	Liabilities
−$500,000 deposit with U.S. bank	−$500,000 deposit of subsidiary

The subsidiary in France then could pay for its imports with its deposit in the U.S. bank. The U.S. exporter may deposit the funds in another bank, in which case the first U.S. bank would lose deposit liabilities and reserve assets of $500,000. The London bank, as a result of the entire set of transactions, would gain $1 million in dollar deposit liabilities, $500,000 in deposits in U.S. banks, and $500,000 in loans outstanding. Of course, the London bank would not earn interest on its $500,000 deposit in the New

York bank. Consequently, it would attempt to further expand its loans, while holding adequate dollar deposits in the United States as a reserve.

More complex Eurodollar transactions could be described. This simple one, however, is sufficient to convey the essence of the Eurodollar market; that is, a German exporter made a loan to a French subsidiary of a U.S. firm through the intermediation of a London bank. All transactions were made in U.S. dollars. None of the parties involved ever saw a dollar bill, since the transactions were made on the books of banks through accounting entries. The bank that accepts a Eurocurrency deposit becomes a financial intermediary helping to channel resources from savers to final users. The Eurocurrency bank can relend the funds deposited to a final user, or it can lend to another bank, which in turn may relend either to a final user or to another bank.

This process of intermediation is illustrated further by an example taken from Gunter Dufey and Ian Giddy.[6] The treasurer of John Deere and Company contacts the Nassau (Bahamas) branch of Continental Illinois Bank to make a $2 million deposit for one month. The Nassau branch (which is staffed in Chicago, only maintaining a nameplate on a building and possibly a set of books in the Bahamas), then contacts the London branch office (which is staffed) to see if they can relend the funds at a profit. The London branch takes the deposit on its books and pays the Nassau branch a slightly higher interest rate. Thus, a second deposit transaction is recorded, this time between two branches of the same bank. The London branch of Continental Illinois, in turn, contacts a broker who keeps track of bids for, and offers of, funds. For a small fee the broker informs Continental of the current bids for funds. Continental sees that Fuji Bank is bidding for $10 million at an attractive interest rate and decides to invest $2 million in a 30-day deposit. Fuji Bank, in turn, lends the $2 million provided by Continental, and $8 million from other sources, to a Japanese trading firm. The $2 million deposit by John Deere and Company thus has made its way from Moline, Illinois to Japan through the intermediation of two banks. All transactions are made in dollars and are handled through book entries of the banks involved.

Why the Eurocurrency Market Exists

The capacity of international financial markets to channel funds in this way provides great benefits to the international economy by bringing together

---

[6] G. Dufey & I. Giddy, *The International Money Market* (Englewood Cliffs, N.J.: Prentice Hall, 1978), pp. 223–226. The example is abbreviated here. For the full institutional detail, it is recommended that the student consult Dufey & Giddy.

savers and investors on a scale and to an extent never before achieved. There are several conditions that must be satisfied, however, for such international financial intermediation to be possible. First, foreign entities (both banks and individuals) must be able to transfer funds in the United States (if the dollar is the currency used in the transaction). After all, each institution that accepts a dollar deposit also acquires an equal deposit in a U.S. bank, which it passes on to the next institution in the chain. In the transaction just described, funds in the Continental Illinois (Chicago) account of John Deere are transferred to an account of the Bahamas branch held by the parent bank in Chicago, and then to an account of the London branch also held in Chicago. Then the funds are transferred to an account of the Japanese trading company, again in a U.S. bank. Such nonresident transfers have to be allowed by the U.S. banking authorities if the intermediation process is to work.

A second condition for the functioning of the market is that institutions and individuals must have the right to hold and transfer foreign currencies among countries. That right did not exist for most countries other than the United States prior to the 1957 reestablishment of currency convertibility in Europe. Consequently, the birth of the Eurocurrency market can be dated from the establishment of convertibility of European currencies in that year.

The market grew slowly at first and by 1967 deposits of foreign currency in banks in major European countries, as well as in financial centers in the Caribbean and Far East, amounted to only $24 billion. The controls on foreign investments instituted by the United States in the mid-1960s, however, shifted demand for funds by U.S. corporations operating abroad to Eurocurrency banks. In a sense, these controls gave the newly established Eurocurrency institutions some infant-industry protection that enabled them to earn higher returns than otherwise would have been possible. With this protection, the market grew rapidly between 1967 and 1970, as is seen in Table 6–5. Rapid growth continued in the 1970s, aided by massive deposits from OPEC countries starting in 1974. By the time U.S. capital controls were eliminated in 1974, the Eurocurrency market was well established; it has continued its rapid growth, although not at the rate experienced in the first half of the 1970s.

The gross size of the market is measured by the gross value of foreign-currency liabilities of the reporting banks.[7] A substantial portion of these liabilities are to other Eurocurrency banks, both within and outside the

---

[7]In the example cited earlier, the $2 million deposit of John Deere would have been counted three times, as liabilities of Continental Illinois branches in Nassau and London, and as a liability of Fuji Bank.

134 THE ECONOMIC ENVIRONMENT OF INTERNATIONAL BUSINESS

Table 6–5 Foreign Currency Liabilities of Reporting Banks (millions U.S. $, end-of-year)

	Gross	Net
1965	24	17
1970	110	65
1971	145	85
1972	200	110
1973	305	160
1974	375	215
1975	460	250
1976	565	310
1977	695	380
1978	895	485
1979	1155	600

Source: *World Financial Markets,* (New York: Morgan Guaranty Trust Co.), various issues.

major financial centers. The net size of the market is obtained by netting out these interbank transactions.[8] By any measure, the Eurocurrency market institutions are quite large. Net Eurocurrency deposits in 1978, for example, were 80 percent of time deposits in U.S. commercial banks and exceeded time deposits in German and British banks.

It is appropriate to compare Eurocurrency deposits with time deposits in national banks, because Eurocurrency deposits are in fact time, not demand, deposits. The Eurocurrency banks are financial intermediaries, just as savings and loan associations in the United States are financial intermediaries. The deposits at Eurocurrency banks thus are in no sense part of the world money supply, and one cannot associate a money multiplier with Eurocurrency deposits any more than such a multiplier can be associated with deposits in savings and loan associations. Eurocurrency banks, rather, are part of the network of financial institutions that channels funds worldwide from ultimate savers to ultimate investors. This point has been made earlier in this chapter, but it is of sufficient importance to bear repeating.

As financial intermediaries, Eurocurrency banks have an advantage in attracting funds because they have lower costs than national banks. They

[8]That is, by netting out deposits by Continental Illinois Nassau branch in London, and the London branch deposit in Fuji Bank. The net deposit is thus only $2 million.

do not have to maintain reserve requirements (5 percent on time deposits in the United States), which immobilizes some assets of national banks. Moreover, their regulatory expenses are lower than those of national banks since they are basically unregulated and do not have to pay such charges as the insurance fee U.S. banks pay to the Federal Deposit Insurance Corporation (FDIC). Eurocurrency banks are not forced by governments to allocate credit in certain ways, and there are no limits on interest rates paid or charged. Finally, these institutions are able to locate in places where taxes are low. Entry is easy, and there are hundreds, if not thousands, of Eurocurrency banks. Competition, together with lack of regulation, helps to keep costs down. Low costs, in turn, help these institutions to bid for funds and compete for loans. As a result, the market has grown rapidly relative to other national and international financial institutions.

Eurocurrency banking centers have grown up where there is economic and political stability, an experienced banking community, good communications with the rest of the world, and little regulation of foreign currency deposits and loans. The most essential conditions are that the banking authorities allow banks to accept foreign currency deposits and do not impose reserve requirements on these deposits. New York is not a Eurocurrency banking center in this sense because U.S. banks are not allowed to accept foreign currency deposits (e.g., D-marks or sterling). Banks located in the United States, of course, still are involved actively in international capital markets through dollar loans to foreigners.

Table 6–6 shows that at the end of 1978 London was the largest international financial center, with foreign loans of $202.8 billion. Banks located in the United States had foreign loans of $129 billion. Of course, a substantial share of the loans out of London also were made by branches of U.S. banks. Branches of U.S. banks in the Caribbean and the Far East (Bahamas, the Cayman Islands, Panama, Hong Kong, and Singapore) had loans of $106.5 billion. Some of these locations, as suggested previously, are not really active banking centers but rather addresses where deposits are accepted and loans are booked in order to avoid regulation, reserve requirements, and taxes that would be imposed if the transactions were made by U.S. banks.

Costs of Using Eurocurrency Markets

Interest rates on Eurocurrency loans are related to interest rates in the country where the currency is issued. Rates on Eurodollar loans are related to interest rates in the United States, and Euromark loans bear an interest

Table 6–6   External Claims As Reported by Banks in Major Financial Markets by Country or Region of Lending Bank (billions U.S. $)

	1975 (Dec.)	1976 (Dec.)	1977 (Dec. 1)	1977 (Dec. 11)	1978 (Dec.)
Banks in European countries[a]	297.3	353.0	433.6	466.2	611.4
Domestic currency	39.2	47.7	59.8	81.4	109.4
Foreign currency (Eurocurrency market)	258.1	305.3	373.8	384.8	502.0
Of which:					
Belgium	14.5	17.4	22.9	22.9	31.8
Luxembourg	24.6	32.0	44.0	44.0	58.3
France	39.0	48.0	62.2	62.2	80.8
Germany, Federal Republic	10.6	14.3	17.3	17.3	20.8
Netherlands	17.3	22.0	27.2	27.2	36.6
Switzerland	16.3	18.4	23.0	23.0	31.4
United Kingdom	118.2	138.0	159.2	159.2	202.8
Banks in Canada	13.8	17.3	18.1	18.1	22.4
Banks in Japan	20.4	21.7	21.7	21.7	33.6
Banks in the United States	59.8	81.1	92.6	92.6	129.0
Branches of U.S. banks in the Caribbean and the Far East[b]	51.1	74.9	91.1	91.1	106.5
Total gross external bank claims	442.4	548.0	657.1	689.7	903.0
Less: double-counting due to redepositing among reporting banks	182.3	218.0	252.3	259.7	363.4
Total claims net of redepositing	260.0	330.0	405.0	430.0	540.0

[a]Up to December 1977 (December 1), the European reporting area covered Belgium–Luxembourg, France, the Federal Republic of Germany, Italy, the Netherlands, Sweden, Switzerland, and the United Kingdom. Since 1977 (December 11) it also includes Austria, Denmark, and Ireland.
[b]The Bahamas, the Cayman Islands, Panama, Hong Kong, and Singapore.
Source: IMF, "IMF Survey," September 3, 1979, *Supplement on International Lending*, (Washington, D.C.: IMF), page 279.

rate related to rates in Germany. As noted earlier, however, Eurocurrency banks are able to operate on narrower margins because their costs are lower than national banking institutions, and they are forced by competition to pass on these lower costs. Consequently, Eurocurrency banks will be able to make loans at slightly lower rates and they will pay slightly more for deposits than banks, say, in the United States lending dollars, or German banks lending marks. Depositors in the Eurocurrency markets will require a slightly higher interest rate because their risk is slightly higher when investing in Eurocurrency institutions than in the country where the currency is issued. The threat that the United States, for example, will not allow transfers between bank accounts of nonresidents increases the risks of a depositor in a Eurocurrency bank as compared to deposits in New

York. Likewise, a borrower in the Eurocurrency market faces higher risks and transaction costs and thus will seek a lower lending rate as compensation.

Besides being linked to the home-country interest rate, the Eurocurrency interest rate on a loan in one currency is related to the interest rate on a loan of another currency by the relationship between forward and spot rates of the two currencies, as well as by the expected rates of appreciation or depreciation of one currency or the other. This is a mechanism that should be familiar to the student already. Interest arbitrage will keep the difference in interest rates in marks and dollars equal to the percentage premium of the forward price of the mark over the spot price. At the same time, speculation will equate the percentage forward premium (discount) to the expected rate of appreciation (depreciation) of the mark; therefore, the interest rate differential (on an annual basis) will equal the expected rate of appreciation of one currency or the other. If the Eurodollar interest rate is 8 percent and the Euromark rate is 5 percent, it can be concluded that speculators are expecting the mark to appreciate by 3 percent per year relative to the dollar.

Eurocurrency loans are made with maturities of several years, but interest rates on these loans are set for shorter periods, usually every six months. The use of such "floating" interest rates is a financial innovation devised to deal with the problem of inflation. Eurocurrency banks generally make loans with maturities that are longer than those on their deposits. In an inflationary environment, where short-term interest rates change rapidly in response to inflationary expectations, banks making longer-term loans are faced with the prospect that the interest rate they have to pay on their deposits could rise substantially above the interest rates on their longer-term loans. The banks are not willing to take such a risk; therefore, they have devised loans in which the interest rate is changed periodically to reflect changes in the cost of funds to the lending bank.

The cost of funds to Eurocurrency banks is the rate of interest at which they can borrow funds as reflected in the London Inter-Bank Offer Rate (LIBOR). The LIBOR is the rate at which a sample of London Eurocurrency banks offers funds for deposit in other banks. The interest rate on a particular loan then usually is set at LIBOR plus a spread that is determined by (1) the extent of competition among banks and (2) the quality of the borrower. In recent years, spreads have been driven down by competition to the point where they are considerably under one percentage point for a prime borrower.

While the spreads charged by Eurocurrency banks have been driven down, the basic interest rate has fluctuated rather dramatically, reflecting changes in short-term credit conditions. Figure 6–1 shows six-month

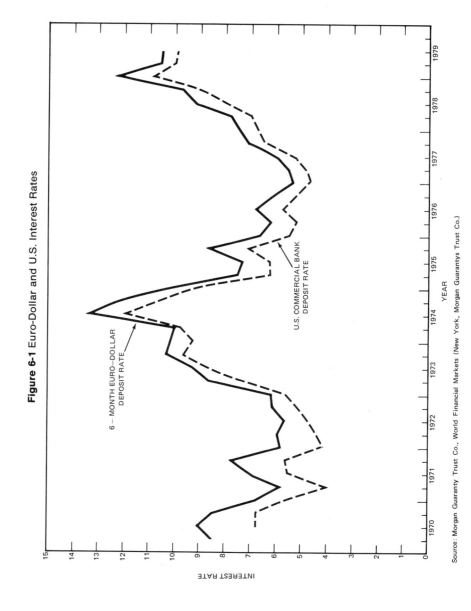

Figure 6-1 Euro-Dollar and U.S. Interest Rates

Source: Morgan Guaranty Trust Co., World Financial Markets (New York, Morgan Guarantys Trust Co.)

138

Eurodollar rates (bid rates rather than offer rates) as they were at the end of each quarter for the period 1970 through 1979. Also plotted in the chart are commercial bank deposit rates in the United States on certificates of deposit. Eurodollar six-month interest rates rose to a peak of 13.4 percent at the middle of 1974, then fell to a low of 5.4 percent at the end of 1976. Thereafter, rates rose steadily to the end of 1978, dropping back briefly during the first half of 1979, only to rise to a new peak by the third quarter.

As is expected, deposit rates in U.S. banks have been consistently below the rate paid by Eurobanks on dollar deposits; however, the differential has narrowed since the early 1970s, probably reflecting the relaxation of U.S. controls on capital outflows. Those controls, in effect prior to 1974, probably inhibited dollar deposits in the Eurocurrency market, thus making it necessary for Eurobanks to raise their bid rates over the U.S. rate in order to attract funds.

As liquidity in the market has increased in recent years, not only have over-LIBOR spreads charged by banks declined, but loan maturities have increased. In 1975, over 60 percent of publicized Eurocurrency loans had maturities of over 5 years, while over 60 percent had maturities over 7 years in 1978. This is a smaller share of long-term loans than had been achieved in 1973, but with a much greater lending volume in 1978 (see Table 6–7).

Private firms, individuals, and governments in developed countries were the main sources, as well as being the largest users, of funds channeled through international financial intermediaries in 1978 (see Table 6–8). On balance, however, developed countries were net suppliers of funds to the market. All other geographic areas were net users of funds, including, surprisingly, oil-exporting countries. By 1978, the balance-of-payments

Table 6–7 Eurocurrency Credit Maturities (all categories expressed in percentages of total)

Original Maturity	1972	1973	1974	1975	1976	1977	1978
Over 1–3.00	9.5	3.4	2.6	5.5	2.9	2.8	2.8
3.01–5.00	18.3	7.1	12.6	38.2	46.3	15.9	5.2
5.01–7.00	32.3	14.8	26.3	27.3	38.8	65.1	25.3
7.01–10.00	27.8	48.7	43.5	4.2	4.1	11.7	56.3
10.01–15.00	3.4	19.8	10.7	1.0	——	——	——
15.01–20.00	——	0.1	0.1	——	——	——	——
20.01–25.00	——	——	——	——	——	——	——
25.01 and over	——	——	——	——	——	——	——
Unknown	8.7	6.0	4.3	3.8	7.9	4.6	4.6
	100.00%	100.00%	100.00%	100.00%	100.00%	100.00%	100.00%

Source: World Bank, *Borrowing in International Capital Markets* (Washington, D.C.: World Bank), various issues.

Table 6–8   External Lending and Deposits in Domestic and Foreign Currency of Banks in 1978 (billions U.S. $)

	Uses of Funds for Lending to	Sources of Funds from	Net Sources (−) Or Uses (+) of Funds
Developed countries	54.4	83.5	−29.0
Eastern Europe	8.2	2.3	5.9
Oil-exporting countries	17.1	5.9	11.2
Developing countries	25.7	16.0	9.7
International organizations	4.5	2.2	2.3

Source: IMF, "IMF Survey," September 3, 1979, Supplement on International Lending (Washington, D.C.: IMF), page 275.

surpluses of the oil exporters, as a group, had been reduced to the point where they were net borrowers, even though individual countries, such as Saudi Arabia, were still net suppliers of funds. The developing countries were also large net users of funds in 1978, even though they had been small net suppliers of funds to the market in 1977.

Many of the borrowers from international financial intermediaries are governments, particularly in developing countries; however, private firms in both developed and developing countries also have been substantial borrowers. Even when governments are the borrowers, the funds ultimately may reach private firms.

It is difficult, if not impossible, to predict the future growth of private international capital markets. Practically no one in the 1960s predicted the growth that already has occurred, nor did anyone predict the way in which the emergence of these institutions would alter the allocation of savings in the international economy and, in particular, the increase in the funds they have channeled to developing countries. The private international financial intermediaries continue to enjoy certain competitive advantages, so they may continue to grow relative to other institutions. At the same time their growth will be limited by the supply of credit available and the risks inherent in international financial intermediation. Whatever the future growth of international financial intermediation, it is clear that the Euro-currency markets will continue to be a major source of funds in international finance and as such will be of continuing, and probably increasing, importance for international business.

Summary

This chapter provides a broad overview of the development of international capital markets. It has been seen that there has been continued change in international capital flows, with private and public investors emerging at different times as the main foreign sources of capital for international trade and investment. In recent years, private capital flows through commercial banks have come to dominate international capital markets and now provide a degree of integration in the international economy that has no historical precedent. Eurocurrency markets will continue to be a major source of funds in international finance and to hold an important place in international business.

SELECTED READINGS

Adler, John, *Capital Movements and Economic Development* (London: Macmillan; New York: St. Martins, 1967).

Bell, Geoffrey, *The Eurodollar Market and the International Financial System* (New York: Halstead, 1976).

Cairncross, A. K., *Home and Foreign Investment, 1870–1913* (Cambridge, Eng.: Cambridge University Press, 1953).

Dufey, Gunther, & Ian Giddy, *The International Money Market* (Englewood Cliffs, N.J.: Prentice Hall, 1978).

Dunning, John, *Studies in International Investment* (London: Allen & Unwin, 1970).

Friedman, Milton, "The Eurocurrency Market: Some First Principles," *Morgan Guaranty Survey,* (New York: Morgan Guaranty Trust, October 1969), pp. 4–14.

Hughes, Helen, "Debt and Development: The Role of Foreign Capital in Economic Growth," *World Development,* February 1979, pp. 95–112.

Jenks, L. H., *The Migration of British Capital to 1875* (New York: Alfred A. Knopf, 1927).

Lewis, W. Arthur, *The Evolution of the International Economic Order* (Princeton University, Woodrow Wilson School, 1977).

Little, I. M. D., & J. M. Clifford, *International Aid* (Chicago: Aldine, 1966), Chapter 1.

U.N. Commission on Transnational Corporations, *Transnational Corporations in World Development: A Re-examination* (New York: U.N., 1978).

U.S. House of Representatives, Committee on Banking, Finance and Urban Affairs, Subcommittee on International Trade, Investment and Monetary Policy, *Hearings, The Eurocurrency Control Act of 1979* (Washington, D.C.: U.S. Government Printing Office, 1979).

CHAPTER 7

National Economic Policies

INTRODUCTION

The preceding chapters provide some understanding of the dimensions of the international economy; discuss the theory of comparative advantage as a basis for trade and shifting competitive positions; explain the balance-of-payments accounts and the functioning of the foreign exchange market; and, finally, explore the development, functioning, and future of the international monetary mechanism. The present chapter brings together these various concepts and fields of investigation in an analysis of national economic policies as they are applied to international trade, international investment, and international finance.

Countries do not always adhere to the "rules of the game," even in cases where such rules have been delineated quite clearly. Moreover, as with any set of rules, and especially complex ones attempting to govern national behaviors in an international arena, there are many loopholes that allow sovereign states to superimpose unilaterally their own wills on the system. This independence has done much to frustrate the smooth functioning of the international monetary system as originally planned by its founders at Bretton Woods in 1944. For example, in August of 1971 the U.S. Government unilaterally imposed a 5-percent surcharge on manufactured imports entering this country. This move, apparently taken without prior consultation with other governments, was part of a series of actions intended to emphasize the American desire for an international solution to its chronic balance-of-payments deficit. In a larger context, however, the imposition of an added tariff by the United States was typical of one source of new economic policies that directly affect multinational business operations. Countries adopt policies as strategic devices to attain particular economic goals. When the strategies succeed, as with the U.S. import surcharge, the policies might be modified or reversed entirely, but many long-standing policies owe their origin to an unsuccessful effort by a government to acquire concessions from other countries in bilateral or multilateral negotiations.

Such a cause, of course, is by no means the only reason for the existence of national policies affecting international trade and finance. All countries experience internal economic difficulties from time to time, and these may motivate governments to take some type of remedial action. Frequently these actions are directed to the international sector, partly because administrative steps are usually simpler to implement there and partly because the major direct effects of such actions are felt by individuals and groups outside the government's constituency. For example, unemployment in an industry might be ameliorated by erecting one or another of several possible impediments to imports in the industry's markets. On a larger scale, general unemployment could stimulate a more general response, such as an overall import surcharge. Another example is the close regulation of agricultural products by many countries to make possible crop-support programs for domestic farmers. All of these policies attempt to facilitate internal economic problem solving by insulating the domestic economy from potentially disruptive external influences. The extent to which these measures work in fact is a function of many factors, not the least of which is the response of other governments.

This chapter discusses many of the economic policies that have been undertaken by national governments and that have had fairly direct impact on international businesses; however, the chapter provides but a summary sketch. Rather than being exhaustive, we transmit some notion of the scope of these measures with respect to trading relationships. All nations adopt policies that in some way affect their international trade and financing. Indeed, the range of these activities, on a worldwide scale, is seemingly limitless. The purpose of the following paragraphs, therefore, is simply to introduce the types of existing policies. This introduction, it is hoped, will serve as a warning to future international business managers that when decisions are made in a world context, specific governmental policies affecting the decisions should be taken into account. Although this mandate might seem obvious, any experienced international executive can cite numerous examples where an overlooked restriction had deleterious effects on the results of an investment or trade deal.

POLICIES PRIMARILY AFFECTING TRADE FLOWS

Perhaps the most pervasive form of consistent interference with the free flow of trade is the import tax or tariff. In general, tariffs can be classified into two types: *ad valorem,* where the tax is a percentage of the product's import or sales price; and *specific,* where the tax is an absolute amount per unit of the imported good. For example, if the tax is *ad valorem* at 10 percent and the import price is $10, the cost to the importer including tariff is $11 per unit. Should the price of the good fall to $9 per unit, then the cost to the importer would be $9.90 per unit, including tariff. If, on the other hand, the tariff is *specific,* let us say $1 per unit, the tax remains the same regardless of the import price; thus, a low-priced unit bears the identical tax borne by a high-priced unit and hence is taxed at a higher proportional rate. This type of tariff can be highly discriminatory.

Although the economic effects of the two types of tariffs are generally similar, there is one rather important difference. In periods of rising prices, the absolute amount of tariff collected tends, with an *ad valorem* tax, to rise. Conversely, inflation reduces the proportionate effect of a specific tariff. Thus, in a period of generally rising prices, specific tariffs can become comparatively innocuous merely through the passage of time. Perhaps for this reason, *ad valorem* tariffs are far more common in most countries.

Tariffs are incorporated into the tax structures of countries for a variety of reasons. In some instances, the origin of a particular tariff might be traced back to a time when import taxes were the chief source of governmental funds, usually early in a nation's development. Even today, tariffs represent an important revenue source for many less-developed countries. As economic development occurs, however, tariffs generally become a progressively smaller proportion of tax revenue, and the rationale for maintaining them or introducing new ones therefore shifts.

One of the chief reasons for industrialized countries to foster tariffs, and one certainly familiar to any business executive, is the protection of domestic industries. If imports were sold in a home market before a tariff, the tax almost inevitably would result in a higher domestic price, greater sales for home firms, and a reduction of imports. These effects are demonstrated graphically in Figure 7–1. Here, S_D and S_F represent domestic and import product-supply curves, respectively. $S_D + S_F$ is their horizontal summation and D is total domestic demand. In the absence of imports, E clearly would be the equilibrium solution; however, with a supply of imports

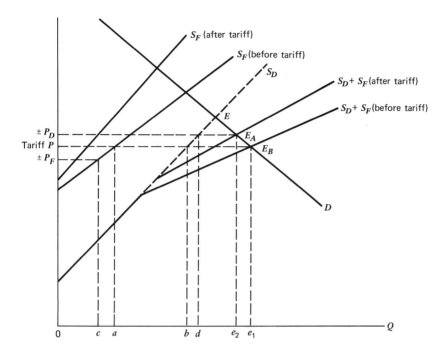

Figure 7–1. Economic effects on an *ad valorem* tariff.

available at lower prices, imports would expand and the market price would fall until, under free-trade conditions, a new equilibrium would be determined at E_B. Total market sales would be $0e_1$ divided between imports $(0a)$ and domestic production $(0b)$, with foreign and home prices equalized at P.

An *ad valorem* tariff has the effect of separating domestic and foreign prices by the amount of the tax. This effect can be represented by an upward shift in the foreign supply curve by the tariff amount. Since the tariff increases as the import price rises, the slope of the after-tariff foreign supply curve is greater than the before-tariff curve. The new equilibrium position with a tariff is denoted by E_A, with foreign suppliers furnishing an amount $0c$ and domestic firms producing the quantity $0d$. The tariff is represented by the difference between P_D, the domestic price, and P_F, the foreign or "world" price. Domestic production increases by bd and imports decline by ca; the market price rises by $P_D - P$ and, because of this change, total market sales decline by e_2e_1.

Several interesting points emerge from this rather elementary example. First, clearly the domestic price level *must* rise as a consequence of the tariff, except in the unusual case where the demand curve is horizontal, indicating an infinitely elastic demand.[1] This increase in price encourages all domestic suppliers to expand output, including those whose costs prohibited them from entering the market under free trade. More efficient producers, of course, enjoy greater sales and larger profits, even though their marginal (and average) costs are higher than in the before-tariff case. This implicit support for a higher domestic price is the reason why tariffs are termed protective and why producers in industries being harassed by lower-price imports frequently seek tariff relief. Two points, however, should not escape our attention. First is the obvious corollary that while tariffs do give domestic suppliers a respite from their competitive battle with producers in other parts of the world, they also force consumers to pay higher prices for goods purchased; therefore, tariffs generally are not in the interests of consumer groups, and, to the extent that they have been able to, such groups have opposed tariffs.

The second point deserving attention is the effect of a tariff on resource allocation within the whole economy. We have seen that even though the higher price resulting from the tariff lowers total purchases of the protected product, domestic firms increase the absolute amount of their own output. Assuming a fully employed economy, this expansion necessarily draws resources away from other producing sectors. Although the process through which this reallocation takes place is rather complex, in general an expansion in the protected industry raises costs for all other industries, reducing their demand for the various factors of production. It can be said, therefore, that tariffs tend to distort the allocative mechanism and shift resources from more efficient to less efficient sectors of the economy. Among the more productive sectors, whose costs are increased, are the export industries. From a purely domestic resource-allocation viewpoint, the somewhat surprising conclusion is that tariffs in one part of the economy tend to reduce the ability of other sectors to compete in world markets.[2] Where exchange rates are inflexible, therefore, the addition of a tariff in one import market might increase the demand for tariffs in other markets as well, as firms seek to mitigate the effects on them of the original tax.

---

[1]For students not familiar with the concept, price elasticity of demand is a measure of the responsiveness of market sales to changes in price level. Specifically, the elasticity measure is the ratio of the percentage change in sales to the percentage change in price level; thus, an infinite elasticity of demand would indicate that suppliers could sell as much as they desired at the prevailing price. The elasticity concept is very common and is useful in analyzing economic problems. The concept can be applied on the supply side as well, where the elasticity of supply is the percentage change in the amount suppliers offer on a market, divided by the percentage changes in market price.

[2]It could be argued that the effects of the tariff on the rest of the world would reinforce this tendency. Developing this argument would be a good student exercise.

Our example based on Figure 7–1 also shows that a tariff usually has the effect of reducing the world price (P_F) of the taxed product. The likelihood of this occurring is stronger if the importing country looms large in world trade, like, for example, the United States. Only when the elasticity of foreign supply is infinite will the world price level remain unaffected, and this condition is not likely to hold when the imported goods represent a substantial proportion of the foreign firms' total production. This fact means that a tariff imposed to raise the domestic price of a product by a certain percentage in general must exceed the desired percentage increase in price. Moreover, if foreign supply is comparatively inelastic, a "normal" tariff might result in only a minor shift in the domestic market price, providing little shelter for local firms. In such cases, tariffs are inadequate as a protective device, and other means, such as quotas, typically are utilized in their place. Mainly for this reason, quotas now are used in the United States to protect both the steel and textile industries from overseas competition.

A quota *can* have the same economic effect as a tariff, but this outcome is by no means necessary or even usual. Figure 7–1 shows that restricting foreign firms to shipments no greater than $0c$ through a quota would shift the market equilibrium point from E_B to E_A, as with a tariff equal to $P_D - P_F$. Since no tariff is collected, however, the difference between the domestic and foreign price must be accounted for in another way. There are at least three possibilities. The proceeds might accrue to foreign exporters if, by working in concert, they agree to charge P_D for imports, despite their ability to sell at a lower price. Or, if foreign exporters are less well organized, monopolistic importers might drive the import price down to P_F, absorbing the difference between P_D and P_F as their profit. In the normal case, an import price somewhere between P_D and P_F might be expected, with exporters and importers dividing the proceeds. Finally, the government might decide to sell the quota to the highest bidder, in which case the amount gained would be close to that found under a tariff.

Because governments typically do not auction quotas, however, businesspeople should be aware of the difference between tariffs and quotas when supply conditions in either the domestic or foreign sector shift. For example, under a tariff, a rise in domestic production costs without a commensurate increase in foreign costs would have the effect of raising domestic prices while reducing total market sales and increasing imports. Obviously, under these circumstances, the amount of the product furnished by home suppliers necessarily would decline, both because demand at the higher price is lower and because importers would increase their market share. By way of comparison, a quota generally would result in an even higher market price with a smaller decline in domestic supply. Finally, it also is clear that changes in foreign supply conditions have less effect on domestic markets under a quota than with a tariff. For example, an increase in foreign producers' costs would have no effect at all on home markets until the foreign supply curve (S_F, before tariff) had shifted upward by an amount that would make the quota unnecessary. With a tariff, on the other hand, any change in foreign supply conditions would affect domestic prices, unless the tariff were prohibitive, that is, prevented any goods from being imported. Quotas, in other words, more adequately insulate home markets from "disruptive" external influences and for this reason generally are preferred by businessmen in the affected industry. If there is to be a trade impediment, however, economists and others concerned with overall re- source allocation prefer tariffs because tariffs allow the price mechanism to operate, albeit in a distorted fashion.

Protection of the Agricultural Sector

A particularly common form of protective system is the set of tariffs and quotas designed to shelter markets in nearly all developed countries from imports of temperate-zone agricultural products. The need for protection arises from the tendency in most of these nations to subsidize their agricultural sectors through price-support programs of one type or another. Because the artificially maintained price would stimulate additional output, support programs typically incorporate a system of acreage controls to limit or even to prevent output expansion. Obviously, the government's ultimate purpose is the support of farm-family income and not the accumulation of crop surpluses in storage; however, the viability of the whole program depends not only on limiting domestic production but also on preventing the importation of the same commodities from overseas suppliers. For this reason, agricultural price-support programs always are coupled with import controls through tariffs or quotas.

An especially onerous form of this control is found currently in the European Community, where price supports are *not* joined with acreage controls. The result has been a rapid rise in output of many products previously imported from other parts of the world, including the United States. To prevent these lower-priced commodities from eroding the support programs, the community maintains a set of tariffs on these products that bring the final import price (including the tariff) to an amount slightly in excess of the support price. Imports, therefore, become the residual, supplying only the amount not available domestically at the support price. Because both the world price and the support price vary from year to year, the tariff also must be altered. For this reason, the program is called a *variable levy* system. The problem with the system is obviously the lack of production controls on domestic output. This tends over time not only to displace imports from former suppliers but also to generate surpluses. These excesses are marketed outside the community at world prices that usually are well below support prices. To finance the export of these artificially generated surpluses, the system uses export subsidies financed from the import tariffs on other agricultural products. Needless to say, former exporters have complained loudly about this Alice-in-Wonderland system, but their outcries have been relatively ineffective, in part because the system is not markedly different in its essentials from similar programs in the export countries. In recent years, however, the problem has been blunted by a rapidly expanding worldwide demand for many agricultural products. This demand has caused world prices to increase, in many instances, above the support prices.

It should be noted, however, that both Europe and the United States have experienced rapidly rising productivity in their agricultural sectors. As a result, farm populations have declined, even though output has risen. It might be anticipated, therefore, that the political pressures to support agricultural incomes in both areas will become less intense as time progresses.

The Notion of an Effective Tariff

Thus far, we have considered the protective effect of a tariff as being directly related to the amount of the tax as a proportion of a product's final selling price. The natural conclusion that might be drawn from this analysis is that an *ad valorem* tariff of, say, 20 percent on one product provides greater protection to producers of that item than a 10 percent tariff on another product. Moreover, if downward tariff revisions were to be negotiated, the more likely candidate for reduction would be the higher tariff, if for no other reason than more room for adjustment clearly exists there. In more detailed analysis, however, it develops that the nominal tariff on a good is not necessarily an accurate indication of the actual effect of the tariff structure on producers of that product. For this reason, the notion of *effective* tariff protection lately has received increasing attention, both from economic theorists interested in overall resource allocation questions and from policymakers concerned with the effects of tariffs on particular industries. Our focus here is predominantly with the latter type of problem.

The difference between nominal and effective protection can be shown most easily by reference to a hypothetical example. Suppose that the world price for black-and-white television sets of a particular size is $100 and that the cost of manufacturing sets, aside from purchased and imported components and raw materials, is $50 in the United States. For simplicity, we can assume that component purchases are equally costly for all world producers of television sets. Suppose now that the United States imposes an *ad valorem* tariff of 20 percent on finished sets, with no tariff on imported parts and materials. If we assume no change in world prices, the tariff would allow a price increase for United States-made sets to $120, thus affording domestic manufacturers of the product a measure of protection from overseas competition. How much protection? Clearly, if the cost of purchased components and materials is the same for all producers, then domestic companies can spend, after the tariff, $70 on their own operations instead of the $50 previously possible. Thus, in terms of *value added* to the sets by these firms, the effective protection rate is not 20 percent, the nominal tariff rate, but 40 percent, the proportional increase possible in the value-added figure. In general, ignoring tariffs on inputs, the rate of effective protection is given by:

$$T_E = \frac{T_N}{V \div P} = \frac{P T_N}{V}$$

where T_N = nominal *ad valorem* tariff
V = value added in the domestic operation before the tariff
P = selling price before the tariff

The effective rate is the nominal rate divided by the proportion of value added in the domestic operation to the before-tariff sales value.[3]

Two consequences of the effective-rate calculation are worthy of mention: (1) the degree of effective protection increases as the value added

[3]In more general form, the formula can be expressed:

$$T_E = \frac{T_i - \sum\limits_{j=1}^{n} a_{ij} T_j}{1 - \sum\limits_{j=1}^{n} a_{ij}}$$

where T_i is the nominal tariff on output i, T_j is the nominal tariff on inputs j, and a_{ij} is the intermediate input coefficient of input j equalling the price ratio P_{ij}/P_i. P_{ij} is the price of the jth input, and P_i is the price of output i. Note that the quantity $(1 - \sum a_{ij})$ represents the proportion of value added before the tariff, and the quantity $[(1 + T_i) - \sum a_{ij}(1 + T_j)]$ is the proportion of value added after the tariff. Since

$$T_E = \frac{\text{value added after tariffs} - \text{value added before tariffs}}{\text{value added before tariffs}}$$

the generalized formula can be derived easily.

by domestic enterprises declines and (2) a tariff on imports used in the productive process reduces the level of effective protection.[4] The first point is obvious from the method of computing an effective tariff, but it is nonetheless extremely important in actual practice. For example, most industrialized nations import raw agricultural products from tropical areas duty free but place a modest tariff on processed forms of the same product. Thus, coffee beans would be imported without tariff, while freeze-dried coffee packaged in jars would be subjected to a small duty of, say, 5 percent *ad valorem*. The tariff would not appear to be particularly significant, especially when compared with an average tariff rate on imports that typically might approximate 10 percent; however, if the cost of processing the raw product represents only a small part of the item's final selling value, as would be true of many agricultural goods, then the *effective* tariff can be very high. In our coffee example, processing costs might be only 10 percent of the wholesale price of a jar of coffee, with the remainder being the cost of imported beans. If this were true, the effective rate of protection on coffee processing would be 50 percent (.05/.1). It is little wonder that potential processors of raw agricultural commodities located in less-developed tropical regions complain bitterly about even the low nominal tariffs assessed by the industrialized consuming countries. To compete, foreign processors would have to have costs no higher than two-thirds (in the coffee example) those of their competitors behind the tariff wall.

The fact that tariffs on inputs into a productive process reduce effective protection for that process helps to explain the common observation in developed countries that tariffs tend to be highest on final goods and progressively lower on intermediate products. Duties on intermediate products can be thought of as a tax on the purchaser of such items, raising his costs of operation. Obviously, a given duty on the final good provides less and less protection as input prices are raised above the world level by tariffs. In fact, if *all* inputs were to be taxed at the same rate as the nominal tariff, the effective and nominal rates for the industry would be equal. For this reason, manufacturers of final products tend to resist additional taxes on needed component items, and the tariff structures of most developed countries reflect this influence.

A somewhat dated idea of the relationship between nominal and effective tariffs for major industrial areas can be obtained by perusing Table 7–1, which gives the nominal and effective tariff rates of 1962. Most effective rates, as expected, were considerably higher than corresponding nominal rates in all industrialized countries; however, for some products

---

[4]This result can be seen using the generalized formula given in footnote 3. As T_j rises, the numerator declines, hence T_E decreases.

Table 7–1 Nominal and Effective Tariff Rates, 1962 (selected products)

Products	United States		United Kingdom		European Communities		Japan	
	Nominal	Effective	Nominal	Effective	Nominal	Effective	Nominal	Effective
Clothing	25.1	35.9	25.5	40.5	18.5	25.1	25.2	42.4
Rubber goods	9.3	16.1	20.2	43.9	15.1	33.6	12.9	23.6
Glass	18.8	29.3	18.5	26.2	14.4	20.0	19.5	27.4
Steel-rolling-mill products	7.1	−2.2	9.5	7.4	7.2	10.5	15.4	29.5
Metal manufactures	14.4	28.5	19.0	35.9	14.0	25.6	18.1	27.7
Agricultural machinery	0.4	−6.9	15.4	21.3	13.4	19.6	20.0	29.2
Nonelectrical machinery	11.0	16.1	16.1	21.2	10.3	12.2	16.8	21.4
Electrical machinery	12.2	18.1	19.7	30.0	14.5	21.5	18.1	25.3
Automobiles	6.8	5.1	23.1	41.4	19.5	36.8	35.9	75.7
Bicycles and motorcycles	14.4	26.1	22.4	39.2	20.9	39.7	25.0	45.0
Precision instruments	21.4	32.2	25.7	44.2	13.5	24.2	23.2	38.5

Source: Bela Balassa, "Tariff Protection in Industrial Countries: An Evaluation," *Journal of Political Economy,* (73:6), 1965. Reprinted by permission of The University of Chicago Press.

the effective tariff rate was lower, actually becoming negative for steel-rolling-mill products and agricultural machinery in the United States. This reversal took place because tariffs on intermediate inputs in these industries were much higher than the tax on finished products. For example, in an industry with no tariff on the final product, tariffs on imported components would have the effect of simply raising total costs for firms in the industry. Such tariffs, therefore, obviously diminish the ability of final-product manufacturers to compete with foreign producers not faced with the intermediate tariff.

OTHER TYPES OF TRADE POLICIES

Explicit tariffs and quotas are by no means the only devices used by nations to regulate trade flows. Included in the panoply of barriers found in various parts of the world are "special" quotas that ostensibly are intended as short-term mechanisms but that in fact frequently become semipermanent. One example is the "voluntary" quota used by the United States on products where ordinary tariffs allow unacceptable amounts of imports. These quotas, found in products as diverse as textiles, steel, and beef, are not in a technical sense quotas at all but are instead controls established by the exporting countries. The stimulus for "voluntary" regulations by the exporters, however, usually is the threat of tougher import controls if cooperation is not forthcoming; but whether voluntary or not, the restrictive effects of a quota, discussed previously, cause distortions in the pattern of trade that would not exist in their absence.

One proposal for eliminating the need for "voluntary" quotas begins with the assumption that the federal government always will take steps to alleviate the gross dislocation of a domestic industry by foreign trade. When such a threat exists, this proposal would limit the growth rate of imports to the rate of expansion of the relevant domestic market as a whole, in other words, limit imports to a fixed market share. Congressional bills to provide for such "orderly" growth of imports have been introduced regularly in recent years, but as yet none have passed into law. The reasons for reluctance to accept the idea are not difficult to understand. First, if applied at all widely, this proposal would tend to lock trade into the existing pattern and would prevent the reallocation of resources to their most efficient use. In this respect, it is similar to the thoroughly discredited notion of a "scientific" tariff proposed frequently in the past. This duty would have set the tariff as the difference between foreign and domestic costs, which clearly would have destroyed any basis for trade, aside from a taste by consumers for foreign-made goods. In addition, however, there are a number of purely pragmatic considerations that would cause difficulty.

For example, to calculate the allowable market percentage for imports, it would be necessary first to define precisely the market boundary in terms of both product characteristics and geography. Would all steel products be included, or would the market definition be restricted only to certain types and grades for which imports were a particular problem? Would a national market percentage be the guide, even if it allowed a flood of imports to inundate a local market to a much higher percentage? The answers to such questions are critical to the potential program's administration and its effects on trade generally. Thus far, Congress has chosen to leave that particular Pandora's box closed.

The same type of problem arises, however, when nations attempt to regulate other forms of foreign competition. The most obvious example is the protection of home markets from the possibly harmful effects of international price discrimination (pejoratively called "dumping") by competitors in the market receiving the low-priced goods. Since the economics of price discrimination are well known, we need only state here that a profit-maximizing monopolistic firm or industry in one country can increase its profitability under certain conditions by charging lower prices for exports than for the same products sold in its own home market. When the price differential cannot be explained by differences in the cost of serving the two markets, dumping is said to have occurred. Most industrialized countries have antidumping regulations that ostensibly are intended to control the possible excesses stemming from the practice. In particular, national governments generally wish to prevent predatory dumping, a form of discrimination where the purpose is to gain control of a market by systematically destroying competitors through artificially low prices.

The U.S. antidumping law serves as a typical illustration of these regulations. Under our law, a discriminatory price found to be harmful to a domestic industry is nullified by a special tariff calculated to be the difference between the price here and in the country of origin. It is important to note that a discriminatory price, in itself, is *not* sufficient to warrant an antidumping duty; injury to a local industry also must be shown. The reason for this two-part condition is simply that consumers tend to gain from lower prices from any source, and unless someone, usually a domestic industry, is adversely affected, the price should be allowed to stand. Less-developed countries where such industries are nonexistent frequently do not have antidumping regulations. Also, the fact that both conditions are required for the special tariff means that periodic dumping of distress merchandise by foreign exporters falls outside the law's effective purview. Only discrimination of a persistent type is subject to control.

In some instances a lower export price is made possible by an implicit governmental subsidy for exports, embodied in special tax rebates or official assistance in financing arrangements. Most governments encourage exports as a matter of public policy, and, although direct subsidies are disallowed by international agreement, a variety of indirect means commonly are employed. Where subsidization of exports can be demonstrated, importing countries usually do not counteract this assistance through antidumping regulations; instead, they use a similar device called a countervailing duty. However, exporters from one country, confronted with subsidized competition from another nation in yet a third country, where the government of the third country chooses not to employ a countervailing duty, typically have no protection from the subsidy's effect. For this reason, overt subsidies are not usually important where both exporting and importing countries are producers of a traded item. They can be a critical determinant of sales in other world markets, however.

A variety of other means exist by which national policies discriminate against importers in favor of local producers. One that particularly affects U.S. exporters is the tendency of many nations in generating governmental revenues to utilize such indirect taxes as the value-added tax that is so common in Europe. Because they are theoretically a consumption levy, these taxes frequently are not applied to exports and, for reasons of equity, are sometimes added to imports. In contrast, the United States relies heavily on the corporate income tax, which is not rebatable on our exports and which is not applied to imports. Many companies in the United States believe that this single difference in tax structure places U.S. exporters at a significant disadvantage vis-à-vis their European competitors.

Attempts to alleviate this problem have been made. One method has been for companies to establish a special export subsidiary to which goods destined for other countries are transferred. The latest example of this type of method is the Domestic International Sales Corporation (DISC), a creation of the Revenue Act of 1971. DISCs are usually separate export sales corporations that can be established by individual companies, even rather small companies, or by groups of firms. The earnings of DISCs are not subject directly to U.S. corporate income taxes. Instead, DISC shareholders, usually the parent firm(s), are taxed on half of the DISC's current earnings, while taxes on the other half can be deferred indefinitely. Thus, for a corporate owner, DISCs simply defer half of the tax on normal export income. Interestingly, the tax-deferred income can be used for essentially interest-free loans to the parent for the purpose of further stimulating exports. Earlier versions of entities established to reduce taxes on export income were Webb–Pomerene associations and Western Hemisphere Trade Corporations. All such mechanisms implicitly subsidize export sales in an indirect way.

The list of other devices used by one country or another to favor domestic industries is virtually interminable. Frequently, product standards are established that inherently give local producers an advantage, or taxes are structured in such a way that outside manufacturers are taxed at different rates than are insiders. The automobile industry provides instances of both phenomena. The developing safety standards of the United States might specify a minimum acceptable distance between the windshield and a passenger's head that would implicitly discriminate against smaller cars from overseas. On the other hand, excise taxes in other nations based on weight would tend to favor lighter foreign cars. The point is not that these laws intentionally favor local producers but rather that their establishment, for whatever reason, often works out to be relatively more beneficial to these firms. This is especially true when local company representatives are the majority members of the standards boards. In any case, taxes and product standards are very important in industries as wide ranging as pharmaceuticals, meat, electronics, and electrical appliances. From an economic viewpoint, the effect of these regulations is to raise foreign manufacturers' costs because of the special requirements of export markets.

The range of nontariff barriers to trade found in the world is virtually limitless, and little would be served in exhaustively enumerating them here. Their importance in restricting trade, however, should not be minimized. As tariffs have tended to decline through multilateral negotiations, as discussed in the next section, other types of barriers have become relatively more influential. Those who are interested in business ought to be acutely aware of the effects of quotas and other restrictions, not only in reducing trade but also in distorting resource allocations. For example, quotas raise domestic prices for the protected industries and, where the products are incorporated in other goods, increase the cost of these items. It has been estimated that the "voluntary" quotas on steel in the United States produce a 50-cent reduction in the trade balance for every dollar's worth of steel kept out, because the products incorporating steel are made more costly.[5] Trade barriers tend to build inefficiency into the economic apparatus of a country by encouraging high-cost producers to expand output and, as indicated previously, by raising costs for more efficient companies. Clearly, it makes little sense to reduce tariffs only to replace them with more onerous forms of restrictions.

In concluding this section on import barriers and export subsidies, it should be noted that many such devices have been initiated for balance-of-

---

[5]Testimony of Robert E. Baldwin before the Joint Economic Committee's Subcommittee on Foreign Economic Policy, *Hearings on a Foreign Economic Policy for the 1970's,* 91st Congress, Second Session, September 29, 1970. Baldwin cited work by Gerald Lage.

payments purposes. Bound by fixed exchange rates, national governments simply have attempted to alter relative prices through policy measures in order to improve their trade balances. It should be readily apparent, however, that when *all* countries incorporate trade restrictions, the result must be self-defeating. World prices become distorted, and production tends to be inefficient. Even where policy measures are confined to particular industrial sectors, as has been the case recently in the United States, the consequences often have been far different than the original intentions.

What, then, becomes of the rationale for either trade restrictions or subsidies when exchange rates are no longer fixed but instead are more free to adjust to foreign exchange market conditions? Clearly, any balance-of-payments arguments are far less persuasive. Consider, for example, the likely exchange-rate consequences of a country's unilaterally assessing a new and uniform tariff of 10 percent on all imports. Presumably, the tariff would improve the nation's trade balance, but this almost immediately would have the impact of increasing the demand for the country's currency, thus raising its relative value. In all probability, the exchange-rate adjustment in the end would offset the tariff increase, leaving the trade balance in approximately the same status as before the tariff change. With flexible exchange rates, general tariffs cannot be justified by balance-of-payments considerations. It is still true, of course, that individual industries might benefit from more specific protection.

At least one implication follows directly from this line of reasoning. Tariff or subsidy schemes that are applicable to all industrial sectors tend to be under some pressure today for removal. For example, the U.S. Congress seems to see far less justification for DISC tax advantages for corporations in 1980 than it apparently did in 1971.

INTERNATIONAL COOPERATION ON TRADE POLICIES

Mutual efforts by governments to harmonize their disparate policies toward trade have taken essentially two directions. On the one hand, wide-ranging international negotiations have occurred periodically under the auspices of the General Agreement on Tariffs and Trade (GATT), of which more than 70 nations now are contracting parties. On the other hand, smaller groups of nations, most importantly and conspicuously in Europe, have banded together in economic unions. The ostensible purpose for such unions generally has been the reduction of tariffs and other barriers to both trade and investment between member countries. Each of these movements is discussed in turn in the following paragraphs.

Trade Negotiations under GATT

The General Agreement, reached in 1947, has served as the primary forum for multilateral negotiations for reduced barriers to international trade. In its original provisions, GATT was founded on the principle of most-favored-nation treatment, through which trade concessions granted by any member in bilateral negotiations with another country were to be extended automatically to all other members. This is to say that preferential arrangements between countries generally were forbidden, although important exceptions, discussed later, were allowed and have been extended subsequently. Quantitative restrictions, that is, quotas, were condemned, although again important exceptions were granted for agricultural products and for the protection of so-called "infant industries" in the less-developed countries. Under these general arrangements, several rounds of tariff negotiations have taken place and significant reductions in world tariff levels have resulted. The principle under which GATT was formed, that the world's economic welfare would be served best by unobstructed trade, has become widely accepted. Accordingly, the institution now is listed among the permanent agencies of the United Nations.

The less-developed nations, however, have not been satisfied with the working of GATT as it affects them. Their major objections center on three matters. First, poorer nations believe that GATT tariff negotiations have been largely a rich man's game, in the sense that reciprocal tariff concessions have involved products that are of interest predominantly to already industrialized countries. The developing countries, being relatively unimportant in the production of such items, have had little or no bargaining leverage for forcing tariff revisions in products they potentially could export. GATT also allows countries to protect systematically certain agricultural markets with quota arrangements; in some cases, these primary markets would offer opportunities for expanding less-developed-country exports. Finally, GATT permits developed countries to utilize a fairly wide range of "exceptions" to tariff reductions where the concession results in unacceptable disruptions to domestic markets. For example, in the United States the device used has been the "escape clause," where if the additional imports resulting from a lowering of tariff rate were injurious to a domestic industry, the rate change could be rescinded to allow time, at least in theory, for the industry to make an orderly adjustment to the altered market conditions. The developing countries claim, not without justification, that exceptions frequently have involved products of interest mostly to nations at a lower stage of industrialization; hence, the developing countries are for all practical purposes virtually excluded from the bargaining process because there is nothing to bargain about.

In recent years, some tangible recognition has been given by the major trading nations to these complaints, but final solutions to the problems will require much more time and effort. For example, in 1966 a chapter was added to GATT, one giving implicit encouragement to relaxing the principle of most-favored-nation treatment. It also allows for the possibility of discriminating in industrial-goods tariffs in favor of the poorer countries. In addition, the less-developed countries no longer are expected to establish reciprocal tariff concessions to acquire the benefits of lower tariffs elsewhere in the world, and they are allowed considerably more flexibility than the developed nations for establishing tariff and quota structures commensurate with their own developmental needs. For example, according to the multilateral trade negotiations concluded in April 1979 (The Tokyo Round), developing countries are allowed to introduce trade restrictions to attain general developmental goals, sometimes without prior notice or consultation. On the other hand, attractive tariff concessions by the industrial nations are likely to be in low-technology product industries. Such industries already are in difficult competitive straits in most developed countries. Meaningful concessions for these industries, politically, require some form of readjustment assistance for affected workers and firms. As yet, efforts to develop readjustment programs have not been notably successful.

The Tokyo Round also resulted in a variety of other trade-liberalizing agreements among the 99 participating countries. Tariff rates, already low for most products due to negotiations of earlier years, are to be reduced another one-third, to take effect over the next eight years. Initially the higher tariffs are to be cut the most, and, in total, new concessions will affect well over $100 billion in trade. In addition, the negotiations for the first time focused on various nontariff barriers that, as a consequence of success in tariff reductions, had assumed relatively greater importance in obstructing trade. National governments addressed such issues as uniform customs valuation procedures, equitable government procurement policies, import licensing rules, export subsidy practices and even biased technical and safety standards.

Cooperation through Economic Union

The General Agreement, from its inception, also relaxed the objective of most-favored-nation treatment for all parties in another very important instance: countries are allowed to establish either free-trade areas of customs unions. Under a free-trade area, participating countries eliminate trade barriers for trade among themselves, while each maintains its own set of tariffs and quotas against outside members. Obviously, because these remaining barriers generally are not the same in each country, some mechanism must be incorporated to prevent transshipment of goods from low- to high-tariff countries within the area. A customs union takes the process one step further by unifying the external tariff rates to be charged by all members to outside countries. In the years since the formation of GATT, both free-trade areas and customs unions have been attempted in various parts of the world with varying degrees of success. However, because of its importance in the world economy and because it amply illustrates both the problems and opportunities for businessmen inherent in economic union, discussion here centers on the European Communities (EC), better known as the European Common Market.

The rationale for excepting economic unions from the nondiscrimination provisions of GATT is simple in principle; in fact, however, it is far from simple. The reason for the exception seems to be that any substantial reduction in overall tariffs, even when involving only a limited set of countries, is a step toward free trade and therefore must be considered as economically beneficial. However, the inherently discriminatory features of an economic union can be harmful to nations outside the union. Moreover, a common market can lead to resource reallocation that is inefficient in the sense that producers of goods, after the union, might be *less* efficient than the producers who made the same items beforehand. The possibility exists that an economic union can be deleterious to the interests of both member and nonmember countries.

Why might this occur? To answer this question, we consider here a common market in which all trade barriers between member countries are removed and a common set of tariffs is established on shipment from outside the market. Typically, the common set of external tariffs would be computed by some process of averaging the preexisting duties of member nations. For a given commodity, therefore, the resultant common tariff would be higher than the previous tariff in some member countries and lower for others. The union's discriminatory effect is the fact that producers in one member nation shipping to another no longer face a tariff barrier, while outside producers confront the residual tariff of the union as a whole. The distribution of the costs and benefits of this discrimination determine whether or not the common market is, in net, salutary from an economic welfare viewpoint.

Two major shifts in the locus of product supply occur as a consequence of the union. The first involves only internal suppliers, where, as a result of tariff reductions, some products that had been made domestically in member countries behind the tariff now are imported from another country. This movement occurs solely because an individual country's tariff enabled **inefficient production to be carried on before the market was formed that** has not been possible afterward. Production is shifted from more costly domestic suppliers to less costly imports from other member countries. This process is called "trade creation." From an economic viewpoint, this type of change clearly is beneficial because it results in further product specialization, lower costs, and lower consumer prices. The other shift, however, has the opposite effect. Here, as a result of the common external tariff, outside suppliers who formerly exported to member countries are displaced by inside suppliers. Clearly, this substitution implies that the cost of acquiring the products now must be higher, because if the internal suppliers had been more efficient, they would have been serving the market before the formation of the common market. This shift extinguishes trade and, consequently, is known as "trade diversion." It obviously reduces economic welfare, both for consumers within the union and for outside suppliers.[6] Trade diversion also results in productive resources being allocated to uses not dictated by efficiency conditions.

From the standpoint of short-run trade effects, it is possible in principle to ascertain the net economic welfare implications of a common market by determining the likely trade-creating and trade-diverting tendencies. In general, if all countries of a union produced most of the goods consumed, one might anticipate that trade creation would be more important than diversion. Conversely, if only one or two inside nations are producers of, say, manufactured goods, with the remainder being supplied by outsiders, then the expectation would be that trade diversion might predominate. These observations can be summarized by stating that the advantages of forming a common market tend to be greater for countries that produce like items and tend to be smaller when member countries are more complementary in their produce offerings. On this basis, it probably can be asserted that the European Community had a net beneficial effect on economic welfare because the member countries are industrialized and similar in economic structure. The efficacy, however, of a union of less developed countries, each producing mainly individualized raw commodities, would be questionable unless other benefits were anticipated. One such benefit might be the possibility of generating lower production costs by constructing larger, more efficient plants.

The European Community (EC), originally comprised of six countries (France, West Germany, Italy, Belgium, Luxembourg, and The Netherlands), was one of two trade areas formed in Europe in 1959. The other,

---

[6]We consider here only productive effects and therefore assume a fixed pattern of consumption. It is possible that the benefits from increased consumption of internally produced items will be more important than the loss of benefits because of a less efficient source. In general, goods will be cheaper to consumers even when trade diversion occurs.

the European Free Trade Area (EFTA), consisted of seven countries around the periphery of the continent. Since formation of the two areas, however, three additional nations (the United Kingdom, Denmark, and Ireland) have joined the EC and two others (Greece and Portugal) have applied for membership.[7] The two trade areas now account for over one-fifth of total world trade.

Efforts by the EC and EFTA to reduce progressively their internal tariffs have been outstandingly successful. Figure 7–2 depicts the 10-year total dismantlement of industrial tariffs within each of the two areas. By 1968, internal industrial tariffs had been entirely eliminated. Beyond these reductions, however, were tariff cuts *between* the areas, also shown in Figure 7–2. Inter-area tariffs were dropped completely in 1977. As a result, Western Europe today is virtually a single, large, free-trade area.

EXPORT CONTROLS

Many nations not only regulate trade inflows but, for one reason or another, also monitor and control exports. In the major Western industrialized countries, such controls typically are far less pervasive than for imports. In fact, as we have seen, export subsidies are more often the rule. Still, a brief review of U.S. controls on exports should provide insight into the rationale

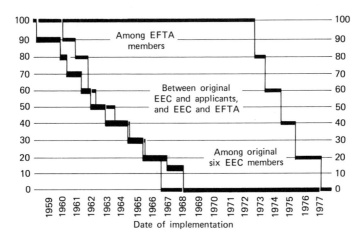

Figure 7–2. The progressive dismantlement of industrial tariffs on intra-European trade (percent of original tariff rates). (*Source: IMF Survey,* International Monetary Fund, Washington, D. C., July 4, 1977.)

[7]The U.K., Denmark, and Portugal were European Free Trade Area members.

underlying such constraints. Even though the American government is generally committed to export-promotion activities, it does impose minimal controls to insure that exports do not interfere with national security or foreign policy objectives.

Perhaps the most significant limitations applied to U.S. exports concern strategic goods and technology. The Export Administration Act of 1979 controls certain exports of goods and technological information, particularly where the sales have potential military applications. Specifically controlled are exports to the Soviet Union and its allies and to the People's Republic of China. The list of items believed to have detrimental security implications is changed from time to time in consultation with other NATO countries and Japan.

The need for consultation arises from the inherent difficulty of controlling technology flows without fairly uniform compliance by all competing nations. Obviously, it would make little sense for U.S. producers to be constrained from exporting materials only to have manufacturers in other nations shipping similar products. American controls also extend to manufacturing subsidiaries of U.S. corporations abroad. If regulated products differed significantly between countries, some items could be restricted for U.S. subsidiaries, but not for other firms in the same country. The argument has arisen repeatedly that since the American-controlled subsidiaries in fact are incorporated in the host country, U.S. controls over the movement of strategic goods interfere with the internal affairs of another nation. Consultation hopefully avoids most such disagreements.

In addition to strategic materials and technology, the U.S. government maintains more general controls over nuclear exports. The purpose of these restrictions is to prevent the possible misuse of the exports in the production of nuclear explosive devices. In determining whether or not nuclear facilities and materials can be licensed for export, the government considers the item's proposed use, whether the potential recipient has signed the Nuclear Non-Proliferation Treaty, and whether guarantees insure that the exports will not be diverted to use in producing weapons.

Other regulations affect a variety of other export goods. For example, all military weapons sales must be approved. Crime control and detection equipment must be licensed, except for sales to close allies of the United States. Some sales of construction equipment and trucks, capable of being diverted to military use, are restricted when the potential recipient country has engaged in or supported terrorist activities or when a threat to neighboring countries is considered imminent. Finally, virtually a complete embargo exists on exports to Cuba, North Korea, and Vietnam, countries where normal relations are not deemed possible.

STATE TRADING

Comparatively few American business executives have been heavily involved in dealing with state-owned enterprises. Occasionally, a country's export sales are consolidated by a state trading organization, as with commodity exports from some less-developed countries. Sometimes imports are purchased by a centralized state-controlled body whose original purpose might have been the regulation of all sales within the nation. Examples of this phenomenon in some European countries are state purchases of alcoholic beverages and tobacco products. For the most part, however, international buyers and sellers of the large preponderance of manufactured goods in Western nations deal in markets where prices are determined mainly by the interplay of supply and demand.

With increasing official emphasis being placed on opening trade and other economic relations with nonmarket economies in China, the Soviet Union, and Eastern Europe, there is ample reason to believe that multinational businesses will have to become accustomed to new trading situations. Although it is difficult to forecast precisely how the new relationships will evolve and what governmental policies will become necessary, some of the general problems of negotiating with state trading organizations are already apparent. For example, on the U.S. export side, state trading concentrates the purchasing decision for very large amounts of a product in a single body. This quasi-monopoly power in the state enterprise provides immense leverage in negotiating with individual private firms scattered around the world. The outcome typically would be a price substantially below one negotiated between parties of more equal bargaining strength. One solution to this type of dilemma is to deal with state traders only through a monopoly of sellers or through a government negotiater, which amounts to the same thing. Such a device frequently has been used for trade in raw agricultural commodities like wheat, corn, or cotton. For manufactured products, however, this type of arrangement would entail a substantial policy change in the export marketing techniques now used. Also, industrial items should, in the course of time, become the more important exports to the Communist countries.

State trading organizations, however, also cause difficulty for businesses in free-import markets. Here the root of the problem is the basis on which selling prices are established. In the absence of tariffs and subsidies, prices in an open market should bear some relation to the comparative costs of production and, all other matters being the same, orders should gravitate to the lowest cost or most efficient supplier. When one of the competitors is a state enterprise, however, the situation becomes more complicated for two reasons. First, costs (and, therefore, prices) used by a state-controlled organization are not comparable to those typically derived in a market-oriented economy. Some costs—for example, capital charges—are not even explicitly considered in many Eastern-bloc countries. Second, even if costs were comparable, the domestic market price in such a country need not be related to these costs. Price decisions in a "command" economy frequently reflect considerations entirely divorced from production costs or demand conditions. The allocation of resources is not left to the market mechanism but depends instead on the economic objectives of central planning officials.

The problem of realistically comparing prices can be illustrated by using the regulation of dumping as an example. In most market economies, the existence of dumping would be determined by a comparison of export prices with the equivalent prices in the exporting country's normal market. The implicit assumption in this calculation is that while the exporting firm or industry might increase its profitability by discriminating between markets, it would not for long maintain unprofitable prices in its major market. The "normal" price must, therefore, have some basis in the firm's cost of production. However, where this assumption no longer holds true, as with, say, the Eastern European countries and the Soviet Union, then the problem of even ascertaining when dumping has occurred is impossibly difficult. A similar problem exists in the more usual situation where a foreign company manufactures a particular item for export that is not sold in the same form in the normal market. Again, price comparisons are ruled out. In such cases, the American regulation would call for estimating the foreign production cost, including a normal profit, by using either the price of a similar product or by applying foreign factor costs to some known technology and building up an artificial cost figure. In the planned economy, however, factor prices may be no more realistic than the product price in terms of their relationship to relative factor scarcity, and cost estimates again would be meaningless. Clearly, the range of trade policies established for market economies will need to be adjusted as the importance of trade with planned economies increases.

POLICIES PRIMARILY AFFECTING FINANCIAL FLOWS

In addition to the multitude of national policies related to trade, there exist in many countries rules and regulations intended to control international investment activity. Even in the United States, probably the country with fewest capital constraints, strict controls in the past have been applied to direct investment by American corporations abroad and to long-term foreign loans by domestic banks to corporations overseas. Other countries also restrict capital outflows, but much of their attention also is directed toward managing foreign investment within their borders. Although the regulation of such foreign investors has been particularly important in less-developed areas, it is by no means confined to countries there. Industrialized nations such as Australia, Canada, and France have become increasingly sensitive to the impact of investments from other countries, especially the United States. Finally, many countries have policies intended to ration the supply of scarce foreign exchange among various users. These policies in part have the effect of restricting import trade, but they also influence the availability of local funds to foreign investors.

This section reviews some of the types of policies confronted by corporate investors when crossing national boundaries. The viewpoint is predominantly American, although many of the policies discussed would affect firms from other countries as well. Because the range of these regulations is extremely diverse, no attempt is made here to be exhaustive.

Regulation of Capital Outflows

The original justification for most countries to restrict capital outflows has been rooted in concern over balance-of-payments deficits. Under the quasi-fixed exchange-rate system existing prior to 1973, one tempting method for reducing such deficits was to force down the large debit item represented by long-term capital outflows. This became especially true when other means, such as increasing trade barriers, were effectively constrained by international agreements. The obvious rationale for wanting to cut down overseas investment flows has been the feeling that such a reduction would have virtually an immediate impact on the payments accounts, while alternative means, even if available, would have required considerably longer.

The strategy of focusing on the reduction of foreign investment flows frequently has had a second target related to improving domestic economic conditions. The idea has been suggested that making it more difficult for companies to invest elsewhere would have the corollary effect of increasing the domestic supply of capital funds. Presumably, this would lower long-term borrowing rates, making otherwise unattractive domestic investment opportunities more feasible. Corporate investment would be increased, acting as a stimulus to the economy as a whole. This type of argument was used to justify the American move to direct investment controls in the 1960s. It should be noted, of course, that if all countries followed such policies, capital markets would become segregated, with any benefits to one country being offset by costs elsewhere.

In the United States, there have been proposals from time to time to change the tax laws applying to multinational corporations for the purpose of modifying foreign investment flows. Generally, under American tax law, corporate taxes on foreign-based income are paid only when a dividend to the domestic parent firm is declared. Some observers believe that this unequal tax treatment between domestic and foreign sources of income implicitly discriminates against domestic investment. Investments, which in every other way would be identical, would be more attractive overseas because of the tax-deferral provision. Therefore, treating both sources of income the same for tax purposes in this view, would remove an artificial subsidy to overseas private investment and would assure that taxpayers in like situations would be taxed equivalently.

Needless to say, businessmen with foreign subsidiaries are strong in their negative reaction to the tax proposals. In part, their arguments are directed to the proposed taxation scheme itself and their differing views on tax neutrality and equitability. In part, however, the business position attacks the fundamental notion that foreign private investment is deleterious to the balance of payments; they assert that, in fact, exactly the opposite is true. With respect to the first argument, businessmen state that their overseas subsidiaries primarily compete with foreign-based enterprises in countries where the U.S. investments are domiciled. Therefore, to saddle these subsidiaries with American taxes is tantamount to placing these businesses on an unequal competitive footing with their most important rivals. Tax equitability, in this view, should not be based on comparison with other U.S. firms but, instead, with companies in the same competitive environment.

The other argument is the more important for our purpose here, because it has been raised repeatedly in debates on the need for further controls over foreign investment activity. The critical question from a balance-of-payments viewpoint is whether or not direct investment contributes to a deficit. Government officials favoring investment controls have answered "yes," while international business executives have answered emphatically in the negative. The "true" answer to this question depends on the time perspective chosen, and it is empirically difficult, if not impossible to determine. Investment in the immediate sense obviously is recorded as a capital outflow contributing to a deficit. In the longer run, however (and the length of run is the unascertainable variable), direct investment has a number of other effects that can interact in a rather complex fashion. An enumeration of some of these effects illustrates the point.

1. Some investment is made in kind, and where this occurs the capital outflow is offset by the export of real goods.

2. The output of foreign subsidiaries might displace former U.S. exports to the region and, in some instances, might ultimately be exported to this country, in both cases increasing the deficit.
3. On the other hand, foreign subsidiaries often are important customers for exports from the parent company of spare parts, replacement equipment, and semiprocessed goods.
4. Foreign subsidiaries pay significant fees to parent companies for management services, license agreements, and the like.
5. Foreign investments are made to earn profits, and interest and dividend flows are a most important credit item in the U.S. balance of payments.

Business persons, taking a longer view, have asserted with considerable justification that the net effect of direct foreign investment has been positive; that is, the balance of payments has been improved. Government analysts, on the other hand, have claimed that the benefits from investment cited by business would have continued from investment already in place and that, within a 5- to 10-year span, new outlays were detrimental to the country's deficit position.

Early efforts to revise the tax laws for foreign subsidiaries were only partially successful in terms of the government's objectives. Profits in overseas subsidiaries incorporated in so-called "tax haven" countries became taxable as earned. These countries had very low or nonexistent corporate income taxes and were used under the old law by multinational companies to accumulate funds for reinvestment around the world. To the extent possible, profits were shifted from areas having corporate taxation to the tax-haven country through organizational devices such as establishing a sales division in the haven and using transfer prices as a means to move profits to that division. In this single case, Congress seemed to agree with the administration view that tax deferral was equivalent to a tax-free loan by the government in support of foreign investment. Investments in countries not deemed to be tax havens were still allowed the tax-deferral privilege.

While the Federal government has not yet eliminated tax-deferral provisions for the great preponderance of U.S. investment abroad, it has in the past taken rather drastic measures to control investment outflows. For example, direct investment was curtailed in 1965 with a "voluntary" restraint program under which over 500 large nonfinancial corporations were asked to "expand the net balance of their export of goods and services, plus their repatriation of earnings from the developed countries, plus their repatriation of earnings from the developed countries, less their capital outflows to such countries; and also to repatriate their liquid funds."[8] Voluntarism, however, was abandoned in 1968 in favor of a complex and mandatory set of foreign investment regulations. Under these rules, investors were severely constrained from transferring funds from the United States, especially where such transfers involved another industrialized country. The regulations, under fire from their beginning as being counterproductive, were discontinued in 1974.

U.S. private long-term capital outflows have been restricted in other ways as well, most importantly through the interest-equalization tax. This tax, which applied to interest earnings of U.S. residents who invest in foreign securities, was put into effect to counteract the tendency for foreign companies to raise funds in the New York capital market. For these firms, New York represented a low-cost source of supply for capital, even though the rate of return to the American investor exceeded the return available from U.S. securities of equivalent riskiness. That is, the difference in long-term interest rates between the United States stimulated capital outflows, as might be expected whenever arbitrage opportunities exist.

The interest-equalization tax was intended to eliminate this differential by taxing away the incremental gain from the foreign security. Private borrowers and lenders once again proved to be an ingenious lot, however, and found other means to take advantage of the original economic stimulus. In this case, when New York security flotations were stopped, long-term foreign loans by U.S. banks rapidly increased. As a result, although originally limited to individual security purchasers, the tax was extended to apply to financial institutions as well. Foreign borrowing in the New York market was reduced markedly, and investment funds generally became scarcer in Europe and elsewhere. Interestingly, because the overseas return to capital increased, the incentive for foreign direct investment also was enhanced; the upshot was that U.S. direct investment reached record levels in 1967, especially in Western Europe, which led to the investment restrictions discussed previously.

It is apparent that U.S. balance-of-payments problems led to a series of steps directly affecting the freedom of multinational business executives in this country to use funds here for investment purposes elsewhere in the world. Some of the implications of these policies for corporate decision making are pointed out in later chapters. For now, we observe that similar policies exist in many other countries, both developed and less developed, where a history of balance-of-payments deficits can be seen. Whether or not this variety of capital constraints found in the world actually accomplishes the task for which these constraints were designed, especially in highly complex economies like the United States, is a subject that has been argued at length, not surprisingly with somewhat ambiguous results. Two points emerging from these discussions, however, can be mentioned in concluding this section:

1. Even though controls on private foreign investment might reduce capital outflows in the short run, the likelihood is that such constraints are counterproductive in the longer period, because balance-of-payments benefits from investment tend to become more important as the investment matures.
2. Controls on capital flows are likely to become increasingly severe and pervasive, as evidenced both with direct investment regulations and the interest equalization tax in the United States. The reason relates to the fungibility of money in a complicated world economy. If one international financial transfer mechanism is prevented from working, other methods develop to accomplish the same end, assuming that the original stimulus to the transfer continues to exist. Thus, if controls are to be effective they must become more and more comprehensive and complex.

Regulation of Capital Inflows

Foreign investors not only must take into account various restrictions on capital outflows, but increasingly they need to be cognizant of the rules controlling investments established by governments in *recipient* countries. At the extreme, host-country governments have on occasion expropriated foreign investments within their borders when the behavior of the owners of the property seemed for one reason or another to conflict with the interests of the government. Even where such drastic actions have not taken place, however, the host government frequently has taken steps to assure that the foreign investment meets the long-term needs of the economy. As foreign (especially American) investment has expanded in many nations, so also has the desire of these countries to wield some control over it; yet, the ability of individual governments to accomplish their wishes has been somewhat constrained by the very factors that have made international capital movements so important. This section explores the interplay of these forces with particular reference to direct investment, which, for most recipient nations, seems to cause the most difficulty.

In the larger industrialized countries of Europe, the concern with outside investors has centered mostly on two issues. The first of these is the tendency for foreign investment to concentrate in a few industries, usually those associated with higher levels of technology, such as electronics or computers. While overall levels of foreign investment might be quite small compared with total net capital formation, in the high-technology industries the proportion can be much higher. In some instances, the larger part of an industry's output is controlled by foreign investors. When this occurs, governments become concerned about the development of an internal technological capacity not dependent on progress in other countries. This worry is founded partly on perceptions of national security requirements, but it is also the product of feelings of national pride.

The second problem European countries have found with outside investors, particularly Americans, has been the foreigner's frequent unwillingness to play by reasonably well-established "rules of the game." Sometimes dissatisfaction has been based on the outsiders bringing along unfamiliar competitive techniques that wreak havoc on monopolistic practices previously utilized. For example, implicit pricing and market sharing agreements generally have not been respected by U.S. investors. Sometimes dissatisfaction also has focused on the apparent ability of American corporations to evade governmental policy restrictions that would apply to domestic companies. One repetitively cited example concerns the policy of some European governments to foster the location of new industry in low-income areas and, therefore, to discourage or even prohibit the use of sites in already industrialized locales. The foreign investor, to whom the government also would like to apply the policy, is not without leverage in such a situation because he has the option of either locating in another adjoining country or, indeed, sometimes withholding the investment altogether. This tendency to play off one government against another, which probably has been far less important than frequently is implied, has nonetheless been a source of irritation to some European governments.

Part of the reason for governmental frustration on issues of the type just mentioned has been the perfectly normal desire to acquire the distinct benefits from foreign investment while minimizing various perceived costs. Most countries encourage investment by outsiders because the new factories and offices increase total productive capacity, raise real wages and taxes, and frequently introduce new technology and entrepreneurial methods. Balanced against these benefits are certain costs. Some of these, like the matters alluded to earlier, are implicit and difficult to measure, but others, such as repatriated profits or, perhaps, the subsidies used to attract investment, are more explicit. In some cases, particularly in less-developed countries, foreign investment can result in costs exceeding benefits, especially when the preponderant amount of investment capital is raised within the country. As a general rule, however, countries desire foreign investment because they derive substantial benefits from it.

The problem to be faced in the countries wanting foreign investment capital is how to create a competitively hospitable climate for outsiders while maintaining control over some aspects of the investors' behavior. Many observers believe that in the absence of some form of international agreement, real control by any individual nation over the activities of a large multinational corporation is simply impossible. This alleged governmental impotence in the face of raw corporate power has been the subject of considerable investigation in recent years. While the findings of these studies are not always persuasive, there seems to be little question that governments will be taking more joint actions in regulating multinational corporations and in improving the investment recipient country's bargaining strength with the companies. Already, the Common Market nations have set forth international rules for that group of countries. In addition, multinational corporate guidelines have been promulgated by both the Organization for Economic Cooperation and Development (OECD) and the United Nations. Oil-producing countries have demonstrated clearly the advantages of joint bargaining with the integrated oil firms by extracting major concessions that most observers believe could not have been forthcoming without concerted action. The likelihood is, therefore, that multinational companies will need increasingly to be cognizant of developing international regulations as well as the host of differentiated rules set forth by individual countries.

In less-developed countries, policies affecting foreign investment generally are motivated (1) by balance-of-payments considerations, (2) by the desire of host governments to direct investment into areas contributing most to economic development, or (3) by concern over political control of economic resources within the country. In the first category are policies restricting dividend repatriation, rationing the acquisition of foreign exchange for various corporate purposes, or regulating the use of transfer pricing arrangements to shift profits among corporate units. In the second grouping are rules governing industries where outside investment is to be permitted and various requirements for the purchase of locally produced components. The third category includes governmental demands that corporate control, particularly in certain sensitive areas like broadcasting and public utilities, remain in the hands of host-country citizens. Each of these policy areas is discussed at some length in Chapter 18.

Two policy matters, more prevalent in less-developed than in industrialized countries, do have direct impact on business decisions and deserve further description. The first of them, already mentioned, concerns the perpetual proclivity of developing countries to encounter balance-of-payments difficulties and acute shortages of foreign exchange. One typical method used to harbor scarce currencies is the simple device of erecting a system of multiple exchange rates. All exporters usually are required to sell their foreign exchange earnings to the government or its agent at an established rate, and each prospective user of foreign funds is assigned a purchasing exchange rate that depends on the particular purpose to be served. Thus the rate structure might call for an "official" exchange rate of, say, 20 pesos per dollar, and all dollars earned would be traded for local currency at this rate. On the other hand, importers of assembled automobiles and other "luxury" goods might be required to pay 40 or more pesos per dollar to acquire the hard currency necessary to make the purchase. Importers of more needed items, such as machinery, spare parts, or medicines, typically would be allowed a rate approximating the official figure. Other purposes, like dividend repatriation by a local subsidiary of a U.S.-based company, also might be subjected to higher exchange rates. Also, as in most rationing schemes, multiple exchange-rate systems usually are accompanied by currency "black markets" characterized by fluctuating prices determined by the particular market conditions. The rate in the black market, which might be well above any rate in the official structure, can be a better indication of the nonexistent "free" rate. For this reason, it frequently is used as a barometer of likely change forthcoming in the government-maintained exchange rates.

The widespread popularity of exchange-control systems among developing countries can be explained by the fact that these systems offer many of the advantages of more elaborate sets of regulations without some of the disadvantages. For example, exchange control clearly can be used as a very flexible device for governing trade flows, particularly imports. Considering the high rates of inflation and chronic balance-of-payments deficits faced by most developing countries, manipulation of exchange rates to control trade flows is much simpler than continually adjusting quotas and tariffs to accomplish the same end. Explicit measures to control trade, such as tariffs, generally result from international agreement and are difficult to modify in dynamic circumstances. Exchange controls, on the other hand, are allowed by the IMF in situations of chronic balance-of-payments disequilibrium, and can be altered quickly as conditions dictate. From the viewpoint of the international investor, however, such controls become a highly unpredictable element of the environment that can have gross effects on his own trade and financial operations.

The other policy area that differs substantially between rich and poor countries is the possibility of governmental expropriation of foreign-owned property. Few corporations worry about expropriation in the developed regions, but in the less-developed areas it is a real and, some believe, increasingly likely problem to be faced. Expropriation of property by a sovereign government generally is condoned in international law, provided that "just compensation" for the property is made. Typically, the property is nationalized for any of a number of reasons: (1) the host government might change radically in composition and outlook, as in Cuba or Chile, with the result that prior agreements with foreign firms appear to be against the newly defined national interest; (2) subsidiaries might operate in a manner found by the host government to be detrimental in some dimension, including such matters as insufficient numbers of local citizens in managerial positions, lack of a high enough proportion of local content in purchased inputs, or even overt attempts by the company at influencing political decisions; (3) the need for outside private ownership might decline, as might be the case where new foreign technology becomes less important to the continued functioning of the enterprise. Also, governments have numerous methods short of overt expropriation for increasing control over the activities of foreign subsidiaries. For example, rules can be established governing the composition of ownership, employment practices, or sources of raw and semifinished goods; or new forms of special taxes might be applied. Sometimes measures of this kind drastically reduce the subsidiary's profitability; for this reason, they have been referred to as "creeping expropriation." Few parent firms would continue for long to operate foreign subsidiaries at a loss.

Business firms are not totally defenseless when confronted with a decision to invest in a country where expropriation might be a problem. First, investors frequently provide services that would be difficult, if not impossible, for the country to provide on its own. Access to the fruits of research and development can be one such benefit, but it is by no means the only one. For instance, for subsidiaries established for the purpose of exporting either raw or manufactured commodities, the parent firm might provide ready access to already developed distribution channels, a form of monopolistic advantage. Without this outlet, the developing country would have to duplicate the channels at potentially very high cost. Also, in instances where the American government has a negotiated agreement on expropriation with the host country, businessmen can insure against the practice through the federal government. Even where such agreements do not exist, there are obvious pressures on host-country governments against expropriation, especially in countries desiring the continued flow of outside investment capital. In general, however, the best defense against expropriation is the maintenance of economic advantages for the host country obtainable only through the outside investor's continued participation.

Summary

This chapter has outlined in a rather abbreviated way the various types of governmental economic policies directly affecting multinational business operations. In part, the policies are directed toward the regulation of trade flows and include elements such as tariffs, quotas, and export restrictions. In part, policies relate to the control of investment and other types of financial activity, and these efforts have come both from investing and recipient countries. There are, of course, additional policy areas that have not been discussed. For example, all countries set forth for firms requirements stemming from national defense or full-employment considerations. Some countries are concerned about aspects of the transfer of technology by international companies or the contributions of these firms to economic growth. It is not the purpose of this chapter to point out the innumerable variations in policy practices by individual countries; such a task would necessitate far more space than the length of this book permits. Instead, we have provided some perspective on the general nature of governmental policies and the economic motivation for their existence.

In the succeeding chapters we will return frequently to the effects of such policies on the decisions of the firm in selecting the form and location of international operations, in selecting technology, in deciding on financial arrangements, and, most importantly, on dealing with conflicts with host-country governments.

In the next two chapters, the methods of entering international business will be discussed. Chapter 9 will concentrate on those methods that do not rely heavily on the use of direct foreign investment, for example, exporting, licensing, and the sale of technical aid and management services. Again, however, these chapters will call into play the theory of comparative advantages as it applies to firms competing abroad.

SELECTED READINGS

Bergsten, C. Fred, Thomas Horst, and Theodore H. Moran, *American Multinationals and American Interests* (Washington, D.C.: Brookings Institution, 1978).

Cohen, Benjamin I., *Multinational Firms and Asian Exports* (New Haven, Conn.: Yale University Press, 1975).

Dunning, John H. (ed.), *Economic Analysis and the Multinational Enterprise* (New York: Praeger, 1975).

Grubel, H. C., "Effective Tariff Protection: A Non-Specialist Guide to the Theory, Policy Implications, and Controversies," in H.G. Grubel and H.G. Johnson (eds.), *Effective Tariff Protection, General Agreement on Tariffs and Trade,* Geneva, 1971.

Krauss, M., "Recent Developments in Customs Union Theory: An Interpretive Survey," *Journal of Economic Literature,* June 1972.

Krueger, Anne O., *Liberalization Attempts and Consequences* (Cambridge, Mass.: Ballinger Publishing, 1978).

Lipsey, R. G., "The Theory of Customs Unions: A General Survey," *Economic Journal,* September 1960; pp. 496–513, reprinted in R. Caves and H.G. Johnson (eds.), *Readings in International Economics* (Homewood, Ill.: Irwin, 1968), pp. 261–278.

Robinson, Richard D., *National Control of Foreign Business Entry: A Survey of 15 Countries* (New York: Praeger, 1976).

Streeten, P., "Trade Strategies for Development," *World Development,* Vol. 1–6, 1973, Raymond Vernon and Louis T. Wells, Jr. (eds.), *Manager in the International Economy,* 3rd Edition, (Englewood Cliffs, N.J.: Prentice Hall, 1976).

CHAPTER 8

Changes in the International Economy

INTRODUCTION

As the decade of the 1980s begins, the world economy is very different than when the first edition of this book was written in the early 1970s. Some of the changes in the world economy since then have been dramatic, like the sudden and huge increase in oil prices in late 1973. Others have been more subtle, like the emergence to economic prominence of a new group of countries, including such semi-industrial countries as Brazil and Korea. The world moved from a fixed to a floating exchange-rate system in the 1970s, and inflation became a worldwide fact of life. International money and capital markets have developed to the point where they are a major source of financing for investment throughout the world, including some developing countries formerly dependent on official aid for foreign capital. Taken together these changes—the increased price of energy, floating exchange rates, the emergence of semi-industrial countries, the development of international capital markets, and world inflation—make the world of 1980 a very different place in which to do business than was the world of 1970. Firms engaged in international business must take these changes into account as they plan their strategy for the 1980s; therefore, the purpose of this chapter is to provide a framework for viewing the world economy as it now exists.

OIL PRICE INCREASES

Of the major changes that took place in the 1970s, the adoption of a floating exchange-rate system and the emergence of Eurocurrency financial markets already have been discussed in earlier chapters. The most dramatic event, and one central to many of the other changes, was the rapid increase in oil prices, which was most marked in late 1973 but began earlier in the decade. Oil prices reached their lowest point in real terms during 1970, and then began a slow but steady rise until the abrupt jump in 1973. Oil prices then tended to decline somewhat in real terms as price increases failed to keep up with inflation. In 1979, however, another abrupt increase raised oil prices to new highs: the price of Saudi Arabian light crude rose to over $25 per barrel by the end of 1979, double the level in 1978 (see Table 8–1). Most observers now believe that oil prices will continue to increase from the 1979 levels at about 3 percent per year in real terms.

The cause for the rapid increase in oil prices often is laid to the emergence of the cartel of petroleum-exporting countries (OPEC); however, it is clear that the strength of the cartel was increased by the rapid growth in the demand for oil relative to production in the consuming countries. It was seen in Chapter 1 that in both the advanced industrial countries and in the oil-importing developing countries energy consumption grew by 1.5 percentage points per year faster than production, thus requiring large increases in imports. Increased oil prices, therefore, probably reflect an actual and prospective shortage of oil as much as they do actions of the OPEC cartel.

While the reasons for the oil price increases may be debated, the effect is clear. The high price of oil has shifted relative prices of inputs into both production and consumption, setting off a series of structural adjustments in the world economy that have not yet been worked out fully. At the same time, because oil importers have not been able to reduce consumption while maintaining a growing level of economic activity, a structural imbalance has been created in the world economy, giving oil exporters more-or-less permanent balance-of-payments surpluses, while importers, as a group, have large deficits. Both of these factors increase the vulnerability of the

Table 8–1 Realized Prices for Saudi Arabian Light Crude Oil (U.S. $/barrel)

	1950	1955	1960	1965	1970	1973	1974	1975	1976	1977	1978
Current $	1.71	1.93	1.50	1.33	1.30	2.70	9.78	10.72	11.51	12.40	12.70
Constant 1978 $	6.60	5.85	4.32	3.83	3.48	5.00	14.49	13.76	14.53	14.29	12.70

Source: World Bank, *Commodity Trade and Price Trends (1979 Edition)*, (Washington, D.C.: World Bank), p. 94.

world economy to other shocks and make economic growth and stability more difficult to achieve.

The change in relative prices brought about by increased oil prices has had many side effects that were not anticipated entirely. For example, the price of molasses now seems to be related to the price of oil! The reason: molasses can be used to make alcohol, which is a substitute for gasoline. The substitution becomes profitable when oil prices are above $25 to $30 per barrel in 1979 figures. On the other hand, oil price increases caused a decline in copper prices, at least for a period of time. The higher price of energy caused consumers of electric power to reduce the rate of growth of their consumption. As a result, there was less need to build new power plants, which are among the most important users of copper for generators, circuit breakers, transformers, and distribution lines. The reduced copper demand caused prices of copper to decline. The price of aluminum, on the other hand, increased because the higher prices of gasoline induced auto-mobile manufacturers to reduce the weight of their cars by substituting aluminum for heavier metals. Increased demand drove up aluminum prices.

The oil price increases, which had their full effect first in 1974, increased the current account balance-of-payments surplus of the OPEC countries to $65 billion in that year. Declining oil revenues as a result of the 1975 recession in the industrial countries, together with rapid growth in imports into the OPEC countries, cut that surplus in half. The surplus remained at about $30 billion in 1976 and 1977, falling then to about $5 billion in 1978 as revenues of oil exporters again fell, while OPEC imports continued to rise. With the doubling of oil prices in 1979, however, the surplus again rose to about $50 billion, with further increases to over $100 billion estimated for 1980. It now is expected that that surplus at least will be maintained.

The effect of these OPEC balance-of-payments surpluses is to create the "recycling problem" and the world debt problem. The OPEC surpluses, of course, are mirrored by current account balance-of-payments deficits in the countries outside OPEC. These deficits have to be financed in some way, for otherwise the importing country would have to reduce economic activity sufficiently to eliminate or at least substantially reduce their deficit. Thus, the recycling problem is how to induce the OPEC countries with balance-of-payments surpluses to continue to export their oil in return for financial claims, and how to find ways for them to channel the credit that is created into the countries with balance-of-payments deficits.

After 1974, tbe OPEC surplus was recycled in part through the Eurocurrency markets, as was seen in Chapter 6. OPEC oil exporters invested the proceeds from their sale of oil in commercial banks. The banks, in turn, made loans to oil-importing countries. In addition, the OPEC surplus was recycled in part through the United States; OPEC countries invested in U.S. securities and the U.S. in turn ran a current-account deficit with other oil importers. Finally, the OPEC surpluses were financed by direct loans from the OPEC countries—and the financial institutions they created—to oil-importing countries, particularly developing countries.

The effect of recycling, of course, is the build-up of foreign debt in the world economy. There has been particular concern about the debt of developing countries, reaching $315 billion at the end of 1978, and the debt service of $51 billion in 1978. Developing countries, however, are not the only ones having run up substantial foreign debt. Some industrial countries also have increased their foreign debt, and, as was seen in Chapter 1, even the net foreign assets of the United States have declined in recent years in response to balance-of-payments deficits.

Among the developing countries, external debt and debt service have become increasingly concentrated in a few countries. Of the $315 billion in medium and long-term debts outstanding at the end of 1978, 45 percent was owed by 7 countries. The large borrowers have been among the most dynamic countries, and their borrowing reflects the need to sustain their rapid economic growth. The emergence of this group of developing countries to prominence has been one of the significant features of the 1970s, the implications of which are discussed in the following section.

INCREASED COMPETITION IN THE WORLD ECONOMY

That the rapid economic development of a group of relatively poor countries has important implications for the structure of the world economy cannot be doubted. A group of 15 or so developing countries grew so rapidly in the 1960s and 1970s that in several respects their economies are more like the advanced industrial countries than they are like the other developing countries. As a result, they are called semi-industrial countries, or newly industrialized countries (NICs). They include Brazil, Colombia, Mexico, and Argentina in Latin America; Greece, Portugal, Spain, Yugoslavia, and Turkey in Southern Europe; Egypt and Israel in the Middle East; Korea, Taiwan, Hong Kong, Singapore, and the Philippines in Asia. These countries followed various economic development strategies, but as a group they have achieved very high rates of growth in their gross domestic product (GDP) over quite a long period of time—6.3 percent per year over the period 1960 to 1977. They have been able to translate these high growth rates into rapid growth in per capita growth of national product—4.4 percent per year—because in many of these countries the population growth rate has now fallen to less than 2 percent per year. The economic structure of these countries has been transformed in a short period of time, with the proportion of the population in agriculture falling from 54 percent in 1960 to 35 percent in 1977. Over the same period, manufactured exports rose from 22 percent of the total to 58 percent for the group as a whole, with much greater gains in individual countries. This group of countries now has a total gross domestic product greater than that of Japan. Brazil alone has a GDP that is one-fourth of Japan's. Together, they have become a significant force in the world economy.

The emergence of this group of countries has both increased opportunities for firms in the advanced industrial countries, because most direct investment in the poorer countries of the world is concentrated in these countries; it also has presented a new source of competition in the world economy. Just as the emergence of Japan in the 1960s increased competition for the established advanced industrial countries, so the semi-industrial countries are transforming the world economy now.

Competition occurs at all levels. These countries constitute a new and important source of demand for raw materials. Except for Mexico and Argentina, all the semi-industrial countries have become important oil importers, for example. At the same time, they have become competitors in many export markets. The Far Eastern semi-industrial countries have become competitors, even with Japan, in the sale of textiles and garments. Semi-industrial countries now are exporting increasing quantities of iron and steel, and Brazil has become the world's third largest soybean exporter.

Not only are the semi-industrial countries becoming more important in international trade, but firms in these countries are beginning to compete with those in the advanced industrial countries in other ways. The abilities of Korean construction companies are legendary. In Korea they seem to be able to construct any plant at less cost than would be required elsewhere, and they have competed successfully with Western firms for contracts in the Middle East. Some Asian textile companies are investing in plants in other developing countries and other firms are exporting technology. A Mexican firm, for example, has one of the few successful methods for making sponge iron by the direct reduction process. Sponge iron can be an input into steelmaking, replacing pig iron from the traditional blast furnace.

The increasing importance in the 1970s of semi-industrial countries only has added to the competition in the world economy that had faced U.S. multinational enterprises during the growth of European and Japanese multinational firms in the 1960s. Chapter 1 pointed out that European (particularly Swiss and German) and Japanese firms have increased their share of the world stock of direct investment. In addition to the entry of German and Japanese firms into international production, competition has been increased by industrial diversification of firms already engaged in international production. A firm in one industry often will establish a subsidiary in another industry. As a result, there are now many more subsidiaries of foreign firms competing in individual markets than was the case in 1950 or even 1960.[1]

The effect of this new competition has been to limit the range of pricing and other options open to any individual firm. Also, as will be discussed in Chapter 17, it improves the bargaining power of host countries in setting the terms on which foreign firms may engage in production; consequently, it is clear that the competitive environment now is more difficult for firms engaging in international production.

INFLATION

Increased competition has been accompanied by increased instability in the world economy. Instability in the international economy is reflected in the increased rate of world inflation experienced in the 1970s. It is difficult to construct a single index of price increases in a wide range of countries because the increases have taken place in different currencies, while exchange rates between those currencies have changed; however, Table 8–2 shows one index of the prices of manufactured exports from developed countries as measured in dollars. Because it is based on dollar prices, the index has been influenced not only by price increases, but by the depreciation during tbe 1970s of the dollar relative to other currencies.

The picture of inflation painted in the table is startling. After a decade of virtual stability during the 1960s, prices in dollars began to increase rapidly even before oil prices were increased in late 1973. Price increases reached a peak in the 1973 to 1975 period that included the quadrupling of

Table 8–2 Index of Inflation in Manufactured Exports (1979 = 100)

	1959	1969	1971	1973	1975	1977	1979
Index	29.8	31.0	37.3	49.7	71.7	80.0	100.0
% annual increase		0.4	9.7	15.4	20.1	5.7	11.8

Source: World Bank, *Commodity Trade and Price Trends (1980 edition)* (Washington, D.C.: World Bank), page 32.

[1]Knickerbocker shows that the average number of subsidiaries in each industry and country increased from 1–2 in 1950 to 4–5 in 1970. In 1950 there were only 38 instances in which 6 or more subsidiaries were producing in the same industry and country, whereas there were 357 such instances in 1970. See Frederick T. Knickerbocker, "Market Structure and Market Power Consequences of Foreign Direct Investment by Multinational Corporations," (Washington, D.C.: Center for Multinational Studies, 1976), Occasional Paper No. 8, pp. 50 & 52.

oil prices. Price increases then moderated somewhat in 1975 to 1977 in the face of a worldwide recession, only to accelerate again in the 1977 to 1979 period.

What is to account for the upsurge of inflation in the 1970s? It is clear that the entire burden cannot be laid on increased energy prices extracted by OPEC, although those increases contributed to the problem, for the acceleration of prices had begun prior to the major oil price increase in late 1973. An important cause of international inflation has been the rapid growth in the supply of money, particularly in the United States, which began in the late 1960s. This growth in the money supply led to U.S. balance-of-payments deficits and the accumulation of reserves in other countries. The expansion of international reserves, in turn, led some other countries to expand their money supplies and thus contribute to world inflation. Germany and Japan, however, have been notably successful in controlling inflation, even though they also have accumulated the largest stocks of international reserves.

The effect of inflation is to increase uncertainty for firms engaged in international business. Inflation changes relative prices of inputs and outputs. Differential rates of inflation lead to changes in exchange rates. Loans in the international capital markets are made at floating interest rates so that interest charged on loans can be changed to reflect changes in the cost of money to the lending institutions. Long-term financing is less attractive to both borrowers and lenders, and long-term contracts for sale or purchase of material become more complicated to negotiate. As a result of all these factors, long-term planning is more difficult in an inflationary environment and managers have to spend more time on hedging the effects of inflation, leaving less time for production estimates.

THE FUTURE

Many of the new developments in the world economy that took place in the 1970s were interrelated. The very strong push for economic growth in the 1960s, aided by rapid expansion of monetary demand in the United States, provided the environment for rapid growth of the semi-industrial countries. It also released inflationary forces that ultimately resulted in the demise of the fixed exchange-rate system and set up the conditions precedent to the oil price increase in 1973. Oil price increases now help to fuel inflation by pushing up costs and by creating balance-of-payments deficits in oil-importing countries; the deficits are financed with the creation of credit. That credit is distributed through the expanded and more efficient international capital markets to oil-importing countries. The availability of financing through international capital markets, and the system of floating exchange rates, may help to perpetuate the inflationary environment by removing balance-of-payments constraints on domestic monetary policy.

The world of the 1980s clearly will be a more difficult one for international business. It will be difficult to maintain healthy growth and development in an interdependent world economy in the face of all of the structural problems that have been described. The dangers come from several sources:

- Oil-exporting countries may not continue to supply the amounts of oil required for continued growth.
- The existing financial system may be unwilling or unable to finance balance-of-payments deficits of oil-importing countries.
- Oil importers may resort to protection or deflation to reduce their payments deficits.

A continuing supply of petroleum is absolutely essential during the time it will take for conservation measures to take hold and alternative sources of energy to be developed. If oil supplies were disrupted either because exporting countries were unwilling to continue to export on credit or because of political difficulties in a major exporting country, an immediate contraction of the world economy would follow. There is little slack in the international energy system that could compensate for reduced exports by a major supplier. The tightness in the energy supply system gives greater importance to the efforts now underway to conserve energy use and to find new supplies.

Even if exporters are willing to continue to supply petroleum, the international financial system may have difficulty in financing the resulting balance-of-payments deficits of oil importers. The private international capital markets were able to handle the financing of the OPEC surplus in 1974 through 1978, but there is now considerable doubt that the enlarged deficits in 1979, and those projected for later years, can be financed in the same way. The reason for this pessimism is that oil-importing countries already have large debts, and the financial institutions have large exposures to particular countries. Prudence requires that additional lending be scrutinized carefully by each lending institution. Default on loans outstanding by an important country might be the event that would precipitate contraction of financing through private financial institutions. It is important, therefore, that other financing mechanisms be found to help carry the burden of recycling the OPEC surplus, now being borne mainly by private commercial banks.

If the financing of deficits becomes difficult at normal levels of economic activity, the response of oil-importing countries will be either to restrict imports of other commodities or to reduce economic activity in order to reduce balance-of-payments deficits. Either of these moves, if carried far enough, could have a cumulative effect on the world economy, leading to large reductions in economic activity and possibly to financial collapse. Restrictions by the advanced industrial countries of manufactured imports from semi-industrial developing countries would force these countries, in turn, to restrict imports and could even force them to default on their loans from the private international capital markets. That would lead to a reduction in loans that would force further reductions in economic activity.

Threats of protection and trade restrictions have reappeared in recent years in the advanced industrial countries, even as the multilateral trade negotiations (MTN) have been brought to a successful conclusion. The MTN could lead to a major liberalization of international trade, particularly through the reduction of nontariff barriers to trade (for example, quotas). At the same time other protection measures have been put in place including:

- New quotas on imports of textile products into the European Economic Community.
- U.S. restrictions on imports of consumer electronics from Korea and Taiwan.
- Restrictions on imports of steel into Europe and the United States.
- Subsidies to declining industries that have the effect of reducing imports.[2]

Clearly, as the decade of the 1980s begins, the interdependent world economy is increasingly delicately balanced. International trade, capital flows, and energy are strands in an economic web that link nations together. A break in one strand jeopardizes others, so there is little margin for error in setting economic policy. The nations of the world thus face the challenge of setting policies that will permit continued growth and development in a context of severe constraints and with the prospect of dire consequences in the event of failure.

Summary

This chapter has reviewed the series of extraordinary events that characterized the world economy of the 1970s. Rapid growth of demand, together with formation of the oil-exporting cartel (OPEC) led to rapid upward movement in petroleum prices, a movement that showed no signs of abating as the decade closed. These price increases had subsidiary impacts. First,

[2]World Bank, *World Development Report, 1979* (Washington, D.C.: The World Bank, 1979), pp. 21–22.

and probably most importantly, oil-importing countries began to run substantial deficits in their balance-of-payments and, conversely, exporting countries accumulated surpluses. The problem was especially severe for less-developed importing nations. These payments imbalances, in turn, placed great strain upon the international monetary system, because some means had to be found to move funds from surplus countries to deficit countries. In this enormous task, the world's commercial banks played the major role.

Another impact of oil price increases and efforts to finance balance-of-payments deficits has been global price inflation in all products. Inflation has added to the uncertainty of business operations, especially for multinational corporations. Combined with this uncertainty, U.S. multinationals have been confronted with increasing competition, not only from other major industrial countries but also from companies in newly emerging but less-developed nations.

With the effects of such events still incomplete, the next decade clearly promises to be a difficult one for business managers and governmental policy makers. The challenge is to foster continued economic and social growth in the face of increasingly fragile world trade and financial relationships.

SELECTED READINGS

Adelman, Morris, *The World Petroleum Market* (Baltimore: Johns Hopkins University Press, 1972).

Bergsman, Joel, "Growth and Equity in Semi-Industrial Countries," World Bank Staff Working Paper #351 (Washington, D.C.: World Bank, 1979).

Cordon, W.M., *Inflation, Exchange Rates and the World Economy* (Chicago: University of Chicago Press, 1977).

Houthakker, Hendrick, *The World Price of Oil* (Washington, D.C.: American Enterprise Institute for Public Policy Research, 1976), p. 37.

Knickerbocker, Frederick T., "Market Structure and Market Power Consequences of Foreign Direct Investment by Multinational Corporations" (Washington, D.C.: Center for Multinational Studies, 1976), Occasional Paper No. 8.

Morgan Guaranty Trust Company, "The Response to Higher Oil Prices: Adjustment and Financing," *World Financial Markets,* March 1980, pp. 1–13.

de Vries, Rimmer, "The International Monetary Outlook for the 1980s: No Time for Complacency," *World Financial Markets,* December 1979, pp. 1–13.

World Bank, *World Debt Tables,* Volumes I and II (Washington, D.C.: World Bank, 1979).

World Bank, *World Development Report, 1979* (Washington, D.C.: World Bank, 1979), Chapters 3–7.

Two

DECISION-MAKING PROCESSES OF THE INTERNATIONAL FIRM

We now leave the broader questions related to the international economic environment and take up a set of topics dealing more specifically with corporate management. In fact, our focus is even more restricted now, since in Part II we will discuss mostly decision-making activities of firms with manufacturing operations abroad. Early chapters in this section will examine the various methods used by companies to engage in international activities and will review why many firms ultimately choose to make significant investments overseas. Other chapters will be devoted to investment decisions, sources of capital, selection of technology, the management of a multinational corporation's financial resources, selection of organizational form, and the staffing of the enterprise.

Part II, therefore, is intended to provide a more detailed perspective on the unique problems associated with managing large international companies.

CHAPTER 9

Assessing the International Market: Exporting, Licensing, and Service Agreements

INTRODUCTION

Internationalism on the part of private firms is explored in this chapter. Although most of the data utilized are for companies headquartered in the United States, the principles demonstrated apply equally well to most other countries. While this chapter will deal with approaches not usually involving direct foreign investment, the following one, Chapter 10, will concentrate on forms of direct foreign investment.

Firms have several vehicles by which they can engage in international commerce. They can export or import goods. They can buy or sell know-how through licensing and franchising agreements. They can invest in countries around the globe, away from their home country, and they can finance transactions arising from trade in goods and services and in international investment. Within a single host country, a multinational firm may have the following:

1. Export arrangements between the subsidiary in the host country and the parent firm in the home country.
2. A franchise arrangement with a distributor.
3. A licensing arrangement and technical aid contract with a supplier.
4. Facilities for the importation of parts and supplies.
5. Wholly-owned assembly facilities.
6. A joint venture and a management contract with a local firm or another multinational firm.

A host of private institutions, and connections between them, tie most of the world's economy into a closely knit complex. Decisions of great significance to peoples widely separated by space are made everyday by large corporations, whether they be manufacturers, importers, bankers, or producers of raw materials. A North Sea oil find by Exxon is important to European consumers, British citizens, and American stockholders. Chrysler Corporation's decision to enter a joint venture in Japan to produce Dodge automobiles has affected U.S. and Japanese auto workers, U.S. and Japanese consumers, and stockholders in both countries. An interminable list of such decisions and developments could be made; however, few people would be interested. Decisions such as these have become commonplace and hardly of headline significance.

MOTIVATIONS FOR ENTERING INTERNATIONAL BUSINESS

Two major questions will be examined here: (1) why do firms engage in international business? and (2) which arrangements do they choose and why? With the existing state of economic theory and available empirical data, these questions cannot be addressed with great precision; yet the theory does provide insights and aids in outlining general tendencies.

There are numerous reasons why firms may wish to engage in international operations, but they all have to do with meeting someone's demands for goods and services. The firm itself may be highly instrumental in creating that demand, as has been true of the Coca Cola Company. That a Peruvian Indian and a Japanese banker have heard of and ingested a bottle of "Coke" is no mere accident. Markets do not arise full blown; they must be built. This maxim applies whether we refer to soft drinks or television sets. What is important is that few products are designed exclusively to serve international markets. A common sequence in the development of production and marketing is shown on the following page.

This pattern is not always followed precisely, but is descriptive of a wide variety of international business developments. Whether the final stages of producing in low-cost countries for export to high-cost countries are completed depends on the nature of the product, its methods of production, the costs of transport, and tariff and/or other barriers that may be levied against it. There are many variations on the theme. If the local market is very small and scale economies great, local production in a foreign country may never emerge; or, even though a country has a large market and inexpensive common labor, a commodity may not be produced there because complementary technical skills and know-how are lacking. Of course, there also are some commodities that require highly specific resources. Bananas grow well only in the tropics, and one needs a plentiful supply of sturgeon to produce caviar.

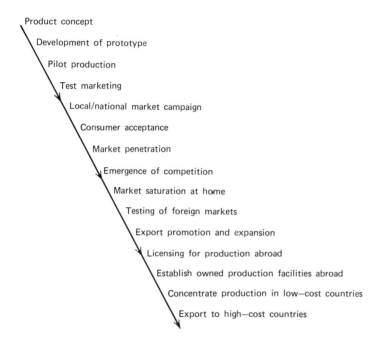

Product concept

Development of prototype

Pilot production

Test marketing

Local/national market campaign

Consumer acceptance

Market penetration

Emergence of competition

Market saturation at home

Testing of foreign markets

Export promotion and expansion

Licensing for production abroad

Establish owned production facilities abroad

Concentrate production in low—cost countries

Export to high—cost countries

Firms engage in international business based on their profit motivations; yet, seemingly similarly endowed firms in the same industry do not always approach international business in the same way. Why do they choose different forms to serve foreign markets? Is one firm rational and the other irrational? Possibly, but probably not. Much depends on timing and the perceived stage of development of the market being served. It also has to do with the global strategies of multinational firms in competition with one another. Each multinational firm has certain comparative advantages in technology, relations with host-country governments, distribution channels, and location of production facilities throughout the world. Each must study the trade-offs of serving different markets in different ways, arriving at a configuration of production, research, and marketing facilities that as closely as possible optimizes the firm's strengths in relation to the competition. This is why we find different companies approaching the same markets in somewhat different ways.

Each firm exploits its advantages in the drive for survival and profits, a drive that often pushes it into the international arena. Firms may become international either to develop new markets or to acquire new resources, and in so doing they either fatten profit margins on existing products or reduce costs of production. Sometimes they do both.

In the case of manufacturing firms, most products historically were made first at home and eventually exported; however, with the passage of time, manufacturing firms have shifted gradually to simultaneous worldwide production and distribution of nearly identical or similar models of their products in many countries. On the other hand, firms concerned mainly with the extraction, processing, or selling of raw materials most frequently entered foreign countries to obtain the resources needed to serve growing markets in their home countries. With growth in other markets, however, the installation of processing capacities on foreign soil has become attractive; thus, we see many installations around the globe, widely separated by space but owned or controlled by a single firm.

To summarize, firms can export and/or import; can license others to produce their product or use property rights such as trademarks, patents, and copyrights; can invest in their own facilities to produce abroad; and can sell technical and managerial know-how on contract. All of these methods involve problems that are peculiarly different in an international, rather than a national, context.

ASSESSING THE INTERNATIONAL MARKET

The search for markets can be viewed as the major reason that multinational firms came into being. If there were not multiple national markets, there would be no need for these large, diversified, yet in many respects highly specialized enterprises. In general, it is their breadth of knowledge of so many markets and market opportunities that allows them to be so successful. A major problem that confronts any firm in assessing markets is the degree to which it must tailor its products and marketing methods to individual national or subnational markets. Ideally, the firm would prefer to approach every market in the same way, using the same product and the same marketing methods. This would be a *standardized* approach, which takes advantage of economies of scale and, accordingly reduces the direct costs of getting the product produced and to the marketplace.

We can cast the problem of international marketing into a framework that has come to be known as the marketing mix. The marketing mix refers to the product and its design, pricing, promotion, and distribution channels. In addressing the question of standardization, one must ask the following: (1) to what extent can a particular product be sold in more than a single market? (2) to what extent can the product be priced identically in two or more markets? (3) to what extent can the same promotional methods that are used at home be used in markets abroad? and (4) to what extent are the distribution channels in other markets similar to those in the home country? If there were no differences between countries, there would be no need to consider the issue of the extent to which one can use a standardized approach. The trick for international marketing is simply to identify those instances when foreign markets will not accept a standardized marketing mix. To serve some markets, it is necessary to develop a specialized product and specialized marketing techniques to sell that product.

There are many combinations of methods of getting a product to the marketplace; where firms have an entire product line made up of several products, there may be a different approach for each product in that line. For example, some automobile manufacturers produce automobiles in Brazil using an American design, a European design, and a local design. All three automobiles end up in the product line to serve the needs of that market. In a few instances in Brazil, to fill out the product line, some products also may be imported. The decision as to how to structure the product line and which aspects to standardize is a complex question for large, diversified companies that have many products in their product line.

THE DIFFERENCES BETWEEN INTERNATIONAL AND DOMESTIC MARKETING

International marketing is different from domestic marketing because countries differ from one another. They differ in culture and the values that are held by their populace. Even within a single country, value systems may differ from region to region. Not everywhere is the attitude toward business and marketing the same. In some countries, business, particularly private business and private ownership, is looked upon with some distrust. Also, the attitude toward certain types of products differs across countries. Religion may play a part and language can be a barrier. For example, it may not be feasible or even advisable to translate promotional materials from, let us say, English into French. Some phrases that might be perfectly suitable in the United States in promotional materials would be considered offensive, inane, stupid, or perhaps totally misleading when translated into French for use in the French market.

Other variables that impinge upon the selection of marketing mix include such things as the socioeconomic situation in the country, the age distribution, income level, income distribution, level of literacy, and the population's life expectancy. The degree of urbanization and the density of population may tell us a great deal about the extent to which there will be certain types of marketing institutions available for product distribution. Also, the availability of transportation and of communication media such as telephones, television, mail, radio, newspapers, and magazines, can affect the way in which we distribute the product and bring to the attention of consumers the fact that the product is available in various types of distribution outlets. Pricing will depend a great deal on income level, degree and level of industrialization, availability of credit for both consumer and wholesaler and retailer levels of trade, and the type and scope of competition that one confronts, either from domestic producers or other producers from abroad. The industrial structure existing in the country also will have some bearing on the types of products one can sell in a particular country. For example, if the level of industrialization is quite low, with very little in the way of a metal machining industry, then we could surmise that the market for machine tools and machining equipment would be relatively small. Finally, in international marketing, the seller will be exposed to risks of loss in foreign exchange.

In addition to having to look at these variables in terms of standardizing the product mix, exporters and multinational firms must examine the different strategies they may follow in serving a foreign market. Usually, foreign marketing begins by exporting from the home country, but once export markets achieve a certain level, the enterprise chooses to produce abroad to serve those markets. Once a company makes this decision, it becomes a multinational firm. In other words, it is producing in two different countries to serve at least two different markets. Even a purely exporting company, however, can take on many of the characteristics of a multinational firm. It need not produce at home always to serve foreign markets. It can purchase the output of producers in third countries to serve either the home market or the market of another country. In some respects, large trading companies, especially such as those in Japan, take on many of the characteristics of the large multinational firms we have become familiar with in the United States and parts of Europe. Most multinational firms use some combination of exporting, production in the host country, and purchases from other enterprises to serve their markets. They also may engage in what are called intracorporate transfers. They may serve a market by exporting from the home country to a subsidiary in the host country, by exporting from another subsidiary in still another country to that same subsidiary, or the subsidiary itself may produce a part or all of the product line. In addition, the subsidiary may import still other products from independent producers located in another country or purchase some of its total output from local producers that may be either domestically or foreign owned. These comments merely demonstrate the complexity of the logistical problems confronting multinational enterprises.

It also should be recognized that the multinational firm must be concerned about its total worldwide marketing effort. In the interests of efficiency and economy, the multinational firm is likely to attempt to standardize as many aspects of the total marketing mix as it can, across as many countries as possible. The trick is to be able to identify those instances where it would not be suitable to use a standardized marketing approach.

THE ADVANTAGES OF STANDARDIZING THE MARKETING MIX

There are several advantages to standardizing the marketing mix across countries. The first is the achievement of economies of scale in production, the use of promotional materials, the distribution system itself, and the development of an identity for the product or products sold. The achievement of economies of scale in these aspects of marketing brings about lower costs and hence the ability to make possible a lower product price than otherwise would be the case.

Standardization of the product itself across all or several national markets has been quite a useful strategy for the Japanese automobile makers and producers of electronic equipment. The Japanese, for example, have not attempted to produce a full line of automobiles. All of the Japanese automobile companies produce relatively small, fuel-efficient automobiles. These are suitable not only for the Japanese and European markets, but they also have made substantial inroads into the U.S. market. By standardizing and centralizing their production in Japan, the Japanese automobile makers have been able to take advantage of economies of scale in production. A relatively standardized marketing approach, worldwide, has allowed the Japanese companies to produce a narrow product line that is sold in all markets. The American automobile manufacturers, on the other hand, have attempted to produce a full line of automobile products, but with emphasis in the United States on larger cars rather than the small, fuel-efficient cars they produce in Europe and elsewhere. Also, U.S.-based automobile manufacturers, in contrast to the Japanese, have tended to provide more specialized treatment of their product line for individual country markets. It seems somewhat ironic that the U.S.-based companies, historically the leaders in standardizing the marketing mix within the industry, are now in a position of being unable to approach the international market with a standardized product line in the same way that Japanese and European-based automobile firms can. Japanese and European companies do not produce specialty products for individual markets; rather they market basically the same product internationally that they market at home. The U.S.-based companies, on the other hand, do not market in the international arena very many units of the products they produce for the U.S. market. Most of the products that are marketed in other countries tend to be either identical to or offshoots of products originally produced for the European market.

There are other advantages to standardizing the marketing mix, beyond those of economies of scale as previously described. Costs of production also can be reduced by standardizing such things as maintenance manuals, promotion materials, warranties, spare parts, service manuals, and even such things as sales training manuals. It also can be risky, however, to attempt to standardize all of these aspects of the marketing mix. Promotional materials suitable for the U.S. market may not be suitable in another culture, even when there is no need to translate them into another language.

Sales training is simplified by having a common product and common promotional materials. A standardized product line is in many respects much easier to sell. Indeed, as we can note in the U.S., such items as radios, television sets, refrigerators, freezers, and washing equipment are sold in discount stores with very little sales assistance to the customer. In fact, these products even are sold via mail order by such companies as Sears, Montgomery Ward, and J.C. Penny. By standardizing the product line and having warranties, the product in many respects sells itself. A highly skilled sales force is not necessary in the U.S., however, consumers in many other countries are not yet as sophisticated as the American consumer. There may be regional tastes and national requirements of one sort or another, including legal requirements, that make it impossible for international marketers to market a standardized product line in a standardized way. Finally, standardization allows for improved market planning, including worldwide product introductions, designs, common color schemes and decorative items, and common promotional and training materials.

Customs may be sufficiently different that promotional and other materials require reworking. For example, a promotional campaign used in the United States may be unsuitable for use in Great Britain. Fortunately, advertising agencies and market-research organizations also have become multinational; thus, tailor-made services can be found in most countries.

In some instances, it is almost necessary to introduce certain new products on a worldwide basis. In the toy industry, a great deal of effort may go into designing a new line of toys. Once the toys are designed, however, it is easy in many instances for foreign manufacturers to copy them thus, it ordinarily does not pay the designing company to obtain patents. Even if a particular toy or toys were patentable in the United States, some countries might not observe the patents and would allow local manufacturers to produce and sell copies of the toy in the home market and perhaps international trade as well. Thus, it pays for the multinational toy company to introduce its new products in all markets simultaneously.

Pirating of designs and selling of copies, including logos similar to those on the original, has become a large-scale business worldwide. For example, the famous Levi blue jean is being copied, as are Mattel toys and even UCLA tee-shirts and totebags. It is not unusual to see sweatshirts or tee-shirts with the illegally reproduced logo of an American university being displayed and worn in Europe, Latin America, or Asia. These universities generally receive no royalties for the use of their logo; indeed, the logo ordinarily is used without permission. The same happens, in a few countries, with commercially recognized logos, trademarks, copyrights, and patents.

One variable we have not discussed as part of the marketing mix is price, yet it is very important as a competitive device. A serious question for international marketers is whether or not they should try to standardize prices for each of their products in all markets where they are sold. Certainly, there are limitations on the extent to which price differentiation can be used across markets. If one attempts to offer the same product in two different countries' markets at substantially different prices, an enterprising individual or group may begin to buy that product in the low-priced market and ship it to the high-priced market. Usually, if there are wide variances in the price of a product across countries, it is because of legal differences among those countries. For example, one finds automobiles and consumer appliances in one country priced at two or three times the price one would find in the United States. The question is: Why? The reason usually is that the high-priced country has imposed protective tariffs on these items to induce their production at home rather than abroad. Disregarding differences brought about by such interventions, we should see prices being related to the cost of serving the market. In other words, small, difficult-to-reach markets should have prices that are higher than those for the same product or products in large, efficient, easy-to-reach markets. Generally, this is what we do see. Prices in developing countries are often considerably higher than prices for the same product in advanced countries, even when these products are imported ratber than produced in the host country. If differences become larger than those brought about by cost alone, then there is roon for product arbitrage whereby merchants can buy in the low-priced market and sell in the high-priced market.

PROBLEMS WITH STANDARDIZATION

While standardizing the product mix has advantages, there are also some disadvantages. Arguments against standardization, in many instances, may be so overwhelming that specialized approaches will be adopted for individual country markets. Indeed, it may not be possible to view the international market as a single large market. It may be impossible to reach some national markets with a standardized approach. Available distribution channels may not allow for standardization, or the same types of media as those used in the home country may not be available. For example, television is not so widely owned and used in developing countries as in advanced ones; thus, if most of a firm's promotional effort and advertising are directed to the consumer via television rather than other media it will not be possible to use the same techniques as those used in the United

States, Canada, Australia, and Europe. In any case, promotional methods usually are sensitive and are one of the least standardized of all aspects of the marketing mix. Even if one used the same promotional messages— photographic layouts and the like—it often is necessary to translate these into another language. Product standardization may even be out of the question. For example, Americans are quite accustomed to having large refrigerator–freezer combinations. Such large units are not suitable for many markets outside of the United States. The limitation is simply that most countries have not achieved the same level of home ownership that is true of the United States. Stated differently, most people the world around are apartment dwellers rather than homeowners. Apartments generally have not been built along the scale that is required by an American type of product. Kitchens are much smaller and are not built to accommodate large refrigerator–freezer units. This stems in part from marketing customs and distribution channels in these countries. The large supermarket with its enormous variety of frozen foods and packaged meats is not so common elsewhere as it is in the United States. The move to large, combination grocery stores is a recent phenomenon outside of the United States, "recent" meaning within the past 10 to 15 years. Thus, the marketing channels are not prepared to provide the wide variety of foodstuffs familiar to Americans. It is common, in Europe and elsewhere, to see householders conduct their food shopping on an almost daily basis; thus, there is less need for a freezer or large refrigerator to store a week's worth of food.

A good example of inappropriately attempting to use the standardized marketing mix in a foreign market is provided by the Polaroid Corporation's experience in the 1960s. Prior to the time it entered the French market with its line of cameras and film, it had marketed cameras in the United States, using heavy doses of television advertising. In television commercials, Polaroid could demonstrate the use of instant photography and the Polaroid camera as it would be used by the customer. There was very little need on the part of salespersons in retail outlets to demonstrate the camera and to use specialized selling techniques. In France, however, television ownership was at a much lower level than in the United States moreover, commercial advertising is not allowed over the publically owned television networks in France. Thus, television in France proved not to be an ideal medium for the product's advertising and demonstration. It thus, was necessary for salespersons to understand the product and be able to demonstrate it effectively to potential customers. Unfortunately, Polaroid neither expended much effort on training retail salespersons about the product nor offered retailers many incentives to demonstrate the product. Indeed, there appeared to be some disincentive because the retailer had to buy the film used in the demonstrations. This was not conducive to stimulating the retailer to demonstrate the product. Polaroid should have designed a specialized marketing mix[1] with respect to price, promotion, and distribution channels for its line of cameras.

The stage of the product life cycle also may differ between countries, with some countries further along than others; therefore, it may not be possible to introduce a product simultaneously in every market. For example, it is particularly true in developing countries that the more adorned and accessory-laden versions of products often are not marketed. The number of consumers who are sufficiently affluent to purchase such items is just too small to make it worthwhile. To illustrate, in the sewing-machine industry most producers provide a low-priced machine to developing countries that they normally do not sell in advanced countries. Higher-priced machines which are electronically controlled and capable of producing a wide variety of stitches may not be sold at all in developing countries simply because the machines are too expensive. In such countries, for detailed and elegant sewing a skilled seamstress is employed, rather than a machine. The stage that the country exhibits in the product life cycle has a great deal to do with the level of per capita income, the degree of urbanization, and several other factors. Related to these variables also will be the degree to which the average customer would wish to have the more expensive versions in a product line.

Only through research and experience can an enterprise determine whether it should or should not standardize its marketing mix when entering a new market. It seems reasonably obvious that an enterprise normally cannot provide a specialized product and marketing approach for each and every national market. Some markets are simply too small to warrant such a strategy, and the costs would be much too high for the amount of sales volume that could be generated. It is a far cry from this situation to one in which the enterprise produces perhaps three or four different types of products performing the same function but sufficiently different from one another that they appeal to different types of markets. This strategy generally has been pursued by American automobile companies. They have produced a product that is aimed at the U. S. market but that, since World War II, has not sold well outside of the United States and Canada. In response to developments in the European automobile industry, American companies developed a different product version for the European market. For the most part, the American companies have used primarily the products produced in Europe, rather than in the United States, to serve

[1]Robert D. Buzzell, "Polaroid France (S.A.) Marketing, Planning in a Multinational Company," in Warren J. Keegan (ed.), *Multinational Management,* Englewood Cliffs, N.J.: Prentice Hall, 1974), pp. 439–468.

markets in developing countries. What is important is that enterprises cannot always use a standardized product, standardized promotional materials, and the same distribution channels everywhere, simply because (1) the product may not be suitable for servicing each and every market, (2) promotional materials and approaches may not be suitable because of the cultural content involved, and (3) the distribution channels across countries may differ.

There are dangers of attempting to carry the standardization process too far. For example, in the 1970s, several companies were selling baby formulae which they had developed to supplement or substitute for human breast milk. The product was first sold in the already advanced countries and served the purpose of providing a high-protein diet for nursing babies. The formula provides a complete diet for the child and can be mixed either with milk or water. It can be fed to the baby using a typical nursing bottle. Care must be taken, however, that the milk or water used to mix with the formula and make it a liquid is reasonably pure and uncontaminated. Also, the formula should either be mixed in very small batches or, if mixed in larger batches, it should be refrigerated adequately. In some developing African countries, many babies died because these conditions were not met. The users of the formula, namely the mothers of the babies, were inadequately trained to use the mix. They used contaminated water to mix the formula, they did not refrigerate it adequately, and they did not follow the directions for mixing the formula in terms of the amount per feeding. The consequence was that hundreds, if not thousands, of babies died, either of starvation or of infections in their digestive systems emanating from the buildup of microorganisms in the formula. All of this occurred despite the fact that the product was introduced through medical clinics where the mothers were given some training in the use of the product by qualified doctors and despite the fact that the manufacturers of the formula provided instructions on the package in the native language. It appears, in retrospect, that the companies did not pay enough attention to the marketing mix and the problems connected with an illiterate and ignorant group of consumers. Surely not all of the mothers who used the formula were in fact trained by the doctors. There must have been a great deal of word-of-mouth advertising on the part of the users. Thus, some, if not most, of the formula ended up in the hands of unqualified users. In this particular instance, the product was priced too high for the income groups it was aimed to serve. Native women did not have sufficient money to purchase enough of the formula to adequately feed the child. They ended up skimping on the amount per feeding and, in many instances, children died of malnutrition. This was the exact opposite result of that desired by the formula's producers; in fact, the formula was designed to improve the nutrition of children in poor and backward countries, rather than to cause debilitation and death. Perhaps with a better designed marketing approach the problem could have been averted. This further magnifies the importance of good market research in international business. Without adequate information, it is impossible to design an appropriate marketing mix for the international market where there are national markets involved that differ from one another. The following section will discuss how we can go about developing information to classify countries in which the same marketing mix might be appropriate.

RESEARCH METHODS FOR IDENTIFYING MARKETS HAVING SIMILAR CHARACTERISTICS

Some of the research in marketing in recent years has attempted to deal with the problem of identifying markets that have similar characteristics. The philosophy behind these efforts is that if countries have similar socioeconomic and other characteristics, we might then be able to group them together and use the same marketing approach in all of these national markets. Partially, it is a philosophy that suggests that the international market can be segmented into groupings of countries. Historically, the primary method of grouping countries is by geographic location. Large multinational firms or large trading companies would, and for the most part still do, organize themselves into an area structure for purposes of international sales. For example, there might be a sales division for Europe, with second, third, and fourth divisions for Latin America, Africa, and Asia and the Far East. Within these area groupings, each country would have a separate sales organization. This approach ignores all of the other characteristics of markets except geographic location. It does not take into account that a country in Latin America might have more in common with a country in Africa than it does with its immediate Latin American neighbors. The commonalities might be based upon the level of income, the degree of urbanization, the degree to which there is a native population as opposed to a population of immigrants, and so on.

If one had a method of grouping countries, other than simply by their geographic location, it then might be feasible for an enterprise to design some different approaches to marketing its product line internationally. The question becomes: How does one go about identifying groups that seem to cluster together even though they may not be geographically near to one another? One such method has been offered by Sethi & Holton.[2] The Sethi–Holton methodology involved the use of 29 political, socioeconomic,

[2]S. Prakash Sethi & Richard H. Holton, "Review of Birkel, Leander, et al., 'Comparative Analysis for International Marketing,' " *Journal of Marketing Research,* Vol. 6, November 1969, pp. 502–503. Also see S. Prakash Sethi, "Comparative Cluster Analysis in World Markets," *Journal of Marketing Research,* Vol. 8, August 1971, pp. 348–354.

trade, transportation, communications, biological, and personal consumption variables. Using a technique called factor analysis, they examined these 29 variables for 91 countries. This analysis yielded 7 country groupings, plus the United States as a single unique object (not similar to the countries in the other 7 groups).

While in some of the groups geography seemed to play a dominant role in establishing the cluster, it was generally true that there was a mix of countries from different geographic areas in some of the other groups. For example, in one group, tbe following countries were included: Argentina, Chile, Costa Rica, Greece, Israel, Italy, Jamaica, Panama, Spain, Uraguay, and Venezuela. The point is that as the world becomes a more complex place, it would be useful to have a method that would simplify the classification of countries for purposes of market development. Sethi & Holton's method helps in this respect. At the same time, perhaps there is a homogenizing influence loose in the world. With television, communication satellites, radio, and so forth, the familiarity of people, even in remote places of the world, with modern technology, products, and services has been enhanced greatly. The multinational firm, through its marketing efforts, has exposed populations around the globe to new products and new concepts. Because of this, perhaps, the job of designing the marketing mix has become simplified through time. It is also true that as countries become more sophisticated and more and more affluent they become more demanding of diversity. The consequence is a profliferation of products and services and of distribution channels. Because of this, the marketing-mix problem has been made more complex even though the world, in some respects, is becoming a more uniform place. It is nevertheless true that the tastes of average consumers have been broadened to include a much wider variety of consumption patterns than was common in earlier times.

CONSUMER PRODUCTS VERSUS INDUSTRIAL PRODUCTS IN STANDARDIZED MARKETING MIXES

Generally, it is easier to standardize the marketing mix for industrial goods than for consumer goods. Industrial goods almost invariably are purchased by people who have considerable expertise regarding the product's technical capabilities and specifications. Buying a fork-lift truck is much different from buying an automobile. The person who buys a fork-lift truck is much more likely to be highly knowledgeable about how that machine functions and how well it can perform the activity for which it is designed. By contrast, the typical consumer who purchases an automobile from a retail dealership may know how to drive and read the instruments but is unlikely to know what the technical specifications and tolerances are for the machine.

Usually, for highly technical products, the marketing mix will be standardized to a greater extent than for less technical or simpler products. This may seem anomalous, but in such highly technical products as a jet airplane, a large mainframe computer, sophisticated machine tools, and the like, special versions of those products usually are not made for different markets. An individual copy of each of these products might be tailored to some extent to a specific customer's needs, but there would be no general effort made on the part of the manufacturer to produce a specific version of that product for a particular national market. Any specialization or diversification of the product line is likely to be centered around the types of problems that customers encounter rather than around any type of national preference or language difference. Promotional and advertising materials, plus manuals for service, maintenance, training, and the like would be specialized for products such as this only insofar as there may be a need to produce them in the language of the country involved. It is more likely, however, that these materials will be reproduced only in three or four languages. Anything beyond this in terms of translating materials into still another language would probably be up to the customer rather than the seller. Products such as processed foods, clothing, furniture, books, and many household items involve personal taste to a large degree, and often these must receive a specialized marketing mix for specific national markets and even subnational ones. However, these tend to be products where economies of scale are less important. The point is that without specialization these products would not be successful in certain national markets unless given specialized treatment.

EXPORTING AND IMPORTING AS FORMS OF INTERNATIONAL BUSINESS

World trade currently approximates $1,500 billion per year and is growing at nominal rates of between 10 percent and 15 percent per year; thus, exporting and importing are important and growing forms of business activity. Some countries are highly dependent on trade, with as much as 50 percent of their national product going to export markets. The Netherlands, Ireland, Belgium, Malaysia, Kuwait, Norway, and several others fall into this category. At the other extreme is the United States, with only about 8 percent of its national product going to foreign markets. Yet the United States, because of its large economy, is also the world's largest trader. Although calculations are very crude, world trade can be thought of as constituting about 10 percent of world product—not an inconsiderable sum—and well worth examining.

Methods of Exporting

For every exporter there is an importer, and these two roles may be combined into a single organization. Some multinational corporations act as their own agents, with one subsidiary exporting to another. Creole Petroleum in Venezuela exports crude oil in parent-owned tankers to parent-owned refineries in the United States. In so doing, Exxon, the parent, acts as its own forwarding, transferring, and receiving agent. There are many similar arrangements among multinational firms, whether they produce automobiles, farm machinery, computers, or pharmaceuticals. Where these arrangements exist, they usually are a part of worldwide operations that also involve ownership of assets located in two or more countries. Rather than deal with this complicated milieu, we shall stick to simpler forms. The principles apply universally whether the transaction involved is consummated through independent exporting and importing agencies or through agencies that are captives of multinational organizations.

For the smaller firm, exporting is the simplest and least risky method of entering the international arena. How does exporting take place? Actually, there is little mechanical difference between an export sale and a domestic one, with the exception of dealing in a foreign currency. The export agency may be a broker operating on commission, a wholesale distributor, or an export management company. The product may be sold on contract at a specified price, or it may be sold on consignment, that is, shipped abroad to an importer to be sold for what it can fetch in the foreign market with payment made when the product sells.[3] The export agency handling the sale may be either an independent entity or an operating arm of the firm itself. Many large firms have an international division that is responsible for handling export sales; however, most firms use the services of independent agencies that specialize in export and import sales. Even those firms that have their own export division often use independent houses to reach small or highly specialized markets. There are several types of relationships export agencies can have with their clients. They may or may not be assigned responsibility for the goods being sold. Instances where they are not include the roles of purchasing agent, export merchant, and export broker. When playing the role of purchasing agent, the export

[3]For a discussion of various organizational forms taken in export trading, see James Green, *Organization for Exporting,* Studies in Business Policy, No. 126, National Industrial Conference Board, New York, 1968.

agency buys for the account of an overseas customer, is paid by that customer, and hence does not represent the exporter. An export merchant buys on his own account and operates on a markup. Sales through purchasing agents and export merchants are identical to domestic sales, since the exporter is not involved in transacting business in a foreign currency. Export brokers operate on commission and represent the exporter. They do not assume exchange risks, do not take possession of goods, and usually are involved in sales of commodities rather than manufactured goods.

A second set of client relationships does involve assignment of responsibility to the export agency: in such a case, the export agency is responsible to the manufacturer for the development of markets and customer relations. This does not mean that they take possession of the goods or bear the risk of changing currency values, however. Included here are the combination export manager, export distributor, export commission representative, cooperative exporter, and foreign freight forwarder (See Table 9–1). Of these, only the export distributor assumes financial risk, by taking possession of the goods and dealing in two currencies. The combination export manager, a combination of export commission representative and export distributor, also assumes risk insofar as he fills the distributor's role. Usually, export distributors and commission representatives handle several accounts and fill multiple roles; thus, most houses can be considered to be

Table 9–1

Type of Agency	Who Does Agency Represent?	Who Bears Foreign Exchange Risks?	Is Agency (first col.), Responsible for Promotion of Product and Market Development?
Purchasing agent	Foreign importer	Foreign importer	No
Export broker	Exporter	Exporter	No
Export merchant	Self	Export merchant	No
Combination export manager	Exporter	Agency, if fills export-distributor role	Yes, if filling export-distributor role
Export distributor	Exporter and self	Export distributor	Yes
Export commission representative	Exporter	Exporter	Yes
Cooperative exporter	Self and other non-competing exporters	Exporter	Yes
Foreign freight forwarder	Shipping firms	Exporter or importer	No

combination export managers who operate in their own names as well as those of several manufacturers.

A cooperative exporter is a captive organization of a single manufacturing firm; however, it will take on the accounts of other manufacturers whose goods do not compete with those of the owner–manufacturer. For example, a manufacturer of drapery materials that has its own export division would be willing to act as export manager for complementary products such as curtain and drapery rods and drapery hooks sold under the brand name of other manufacturers.

The foreign freight forwarder is licensed by the Federal Maritime Commission. He is an expediter who specializes in traffic operations, customs regulations, and shipping rates and schedules. He handles goods from port of exit to port of entry and for this service receives a brokerage fee from the shipping lines or transportation firms whose space he books.

With the exception of export distributors and merchants, export agencies do not take possession of the goods involved. Their main function is to bring buyer and seller together, to arrange for transportation and insurance, and to assist with the clearance of customs and other regulations. This they do for a fee or commission.

The economies of choosing an export agency are governed by the size, nature, and number of sales involved, plus nature of markets being served. If the export business is large and continuous, the firm probably will choose to establish its own export division. When one uses a broker or export manager, he is buying expertise and information. If sales are large and frequent to a set of well-known customers, there is no need to continuously purchase information because the information becomes ingrained in the organization; thus, the large firm most likely can reduce its sales costs by establishing its own export organization. Often this is done by firms that have overseas distributors and well-known contacts. Under these circumstances they can act as their own intermediaries.

For small firms or for specialized sales by large firms, an independent intermediary is highly useful. Small firms seldom can afford to develop an overseas sales network. For this reason, they usually select an export distributor who operates like a large wholesaler. Essentially, the export distributor provides a sales network for the small firm and also carries the burden of foreign exchange risk. One of the disadvantages of using an export distributor is the lack of control the client firm has over markups, credit, discount policies, and development of customer relations. All of these functions are performed by the export distributor. For this reason, some small and medium-sized firms choose to use an export commission representative. This form allows the client firm to exert greater control over pricing, credit, and customer relations. There also is greater opportunity to know one's customers; their identity is not concealed, as it is when using export distributors. Export commission representatives use the same overseas outlets that a firm would use if it were exporting directly. Generally, this knowledge can be accumulated by the firm itself, and if and when sales achieve sufficient volume, the firm can establish its own export organization. This is not accomplished so readily when the export distributor is involved. The major disadvantage of the commission representative as compared with the export distributor is that the exporter must bear all of the risks, including that of dealing in foreign exchange.

Export agencies, regardless of their form, usually ask for exclusive rights to sell the product in certain markets. For small firms this might entail exclusive rights on a worldwide basis for the entire product line. For larger firms, exclusive rights may be given for only certain products and certain regional, national, or subnational market territories. Once agreement is reached on the area and products where exclusive rights are to be given, a contract or franchise is signed. Initial contract duration is usually one or two, but sometimes three years. The contract then is renewed on a year-to-year basis, with either party having the right to cancel the contract on 60 or 90 days' notice.

Some Problems in Exporting

Once the exporter has gotten over the hurdle of choosing an export agency, he confronts numerous other problems connected with export sales. Many exporters deal in standardized, graded commodities where little in the way of marketing expertise is involved, but what about the manufacturer who wishes to export cosmetics, apparel, processed foods, or some other good where demand is connected intimately to consumer tastes, attitudes, and customs? Exporting then becomes a much more complex story. As with the introduction of new products to any market, there may be 10 failures for every success. That one national market accepts and embraces a product does not mean that every national market will; thus, the first set of critical problems facing the international firm is that of market development and user acceptance.

The following example should be helpful in demonstrating this point. Initial attempts by Japanese automobile manufacturers to enter the U.S. market were rebuffed badly by American consumers. Indeed, Toyota was hardly noticed. Its entry and exit in the early 1960s hardly left a ripple. Toyota reworked its strategy. It upgraded its product, hired a witty and skillful American advertising firm, and established solid distribution networks. Its second entry into the U.S. market only could be called a resounding success. The Toyota was Americanized by product design, advertising, and marketing strategy. Today, Toyota is recognized as an economical, stylish, high-quality product. There are many other examples of the post-World War II Japanese export drive, which had much to overcome in terms of historical images and perceptions of Japanese goods.

The point to be made here is that exporting may entail little cost, as is true of standardized commodities, or it may entail great cost when much market development is required. Indeed, for some commodities (soaps, detergents, cosmetics, and soft drinks), investment in production facilities abroad entails little more cost and risk than does exporting, simply because the major investment is that of gaining consumer acceptance and marketing channels.

A second set of problems has to do with the policies adopted by governments regarding the products exported by other countries. There is a host of tariff, quota, administrative, and regulatory hurdles and barriers established by national governments with respect to foreign goods. Almost every country espouses the virtues of free trade, yet they simultaneously introduce measures designed to restrict trade. Various and sundry reasons are offered, but restrictions are almost without exception an outgrowth of competitive forces and shifting comparative advantage. As technologies and factor endowments change, the relative costs of production among countries also change. At the margin, one country becomes more efficient and another less efficient in the production of some good. Under these circumstances, pressure for trade restrictions comes from local firms and labor groups in the less efficient country. Many instances exist, however, where trade restriction is a deliberate part of economic policy. The two arguments most commonly used are those of national defense and economic development. The former is encountered repeatedly and most frequently among already advanced countries, while the latter is widely used by developing countries.

Exporters and importers confront numerous restrictions other than those represented by tariffs. Quotas are more insidious than tariffs because they involve administrative control. Under quota arrangements, a country places a ceiling on the quantity to be imported, and all amounts up to that ceiling can be brought in at going market rates; thus, the price mechanism is subverted, and a substitute method of allocation must be used. The method used is administrative fiat: importers are allocated a share of the quota under license. This allows considerable room for corruption, since each quota "owner" receives an abnormal profit on his share. The potential for corruption in the form of payoffs and kickbacks to officials administering the program is always present; moreover, government red tape is compounded. Each importer must report amounts received and periodically must renew his license. There is always uncertainty as to how large the quota will be from year to year. In some countries, quotas also are attended by exchange control, with some goods being given preferential rates of exchange. Exporters to these countries (and their importing agents there) confront extremely complex legal controls that are subject to change on the whim of government administrators.

We also should be aware of straightforward administrative restrictions. Among these are the food and drug laws and regulations on weights, measures, and quality. In many instances, these regulations served, and still serve, the purpose of protecting consumers against impure and fraudulently packaged goods. Conditions have changed since these laws were first established, however. Now they often are used to keep out foreign goods that are directly competitive with those produced at home. When so used, they serve the interests of local producers rather than those of the consumer.

LICENSING, TECHNICAL-AID AGREEMENTS, AND MANAGEMENT CONTRACTS

In recent years, firms have become increasingly aware of their ability to sell intangible resources. Know-how has become an important element of international trade. Rather than export or invest to serve a market, firms now enter contractual arrangements to accomplish their ends. By so doing, they minimize risk and augment income. One vehicle, licensing, also provides a means for smaller firms to enter foreign markets without risking much in the way of tangible assets. The three methods used to sell know-how are licensing, technical-aid agreements, and management contracts.

Licensing

Firms hold proprietary rights to patents, trademarks, copyrights, production processes, and brand or company names and insignia. They can license others to use these rights. Licenses, in turn, may be exclusive or nonexclusive; that is, the licensee may or may not have the exclusive right to use specific property rights in a particular market or group of markets. Licenses must contain clauses indicating jurisdiction. Otherwise, licensees would be in a position to compete directly in any market against the licensor. The licensor usually would like to have some control over which markets are to be served by licensees. This holds true particularly for multinational firms that attempt to efficiently organize production and marketing internationally.

Licensing agreements come in many forms; however, they usually cover either a 5- or 10-year period at a specified percentage return on sales. This percentage averages between 3 percent and 8 percent of sales, depending on the extent and nature of the rights obtained under the license. Some countries limit the amounts that can be paid annually, either in terms of percentage of sales or lump-sum payments. Brazil, for example, does not allow foreign firms to establish licensing agreements with their own subsidiaries operating in Brazil.

Licensing provides a mechanism through which proprietary know-how can be sold without the seller's committing tangible assets to the enterprise. Payment for property rights, however, is often in the form of equity participation. Indeed, the value of know-how is used increasingly by firms to gain market entry and partial ownership in locally controlled firms. As such joint ventures prove their success, the supplier of know-how ultimately may purchase a controlling interest in the firm. This is a particularly attractive method of becoming multinational for smaller firms that are long on technological know-how but short on capital and management talent.

The major advantage of licensing is that it provides a low-cost, low-risk form of market entry. Indeed, there are instances where licensing may be the only method of entry available. For example, several countries tightly control foreign investment and also do not allow certain foreign goods to be imported; thus, both the export sales of goods and investment sometimes are foreclosed as entry routes to foreign markets. Licensing, and especially the licensing of technical know-how, however, often is welcomed. Under these circumstances the firm can exploit its know-how through licensing agreements, even if it cannot incorporate that know-how into products either by exporting or producing abroad.

There are disadvantages to licensing, and these often lead firms to seek financial control of licensees. The major disadvantage is that of having to police the license. Policing, or assuring that the terms of the agreement are being met, is a particularly difficult problem in markets that are small and are not well endowed with technical skills. It should be remembered that licensors risk their reputations. The licensee represents the licensor in the agreed territory and uses the product brand name and perhaps the company name and trademark. For this reason, most multinational firms are extremely conscious of the licensee's ability to respect the company's reputation for quality and dependability. Licensees sometimes are bought out because they are unable consistently to meet quality standards. The licensor often has a worldwide reputation to uphold and also may wish to enter the market later. An inept, poorly policed licensee can spoil the market for such future ventures; thus, licensing may lead firms into international investment much earlier than they had intended.

To summarize, licensing provides a toehold for firms not wishing to invest in a market immediately. It also can provide a lucrative outlet for the controlled sale of property rights. Firms that traditionally have exported and do not wish to invest abroad, but find themselves constrained by government policy, can protect their marketing investments through licensing arrangements. For the small firm it is a low-risk method of trading on one's technical know-how. Licensing also may lead to equity investments and is sometimes the precursor to international investment.

Technical-Aid Agreements and Management Contracts

Technical-aid and management contracts often accompany licensing agreements, or investment, or both; they also may precede or follow the same. They differ considerably from licensing, however, which is much more of a blanket agreement. Technical-aid and management contracts are written for specific services to be rendered by one firm for another. They are much more in the vein of consulting arrangements; indeed, they may be precisely that. Large engineering firms not only may design and construct a plant but, on a technical-aid agreement, may develop the staff and manage the plant through some specified shakedown period. When functioning efficiently, the plant then is turned over to its owners, completely intact. This is called a turnkey operation, one that is ready to go.

In most instances, technical-aid agreements and management contracts involve the use of expatriate personnel who are not citizens of the host country. Usually, but not always, they are citizens of the country where the parent firm is headquartered. The technical-aid agreement indicates the type of services to be received, level of personnel to be employed, and duration over which the services are to be made available. Payment is usually, although not always, on a per diem basis, plus traveling expenses. The aid required thus dictates the amount of payment. Such agreements also may call for expatriate personnel to be resident at the site; that is, quality-control personnel, production managers, foremen, and the like may be provided by the foreign-based firm, on a continuing basis, to the recipient firm, in its facilities.

In this respect, the management contract is similar: expatriate personnel are resident in the recipient firm's facilities. The management contract differs from a technical-aid agreement in that it provides the foreign-based firm with management control over the recipient. Of course, this is not to say that foreign-based firms do not wield some control over placement of technology in a technical-aid agreement. They do indeed. Technical-aid agreements sometimes accompany licensing arrangements. The licensor will grant a license to a local firm only on the proviso that the local firm take on an expatriate who controls the application of technology and assures that quality standards are being met. Technical-aid and management contracts contain a major educational input and often are terminated when the licensee is able to understand and utilize fully the technology, consistent with licensor standards.

Technical-aid agreements and management contracts have several advantages, not the least of which is that they may offer a substitute to the licensing agreement. Indeed, some countries either have disallowed payment of licensing fees or have placed ceiling rates on licensing fees between subsidiaries and their foreign parents. For example, licensing agreements between a foreign-owned parent and its subsidiaries are illegal in Brazil. There appear to be similar moves afoot among several developing countries. The Andean Pact group has disallowed payment of the royalties for intangible technology, presumably meaning the use of trademarks and the like. Where it can be shown that tangible services are rendered, as is the case with technical-aid and management contracts, payments can be made. Thus, in many instances, these contracts may provide for the control and transfer of technical and managerial know-how and can have much the same contractual force of the licensing agreement, with respect to the application of technology.

The data in Table 9–2 indicate the relative volume of licensing royalties and technical-aid and management fees repatriated to U.S.-based firms from several regions.

Summary

It is not feasible in a single chapter to examine every aspect of the marketing mix and how it might or might not be standardized for the national markets that comprise the international market. The approach for some products and for some national markets can be standardized and efficiencies achieved thereby. Some products are more amenable to a standardized approach than are others. Generally, highly technical industrial goods are more amenable to a standardized approach than are consumer goods, especially those consumer goods that involve personal taste and differentiation. Even for standardized products, however, the choice of promotional materials, distribution channels, product positioning in terms of price or quality in a product line, and similar other variables must be tailored for individual national markets. There are some techniques or methods that can be used to simplify the process of identifying national markets that might be clustered together for similar treatment. The efforts of multinational firms have done much to homogenize the world economy and make nations and their consumption habits and patterns increasingly alike along certain dimensions. At the same time, with growing affluence and improved rapid communication and transportation, populations around the world have begun to acquire tastes for a wider variety of goods and services. This

Table 9–2 Income to U.S. Enterprises from Fees and Royalties in 1977 and 1978 (millions U.S. $)

Countries	All Industries		Mining and Smelting		Petroleum		Manufacturing		Service Industries	
	1977	1978	1977	1978	1977	1978	1977	1978	1977	1978
All countries	3,793	4,806	69	66	420	482	2,346	2,814	958	1,443
Developed countries	3,045	3,854	29	34	180	235	2,185	2,610	650	875
Canada	672	727	16	22	36	38	488	538	133	128
Europe	1,860	2,431	—	—	121	174	1,336	1,628	403	628
Japan	302	453	—	—	D[a]	D[a]	246	319	D[a]	D[a]
Australia, N.Z., and South Africa	210	243	13	12	D[a]	D[a]	116	124	D[a]	D[a]
Developing countries	704	881	40	31	226	216	160	204	279	429
Latin America		361	22	27	89	37	123	132	104	164
Africa	82	73	D[a]	3	D[a]	38	7	7	20	25
Middle East	172	234	D[a]	D[a]	D[a]	91	6	11	108	D[a]
Asia and Pacific	112	213	3	1	37	51	24	55	46	106
Other	44	71	—	—	15	30	—	—	29	40

[a]D = Suppressed by the Department of Commerce to aviod disclosure of data of individual companies.
Source: U.S. Department of Commerce, Survey of Current Business, 59: 8, Part 1, August 1979, pp. 36 & 37.

suggests that even national markets are becoming increasingly segmented and, accordingly, perhaps will require more, rather than less, specialized treatment. The methods of exporting, licensing, and using technical-aid and management contracts have been described. Data on the volume and origin of royalties and fees paid to U.S. firms operating abroad have been provided.

Yet to be discussed is the very important subject of international direct investment. This will be examined in the next chapter.

SELECTED READINGS

Alexandrides, C. G., & George P. Moschis, *Export Marketing* (New York: Praeger, 1977).

Cateora, Philip, & John M. Hess, *International Marketing,* 3rd ed. (Homewood, Ill: Irwin, 1975).

Dymsza, Willaim A., *Multinational Business Strategy* (New York: McGraw-Hill, 1972.

Gabriel, Peter, *The International Transfer of Corporate Skills* (Boston, Mass: Division of Research, School of Business Administration, Harvard University, 1967).

Green, James, *Organizing for Exporting,* Business Policy Study No. 126, National Industrial Conference Board, New York, 1968.

Lovell, Enid B., *Appraising Foreign Licensing Performance,* Business Policy Study No. 128, National Industrial Conference Board, New York, 1969.

Robinson, Richard D., *International Business Management: A Guide to Decision Making* (Hinsdale, Ill.: Dryden Press, 1978), Chapter 1.

Terpstra, Vern, *International Marketing,* 2nd ed. (New York: Holt, Rinehart and Winston, 1978), Parts I and II.

Terpstra, Vern, *The Cultural Environment of International Business* (Cincinnati: Southwestern Publishing, 1978).

Wells, Louis T., (ed.), *The Product Life Cycle and International Trade* (Boston, Mass.: Division of Research, Graduate School of Business Administration, Harvard University, 1972).

Zenoff, David, *International Business Management* (New York: Macmillan, 1971), Chapter 4.

CHAPTER 10

Direct Investment and Joint Ventures

INTRODUCTION

Those business methods not ordinarily involving direct investment in foreign countries were discussed in Chapter 9. It is true that firms exporting goods can and do establish their own distribution facilities abroad, and it also is true that such facilities constitute direct foreign investment; however, these are not the types of investments with which we are most concerned. Instead, in this chapter we will focus on those direct investments involving manufacturing facilities, petroleum and mining extraction and processing, and other such operations that are more tightly integrated into the economies of the recipient, or host, countries. We first will examine the wholly-owned, or at least financially controlled, type of investment. After discussing this, we also will review the joint business ventures.

International direct investment is, for the most part, a post-World War II phenomenon.[1] While there was some foreign ownership of assets around the world prior to the war, much of it was associated with colonialism and most was concentrated in the primary producing industries of mining, petroleum, and plantation agriculture. Between investment in the primary

---

[1] Here we refer to investment as being direct investment where the investor has nominal financial control. The Office of Business Economics, U.S. Department of Commerce, defines this as having ownership of 25 percent of the equity for foreign-based firms operating in the United States and 10 percent of the equity for U.S. firms investing abroad.

industries (agriculture, mining and smelting, and petroleum) and manufacturing and service industries, approximately 29 percent of U.S. industrial investments were in the manufacturing industries in 1943. By 1978, manufacturing represented 44 percent of the total (see Table 10–1). Investment as we know it is a modern-day phenomenon. Currently, U.S. firms hold operating control of almost $200 billion worth of assets located abroad, while foreign-based firms control more than $35 billion worth of assets in the United States.

Even though the United States is by far the largest investor abroad, it is not always a dominant factor among foreign investors in some countries. Canada, the United Kingdom, the Netherlands, Switzerland, France, Germany, and, more recently, Japan, are also large direct investors abroad. Although much of the French, Dutch, and British investment still flows to former colonies, investment is becoming more diversified industrially and geographically.

There are three basic types of foreign investment: (1) horizontal expansion of production abroad of the same or similar products produced at home, (2) vertical integration or production abroad of raw materials or intermediate goods to be processed into final products in the home country, and (3) conglomerate expansion or the production abroad of final products not similar to those produced at home. The first and second are by far

Table 10–1   Industry Composition of U.S. Direct Investments (millions U.S. $)

Year	All Industries $	%	Mining, Petroleum and Agriculture $	%	Manufacturing $	%	Service Industries $	%
1929	7,528	100	3,182	42.3	1,813	24.0	2,533	33.7
1936	6,691	100	2,588	38.7	1,710	25.6	2,393	35.7
1943	7,862	100	2,869	36.5	2,276	28.9	2,718	34.6
1950	11,788	100	5,108	43.3	3,831	32.5	2,849	24.2
1957	25,262	100	12,096	47.9	8,009	31.7	5,157	20.4
1959	29,735	100	13,943	46.9	9,692	32.6	6,100	20.5
1965	49,328	100	19,083	38.7	19,339	39.2	10,905	22.1
1969	70,763	100	25,620	36.2	29,450	41.6	15,692	22.2
1972	94,031	100	33,530	35.7	39,478	42.0	21,024	22.3
1977	149,848	100	38,493	25.7	66,033	44.1	45,323	30.2
1978	168,081	100	40,322	24.0	74,204	44.1	53,553	31.9

Percent Annual Growth

Year	All Industries	Mining, Petroleum, and Agriculture	Manufacturing	Service Industries
1929–1978	6.5	5.3	7.9	6.4
1928–1959	4.7	5.0	5.7	3.0
1959–1978	9.5	5.7	11.3	12.1
1969–1978	10.1	5.2	10.8	14.6

Source: U.S. Department of Commerce, *U.S. Business Investments in Foreign Countries* (Supplement to the Survey of Current Business, 1960), and various issues of *Survey of Current Business*.

predominant. In vertical integration, backward integration into the production of raw materials and intermediate goods represents much more in the way of total investment than does forward integration into wholesaling and retailing. In the early days of direct foreign investment, horizontal expansion was more typical of manufacturing firms and vertical integration was more typical of primary industries. Although this still tends to be true, elements of both are apparent in the investment patterns of large manufacturing firms and those in the extractive industries. Manufacturers increasingly are becoming vertically integrated, and their operating subsidiaries are becoming more highly specialized. Also, petroleum companies are expanding horizontally, with refineries and marketing outlets becoming more geographically dispersed. There is interpenetration of one another's markets all along the line by international firms. Conglomerate expansion or product diversification across national boundaries, however, are of little significance in the total value of direct investments.

VOLUME AND LOCATION OF U.S. DIRECT INVESTMENTS

As can be seen from Table 10–1 on the industry composition of U.S. investments, the decade of the 1950s (1950 to 1957) was very much one of investment in primary industries (largely petroleum production and refining). By the 1960s the rapid buildup of primary production had largely run its course and the emphasis had switched mainly to manufacturing and, to some degree in the 1970s, to tertiary industries.

Despite the efforts of developing countries to attract foreign investments, especially in manufacturing, their share in total investment has been shrinking continuously since 1957. Even in petroleum and mining, usually thought to be the forte of several developing countries, most recent investment has flowed to advanced, rather than developing, countries. This, in part, reflects the build-up of downstream stages of production and marketing, but it also reflects continued exploration for oil. Many recent finds have been in advanced countries; moreover, much of the crude production capacity in developing countries has been nationalized since the early 1970s. This has reduced the share of petroleum in total value of direct investment.

The most disturbing fact about the data for earlier years, shown in Table 10–2, was that developing countries, despite major efforts, were unable to increase their share of foreign investment in the manufacturing sector. Their share by 1972, as a percentage of this, was smaller than it had been 15 years earlier in 1957. Less than 17 percent of total direct investment in manufacturing is located in developing countries; however, this trend is reversing itself as more developing countries become increasingly industrialized.

Table 10–2   Percentage Distribution of U.S. Direct Investments

Industry and Year	Advanced[a] Countries ($)	(%)	Developing[b] Countries ($)	(%)	Total (millions of dollars)
All industries[c]					
1957	13,906	57.41	10,315	42.59	24,221
1963	25,541	65.94	13,192	34.06	38,733
1969	47,701	70.45	20,001	29.55	67,702
1972	64,114	71.80	25,186	28.20	89,300
1978	120,741	74.80	40,466	25.10	161,207
Petroleum					
1957	3,568	42.46	4,837	57.54	8,405
1963	6,457	50.80	6,253	49.20	12,710
1969	10,447	57.32	7,830	42.68	18,277
1972	14,200	58.97	9,878	41.03	24,078
1978	26,415	85.37	4,525	14.63	30,940
Mining and smelting					
1957	1,070	44.29	1,346	55.71	2,416
1963	1,732	51.70	1,618	48.30	3,350
1969	3,315	58.82	2,321	41.18	5,635
1972	4,420	61.97	2,712	38.03	7,132
1978	4,670	66.52	2,349	33.48	7,020
Manufacturing					
1957	6,591	82.30	1,418	17.70	8,009
1963	12,385	83.17	2,505	16.83	14,890
1969	24,282	82.45	5,167	17.55	29,450
1972	32,825	83.15	6,652	16.85	39,477
1978	60,135	81.04	14,071	18.96	74,207
Other industries					
1957	2,556	47.42	2,835	52.58	5,392
1963	5,888	67.63	2,819	32.37	8.707
1969	9,657	61.54	6,035	38.46	15,692
1972	12,669	68.06	5,944	31.94	18,613
1978	29,522	60.20	19,520	39.80	49,041

[a] Canada, Europe, Japan, Australia, South Africa, and New Zealand.
[b] Latin America, Western Hemisphere dependencies, Asia, and Africa.
[c] Excludes international shipping and unallocated.
Source: Survey of Current Business, U.S. Department of Commerce, various issues.

MOTIVATIONS TO INVEST ABROAD: THE DIRECT FOREIGN INVESTMENT

There are three major hypotheses that attempt to explain why firms make direct investments abroad:

1. The first is the basic neoclassical profit-maximization thesis. An extension of this formulation brings in the concept of portfolio effects, including the trade-off between riskiness and rate of return.
2. The second suggests government intervention (protectionism) as the motivating influence for direct foreign investment.
3. The third grows out of the theory of industrial organization or oligopoly theory, which suggests that firms have different competitive strengths to exploit. This theory does not deny the notion of profit maximization or portfolio effects, but it is the only one that provides a rationale for seeking managerial (operating) control over foreign investments, which we see occurring in direct foreign investments.

All of these hypotheses have profit maximization as their central thesis, but it should be noted that there are other competing formulations that suggest growth or market share rather than profits as the primary objectives. In the preponderance of the literature, however, profit maximization is central and in virtually no instance is it left out entirely as being a very important motivating objective.[2]

The traditional neoclassical theory of international investment suggests that capital moves in response to a change in relative rates of return on securities in two or more countries. Thus, a profit-maximizing enterprise would invest in countries where rates of return are highest and would disinvest in countries where they are lowest. In the more recent version of the theory, firms also would be expected to diversify their investments among countries in such a way that the risk-discounted rate of return is greatest for the entire portfolio of investments.

Stated differently, the quality of returns also is important. One would prefer a steady stream of earnings rather than one that fluctuates violently from highly positive to very negative from year to year. Indeed, each of us would be willing to accept a lower average return if simultaneously we could avoid or reduce the year-to-year fluctuations. This is the risk–return trade-off.[3]

---

[2] For a survey of the literature through 1973, see Guy V. G. Stevens, "The Determinants of Investment," in John H. Dunning (ed.), *Economic Analysis and the Multinational Enterprise* (New York: Praeger, 1974), pp. 47–88.

[3] Here, risk is measured by the variability of the earnings stream over time.

The overall risk of a portfolio can be reduced by diversifying in such a way that the variability of the total stream of savings to the entire portfolio is reduced. By deciding to invest in a country whose stream of earnings demonstrates a low correlation with the earnings from an existing portfolio, the riskiness of the portfolio can be reduced.[4] Stated differently, a high rate of return tends to be more risky than a lower rate of return. If this were not the case, everybody would invest in high-rate-of-return securities, and this would continue until rates of return everywhere became equal. Persistent differences in average rates of return over time can be explained by the relative size of the variance of year-to-year rates around the mean.

A second theory of direct foreign investment argues that firms first export to develop foreign markets for their goods. Once these markets become important, countries often impose protective tariffs so as to elevate costs of serving the market with imported goods. Foreign firms no longer can serve the markets via exportation from their home country; hence, if they are to protect their market they may be forced to invest and establish operating plants within the host country. Neither this theory nor the neoclassical theories per se, however, offer a rationale for the desire to have operating control. For example, an exporter, squeezed out of the market by a protective tariff, could license or otherwise contract with a local firm to produce the product. This happens occasionally, but more often those exporters who invest in response to the tariff end up with financial control of the investment.

There seems to be only one theory of direct foreign investment that is consistent with the great desire for control. It is rooted in the theory of oligopolistic competition: firms that invest abroad have peculiar advantages and can earn monopolistic rents based on these advantages. The advantage may be a patent, a proprietary secret process, economies of scale either through vertical or horizontal integration, discovery of superior raw materials, or strong differentiation of products through advertising, styling, or performance. Other advantages include worldwide sourcing of capital and the ability to locate working capital strategically. Optimum exploitation of these advantages, from the firm's point of view, calls for control. If control were not the most profitable route, then we should observe much more in the way of licensing others to exploit these advantages and/or much more in the way of straightforward portfolio investments not involving control.

---

[4]See Hiam Levy and Marshall Sarnat, "International Diversification of Investment Portfolios," *American Economic Review,* 60:4, 1970, pp. 668–675, Table 1.

This is not to deny that substantial amounts of foreign investment actually take place in nondirect form, that is, purely a matter of an investor becoming a minority stockholder with no managerial position; but most of such investment is made by individuals, pension funds, mutual funds, and occasionally a business firm seeking to find a return on idle funds. Moreover, most so-called portfolio investments (as distinct from direct investments) are in the form of commercial deposits, short-term bonds, and long-term bonds, rather than in the common-stock shares of foreign firms. To illustrate this point, at the end of 1978, private holdings of foreign assets by U.S. citizens and corporate entities amounted to $377 billion. Only $11 billion, however, was invested in corporate stocks. Direct investment, by comparison, made up $168 billion, or 45 percent of total U.S. assets held abroad. Table 10–3 is supportive of this notion.

Table 10–4 futher supports the argument regarding the great desire for financial control. Of over 13,000 subsidiaries studied by the Harvard Business School Multinational Enterprise Project, about 90 percent involve financial control. Indeed about 70 percent of all subsidiaries could be considered wholly-owned. Moreover, there seems to be little inclination for owning firms to relinquish control or even greatly reduce their share of the equity capital. There may have been a modest move over time toward greater use of the minority joint venture, particularly in the developing countries and in former British dominions.

One may ask why most international investment is undertaken by large firms. There is, at least, one ready answer. They are in a better position to assume the risks associated with operating in a multicultured world where there are differences in language, customs, attitudes, institutions, and currency values. They can afford the high cost of acquiring information on

Table 10–3 U.S. Privately Owned Assets Held Abroad in 1978 (billions U.S. $)

Total	377
Direct investment	168
Bonds	42
Corporate stocks	11
Claims on unaffiliated foreigners	26
Claims reported by U.S. banks	130

Source: Russell B. Scholl, "The International Investment Position of the United States: Development in 1978," *Survey of Current Business*, (Washington: U.S. Department of Commerce), August 1979, Table 3, page 56.

Table 10–4 Type of Ownership Selected for Newly Formed Subsidiaries by Period and Geographic Location[a]

Country	Wholly-Owned (95 percent +)				Majority and 50 Percent Owned (50–94 percent)				Minority Owned (5–59 percent)			
	1951–1966	1967–1969	1970–1972	1973–1975	1951–1966	1967–1969	1970–1972	1973–1975	1951–1966	1967–1969	1970–1972	1973–1975
Canada	84.2%	92.0%	88.7%	84.6%	9.9%	5.7%	8.3%	8.5%	5.9%	2.3%	3.0%	6.9%
Latin America	66.7	69.9	70.9	63.2	20.3	20.9	16.6	18.0	13.0	9.2	12.5	18.8
Europe	68.9	78.6	77.0	75.1	22.5	15.2	16.0	15.5	8.6	6.2	7.0	9.4
Africa and Middle East	63.1	62.5	65.8	60.9	23.0	21.1	19.8	18.0	13.9	16.4	14.4	21.1
South and East Asia	51.4	54.4	51.4	52.4	26.5	27.0	34.0	31.3	22.1	18.6	14.6	16.3
Australia, New Zealand, South Africa, Rhodesia	70.6	79.7	75.0	71.3	22.0	14.2	16.8	15.3	7.4	6.1	8.2	13.5
Total	68.8	75.9	73.4	69.2	20.6	16.3	17.6	17.6	10.6	7.8	9.0	13.2

[a]Only those subsidiaries where ownership structure was known were included in calculating the percentages. Some 13,158 subsidiaries were included.

Source: Joan P. Curhan, William H. Davidson, & Rajan Suri, *Tracing the Multinationals: A Sourcebook on U.S.-Based Enterprises* (Cambridge, Mass.: Ballinger Publishing Co., 1977), pp. 24 & 25. We have converted their data to percentages.

markets, distribution systems, and sources of finance and technologies. Test marketing of a new product in a foreign market may cost $100,000. To Procter and Gamble, that is a small expenditure relative to total sales or total assets; but for a firm with only $1 million in assets, such a study calls for an expenditure of 10 percent of its capital. To enter the market effectively, it may be necessary to spend the $100,000 to obtain the relevant information. Only large firms can afford the effort, for only they have the resources to exploit the markets uncovered by those expenditures. It is not enough to know that a market exists or has great potential. One also must finance production facilities, distribution channels, advertising expenditures, inventories, and the like. Few small firms have the ability to raise the necessary credit and financing for such major ventures. It is perhaps even more the case in international investment than in national investment: large size confers many advantages. Certainly large size allows for the diversification of investment among different countries; that is, the large firm can take advantage of portfolio effects to reduce its overall risk position.

There is further evidence that a high level of concentration characterizes those industries in which foreign investment is important. All of the U.S.-based firms involved in final assembly of transport vehicles operate abroad. A similar situation exists in agricultural machinery, household appliances, rubber tires and tubes, and aluminum production. All of these are highly concentrated industries dominated by a few very large firms. Where there is investment abroad by these firms, they tend to dominate local firms in their chosen fields of specialization. While large size and an oligopolistically competitive industry may be almost necessary for direct foreign investment, they alone are not a sufficient condition to bring it about. The industries that involve direct foreign investment also are differentiated oligopolies in product groups such as automobiles, farm equipment, electronic equipment, tires, and numerous others where there is either strong technological differentiation or differentiation by advertising that results in distinctiveness in fact (technical) or at least in the mind of the ultimate user (psychological). Except insofar as they may invest abroad to obtain raw materials, we do not see much direct foreign investment in industries characterized as undifferentiated oligopolies, that is industries such as steel, copper, glass, cement, basic fertilizers, basic aluminum, and the like. There may be foreign investments that use the outputs of these industries, but these industries are heavily the preserve of domestic investors. Stated differently, in these basic industries where product differentiation is difficult and technological change slow, the foreign firm has no major advantage over the local firm and hence there is little incentive to invest abroad.

THE JOINT INTERNATIONAL VENTURE

The term "joint international business venture," joint venture for short, has come to mean many things to many people. It sometimes is taken to mean any joint relationship between one or more foreign firms and one or more local firms. Such a broad definition is excluded here. Joint venture will be taken to mean joint ownership of an operation in which at least one of the partners is foreign based.

Joint ventures can take many forms. A foreign firm may take a majority share, a minority share, or an equal share in ownership. While it is not necessary to have financial control to have operating control, some firms refuse to use the joint venture form if it is not possible to have a majority position in ownership. There are firms that have few qualms about holding minority position, however, so long as they can have operating control. They achieve this through technical-aid, management, or supply contracts.

It should be recognized that maintaining operating control sometimes is difficult if one also does not have financial control. Objectives of the participants may diverge; when they do, financial control becomes important. For example, even though a foreign-based firm can wield operating control through contracts, it may not be able to influence sufficiently the composition of the board of directors. The managing group may have thrust upon it, by the board, decisions it does not wish to take. Certainly, at the policy level, this can be critical. Management may wish to reinvest earnings while the majority of the board may wish earnings distributed as dividends. Unless policy issues of this kind can be settled amicably, lack of financial control can prove to be very unsatisfactory, if not fatal.

Many joint ventures emerge as matters of necessity; that is, no single firm is willing to assume the risks entailed, while a consortium of firms is. Large, capital-intensive, long-lived investments are natural candidates for the joint venture. Exploitation of resource deposits often is done by a consortium of several petroleum or mining firms. Roles are parceled out even though each phase of the operation is owned jointly. One firm does the actual mining, another provides transportation, and still another does the refining and extraction. There is a wide variety of combinations. An example, as shown in Table 10–5, indicates some of the possibilities. Each of three firms contributes roughly one-third of the total investment. None has operating control of the aggregate investment, but each has operating control of that part of the total in which its expertise is dominant. This assures that on decisions affecting the total operation each firm is treated equally. Decisions that affect one part of the system are made by the firm most knowledgeable in that field.

Our example illustrates the type of joint venture that firms consciously

Table 10–5 Ownership Pattern of a Large Joint Venture

Phase of Operation	Mining Firm (%)	Transportation Firm (%)	Refining Firm (%)	Value in Millions of $
Mining	51	19	30	1000
Transportation	20	60	20	500
Refining	15	30	55	300
Total	36.4	32.2	31.4	$1800

wish to undertake; however, increasingly, joint ventures are an extension of nationalism and are undertaken as a condition of entry rather than as a permissive arrangement between firms. Several countries now require that there be local ownership participation in new ventures involving foreign equity capital. In some instances, national governments insist on local financial control in a few industrial sectors. In others, almost all new investments must have at least 50 percent local participation. Countries that currently require local equity participation in some industries and in some form include India, Peru, Mexico, the Philippines, Malaysia, and Indonesia.

As noted, the joint venture can pose problems, especially if it is an enforced marriage of partners. For many ventures in small countries, it is difficult to find a suitable local partner, that is, one with sufficient capital and know-how to be able to contribute to the partnership. Unfortunately, the joint venture can operate to reduce competition and to increase the concentration of economic power if the only partner available also happens to be a wealthy family in the host country. In some developing countries, a small handful of families controls the entire locally owned part of the industrial structure. Under these circumstances, a joint venture merely insulates them further from independent, foreign-owned plants that would compete against them. For this and other reasons, the only suitable partner may end up being the government itself. Most multinational firms, however, shy away from such arrangements where possible.

The Japanese multinational firms are much more likely to engage in joint ventures than are European and American firms. One explanation for this is that the Japanese are more recent to the international scene and have had to enter most countries under more stringent conditions than did the European and American firms. Also, the large bulk of Japanese investments (55 percent of the total and 72 percent of manufacturing investments) are located in developing countries where joint ventures are more likely to be preferred to wholly-owned subsidiaries. U.S.-based firms, by contrast, have only 21 percent of their investments in developing countries and 79 percent in advanced countries. Also, over 60 percent of

U.S.-owned investments in manufacturing in developing countries are concentrated in high-technology fields, whereas Japanese firms have about two-thirds of their manufacturing investment in developing countries located in relatively low-technology industries.[5] Since Japanese firms may have less to protect in the way of technology, they also may be more willing to share ownership. Also, they compete in the same industries as do local firms and hence may feel compelled to use joint ventures as a form of protective coloration. Further analysis of these points is provided in the following chapter.

CHOOSING AMONG ALTERNATIVE METHODS

As we have pointed out, if a U.S.-based firm, or other foreign firm, is to engage in international business at all, it must have some advantage over local firms in the host country. A comparative advantage is necessary if the firm is to export. Licensing is possible only if the firm possesses some patent or secret process that can be transferred for a fee. Similarly, direct investment can be successful only if the firm has an advantage over local firms in the host country. Without such an advantage, the U.S. firm would not be competitive with local ones possessing a natural advantage because of inherent knowledge of the market and the culture. Additionally, the U.S. firm would have the disadvantage of operating at a distance from its management center. Consequently, some compensating advantage is required if the U.S. firm is to be competitive. The sources of such advantages include the following:

1. Superior product and production technology.
2. Superior management skills.
3. Preferential access to production inputs, such as capital.

The problem is to determine which method of exploitation—exporting, licensing, or direct investment—is most profitable in each case.

The choice between domestic and foreign production—either by licensing or direct investment—hinges on several factors, among which are:

1. The size of the foreign market relative to efficient plant size.
2. Tariffs on imports.
3. Relative wage rates and labor efficiency.
4. The cost of capital inputs at home and abroad.

---

[5]See R. Hal Mason, "A Comment on Professor Kojima's Japanese Type versus American Type of Technology Transfer," *Hitotsubashi Journal of Economics,* (Kunitachi, Tokyo), 20:2, 1980, Table 1, page 49.

If the foreign market is small relative to an efficient plant, it can be served at a lower cost by producing at home and exporting. Scale economies in production can be realized by serving several markets, including that of the United States, from the same plant. Boeing Aircraft, for example, centralizes its production in the United States and exports to foreign markets because an efficient plant to manufacture jet transports is large relative to the size of any single national market.

If a firm does decide on foreign production, it must choose between direct investment and licensing its technology to a foreign firm. Licensing is possible only when the technology is in a form that can be transferred readily. When such licensing is possible, the choice between it and direct investment depends on the same kinds of factors that affect the more general choice between exporting and foreign production: the size of the foreign market and the amount of capital and labor used in the production process. An additional element in the decision is the fixed costs a U.S. firm must incur in order to produce abroad.

Figure 10–1 may be used as an aid to understanding the importance of

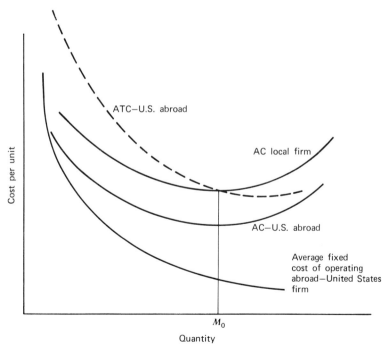

Figure 10–1. Average production costs at various outputs of automobile producers in a foreign country.

these three factors. The figure shows average production costs at various outputs of hypothetical automobile producers in a foreign country. The curve labeled "AC—local" shows average production costs for a local firm, while the curve "AC—U.S. abroad" indicates the average production costs in the foreign country for the U.S. firm at various outputs. In addition to production costs, however, the U.S. firm incurs some fixed costs of operating in the foreign environment. These include costs of investigating the investment opportunity and costs of coordinating the foreign subsidiary's activities with those of the parent.

The minimum market size at which the U.S. firm acquires a cost advantage depends on the magnitude of the fixed costs associated with the foreign operation. Obviously, the minimum market size required is smaller, the smaller are the fixed costs. Smaller fixed costs would shift the average fixed-cost curve, and hence the average total-cost curve, downward in Figure 10–1. The output at which average total cost of the U.S. firm would fall below average cost of the local firm, therefore, would be shifted to the left.

The point to be made is that any firm must be a "low-cost" producer if it is to export. If wage rates or some other major cost of inputs are lower abroad than at home, at some point it may become profitable to shift production to the foreign site. Whether costs can be brought down to a level lower than home production costs (costs in the U.S. in this case), plus transportation costs to the foreign market, depends upon the size of foreign market (economies of scale), the productivity of foreign labor, and the costs of entry (installation of a plant, materials costs, etc.).

Choices Based on Advantages Due to Superior Management and Preferential Access to Production Inputs

Although many U.S. firms may not have a technological advantage over local firms, some have advantages stemming from superior management. It is recognized widely, for example, that Procter & Gamble has a competitive advantage over other firms in certain consumer products because of superior marketing skills. These skills can be exploited, to some extent, by exporting; however, it may be necessary for Procter & Gamble to produce in foreign markets to exploit fully this marketing advantage. Superior marketing skill includes the ability both to identify the characteristics of market demand and to supply the desired products, either in fact or in the mind of the consumer through advertising. Local production is an invaluable marketing aid because it facilitates adaptation of the product and marketing strategies to changes in local market conditions. Moreover, the local plant improves the reliability of supply—a factor that is of particular importance when the product has no special technological advantage.

Some firms have neither superior technology nor superior management skills. This is the situation in the U.S. steel and textiles industries. Few would argue that firms in these industries have a competitive advantage rooted in superior technology or superior management. Much of the new steel production technology, for example, has been developed outside the United States. Firms in these and similar industries only have an advantage over foreign firms, if they have any advantage at all, because they have access to low-cost capital in the U.S. capital market. This access to low-cost capital is more important to firms that use much capital relative to other inputs in their production processes. Neither the textile nor the steel industry employs an abundance of capital relative to other inputs. Consequently, both industries have considerable difficulty in exporting and neither has attempted direct foreign investment to produce final products in any significant degree.

Choices Based on Empirical Research

Two general approaches have been employed to identify the factors affecting foreign investment decisions—surveys and statistical studies. If a researcher wants to know why, when, and where foreign investments are made, one method of obtaining the answers is simply to use surveys that ask these questions of the business executives who make the decisions. Statistical studies, on the other hand, approach the problem in a different way. They attempt to determine whether there is any statistical association between actual investments, on the one hand, and measurable factors (such as tariffs, market size, and capital employed in production), on the other. Statistical association implies that, in fact, there is a connection between the explanatory factors and foreign investment.

Both types of studies, of course, have certain strengths and weaknesses. Surveys can be employed to investigate rather complex decision processes within the firm. Statistical studies usually are limited, by the availability of data and statistical methods, to the identification of simple aggregate relationships. They have the advantage, however, of being able to identify the relative importance of various factors influencing foreign investment on the basis of actual decisions. The surveys are more impressionistic, and it is difficult to attach weights to the various factors. The surveys also suffer from the possibility that the respondent, consciously or unconsciously, may bias the information given to the interviewer.

Surveys and statistical studies of foreign investment are, in fact, complementary. The surveys are useful for investigating the complexities of the foreign investment decision-making process within the individual firm. Out of these investigations may come hypotheses that can be tested more rigorously by using statistical methods. Taking both types of studies together, then, it sometimes is possible to discern some major features of foreign investment.

First, the survey studies agree that foreign investment is not always the result of systematic and rational analysis. Yair Aharoni,[6] for example, has found in a survey of 38 U.S. corporations that the foreign investment decision-making process is initiated by the emergence of a problem, rather than through a comparison with other alternatives. The investigations usually are conducted in general terms using rather crude data, and at any point in the process the investment alternative may be rejected on the basis of subjective feelings about the risks involved.

If the investment decision-making process is not completely rational, the evidence nevertheless seems to indicate that direct investment is related to variables that a rational decision maker should take into account. Both the statistical studies and the surveys tend to agree, for example, that the size of the foreign market is a highly important determinant of direct investment. Several statistical studies have shown that U.S. direct investment in Europe is related to the absolute size of European markets and to changes in market size. Guy Stevens[7] has shown that expansion of existing foreign subsidiaries is related to changes in their sales. Gordon & Gommers,[8] from their survey of U.S. direct investment in Brazil, concluded that:

> More important than any of the specific inducements or hindrances to manufacturing operations discussed in the earlier chapters has been the general conviction among the participating companies that Brazil presents a large and potentially rapidly growing market and that, in general terms, it offers a good environment for the foreign manufacturing company.

The results concerning the effect of foreign tariffs on direct investment are more mixed. The survey studies identify tariffs as one factor that may initiate search for investment opportunities; however, there also are other factors, and tariffs are by no means necessary. Horst[9] shows that U.S. direct investment in Canada has occurred in industries with the greatest tariff protection. There is also some evidence that the trade-diversionary

---

[6]Yair Aharoni, *The Foreign Investment Decision Process,* (Boston, Mass.: Division of Research, Harvard Graduate School of Business Administration, Harvard University, 1966).

[7]Guy V. G. Stevens, "Fixed Investment Expenditures of Foreign Manufacturing Affiliates of U.S. Firms," *Yale Economic Essays,* Spring 1969, pp. 137–198.

[8]Lincoln Gordon and Engelbert Gommers, *United States Manufacturing Investment in Brazil,* (Boston, Mass.: Division of Research, Graduate School of Business Administration, Harvard University, 1962), p. 146.

[9]Thomas Horst, "The Industrial Composition of U.S. Exports and Subsidiary Sales in the Canadian Market," *American Economic Review,* 62:1, 1972, pp. 37–45.

effects of the European Economic Community induced direct investment in Europe. Miller & Weigel,[10] on the other hand, found nothing to relate U.S. direct investment in Brazil during the period 1956 to 1961 to the level of changes in Brazilian tariffs. In fact, substantial investment occurred in capital goods industries with little or no protection.

When we shift our attention to the internal characteristics of investing firms, evidence is more difficult to uncover; however, Vernon[11] has shown that U.S. direct investment in Europe has been concentrated more heavily in the industries that employ the largest percentage of scientists and engineers. This result supports Vernon's contention that direct investment by U.S. firms is made to exploit technological advantages.

Miller & Weigel[12] also found that U.S. direct investment in Brazil was related to possession of a technological advantage, as measured by the proportion of scientists and engineers employed. In addition, however, they found that direct investment in the technologically advanced industries was more probable when the industry employed relatively large amounts of labor in the production process. On the other hand, in industries without a technological advantage, direct investment was more probable when large amounts of capital were employed; thus, it would appear that some firms had a technological advantage over Brazilian firms and invested to reduce labor costs. Firms without a technological advantage, however, invested only when they had an advantage because of their access to low-cost capital.

Summary

Figure 10–2 portrays schematically in a highly simplified form the relationship between the firm, the environment, and the methods of engaging in international business.

The larger the firm and the greater its strengths and international experience the greater will be the likelihood it will find it profitable to risk assets in international investment. The country or countries of choice are determined by the size of the market to be served, availability of natural resources, level of development of the country, and permissiveness of the environment. The larger the firm and the more inviting the environment, the more likely it will be that higher-risk forms of involvement will be pursued.

[10]Robert R. Miller & Dale R. Weigel, "The Motivation of Foreign Direct Investment," *Journal of International Business Studies,* Fall 1972, pp. 67–79.

[11]Raymond Vernon, *Sovereignty at Bay* (New York: Basic Books, 1971), Chapters 2 and 3.

[12]Miller & Weigel, *op. cit.*

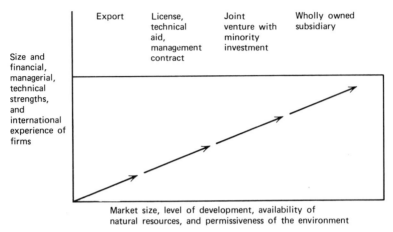

Figure 10-2.

The firm with little experience may wish only to export, but if market development is expensive and protracted, exporting calls for a substantial simultaneous investment of resources. Licensing is the next more sophisticated vehicle; however, it too can be looked on as a form of exporting, an export of know-how. It usually requires commitment of some resources, for example, skilled technicians, or legal counsel to police the terms of agreement. Joint ventures, for various reasons, may be less risky than wholly-owned operations. If they are used as a permissive device to spread risk over a large number of stockholders, they can reduce the risk of large ventures for the individual firm. If they are used as protective coloration in the face of nationalism, they also may reduce risk. Finally, all other things being equal, wholly-owned operations call for the greatest commitment of resources and hence are most risky. The greater control achieved, however, may offset these risks as compared to a joint venture. Decisions can be made more quickly and are not constrained by a partner.

Firms investing abroad tend to be large. The risks are greater in international—rather than in purely national—investments. Large firms are better able than small firms to hedge themselves against risk. As countries become more nearly alike, however, the cost of adaptation for the foreign firm is lessened, and even small firms may find the risks associated with direct foreign investment to be manageable.

SELECTED READINGS

Aharoni, Yair, *The Foreign Investment Decision Process,* (Boston, Mass.: Division of Research, Graduate School of Business Administration, Harvard University, 1966).

Aliber, Robert, "A Theory of Direct Foreign Investment," in Charles Kindleberger (ed.), *The International Corporation* (Cambridge, Mass.: The M.I.T. Press, 1970), pp. 17–34.

Bergsten, C. Fred, Thomas Horst, & Theodore H. Moran, *American Multinationals and American Interests* (Washington, D.C.: Brookings Institution, 1978).

Buckley, Peter J., & John H. Dunning, "The Industrial Structure of U.S. Direct Investment in the U.K.," *Journal of International Business Studies,* 7:2, 1976, pp. 5–14.

Caves, Richard E., "International Corporations: The Industrial Economics of Foreign Investment," *Economica,* 37:49 (N.S.), 1971, pp. 1–27.

Dunning, John H. (ed.), *Economic Analysis and The Multinational Enterprise* (New York: Praeger, 1974).

Gordon, Lincoln, & Engelbert Gommers, *United States Manufacturing Investment in Brazil,* (Boston, Mass.: Division of Research, Graduate School of Business Administration, Harvard University, 1962).

Grubel, Herbert G., & Kenneth Fadner, "The Interdependence of International Equity Markets," *Journal of Finance,* 26:1, 1971.

Gruber, W., D. Mehta, & R. Vernon, "The Research and Development Factor in International Trade and International Investment of U.S. Industry," *Journal of Political Economy,* 75:1, 1967, pp. 20–37.

Horst, Thomas, "The Industrial Composition of U.S. Exports and Subsidiary Sales to the Canadian Market," *The American Economic Review,* 62:1, 1972, pp. 37–45.

Hymer, Stephen, *The International Operations of National Firms: A Study of Direct Foreign Investment* (Cambridge, Mass.: M.I.T. Press, 1976).

Kindleberger, Charles, *American Business Abroad* (New Haven: Yale University Press, 1969), Lecture 1.

Kindleberger, Charles P., & Peter H. Lindert, *International Economics,* 6th ed. (Homewood, Ill.: Irwin, 1978), Chapter 25.

Knickerbocker, Frederick T., *Oligopolistic Reaction and Multinational Enterprises,* (Boston, Mass.: Division of Research, Graduate School of Business Administration, Harvard University, 1973).

Kobrin, Steven, "The Environmental Determinants of Foreign Direct Investment: An Ex Post Analysis," *Journal of International Business Studies,* 7:2, 1976, pp. 29–42.

Miller, Robert R., & Dale R. Weigel, "The Motivation of Foreign Direct Investment," *Journal of International Business Studies,* 3:2, 1972, pp. 67–79.

Stevens, Guy V. G., "Fixed Investment Expenditures of Foreign Manufacturing Affiliates of U.S. Firms," *Yale Economic Essays,* Spring 1969, pp. 137–198.

Stopford, John M., & Louis T. Wells, *Managing the Multinational Enterprise* (New York: Basic Books, 1972), Chapters 7 and 8.

Vernon, Raymond, *Sovereignty at Bay* (New York: Basic Books, 1971), Chapters 2 and 3.

Yoshino, Michael, *Japan's Multinational Enterprises* (Cambridge, Mass.: Harvard University Press, 1976).

CHAPTER 11

Selection and Transfer of Technology

INTRODUCTION

Preceding chapters have examined some of the problems of national policies toward investing firms and the various options open to firms when they decide to become involved in international trade and investment. Chapter 10 has been concerned directly with investment abroad, whether in wholly-owned operations or joint ventures. One critical aspect of such investment decisions is the selection of technology to be used in the venture. Before managers can conduct sensible analyses of alternative investment opportunities—the subject of Chapters 13 and 14—they must have considerable knowledge of the technological options open to them in the pursuit of these alternatives. This chapter therefore examines the economics of technology selection and transfer.

Firms should and do have an appreciation for the need to examine technological alternatives. Much of the success of investment projects depends on the selection of appropriate technologies. For example, economic environments among countries differ regarding wage rates, capital costs, and skills available. What may be an appropriate technology for the manufacture of automobiles in Japan or the United States may be almost totally out of place in the Philippines or Taiwan. In some industries there is a wide variety of technological options, with some technologies using much labor and little capital and others using little labor and much capital.

It also is true that not all industries have a wide variety of processes to choose from. For example, offshore oil drilling may be conducted nearly identically regardless of which country owns the oil. Under similar physical circumstances, the same amounts of capital and man-hours of labor may be used to drill a well on the continental shelf of Indonesia as are used to drill a well in the North sea, despite the fact that labor is cheaper per man-hour in Indonesia than in Great Britain. Why? Simply because there can be little substitution of labor for capital in oil drilling. Fortunately, unlike in oil drilling, there are several different ways to combine labor and capital in the production of most products and services.

Countries, as well as investing firms, should be concerned about the selection of technology, including the industries to be established, expanded, or both. Developing countries should be particularly concerned, given their relative abundance of unskilled labor and low level of ability to generate new capital; yet, as we observe the policies of many countries, including those at low levels of development, we may gain the impression of living in an upside-down world where incentives favor the lavish use of relatively scarce factors of production. Such incentive systems are important to the choice of technology because they distort price relationships among productive factors and lead investors to make decisions that may maximize private profits but leave society as a whole less well off than otherwise would be the case.

Some of the variables considered to be important in making the choice among competing technologies will be examined in this chapter. The development process also will be analyzed, with the focus heavily weighted to the needs of developing countries.

TECHNOLOGY: A DEFINITION

The term "technology" usually is associated with the use of electrical and mechanical power to extend human abilities. Technology can be viewed as a set of man–machine systems designed to accomplish desired ends. The term "state-of-the-art" is used to indicate what can and cannot be accomplished by applying knowledge or technology. Technology thus tends to be considered as not only machinery of some sort but also as a state of collective knowledge and abilities, or know-how. When we discuss technological innovation, we mean that somehow this ability has been extended either by finding new applications for existing know-how or by augmenting our body of knowledge by the creation of new technologies.

The term technology will be taken here to mean a method or technique of accomplishing something, a process of converting inputs into outputs. Raw materials, capital, labor, electrical, and/or other types of energy and management are combined and converted into products and services. We shall refer also to technological alternatives. This means that more than a single method exists to process inputs into the same type of output. For example, a roadbed can be built in many different ways. A primitive technology would use people with picks, shovels, hand drills, sledge hammers, and wheelbarrows. Given enough workers, simple tools, and time, a six-lane roadbed can be built through difficult terrain. An intermediate technology would include animal power, carts, blasting powder, and animal-drawn grading equipment. One can imagine a wide variety of combinations of workers and machines, each representing a "technology." At the advanced extreme of modern roadbuilding, we would be using high-powered tractors, bulldozers, and earthcutting equipment to build the roadbed.

Some of the options can be used to demonstrate what is meant by alternative technologies. Each technology in Figure 11–1 has a unique production function[1] that relates inputs to outputs, that is, shows how labor and capital are combined to move earth. Within each technology, capital can be substituted for labor and vice versa. For example, let us say that each of our output curves represents digging 1 cubic yard of earth and moving it 100 feet in 5 minutes. The curves depict all of of the combinations of workers and machines (picks, shovels, animals, bulldozers, and so forth, are considered machines) that can be used to accomplish this task. As can be seen, people alone, working without some machines, cannot accomplish the task. Nor can machines without people accomplish the task. It is impossible to get some output with one factor working alone.

Suppose we are working with technology 1: we have only picks, shovels, and workers. Initially, we have only one pick and one shovel for every six workers. One worker picks and one shovels, while the other four regain their energy. We are combining much labor with little capital. Now suppose another project is started nearby, and to obtain laborers the new employer must pay higher wages. This forces the wage rate upward on our own project, thus making it more attractive to employ more picks and shovels and fewer workers. We now employ only two workers per pick and two per shovel. We have moved downward and to the right along our product curve, say, from point a to point b in Figure 11–1.

[1]A production function defines a relationship between inputs and outputs. In Figure 11–1 each technology can be described by a general function $Q = f(L, K)$. The quantity of output (earth moved) is a function of the amount of labor and capital applied to the process of earth moving. While there are many types of labor, we can index them into a common unit. The same can be done with capital, that is, an hour's worth of bulldozer time is worth so many sticks of dynamite. Thus, we shall refer to only two factors of production, for the sake of simplicity.

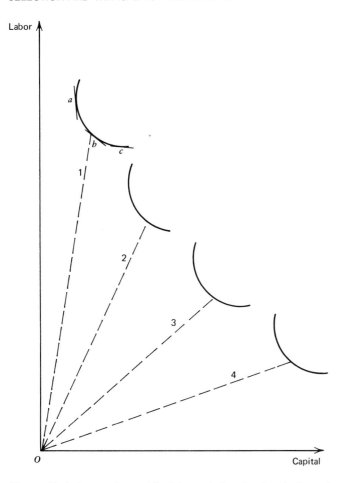

Figure 11–1. 1 = workers with picks and shovels; 2 = 1 plus animals and animal-drawn equipment; 3 = 2 plus some engine-powered equipment; 4 = highly mechanized power equipment with skilled operators.

Suppose, in addition, that the price of picks and shovels falls. We now can employ one pick and one shovel for every two workers and release some of the workers so that we produce at point *c* in Figure 11–1. Throughout we have moved in the direction of substituting capital for labor, as their prices relative to one another have changed. Labor became more expensive and capital less expensive.

There is a key point that needs to be stressed: technological innovation. There are two types of technological change to be examined. The first is improvement to an existing technology. The other we might term technological shift or development of a new process. In other words, we can tinker around and improve an existing process or we can invent an entirely new process to replace the original. Both types of technological change take place side by side. Replacement of the steam locomotive on passenger trains was a matter of tinkering with an existing process. The basic technology of moving people remained unchanged. Replacement of the passenger train by the airplane, on the other hand, was a matter of substituting one process for another, or, stated differently, a new technology for moving people was discovered. Improving an existing process causes a shift in the product curve, whereas creation of a new process creates a new product curve.

To distinguish between entirely different technologies and improvement of an existing technology, suppose in our pick-and-shovel option we find that workers are more productive when the picks and shovels are regularly sharpened. By reallocating workers and machines, we create a specialized group called blacksmiths. Each can sharpen five picks and five shovels per day. We also find that with sharpened implements 1.5 workers can produce what 2 did previously; however, to keep these 1.5 workers going we require 0.25 workers to keep picks and shovels sharpened. We therefore are able to accomplish what we did before with the same number of picks and shovels but with 1.75 workers instead of 2. We now use fewer resources to obtain the same output. This is depicted as an inward shift of our product curve, as shown in Figure 11–2.

Initially, we required l_2 of labor and k_2 of capital to dig and move 1 cubic yard of earth 100 feet in 5 minutes. We now can do it with l_1 of labor and k_1 of capital. We have improved the process, but we still are using pick-and-shovel technology.

As yet, we have not discussed the nature of technological choice. Under what conditions would we choose pick-and-shovel technology in preference to power-equipment technology?

THE ECONOMICS OF TECHNOLOGICAL CHOICE

Economists have developed a theory of choice relating to the technology of production. The key variables involved are the amounts of labor and capital required by each technology, the price of labor, and the cost of capital. This theory is presented in simple form in Figure 11–3. With two different technologies, A and B, which one we choose depends on the price of labor and the price of capital, where we are assuming only 2 factor inputs. Suppose that technology A represents the use of picks, shovels, and wheelbarrows (capital), plus workers (labor). Technology B represents the use of bulldozers (capital) and drivers (labor). Each product curve again represents the digging of 1 cubic yard of earth and moving it 100 feet in 5

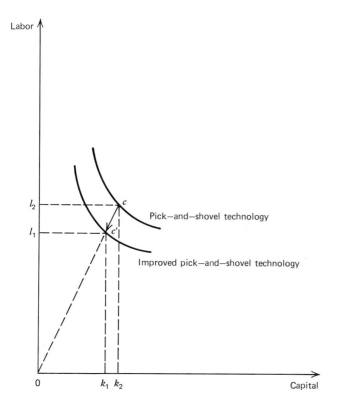

Figure 11–2. Improved technology reflected by an inward shift of the product curve.

minutes. Now, which technology should an earth-moving contractor select? That decision requires knowledge about the prices of capital and labor.[2] If line *a* represents the price ratio between labor and capital, then we would select technology *A* and use l_2 of labor in combination with c_1 of capital. Since technology *A* uses relatively more labor and relatively less capital

---

[2]In strict terms, the so-called price-ratio lines are not price ratios pure and simple. Each line is more precisely a budget line, reflecting the ratio of prices. If we had $1 to spend, given the price ratio, each line indicates the amounts of capital and labor services we could obtain for that dollar. That they reflect price ratios can be seen where P_l = price of labor, P_k = price of capital, and B = budget. The quantity of labor services (Q_l) we can acquire $= \dfrac{B}{P_l}$ and capital services (Q_k) $= \dfrac{B}{P_k}$. If we wish to know the ratio of capital to labor services depicted by each line, that is, $Q_l \div Q_k$, we need only divide $\dfrac{B}{P_l}$ by $\dfrac{B}{P_k}$ because they equal Q_l and Q_k. In so doing, we obtain the price ratio P_k/P_l as the slope of the *lc*.

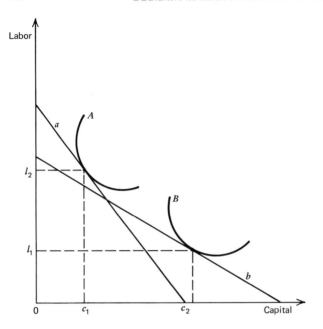

Figure 11-3. Relationships between capital *(c)* and labor *(l)*.

than technology *B,* it is termed the labor-intensive technology and, if labor is cheap in relation to capital, it will be selected. If capital is relatively cheap in relation to labor, however, our contractor would select technology *B,* as would be the case should line *b* prevail rather than line *a* as a reflection of the labor and capital price relationships. Under technology *B,* l_1 of labor would be combined with c_2 of capital; as we can see, technology *B* is the more capital-intensive of the two.

Economic choice occurs only when alternative technologies require more of some and less of other inputs to achieve the same level of output. Some technologies are obviously inferior and therefore are ignored in making the final decision; that is, they use as much of one factor and more of another to yield the same output as would an alternative technology.

Investments are usually long-lived; therefore, business executives must anticipate what may happen to prices—and most especially to the price of labor. One knows how much he is paying for a machine that will last 10 years because he is buying it now. He does not know how much he will be paying the operator of that machine 5 years from now. The businessman must project ahead and make judgments about factor availabilities and their relative prices over time. The selection and adaptation of technology hinge on such factors as market power of the firm, timing of the investment, governmental policies, market size, economic growth, and so on.

VARIABLES AFFECTING THE CHOICE OF TECHNOLOGY

In the previous section we assumed that there was a well-known wage for every type of labor, a well-developed market with well-known prices for every piece of capital equipment, and a well-developed financial market whereby the investor knew what interest rate he would have to pay for the use of financial assets. Implicit has been the assumption that technological change is either absent or at least predictable. These conditions do not hold in the real world, which is fraught with uncertainties. There is a cost involved in obtaining information. A host of questions must be addressed before one can determine the cost of labor, the cost of capital, and the factor combinations and range of factor substitutability for different technological options.

Most variables affecting the choice of technology can be handled by examining three or four variables, that is to say, we can collapse many variables into a few. The critical ones are market size and growth, labor costs, capital costs, the range of technologies available, and the prospect of technological obsolescence.

Market Size and Growth

The first variable to examine is market size, which includes the host country's domestic market plus any exports to other markets from the proposed facility. In addition, some estimate of the rate of market growth is required, along with an assessment of competitors' strategies. This is largely a matter of guesswork, but the investing firm must have some notion of how large the market is and what share it may be able to capture. In many instances, the firm already has established a market through exportation to the host country and consequently has accumulated knowledge regarding market size, rate of growth, government regulations, and the relative position of major firms in terms of product quality, consumer acceptance, distribution channels, and market shares.

In this context, the investor must have an answer to two very important questions:

1. Is the market large enough to accommodate the smallest technologically feasible plant?
2. Can the product be priced high enough to cover full costs and yield our target rate of return to capital?

We can illustrate the problem using long-run average cost curves, which are envelope curves connecting the short-run average cost curves of different plant sizes for each given technology. In Figure 11–4 we have a long-run average cost curve tangent to six different short-run cost curves.

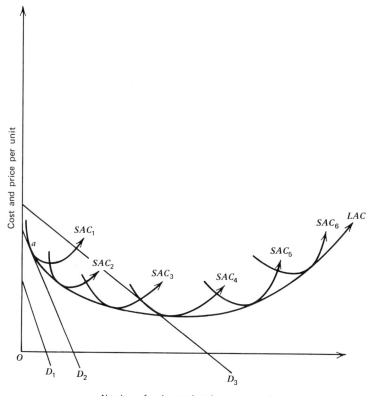

Figure 11–4.

Each short-run curve represents a distinct plant size or alternative technology. Based on exports from its home plant to the local market, the firm initially estimates its demand curve to be D_1. Plainly, the market is too small to sustain even the smallest-scaled plant, as represented by SAC_1. Under these circumstances, the firm would continue to export and not invest in a plant to serve the local market. If, however, the demand curve were D_2 instead D_1, the smallest plant (SAC_1) would be barely feasible. It would cover its average total costs because the market would accommodate a price equal to average unit costs. This is demonstrated by the tangency of demand curve D_2 at point a on both the LAC and SAC_1 curves.

To extend the example further, suppose that the market is growing rapidly. The firm estimates that by the time it can have a plant installed and operating, the market demand will have shifted to D_3. Now we are in a situation of economic choice among competing technologies and plant scales.

In Figure 11–5, we have added a marginal cost curve. We can see that plant size SAC_3 is most profitable. With selection of plant size SAC_3, the entrepreneur would produce at output Q, where long-run marginal cost equals marginal revenue. He would price his output at P and would incur average costs per unit of C. His profit would amount to PQ minus CQ.

The Costs of Capital and Labor and the Availability of Technological Alternatives

As we have indicated already, there are many types of labor and many types of capital. Somehow, in the decision to choose one technology or another, everything must be reduced to common units. Ordinarily, we prefer that these units be monetary ones, with all values so expressed. Whether we converse in dollars, yen, rupees, or rubles, we want a common denominator. To demonstrate this, we use the following example. Suppose

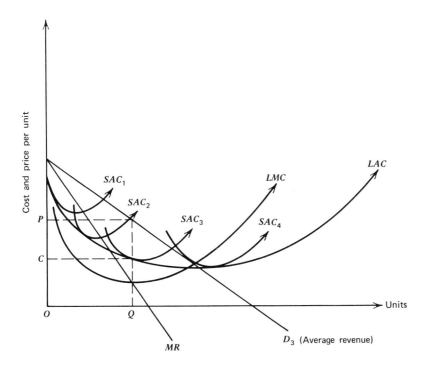

Figure 11–5.

we have the following data on alternative methods of weaving rough cotton cloth[3] in India:

Annual wage rates:	
Unskilled labor	600 rupees per year
Maintenance personnel	1,200 rupees per year
Supervisory personnel	1,800 rupees per year
Accounting staff	2,000 rupees per year
Executive personnel	3,000 rupees per year
Installed value of new machines:	
Throw-shuttle loom	5 rupees
Fly-shuttle loom	50 rupees
Semiautomatic pedal loom	250 rupees
Nonautomatic power loom	1,500 rupees
Automatic power loom	5,000 rupees

With the operating characteristics of the different technologies, we can evaluate them in common terms. We can examine labor costs in terms of so many units of unskilled labor per square yard of cloth produced. Capital costs can be evaluated in terms of so many units per square yard based on machine outputs over time. Table 11–1 presents the operating data. Table 11–2 indicates the investment in machines and buildings and the man-hours of labor required to produce selected amounts of cotton cloth. As is shown in Table 11–1, different types of labor requirements have been indexed or scaled to be equivalent to unskilled labor. From the data in Table 11–2, we can construct an isoproduct curve connecting the input requirements of each technology.[4] We have done this in Figure 11–6.

All technologies have been scaled to a 40-year life to obtain a common base for including the value of buildings. We have plotted the investment in machinery and buildings in thousands of rupees along the horizontal axis. Man-hours expended in thousands have been plotted on the vertical axis. Man-hours are in unskilled labor equivalents (2,496 hours per year and 600 rupees per man-year).

The rental value of capital is assumed to be 10 percent; thus, the trade-off between labor and capital is the use of 600 rupees worth of capital, or 1 man-year of unskilled labor. That is, the rental value of 6,000 rupees

---

[3]This example is adapted from Table 2 of "production Techniques and Employment Creation in Underdeveloped Economies," Asian Advisory Committee of the International Labor Organization, *International Labor Review,* 78:2, 1958, pp. 120–150.

[4]Since we have only point estimates, we cannot construct isoquants for each technology, as was done in Figure 11–1. It should be realized that intersecting each point on the isoproduct curve is an isoquant for that particular technology.

Table 11-1 Operating Characteristics of Alterative Technologies in Cotton Weaving

Characteristic	Type of Loom				
	Throw-Shuttle	Fly-Shuttle	Semiauto-matic Pedal	Nonauto-matic Power	Auto-matic Power
Unskilled laborers per loom	1.25	1.25	1.25	0.50	0.13
Maintenance personnel per loom	0.05	0.10	0.20	0.30	0.40
Supervisory personnel per loom	0.01	0.01	0.05	0.10	0.10
Staff personnel per loom	0.01	0.01	0.05	0.10	0.20
Executive personnel per loom	0.01	0.01	0.05	0.10	0.10
Unskilled equivalents per loom	1.363	1.563	2.217	2.333	2.397
Total annual wages per loom (rupees)	409	938	1,330	1,400	1,438
Per-loom value of building floor space at 25 rupees per square foot	200	250	450	625	625
Economic life of building (years)	40	40	40	40	40
Economic life of equipment (years)	5	10	10	20	20
Annual output per loom (square yards)	1,000	2,500	9,000	10,000	12,000

Table 11-2

| Loom Technology | Rupees of Investment in Machines and Buildings | | | Man-Hours of Labor | | |
| | Number of Square Yards Produced | | | Number of Square Yards Produced | | |
	5,000	10,000	20,000	5,000	10,000	20,000
Throw-shuttle	1,200	2,400	4,800	17,010	34,020	68,040
Fly-shuttle	900	1,800	3,600	7,800	15,600	31,200
Pedal	805	1,610	3,220	3,075	6,150	12,300
Nonautomatic power	1,815	3,630	7,260	2,910	5,820	11,640
Automatic power	4,425	8,850	17,770	2,495	4,990	9,980

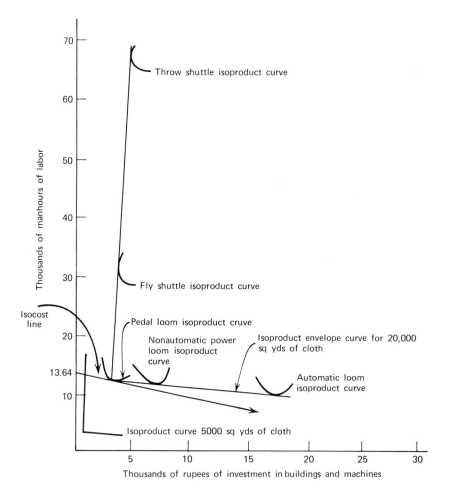

Figure 11-6.

246

worth of capital is 600 rupees and so, too, is the cost of employing one man-year or 2,496 hours of labor. The cost of producing 20,000 square yards of cloth for the five different technologies is:

Throw-shuttle	Rs. 16,835
Fly-shuttle	7,860
Pedal loom	3,279
Nonautomatic power loom	3,524
Automatic power loom	4,176

The isocost line tangent to the 20,000-unit isoproduct curve[5] has a value of 3,279 rupees. For this amount we can have either 13,640 man-hours of labor or the use of 32,790 rupees worth of buildings and equipment, but not both. Table 11–2 shows that we are using 3,320 rupees of capital equipment and 12,300 man-hours of labor to produce 20,000 square yards of cloth using the pedal loom.

It is obvious that we would choose the pedal loom. The cost of capital relative to labor would have to fall considerably before the nonautomatic and automatic power looms would become economical. It also is obvious that the throw-shuttle and fly-shuttle options could never become competitive. Indeed, if we were businessmen we would use these two techniques only if laborers were willing to pay us to allow them to work for us; that is, the wage rate would have to become negative. A zero wage rate would be a line parallel to the vertical axis, and, as can be seen, the curve above the pedal-loom coordinates is inward bending. In other words, to achieve a given output, the pedal loom uses less of both factors than do the throw-shuttle or fly-shuttle processes. Although the example we have just described is rather simple, it can be extended to examine many of the questions raised previously.

There are other considerations that bear on investment projects. We also must be concerned with the length of time different methods require. In our road-building example, might we still choose a heavy-equipment technology because we can complete the roadbed much more quickly? Until the road is completed it cannot be used, and until it can be used it has no value, that is, it produces nothing. Now suppose that a road connecting two cities is expected to reduce transport costs by 5 cents per ton-mile and will carry 50 million ton-miles per month when completed. Every month of delay in its completion then represents $2.million worth of foregone eco-

[5]The isoproduct curve referred to here is an envelope curve connecting the individual isoproduct curves of the different technologies. For an explanation of isocost lines, see footnote 2 of this chapter.

nomic benefit. If with heavy equipment we can complete the road in one year, but with pick-and-shovel technology it would require five years, we would have to forego $120 million worth of economic benefits. Stated differently, pick-and-shovel technology must have assessed against it not only the labor and capital costs it incurs directly, but also the indirect cost of foregone benefits resulting from the time delay in completing the project. Finally, the longer time required means that our expenditure of capital and labor is tied up in an unproductive asset. There is a time value of money that also must be assessed against projects. As just depicted, the pick-and-shovel technology also would incur a greater charge on this account.

Technological Innovation and Obsolescence

Another aspect of technological choice is that of estimating the possibility that one or more existing technologies might become obsolete before the investment project has generated enough net revenue to cover its initial costs.[6] For example, in the early 1950s, a new steel-making process became available: the top-blown oxygen converter. Any businessman investing in steel making just prior to that time should have considered the possibility that existing processes might become obsolete within a relatively short time. The oxygen converter is absolutely cost saving as compared with either the open-hearth furnace or the electric furnace, and it is both labor saving and capital saving but a bit more capital saving than labor saving when compared with the other two processes. The electric furnace is the more capital intensive of the three methods. There is little variation, however, among the three processes in the capital-to-labor ratio. For developing countries, the oxygen process is more nearly in line with their needs. Not only is it the more productive, but it is also the more labor intensive; it employs more labor per unit of capital consumed.

Now suppose a business man already had invested in a steel-making plant prior to the oxygen-converter innovation. Should be scrap his already existing plant and adopt the new technology? The answer, of course, depends on the initial technology selected. If he had selected the open-hearth technology, the answer is yes. If the electric furnace technology was selected, the answer is no. Capital costs are sunk costs that do not enter into the decision; thus, they should be ignored. So long as the plant more than covers its average variable costs (which exclude capital overheads) and these are less than average total costs for the new technology, he should continue operating his existing plant. Total variable costs per ton for the electric furnace are less than total costs per ton for the oxygen

---

[6]An explanation of net present value will be provided in Chapter 13.

converter; thus, if the electric furnace had been installed, the businessman should continue to operate it. If for some reason he had installed the open-hearth rather than the electric furnace, he should scrap his plant even though it might be "brand spanking new" because its average variable costs per unit exceed the total average costs per unit of the oxygen converters. Not only would he have chosen an inferior technology (as compared with the electric furnace that has lower average total costs than the open-hearth's average variable costs), but he would be considerably more vulnerable to technological innovation.

We do not mean to imply from the this that the open-hearth furnace would necessarily be unprofitable in an accounting sense. Indeed, with the appropriate industry structure and pricing practices, it might be quite profitable, that is, more than cover its average total costs. At the same time, however, the electric furnace and oxygen converter are much more profitable.

TECHNOLOGY TRANSFER AND THE ROLE OF MULTINATIONAL FIRMS

Methods of Transferring Technology

Technology transfer is a term that is used widely in the literature of several disciplines.[7] Generally, the term means something different in one discipline than it does in another. Also, there are several terms used almost interchangeably in the literature to refer to technology transfer. In addition to the term "technology transfer," the terms "technology assimilation," "technology diffusion," "technology absorption," "technology transplanation," and "technology transmission" are used to refer to the international movement of technology through foreign investment and/or international trade.

We shall define the term "technology transfer" to include transmission, absorption, and assimilation. This suggests that a complete technology transfer has not been accomplished until a firm in the receiving country is able to operate, maintain, and repair a set of physical capital designed to accomplish some predetermined objective using indigenous personnel. Anything short of this can be considered an incomplete transfer. One extreme form of incomplete transfer is the "technology transplant," which,

---

[7]The material in this section is based on R. Hal Mason, "A Comment on Professor Kojima's Japanese Type versus American Type of Technology Transfer," *Hitotsubashi Journal of Economics,* (Tokyo: Hitotsubashi Academy 20:2, 1980), pp. 42–52.

as the term suggests, is the emplacement of a technology that has not been transmitted to and absorbed by the indigenous workforce. A good example of this was the tractor mechanization of Turkish agriculture during the 1950s and 1960s. Tractors were introduced without adequate attention to the low level of mechanical skills available. Inadequate repair and service facilities resulted in failure of the program. The transplant was rejected.

For the purposes of this chapter, *technology* is defined to include not only physical capital but also that set of technical and managerial skills or software required to operate, maintain, and service the physical capital and effectively tie its output into a marketing and distribution system. Insofar as the enterprise is concerned, there are two types of technology required for a successful technology transfer: embodied and disembodied. Embodied technology is that which is engineered into physical capital or into an organization in the form of knowledge. One might call this the stock of technology available to the enterprise in isolation. Within this stock are certain types of physical and human capital. Technology transfer is complete only when there is a complementary matching between physical and human capital. At such a point, the technology becomes embodied, so far as the enterprise is concerned. If there is not such complementarity, certain aspects of the technology remain disembodied and transfer is complete. There continues to be a need for technology infusion, either in the form of more physical capital or additional human capital from outside the enterprise.

Another way of examining this concept of technology is to view the firm as having certain competitive advantages that are inherent in its ability to internalize a unique set of resources. In so doing, it can choose to limit or even deny access by other firms to these resources. The firm may sell the products or services produced by these resources but may not sell the resources themselves. In this sense, the firm substitutes for the market mechanism and appropriates (collects) economic rents by controlling access to its own unique capabilities. Appropriable rents, arising from superior factors created by the enterprise, include those arising from the application of technology in the creation of products and services or those resulting from the sale of certain aspects of the technology itself. It is within this context that we shall discuss technology and its transfer across national boundaries.

Institutional Arrangements and Methods of Transferring Technology

Using the concepts just given, technology transfer can be examined in terms of the degree to which firms can control access to proprietary technological know-how. Largely, this depends on how difficult (or costly) it is for other firms to duplicate or replicate the technology. The more costly the replication is, the higher the returns and the greater the owning firm's incentive to limit access to the technology. At the other extreme, the easier it is for another firm to replicate the technology, the greater is the incentive for the owning firm to sell the technology outright. This set of conditions tends to explain the variety of institutional devices used to apply technology, devices that differ in terms of the degree to which they permit the owning enterprise to maintain control over or limit access to the technology.

As with any economic decision, the firm must assess the costs of control against the economic returns of control. The degree of control will depend largely upon the amount of economic rent generated by the technology. At one extreme, if there is little in the way of economic rent to be appropriated, the enterprise will not attempt to internalize the decision-making capabilities of the market and will sell the technology competitively in the marketplace.[8] At the other extreme, if appropriable economic rents are sufficiently great, the firm will attempt to deny other firms direct access to the technology by internalizing the decisions of the marketplace and selling the outputs of the technology but not the technology itself. Under these circumstances, the firm will invest abroad in the form of wholly-owned subsidiaries.[9] We thus can examine the institutional arrangements for transferring technology in terms of where they lie between the extremes of free trade—which offers little or no control—and direct foreign invest-ment—which provides the greatest amount of control but not necessarily complete control.

There are various institutional arrangements that are used commonly by international firms to move technology and technological know-how across international boundaries. They are:

1. Direct foreign investment (wholly-owned subsidiary).
2. Joint ventures:
    a. Foreign only (two or more foreign firms)
    b. Majority foreign
    c. Minority foreign
    d. Equally foreign and local.

---

[8]For an interesting treatment of the concepts underlying this argument, see Benjamin Klein, Robert G. Crawford, and Armen Alchian, *Vertical Integration, Appropriable Rents and the Competitive Contracting Process,* working paper, Department of Economics, UCLA, 1978.

[9]Here we take a chapter from the late Stephen Hymer. We have cast the argument in somewhat different terms than those used by Hymer. See his doctoral thesis, which is now available in book form: *The International Operations of National Firms: A Study of Direct Foreign Investment* (Cambridge, Mass.: M.I.T. Press, 1976).

3. Contractual agreements:
   a. Licenses and franchises
   b. Technical-aid agreements
   c. Management contracts
   d. Engineering and consulting contracts
   e. Turnkey plants
   f. Supply contracts
   g. Resource concessions.
4. Debt financing.
5. Combinations of the above.

The types of technology transferred and depth of commitment of the transferor and recipient may differ depending upon which arrangement is used;[10] moreover, the degree to which each of these arrangements limits access to the technology depends to a very great degree upon the nature of the technology itself. For example, the Coca Cola Company can limit access to its technology through a simple combination of franchising and a supply contract because Coca Cola controls the supply of the basic ingredient, the syrup. The formula for the syrup is a closely guarded secret. Coca Cola therefore is able, because of its monopoly position, to appropriate the economic rents through the price of the syrup. There is no need to undertake direct foreign investment in order to appropriate the economic rents. International Business Machines, on the other hand, serves its markets either by sales of business machines and computers (but not the basic technology) in international trade or by producing the machines in wholly-owned subsidiaries operating abroad. It will not engage in joint ventures or licensing, where the basic technology must be shared. In the cases of both Coca Cola and IBM in India, they refused to disclose details of their technologies upon demand of the Indian Central Government, preferring instead to close down operations in that country. Disclosures such as those demanded by India are tantamount to creating one's own competition and destroying the source of appropriable economic rents.

Operating Characteristics of Firms and Technology Transfer

It should be pointed out that the operating characteristics of the firm supplying the technology also have a great deal to do with which arrange-

---

[10]See R. Hal Mason, "Technology Acquisition in the Pacific Basin: Direct Foreign Investment vs. Unpackaged Technology," in R. Hal Mason (ed.), *International Business in the Pacific Basin* (Lexington, Mass.: Lexington Books, D.C. Heath and Co., 1978), Chapter 8, pp. 117–129.

ments will be chosen. Firms differ not only in terms of the extent of appropriable rents available but also in terms of the key strengths that allow them to create appropriable rents. Some firms' technology or know-how requires the sale of a final product in order to capture the rents. Most manufacturing firms fall into this category. General Motors, Ford Motor Company, and other automobile manufacturers prefer wholly-owned subsidiaries in most instances but will enter into other arrangements if necessary. Their preference for wholly-owned subsidiaries probably is related to the greater extent to which they can capture the economic rents. On occasion, however, these firms have been known to engage in licensing and other arrangements that provide less control. Of course, so long as the automobile firms supply most of the basic components and body stampings, they are still in a position, through pricing tactics, to capture most of the economic rents without resorting to ownership of the plants that assemble the final product. Once there is sufficient volume, however, to warrant an integrated automobile complex including foundry, engine plant, transmission plant, axle plant, stamping plant, body plant, and assembly plant, the companies end up with at least a majority joint venture or a wholly-owned subsidiary.

The point is that manufacturing firms such as these find their strength in the logistical and coordinative processes that tie an enormously complex set of technical production processes together into a functioning whole and that must then be balanced against pressures of the marketplace. It is this ongoing total process that constitutes the competitive strength of such firms and yields the appropriable economic rents. The same system placed in inexperienced hands would yield zero or even negative economic rents. The technology or technological know-how is embedded in the system and probably cannot be disengaged easily and sold separately. Any large automobile company can design an automobile production complex and sell it, but it is unlikely that an automobile company can teach someone else how to operate that complex without also taking over technical and managerial control for an extended period of time, perhaps for several years.

Large engineering–consulting firms, such as Bechtel Corporation, Kaiser Engineers, Fluor Corporation, and Babcock and Wilcox, design and build chemical plants, cement plants, fertilizer plants, and the like and sometimes set up management teams to run these plants and train nationals to take them over. In the latter case, the plant is known as a turnkey plant. Seldom, if ever, would these engineering firms take a direct ownership interest. Unlike General Motors or Ford, they do not create appropriable economic rents by being operating companies. Their economic rents are generated by their ability to design, engineer, and build complex plants.

Their strength is that they can marshall large groups of engineers, construction workers, machinery, technicians, and managers to undertake projects that are one (or a few) of a kind. When the project is complete it is someone else's role to provide the operating know-how. Engineering firms do transfer technology, but it is someone else's technology, not their own; they transfer only the end result of that technology, i.e., the plant or construction project. Thus, they normally do not need ownership, licenses, and the like to protect the technological know-how that yields them their economic rents. An engineering or consulting contract is sufficient protection because the technology that can replicate the end product resides primarily in people rather than in physical capital.

Technology Transfer and Economic Development

Large multinational firms are a major source of technology and are key transfer agents. They tend to prefer direct foreign investment as their method of transfer. In many instances, the technologies they transfer were designed for large markets that have an abundance of capital and high-level labor skills. In the developing countries these conditions more frequently do not prevail; markets are small and capital and skills are scarce. Thus, economic theory suggests that we should find these firms adapting their techniques when they invest in developing countires. We would expect them to use much less capital per worker than they do in advanced countries; however, differences in capital-to-labor ratios are not so great as we might expect when we compare the developing countries' manufacturing sectors with the same sectors in advanced countries. Are there any explanations for such an outcome? There are several, as follows:

   Technological fixity of production processes.

   Distorted price relationships in factor markets.

   Imperfect competition.

   Ignorance of market conditions.

   There indeed may be rather narrow limits within any industrial process on how much factor substitution can take place, yet we do see vast differences when comparing the capital-to-labor ratio of one industry with that of others. There are relatively labor-intensive industries, such as textiles, woodworking, light machinery, food processing, pharmaceuticals, footwear, and the like. There also are very capital-intensive industries, such as petrochemicals, chemical fertilizers, electrical generation, and heavy machinery manufacture. Even within so-called capital-intensive sectors, however, many activities are labor intensive. For example, in the electrical equipment field, the wiring of boards is labor intensive. In many industries, activities such as packaging, filling, order picking, materials handling, grading and inspection, and painting and finishing can be done manually rather than by specialized machines. Thus, even if production processes tend to use capital and labor in fixed proportions, all other things being equal, we should see investments in developing countries concentrating in the labor-intensive industries, activities, or both. Yet we find a positive relation between sectoral growth and sectoral capital intensity in developing countries. Capital-intensive industries tend to be growing more rapidly than the more labor-intensive ones.

The technological fixity argument remains an open question; however, the range of capital-to-labor ratios among industries is quite broad. Given this, perhaps we should see more rapid growth of labor-intensive subsectors in developing countries. We have suggested elsewhere that the rapid emplacement of capital and the low employment multiplier in developing countries is due to factor-market price distortions.[11] These distortions, which take the form of capital subsidies and high social overhead costs of employing labor, are a result of industrialization policies and have stimulated capital deepening and a shift away from labor-intensive industries. Technological fixity could be a problem only if the emphasis of industrial policy were wrongly placed, resulting in the selection of an inappropriate mix of projects or industries to be expanded. It should be noted that Wells' research[12] suggests that there are alternative technologies available in several light manufacturing industries he studied; however, in no case did the 10 multinational firms included in the study choose labor-intensive technologies, and only two were using intermediate technologies. By comparison, of the 33 locally owned firms he examined, all but 3 were using much more labor-intensive methods than were the multinationals to produce the same or similar products. Wells suggests that some firms use capital-intensive techniques to assure quality, avoid labor problems, and increase the flexibility of plant utilization.

In a study conducted in Brazil, Morley & Smith examined multinational firms operating in the metal-working industries.[13] While they concluded that

[11]R. Hal Mason and Il Sakong, "Level of Economic Development and Capital—Ratios in Manufacturing," *Review of Economics and Statistics,* 53:2, 1971, pp. 176–178.

[12]Louis T. Wells, Jr., "Economic Man and Engineering Man: Choice in a Low Wage Country," *Public Policy,* 21, Summer 1973, pp. 319–342. The industries or products examined were: plastic sandals, cigarettes, soft-drink bottling, bicycle and betjak tires, flashlight batteries, and woven bags.

[13]Samuel A. Morley & Gordon W. Smith, *The Choice of Technology: Multinational firms in Brazil,* Workshop on Income Distribution and Its Role in Development. Program of Development Studies, Rice University, April 1974, See also Morley & Smith, "Limited Search and the Technology Choices of Multinational Firms in Brazil," *Quarterly Journal of Economics,* 91:2, 1977, pp. 263–287.

there are alternative techniques, they also concluded that the choice among these different techniques does not alter the capital-to-labor ratio by very much, and, accordingly, multinational firms cannot be blamed too much for being insensitive to relative factor prices. They also found that the costs of searching for new or at least different (labor-intensive) technologies may outweigh the reduction in manufacturing costs occasioned by the use of labor-intensive technologies.

Imperfect competitive conditions also may contribute to the problem. Yeoman[14] found little difference in the amounts of capital used per worker in plants located in developing countries when they were compared with amounts for similar plants in advanced European countries. Whether multinational firms adapted technology (scaled it down for small-market and/or labor-abundant situations) depended on (1) the degree of market power (extent of product differentiation) of the firm and (2) the share of manufacturing, labor, and depreciation costs included in the total selling price. Where there is strong differentiation of product and where the share of manufacturing cost in final selling price is low, adaptation of production processes was also low. Under these circumstances, little incentive exists to re-engineer production processes because the savings are small relative to the total value of the product. These conditions typify the pharmaceuticals industry, where Yeoman found little process adaptation; however, in the home appliances field, which is more competitive and has high manufacturing costs relative to final selling price, adaptation was much more extensive in developing-country manufacturing plants. In many instances, technologies are transferred nearly intact from capital-abundant to labor-abundant situations, but one must consider the costs of adaptation in relation to what is to be gained by it. As Yeoman points out, if the gains are small, as they may be in a highly imperfect market, there will be little adaptation. Also, if factor price relations are distorted in developing countries such that they do not reflect relative factor scarcities, technologies are more likely to be transferred intact, again because the gains from adaptation or the cost savings to be achieved are small. The distortions make the factor markets of developing countries appear to be much like those of advanced countries, when actually they are not.

Multinational firms react to local conditions in much the same way as do locally owned firms. Mason[15] found that capital-to-labor ratios differed

[14]Wayne A. Yeoman, "Selection of Production Processes for the Manufacturing Subsidiaries of U.S.-Based Multinational Corporations," unpublished doctoral thesis, Harvard University, April 1968.

[15]R. Hal Mason, "Some Observations on the Choice of Technology by Multinational Firms in Developing Countries," *Review of Economics and Statistics* 55:3, 1973, pp. 349–355.

little when comparing the subsidiaries of multinational firms with closely matched locally owned counterpart firms. This does not support arguments by some that multinational firms are, at worst, ignorant of developing-country conditions and, at best, indifferent to those conditions. The foreign investor, unless he has a complete monopoly, still must face competition from either local firms or other foreign firms; consequently, selection of technology and the factor proportions available can be ignored only at one's peril. Selection of technologies that are inappropriate seems to be rooted in distorted market conditions rather than an inability to substitute labor for capital (technology fixity) or an ignorance of differing market conditions on the part of investing firms.

EFFECTS OF TECHNOLOGY TRANSFER: CONCERNS AND REACTIONS OF HOME AND HOST COUNTRIES

Technology transfer has become an extremely important topic in recent years. Not only is the sale and transfer of technology and technical know-how an important source of income to firms engaged in international business, but it also is important for its effects upon the changing patterns of international trade and investment. For this latter reason, technology transfer has become a controversial subject. Nation-states, whether already developed or less developed, desire the fruits of technology, which include new products, improved productivity, economic growth, and presumably access to the "good life." Controversy arises, however, because technology is largely a phenomenon that involves proprietary ownership rights. Technology is not a freely available factor of production. There are costs incurred in its creation and in its transfer.[16] Moreover, the acquisition of technology usually involves foreign intrusion, either through foreign ownership of the assets used to apply the technology or through contractual arrangements between the nationals who wish to use the technology and the foreign owners of the technology. In the case of foreign ownership, payment for the technology takes the form of profits to the foreign enterprise. In contractual arrangements, payments are usually in the form of royalties or rents paid for the right to use the technology. Whether payment is in profits, royalties, or other forms, there is often controversy in both the recipient and the home country regarding how the economic rents accruing to technology are to be shared.

Recipient countries complain that they are technologically dependent on foreign-dominated enterprises. They also complain that they are paying

[16]See David J. Teece, *The Multinational Corporation and the Resource Cost of International Technology Transfer* (Cambridge, Mass.: Ballinger Publishing, 1976).

too much for the use of technology. Simultaneously, home countries often are concerned that the export of technology is damaging to their economic base and that jobs are being exported. Accordingly, they may feel that foreign recipients of technology are not paying enough for its use. Thus, just as they have on occasion chosen to intervene in the markets for goods and financing, nation-states have begun to intervene in the market for technology and its attendant services. Caught in the middle are the enterprises that hold proprietary rights over the technology being transferred.

Host-Country Concerns

Recipients of technology (host countries) have several concerns about the transfer of technologies, and it is difficult to disentangle technology per se from the larger concerns regarding multinational firms in general. After all, it is largely the multinational firms' know-how (technical, marketing, financial, and managerial expertise) that provides a competitive edge in supplying product and production process technology. It is this know-how that host countries wish to acquire, if not entirely then at least partially. From the earlier analysis, however, it should be clear that there are strong incentives for multinational firms to avoid sharing or transferring certain types of know-how, namely, the types that yield the economic rents. Host countries would like to have greater control and also would like to obtain a share of these rents (reduce the cost of technology). A sizeable number, therefore, have taken measures designed to alter their bargaining power in what they historically consider to have been a one-sided situation. Whether rightly or wrongly, the developing countries have tended to see themselves as weak and impotent in their dealings with multinational firms. Their concerns vis-a-vis technology acquisition can be listed as follows:

1. Technological dependence.
2. Too high a cost for technology.
3. Lack of progress toward an inventive capability of one's own.
4. Inability to obtain appropriate or suitable technologies.
5. Inability to achieve international competitiveness.

These concerns manifest themselves through the policies that host countries take toward foreign firms and toward the importation of specific products.

Most of the following characteristics are embedded in investment regulations and the selection of the priority industries that will receive incentives.

1. Job-creating ability, that is, labor intensity.
2. Export orientation, that is de-emphasis of import substitution.

3.   Nonindigenous technology, that is, new products or new processes to produce existing products, particularly if these technologies result in export capability.
4.   Local participation in ownership and management.
5.   Skill-creating capability, that is, upgrading of existing skills.
6.   Ability of the firm to tie into an international marketing network.
7.   Complementarity rather than competitiveness with local firms.

Some countries have very well-defined requirements for new foreign investments, particularly in those industry sectors enjoying incentives (tax holidays; low-interest loans; training grants; tariff protection; escape from customs duties on imported capital equipment, parts, and ingredients; tax rebates on exports; and tax credits for use of locally supplied capital equipment). There also may be requirements for existing firms to come into line with certain specifications on ownership, royalty rates, employment of nationals, local content, and export sales. Countries do bend these rules in cases considered quite desirable, however, because of the technology being transferred. Wholly-owned subsidiaries can be allowed and royalty rates on licenses may be allowed to exceed the guidelines. For example, the Philippines prefers joint ventures to wholly foreign-owned subsidiaries, but it will allow 100 percent foreign ownership. The Philippines also has an upper-bound guideline of 5 percent of gross sales on licensing royalty rates, but it will allow 7 percent or 8 percent. Whether 100 percent ownership and higher than 5 percent royalty rates are allowed depends very much upon the perceived value of the technologies being transferred to the country. Much the same attitude is displayed in Korea, Thailand, Malaysia, and several other developing countries.[17]

Most countries have some things in common in terms of the apparatus they install to review, monitor, and control technology transfers through direct foreign investment and certain contractual arrangements. They differ in terms of which industries are included in their respective plans. This is what one would expect, given that their resources, objectives, and priorities differ. Virtually all countries that have formalized their review procedures have some or all of the following paraphernalia to be applied to new investments.

---

[17]For a review of investment regulations, incentive programs, and so forth, see Thomas W. Allen, "Industrial Development Strategies and Foreign Investment Policies of the Southeast Asian and South Pacific Developing Countries," in R. Hal Mason (ed.), *International Business in the Pacific Basin* (Lexington, Mass.: Lexington Books, D. C. Heath and Co., 1978), pp. 51–91. See also Richard D. Robinson, *National Control of Foreign Business Entry* (New York: Praeger, 1976).

1. A set of industrial priorities.
2. Incentive programs tied to these industrial priorities.
3. A board of investments (or equivalent agency) to screen new investments.
4. An interagency screening process that usually covers incentives (board of investments), foreign exchange implications (ministry of finance or central bank), capital requirements and ownership structure (board of investments and ministry of finance), investment priorities and technology acquisition (ministry or board of science and technology, ministry of industry and commerce), import and export implications (ministry of trade), and licensing agreements and/or registration of patents and trademarks (board of science and technology and board of patents and commercial registrations).
5. A list of overcrowded industries.
6. An incentive program to disperse new industry away from congested urban centers.
7. A set of rules on ownership structure of the enterprise and the application of patented technology.
8. A list of industries open to nationals only.

In addition, some of the countries have plans under law by which foreign entities must reduce their share of ownership to some specified level by spinning off share (equity) capital to nationals within some specified time horizons. Also, there may be controls over how many expatriates may be employed as a proportion of the workforce, especially as a proportion of those positions involving technical and managerial skills. Through all of these devices there are several objectives being pursued, but it is apparent that the control over technology transfer by foreigners is at least an implicit objective of considerable importance.

It is largely typical that countries do exert some control over the following:

1. Industries open to foreign investment.
2. Ownership and financial structure of enterprises in which foreigners participate.
3. Nature and terms of licensing and franchising agreements.
4. Composition of the workforce and the amounts and types of training undertaken.
5. Location of new or expanding foreign enterprises.
6. Level of repatriated profits and service fees.

Through these controls, the countries can and do manipulate the owners of technology in terms of the types of technology transferred, the degree to which these are diffused or internalized by nationals, and the price paid for the use of these technologies. At the same time, however, there may be adverse side effects in terms of making certain desirable technologies unavailable to the country. The empirical evidence on which we could make a judgment on this aspect of technology transfer controls is virtually nonexistent. Four major tendencies are in evidence. First, there is considerable exchange of information among boards of investments regarding methods of control over foreign participation and technology transfer, as well as the bargains struck in making technology acquisitions. Second, there is a clear recognition that industries differ with respect to the value of their technologies and the terms under which these will be made available. Third, countries differ in terms of the degree to which they see the multinational firm as a vehicle through which national policies can be or should be implemented. Fourth, the countries, at least along some dimensions, see themselves as competing with one another in the acquisition of technology because they are attempting to attract or stimulate many of the same industries. Thus, while there are some areas of cooperation in the exchange of information among countries, there are also areas of competitiveness in their efforts to attract and obtain what are deemed to be particularly attractive industries and technologies.

Before closing this section, a word should be said about the role of the United Nations on the subject of technology transfer. The United Nations has been concerned with the problems of economic development almost from its inception. Over the years it has held several conferences on the subject of technology transfer, technology acquisition, technology creation, and the relation of these to economic development. Recently, the Group of 77 has suggested that multinational firms be subject to a code of conduct on technology transfers.[18] The objective to be achieved is a reduction in the monopolistic power of these firms over the application of technology. Presumably, acquisition costs would be reduced, access to technology improved, and the ability of developing countries to diffuse technology enhanced.

Any code that would be acceptable to the home countries (advanced countries for the most part) would have to be acceptable also to multinational firms and other owners of technology. The consequence is that there may be agreement on the notion of having a code but the developing and advanced countries may be poles apart as to what types of provisions such

---

[18]The Group of 77 is a group of developing countries that are General Assembly members and that initiated the push for a new international economic order to include a code of conduct for multinational firms with respect to their technology-transfer activities.

a code should contain. As is so often the case an effective code of conduct implies controls, but the owners of technology simply may refuse to supply it to any country that tries to impose the provisions of the code rigorously. Moreover, individual countries have shown themselves to be quite capable of dealing with multinational firms. The result simply may be that the issues surrounding an international code have become moot.

Home-Country Concerns and Reactions

It may seem ironic that host countries can and do argue that they are not getting their fair share in technology transfers while simultaneously home countries make the same argument. Of course, they each argue to the same conclusion on different grounds. Hosts argue that they have little or no control over multinational firms, that transactions for technology take place in imperfect markets and hence are too costly, that they cannot obtain the most desirable technologies, that they cannot acquire the ability to create technology because multinational firms throttle any incipient independent technological capability that arises within the host country, and that multinationals do not diffuse technology to local firms. The consequence, so the argument goes, is that the host does not actually acquire the technology, continues to pay monopoly rents to multinational firms, and is destined to remain technologically dependent upon the advanced countries and the technologically well-endowed enterprises harbored there. Despite these protests, several of the developing countries in Latin America and the Far East have shown themselves capable of attracting technology on favorable terms and exerting considerable control over the foreign firms supplying the technology. Some of these countries, including Taiwan, South Korea, Hong Kong, the Philippines, Singapore, Brazil, and Mexico are becoming exporters of certain types of technology, in their own right.

What about home countries?[19] They argue that by transferring technology multinational firms, do the following:

1. Build up production capability abroad and by so doing decrease exports from the home country and even increase imports by exporting from the new foreign facility back to the home country.
2. As a consequence of the first consideration, they eliminate jobs in the home country.
3. Reduce the home country's international competitiveness by mak-

---

[19]For a review of home country concerns, see John H. Dunning, "The Consequences of International Transfer of Technology by Transnational Corporations: Some Home Country Implications," paper prepared for the International Conference on Technology Transfer Control Systems, Phase II, University of Washington, Seattle, Washington, April 1979.

ing technological know-how accessible abroad to countries that do not contribute to the costs of developing new technologies and technological know-how.

4. Reduce the rate of economic growth in the home country.

These arguments are a form of partial analysis that may hold in the short run. When capital and/or technology move abroad, the level of employment of labor in the home country would be lower than it otherwise would have been, all other things remaining constant. Unfortunately, life is never so simple—all other things usually do not remain constant. From a purely nationalistic point of view, one might argue further that, should the home country fail to transfer capital and technology abroad to take advantage of lower-cost labor, some other country will do so. This assumes that there is not a complete monopoly in the supplying country, that is, there are competing sources of supply available to the host country. The consequence would be that international output would expand but the noninvesting country would lose some of its share of world production. Once equilibrium is reestablished, costs of production and international prices will be lower than before the transfer of resources took place. Consumers in the home country will obtain the product more cheaply than before and, if there is not complete specialization, welfare will have been improved. In any case, the home country will be forced to undergo adjustment regardless of whether it or another country is the supplier of the technology. Employment effects will occur such that there will be initial short-run unemployment but with long-run reallocation of labor into other activities. Any costs of retraining and the like will be borne by the home country.

Just as there is an optimum tariff in commodity trade, there also is an optimum tariff (or royalty rate) for technology transfer, whether that transfer is accomplished by licensing or capital investment.[20] The greater the monopoly power of the supplying country, moreover, the greater will be that optimum tariff.

There is another argument that may have more appeal for the introduction of home-country controls over technology transfers. Technological development, particularly in the United States, tends to be a subsidized activity. Through grants to universities and colleges, contracts with research

---

[20]For an examination of the impact of technology transfers abroad on domestic employment in the United States, see Rachel McCulloch and Janet L. Yellen, "Technology Transfer and the National Interest," seminar paper, Department of Economics, University of California, Los Angeles, May 1977. See also Rachel McCulloch, "Technology, Trade, and the Interests of Labor: A Short-Run Analysis of the Development and International Dissemination of New Technology," Discussion Paper No. 489, Harvard Institute of Economic Research, Harvard University, Cambridge, Mass., May 1977.

laboratories, and the like, the federal and state governments contribute to the development of new technology. The hope is that new products and processes will be discovered that in turn will either increase productivity in the production of existing products or elevate the quality of consumption through the introduction of new products, or both. This appears to have been the outcome of such tax-supported expenditures.

Free dissemination of the technology to all comers means that one country (the United States in this case) is subsidizing all users of the technology. Again, the optimum tariff argument can be used. To the degree that they are beneficiaries of the technology, foreign users should pay some share of the technology's cost. Normally, this would be the case in the typical life-cycle analysis, where it takes time for other countries to master the technology. They would pay the marginal cost of the product or service being offered in international trade, which would include the cost of the technology. The time needed for dissemination, is being shortened. For example, in a recent study of 406 innovations introduced in the United States between 1945 and 1975, only 12 percent of new innovations in the 1950 to 1954 period were transferred abroad within three years after their introduction in the U.S.[21] By the 1970 to 1975 period, 65 percent of new innovations had appeared in foreign countries within three years; that is foreign manufacturing plants already had begun competing with domestically owned plants. This shortening of the product life cycle, as the argument goes, reduces the period over which the home country can ammortize, through international trade, the investment in technology that led to the development of the innovation. Transfer of the technology to a foreign location, however, does not necessarily mean that the home country is made worse off, regardless of how shortened the life cycle becomes. The research and development to create an innovation could be done in one country and the manufacturing of the product done in another, with both countries gaining from the process. The country supplying the technology is compensated by lower prices to its consumers. It loses only if there are beneficial externalities that it could have captured if production had occurred at home but that it cannot capture if production occurs abroad.

Except for the optimum-tariff type of argument, arguments to reduce the outflow of technology, like those calling for reductions in trade or investment, are self-serving to some. They almost invariably support the appeals of special-interest groups.

[21]See William H. Davidson, "Trends in the International Transfer of U.S. Technology to Pacific Basin States," *Proceedings of the Academy of International Business Conference on Asia–Pacific Dimensions of International Business, (University of Hawaii, Office of Management Programs, 1979), pp. 86–95.*

Can Both Host and Home Countries Be Right?

Are there any circumstances in which the host and home countries can both be correct in their arguments? As a general rule, the answer is: Only if there is some form of government intervention or if there is imperfect competition. In the actual market situation there often is both intervention and imperfect competition. Also, suppose that the host country believes that there are large externalities to be captured by having the technology used inside its borders, when in fact the externalities are small or non-existent. Nevertheless, based on its belief that they are large, it subsidizes the entry of the technology. In this instance, the precepts of comparative advantage are violated and both countries are made worse off. The appropriate response of home countries in these circumstances would be to take countervailing measures to abort the transfer. Since much of technology transfer occurs in industries subsidized by host countries—especially among the developing countries—and since most home countries do not take countervailing measures, there are possibilities that technology transfer has been misplaced in many instances. Whether it has or not depends upon the beneficial externalities resulting from the transfer. As yet, there has been very little research into this aspect of technology transfer.[22]

The Suitability of Technology: A Continuing Dilemma

One major issue for developing countries is the suitability of the technologies being transferred. Most of the world's technological know-how is harbored in large firms headquartered in already-advanced countries. Most technologies also have been adapted over time to substitute capital for labor because labor has become more expensive relative to capital in advanced countries. These are not the conditions faced by developing countries. They have abundant supplies of unskilled labor and a scarcity of capital and high-level skills. It also appears, at least for the U.S. data, that technologies that use much capital per worker also may be skill intensive.[23] Developing countries may be doubly hampered in their efforts to hasten the process of economic development. Not only are they caught in the vicious circle of low income, low savings, and low capital accumulation, but also what little capital they are able to accumulate cannot be utilized efficiently because

[22]For some further aspects of conflict in technology transfer, see Chapter 17. For an examination of the costs of technology transfer to the owing and recipient enterprises, see David J. Teece, *The Multinational Corporation and the Resource Cost of International Technology Transfer, op. cit.*

[23]See Zvi Grilliches, "Capital–Skill Complementarity," *Review of Economics and Statistics,* 51:4, 1969, pp. 465–468.

existing technologies use capital and skilled labor in relation to unskilled labor in such a way that the available unskilled labor cannot be absorbed.

While we have very few well-conceived empirical studies on the choice of technology, it is nevertheless true that the capital and skills shortages confronting developing countries present a serious problem in the choice of technology, given that modern technologies tend to be both skill- and capital-intensive, relative to the factor endowments available to those countries.

One of the major problems is the use of indiscriminate industrialization policies in developing countries. Most have followed an import-substitution model of development by restricting imports and inducing investment to serve the local market. The result has been a proliferation of small, high-cost plants in most industries. This indicates a lack of adequate planning and control. If more attention had been paid to the selection of technology and to the market-size requirements of economically efficient plants, incentive systems could have been designed to attract those industries having the potential of becoming economically viable and able to compete internationally.

Right now, many developing countries wish to have the domestic capacity to produce chemical fertilizers and similar products where capital requirements per worker are high and economies of scale are great. Efficient-sized plants call not only for large amounts of capital relative to labor, but also for large markets and a ready source of raw materials. Does this mean that developing countries should concentrate only on those industries that are labor intensive and should shun those that are capital intensive? The answer is a qualified no. It is important to choose a mix of industries that, in aggregate, has a capital-to-labor and skilled-to-unskilled ratio that approximates the overall ratio in which the resources are available.

Figure 11-7 demonstrates the problem. We have three dimensions, one for unskilled labor, one for skilled labor, and one for capital. The ray from O to point C_1, S_1, U_1 indicates the amount of new capital, skilled labor, and unskilled labor the economy can make available for new projects this year. If the appropriate mix of projects can be found, all of the available resources can be employed. Suppose, however, that planners choose projects that in aggregate have the ratio of factor inputs represented by the ray from point O to point C_1, S_1, U_2; that is, the projects selected use techniques that are relatively skill and capital intensive. All of the available factors cannot be employed. Some unskilled labor remains unemployed. This is known as the "factor proportions problem."[24]

[24]For a classic treatment, see: Richard S. Eckaus, "The Factor Proportions Problem in Underdeveloped Areas," American Economic Review, 45:4, 1955, pp. 539–565.

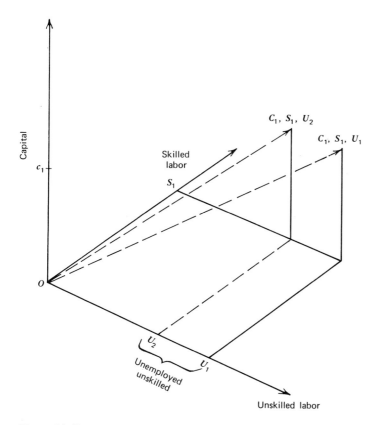

Figure 11–7.

There are other reasons why we might see such a choice. The government may establish incentives and penalties that favor capital-intensive techniques. For example, in already-developed countries, skills are readily available and are supplied in large degree by publicly supported educational systems or by the individual himself. In the developing countries the firm may have to supply many more of its needed skills through its own training programs. This elevates the cost of employing labor. Also, developing-country governments, to attract new investments, may use incentive systems that tend to subsidize the use of capital. As a consequence, the techniques chosen are too capital absorbing and too labor saving for the relative amounts of factors available. It is the induced change in factor price relationships that encourages private investors to choose the more capital-using technologies. The effect on the country, all other things being equal, will be to obtain a lower level of total output than otherwise would have been the case.

One must look at the choice of technology in a general equilibrium framework. Even though a capital-intensive technology may be the least-cost choice for one sector, the decision cannot be taken in isolation. One also must look at what the decision would do to the supplies of factors, particularly capital, then available to other sectors. Although it is true that a country can augment its savings by borrowing abroad, there are limits on how far this can be carried. In the long run, a country ultimately must fall back on its own resources. Today's borrowing must be repaid with tomorrow's saving. If today's borrowing, however, allows the country to become more productive, tomorrow's saving can be greater than it otherwise would have been; consequently, the country will be better off and able to grow more rapidly in the future.

Summary

In this chapter, we have given a definition of technology and have presented a model that links technological choice to relative factor prices where the the factors are defined simply as capital and labor. We have noted that there are many types of capital and labor, but that they all can be indexed into common units. Other variables enter the decision. Certainly market size is critical, since it determines the extent to which large-scale options can be considered. We also have observed, however, that not all industries are subject to economies of scale. Also, technological innovation cannot be ignored.

Empirical evidence shows that firms tend not to adapt technology when moving to developing countries if the gains from adaptation are small. We also discuss the effects of an inappropriate choice of technology on the host country. The host country must be cognizant of the proportions in which factors can be made available; however, an efficiently implemented use of external savings may allow the country to alter its factor proportions over time, thus increasing its rate of growth. This is the desire of host countries. If, however, there are no modern technologies that can accomodate the developing countries' factor proportions, these countries may be caught in a technological backwash.

The role of the multinational firm has been explored. There has been concern that multinational firms are reluctant to adapt technology, yet our own study indicates that their factor proportions in final output differ little from those of locally controlled firms.

Host countries are concerned about control of technology. Multinational firms own the technology and prefer to use direct investment as the vehicle to exploit it. This confronts host countries with a dilemma. They desire technology but wish not to become dependent on an externally controlled force.

There are few clear-cut, empirically tested propositions in the field of technology transfer. Many of the questions raised here call for continued study.

SELECTED READINGS

Baranson, Jack, *Technology and the Multinationals: Corporate Strategies in a Changing World Economy* (Lexington, Mass.: Lexington Books, D.C. Heath and Co., 1978).

Bergsten, C. Fred, Thomas Horst, & Theodore H. Moran, *American Multinationals and American Interests* (Washington, D.C.: Brookings Institution, 1978), Chapters 10 & 11.

Cohen, Benjamin I., *Multinational Firms and Asian Exports* (New Haven, Conn.: Yale University Press, 1975).

Dunning, John H., "Technology, United States Investment and European Economic Growth," in C. P. Kindleberger (ed.), *The International Corporation: A Symposium* (Cambridge, Mass: M.I.T. Press, 1970).

Eckhaus, Richard, "The Factor Proportions Problem in Underdeveloped Areas," *American Economic Review,* 45:4, 1955, pp. 539–565.

Kojima, Kiyoshi, "Transfer of Technology to Developing Countries–Japanese Type versus American Type," *Hitotsubashi Journal of Economics,* 17:2, 1977, pp. 1–14.

Lall, Sanjaya, "Transnationals, Domestic Enterprises and Industrial Structure in Host LDCs: A Survey," *Oxford Economic Papers* (N.S.), 30:2, 1978, pp. 217–248.

Lombard, Francois, "The Foreign Direct Investment Screening Process: The Case of Colombia," *Journal of International Business Studies,* 9:3, 1978, pp. 66–80.

Magee, Stephen P., "Factor Market Distortions Production and Trade: A Survey," *Oxford Economic Papers* (N.S.), 25:1, 1973, pp. 1–43.

Magee, Stephen P., "Multinational Corporations, the Industry Technology Cycle and Development," *Journal of World Trade Law,* 11:4, 1977, pp. 297–321.

Mason, R. Hal, *The Transfer of Technology and the Factor Proportions Problem: The Philippines and Mexico,* Research Report No. 10, United Nations Institute for Training and Research, New York, 1971.

Mason, R. Hal, "A Comment on Professor Kojima's Japanese Type versus American Type of Technology Transfer," *Hitotsubashi Journal of Economics,* 20:2, 1980, pp. 42–52.

Morawetz, David, "Employment Implications of Industrialization in Developing Countries: A Survey," *Economic Journal,* 84, September 1974, pp. 491–542.

Morley, Samuel A., & Gordon Smith, "The Choice of Technology: Multinational Firms in Brazil," *Economic Development and Cultural Change,* 25:2, January 1977, pp. 239–264.

Morley, Samuel A., & Gordon Smith, "Limited Search and the Technology Choices of Multinational Firms in Brazil," *Quarterly Journal of Economics,* 91:2, 1977, pp. 263–287.

Pack, Howard, "The Substitution of Labor for Capital in Kenyan Manufacturing," *Economic Journal,* 86, March 1976, pp. 45–58.

Pavitt, Keith, "The Multinational Enterprise and the Transfer of Technology," in John H. Dunning (ed.), *The Multinational Enterprise* (London: Allen and Unwin, 1971), pp. 61–65.

Peck, Merton J., "Technology," in Hugh Patrick and Henry Rosovsky (eds.), *Asia's New Giant: How the Japanese Economy Works* (Washington, D.C.: Brookings Institution, 1976), Chapter 8, pp. 525–585.

Pickett, James, D. J. C. Forsyth, & N. S. McBain, "The Choice of Technology, Economic Efficiency and Employment in Developing Countries, *World Development,* 2:3, 1974, pp. 47–54.

Reynolds Lloyd G., et al., *Wages, Productivity and Industrialization in Puerto Rico* (Homewood, Ill.: R. D. Irwin, 1965).

Robinson, Richard, *National Control of Foreign Business Entry* (New York: Praeger, 1976).

Strassman, W. Paul, *Technological Change and Economic Development: The Manufacturing Experience of Mexico and Puerto Rico* (Ithaca, N.Y.: Cornell University Press, 1968).

Teece, David J., *The Multinational Corporation and the Resource Cost of International Technology Transfer* (Cambridge, Mass.: Ballinger Publishing, 1976).

Vernon, Raymond, *The Technology Factor in International Trade* (New York: National Bureau of Economic Research, 1970).

Vernon, Raymond, *Storm Over the Multinationals* (Cambridge, Mass.: Harvard University Press, 1977), Chapter 3.

Wells, Louis T., "Economic Man and Engineering Man: Choice and Technology in a Low-Wage Country," *Public Policy,* Summer 1973.

Yeoman, Wayne A., "Selection of Production Processes for the Manufacturing Subsidiaries of U.S.-Based Multinational Corporations," Unpublished Doctoral Thesis, Harvard University, 1968.

CHAPTER 12

Evaluating Foreign Projects

INTRODUCTION

The analysis of investments in foreign projects presents many problems not encountered in domestic projects. Many of these problems stem from the fact that benefits or costs of the foreign project accrue in a different currency than that used to make the investment. The social and economic organization of foreign countries also might be unfamiliar to the investor. Finally, the investor must confront the government of the host country, often as an adversary, in negotiating over the distribution of benefits from the project. All of these elements serve to increase the risk of a foreign investment while increasing the complexity of the analysis. The intent of this chapter is to show how these differences between foreign and domestic investment can be incorporated into an analysis of individual investment opportunities.

Consider the problems of August Thyssen Huette A.G., the largest German steel manufacturer, when it considers investing in a first venture with Brazilian interests in a new steel mill in Brazil. Compare those problems with the ones of Volkswagen investing in a new plant in the United States. The currency used to make both investments, the German mark, has been appreciating in relation to both the U.S. dollar and the Brazilian cruzeiro. Inflation in the United States and Brazil is occurring at different rates than in Germany. How, then, do investors determine the real value of their investments?

Consider the position of a consortium of U.S. investors led by American Smelting and Refining Corporation investing in the Southern Peru Copper Corporation not long after other foreign investments in Peru, including some mining properties owned by members of the consortium, had been expropriated. The foreign exchange problems of that investment will be relatively small, since most of the benefits from the project will be from the export of copper for U.S. dollars. Nevertheless, the risks would appear to be substantial considering the history of government intervention in foreign investments.

Finally, consider the problems of analysis facing Unilever, the giant Dutch–British multinational firm, when investing in a food processing project in Yugoslavia. Yugoslavia is a socialist country where the means of production are controlled by the workers; thus, the "owners" of a plant are the workers in the plant. The workers form a Basic Organization of Associated Labor (BOAL), and select a Board of Directors, which in turn makes all of the policies of the enterprise. How does a foreign firm even invest and own property in such a system? How will profits and their distribution among foreign (Unilever) and local (BOAL) owners be determined?

A method is needed for analyzing all foreign investments in all of the diverse circumstances that may be encountered. The plan of this chapter is first to outline a general approach to analysis—that is, cost–benefit analysis—that should be familiar to most students. Methods of introducing into the analysis factors that are unique to foreign investment then will be outlined. The third section of the chapter will describe ways of analyzing risk and discuss some of the sources of risk in foreign investments. Finally, the chapter will conclude with a presentation of the contrasts between the way an investor might analyze the benefits and costs of a project, and the way in which the benefits and costs of the project may be viewed by the host country.

COST–BENEFIT ANALYSIS

Business firms have employed many investment evaluation techniques at one time or another, but the one most nearly able to encompass all factors relevant to a decision is discounted cash flow analysis, or cost–benefit analysis.

Cost–benefit analysis involves four main steps. The first, and most important, is to specify all of the relevant alternatives. Then the benefits and costs (investments and operating costs) must be estimated for each future year. In the third step these benefit and cost streams are discounted to obtain a net present value of each alternative. Finally, the net present value of the alternatives (including the alternative of doing nothing) have to be compared, and the alternative with the highest positive net present value must be selected for implementation.

Alternatives

The broad alternatives open to a manufacturing firm in serving a foreign market already have been discussed in Chapters 9 and 10. They are: exporting, licensing technology to another firm, or investing directly in the market. Volkswagen considered at least the first and third alternative ways of serving the U.S. market, but as the mark appreciated relative to the dollar, exports became too expensive and Volkswagen ultimately decided to invest.

The number and character of specific alternatives open to a manufacturing firm will depend on how markets are defined. A country suddenly may become a separate market in the eyes of foreign firms if tariff barriers are raised to restrict imports, as many developing countries have done. On the other hand, lowering trade barriers among a group of countries may broaden the relevant market so that it is possible for a foreign firm to consider alternative ways of serving the group rather than serving each individual country. The establishment of the European Economic Community, for example, enabled foreign firms to serve the entire market from one plant. The reduction of trade barriers among countries in the Andean Common Market (Bolivia, Colombia, Ecuador, Peru, and Venezuela) may have the same effect. Plants already have been established as joint ventures between foreign and local firms to produce pneumatic drills and specialty papers, among other items, for the entire market.

Formation of a large common market increases the investment alternatives open to foreign investors. The Ford Motor Company, for example, has distributed its production operations among member countries of the EEC but has completely integrated its operations. Engines are produced in one location, transmissions in another, and body stamping and assembly in still others. In fact, Ford operates in Europe as it does in the United States, with facilities distributed over the entire market area. That would not have been possible without the common market.

A similar integration of automobile production is being developed in the Andean Common Market. Prior to the Common Market, Peru and Colombia each had automobile assembly plants producing a few cars. Since the markets were small, the plants were inefficient and had to import most of the components as "completely knocked down (ckd)" kits. With the advent of the Andean Common Market, an integrated automobile program has been developed for the market area. Each country is assigned one or two classes of vehicles for exclusive production in the entire market, and has to select one firm to produce the assigned vehicle and various components (engines, transmissions, axles, and so forth). The countries are allowed to make agreements with other members for the sharing of production, so that one plant can be established to produce components, such as transmissions, for the entire market.

The automobile program in the Andean Common Market opens up for foreign automobile companies many alternatives that did not exist before. Besides allowing the production, for the entire market area, of a particular model in one country, it also raises the possibility of agreements among countries that would permit a more complete integration of production in the market, as has been done in Europe. General Motors already has taken advantage of this possibility. It has signed agreements with Venezuela and Ecuador whereby GM will build a plant in Venezuela to produce engines and one to produce transmissions in Ecuador. The plants will supply both countries, as well as produce for export outside the Andean Common Market. It would be a useful exercise for the students to formulate the alternatives open to General Motors in the Andean Common Market, and then to follow the strategy actually chosen.

Firms invest abroad not only to serve the foreign market but also to produce for their home market at a lower cost. The U.S. tariff code facilitates this type of investment because tariffs are assessed only on the value added to raw materials and subassemblies that are shipped to a foreign plant for processing and then exported back to the United States. Electronics firms in the United States have taken advantage of this provision by establishing plants in countries with low wages, where components made in the United States are assembled and exported back to the United States. Clothing manufacturers have shipped cut cloth to low-wage countries, where it has been sewn into garments and shipped back.

Mining firms, unlike manufacturing firms, have fewer alternatives because they have to invest where the mineral deposits are located; however, a wide range of alternative deposits exists for most minerals, and there are alternatives for exploration. Perhaps more importantly, there are alternatives to be considered in the location of processing facilities. Bauxite, for example, is made first into alumina, which then is smelted to make aluminum. Alumina may be made at the bauxite mine, or elsewhere. Another location altogether may be chosen for aluminum production. Many aluminum firms mine bauxite at one location, make alumina at another, and make aluminum at a third. Aluminum smelting uses a lot of power, so the third stage usually is located where cheap power is available.

Firms usually do not identify all available alternatives when evaluating foreign opportunities, for costs limit the search for alternatives. Even the cost of designing a complicated plant may be several million dollars, so that it would be prohibitively expensive to evaluate all possible plant sizes and locations. Instead, firms usually consider foreign operations in response to some problem that is raised, such as a threat to an export market from an increase in tariffs of the importing country. They evaluate only those alternatives that will enable them to deal with the specific problem, using their general knowledge of the industry and the region involved to formulate what appear to be relevant alternatives. Of course, in the process, they often exclude alternatives that should be considered. The formulation of the relevant alternatives is probably a more important part of the decision-making process than the application of sophisticated methods to analyze the alternatives.

Measuring Benefits

Benefits and costs come in many shapes and sizes, and considerable ingenuity is needed, particularly in international projects, to specify them correctly. Firms incur costs in foreign projects in order to obtain benefits in the form of sales, fees, and reduction in other costs. Volkswagen may invest in the United States in order to increase sales and also to reduce the cost of supplying the U.S. market. A hotel-management firm such as Hilton or Western International may invest in the equity of a hotel in Mexico, not so much for the returns on equity, but for the fees that they obtain from managing the hotel.

Both benefits and costs of a new operation are measured relative to what would have happened without the new initiative. The benefits of foreign projects are the *additional* sales or fees, or the lower costs relative to those that would have been incurred had the project not been implemented. It is important to stress that benefits are measured relative to what would have happened *without* the project, not *before* the project. Sales or costs that occur before the project is implemented may be a completely misleading guide to what would have happened without the project. Sales, for example, may have grown even without the establishment of a foreign subsidiary, so that attributing all additional sales to the investment in the subsidiary would be overstating benefits.

Volkswagen would have made sales in the United States without its new assembly plant, by supplying the market from plants in Germany and perhaps Brazil. Building the new plant, of course, frees capacity in those plants for sales elsewhere. The benefits of the new assembly plant, therefore, would depend on three main elements:

1. The quantity and price of sales expected from the new plant.

2. The quantity and price of sales that would have occurred without the new plant.
3. The quantity and price of sales that will be possible from released capacity.

Suppose that Volkswagen expects to sell 500,000 units from the new facility at a net price of $4,500 per unit, and that the plant will take two years to reach full capacity. At the same time, suppose that the same number of units could be sold when supplied from foreign plants, but only at a net price of $4,250 because of the transport costs incurred and tariffs paid on imports. Finally, assume that the released capacity can be used to supply other, more distant, markets but only at a lower net price of $4,000 because of higher transport costs. The net benefit of the investment, then, would be $2,125 million per year, composed of a $125 million gain on the sale of 500,000 units produced in the new facility at a higher net price ($4,500 rather than $4,250), and $2,000 million on the sales of 500,000 units from released capacity at $4,000 per unit.

It is useful to note that the benefits depend most heavily on the uses to which the existing capacity can be put once the new plant is in operation and on the price differential of supplying the market with imports as compared with local production. The price differential is relatively small because tariffs are low and transport is efficient. Where there are larger tariffs (or quotas on imports), or transportation is inefficient, benefits of local production will be larger because the price differential will be larger.

In this example, sales directly associated with the project ($2,250 million) overstate the benefits because they exceed the additional sales Volkswagen may expect from making the investment. That is the case even though sales made in the United States as a result of the investment are expected to be made at a higher net price to Volkswagen ($4,500 rather than $4,250). The reason is that existing capacity can be used only to supply sales at a lower net price ($4,000) than Volkswagen would get if it continued to supply the U.S. market from the existing capacity.

Sales from export-oriented projects also may overstate benefits of the project if the sales reduce either the quantity or the price of sales from other facilities owned by the firm. For example, exports of nickel by International Nickel (INCO) from new mines in Guatemala or Indonesia may substitute for production from its Canadian mines. Moreover, expanded capacity and production from the new mines may depress the world market price of nickel, thus reducing sales of existing mines. As another example, a new hotel may divert customers from other hotels owned by the same chain. In these cases, the sales associated with the new investment have to be reduced by the negative effect on other operations of the investing firm, in order to arrive at a realistic estimate of the benefits. Of course, diversion of sales from other plants also will reduce the variable costs of these plants, and that reduction should be counted as a benefit of the new investment.

In fact, the principal benefit of an investment may be lower costs. Investments by U.S. electronics firms and clothing firms in assembly operations overseas had the purpose of reducing manufacturing costs. An important, although not the principal, benefit of many overseas investments is to reduce inventory costs of supplying a distant market. These benefits will be substantial where supply lines are long and storage is costly, as in the case of perishable food products.

Measuring Costs

Costs usually are divided into two main components: investment costs and operating costs. Investment costs are the value of resources put into long-lived assets such as buildings and machinery. Other items, including preoperating expenses, interest coming due during construction, net working capital, and provision for escalation and contingencies, also are usually included in investment costs because sufficient financing has to be raised to cover both these costs and the losses incurred during start-up. Interest paid during construction, however, should not be counted as a part of investment costs when the net present value of a project is calculated. The process of discounting imputes a cost-of-capital employed, and inclusion of any interest payments in the costs of the project to be discounted would be double counting. Likewise, price escalation should not be included as part of investment costs if the analysis is done in constant prices, as is the usual procedure.

Operating costs are the value of current inputs, such as labor, raw materials, and utilities, that are needed for production. While not necessarily wholly variable, the magnitude of operating costs is related to the level of production. The contribution of operating costs to total value of output will vary greatly among products. In the case of labor-intensive products such as garment manufacture, operating costs (mainly labor and cloth inputs) will account for a large proportion of the value of output. In capital-intensive products such as petrochemicals, on the other hand, operating costs will be a lower proportion of the value of output, mainly because capital costs are so large.

Resources used in a project, either for capital or operating costs, are valued in terms of their opportunity costs, that is, by their value in alternative uses. In most instances the opportunity cost of a resource is simply its market price, since that is the amount the firm must give up to obtain command of the resource. Sometimes, however, the opportunity cost may be greater than the market price. For example, the opportunity cost of using executive talent in an overseas project may not be just the salary that is paid the executive. If similar executives cannot be obtained at the same salary, the opportunity cost to the firm may be higher than his salary. The executive in his present position may produce earnings for the firm that exceed his salary. Consequently, when similar executives are not available, use of the executive in the foreign project will reduce the firm's current earnings by an amount that is greater than his salary. That amount is the opportunity cost of using the executive and hence must be taken into account when estimating costs for the new overseas project.

In a few instances, where there is no market for resources owned by the firm, their opportunity cost in an overseas project may be little more than zero. For example, if the resource otherwise would be unemployed, the firm loses nothing by using it overseas. If equipment is obsolete in one country and can be sold only for scrap, then its opportunity cost is merely its value as scrap.

As with benefits, costs are measured relative to what would have occurred if the project had not been done. A U.S. drug firm such as Eli Lilly usually will not have to incur additional research expenditures to produce one of its standard products in Europe; thus, corporate research expenditures should not be allocated to a European investment, even though Lilly will want to price its products overall to yield a return on its research investment. Should a product be adapted to a specific market, however, the costs of adaptation should be charged against the benefits when a project to serve the market is being investigated.

In conclusion, several general concepts should be kept in mind when initiating an analysis of a foreign project. The first is that the costs and benefits of any alternative must be viewed from the perspective of the entire firm, rather than just the particular project. Second, benefits and costs must be measured in relation to what would have happened had the project not been initiated. Projects may affect prices of products as well as quantities, and these price effects must be taken into account as well. The unique characteristics of foreign projects are outlined in the following sections.

FOREIGN INVESTMENTS

Foreign projects are distinguished from those at home by two major characteristics. The first is that at least some of the costs incurred, or benefits obtained, are in a currency that is different either from the one used to make the investment or from the one the firm wishes to use in making dividend payments to shareholders. Exchange rates, therefore, intervene to complicate the analysis of foreign projects and add another factor that will influence the results of the project. The second distinguishing characteristic of foreign projects (whether they be investments, licenses, management contracts, and so on) is simply their foreignness: the firm is operating as an outsider in a different environment. These operations are subject to intervention by the government of the host country because the firm is foreign. Moreover, economic relationships in the foreign country may be different from those the firm is used to at home. Ownership forms may be different, for example, as is the case in socialist countries such as Yugoslavia. Relationships between product prices and prices of inputs such as labor will be different, and will change in different ways than the firm is used to in the United States, so that it may be necessary and desirable for the firm to choose a different production technology, as was discussed in Chapter 11. All of these factors introduce new elements into the analysis of foreign operations and create additional sources of risk. Suggestions are made in this section as to how they might be incorporated into a cost–benefit analysis.

Inflation, Devaluation, and Relative Prices

Firms investing or undertaking any other kinds of operations in foreign countries usually are interested ultimately in recovering returns from their activities in their home currencies; thus, an American firm is interested in getting returns in dollars, and a German firm is interested in profits in marks. At least some of the benefits or costs of an overseas project, however, will be denominated in a different currency; therefore, a firm, as it evaluates a foreign project, is faced squarely with the problem of converting one currency into another.

The rates at which one currency can be converted into another, and restrictions on such conversions, can be the dominant determinant in the success or failure of a foreign project. Changes in exchange rates can have marked effects on the real benefits and costs of a project measured in terms of the home currency of the firm involved. Restrictions on the ability of the firm to convert profits and fees from a foreign currency to its home currency likewise could be of overriding importance. Exchange rates and exchange restrictions have to be introduced explicitly, therefore, into a cost–benefit analysis of a project.

There are many reasons for changes in the exchange rates between two currencies, but the most important is likely to be differences in rates of inflation in the two countries. If prices are rising faster in the United

States than in Germany, it would be expected that the dollar would have to depreciate in value relative to the mark; that is, fewer marks would be needed to buy a dollar. Inflation and changes in exchange rates are bound inexorably together.

Several methods are used by firms to incorporate inflation and changes in exchange rates into the evaluation of foreign projects. One approach, widely used, is essentially to ignore the problem and assume that all relative prices will remain the same despite inflation. It is assumed by those who use this approach that the exchange rates between two currencies will change in exact proportion to changes in price levels in the two countries. In addition, it is assumed that all input and output prices will remain in the same relationship despite the inflation. In the case of a cement plant, for example, it is assumed that as inflation proceeds, cement prices will change at the same rate as fuel prices.

The problem with this approach, of course, is that factors other than relative rates of inflation enter into the determination of exchange rates, as has been seen in preceding chapters (see Chapters 3 through 5, particularly Chapter 4), so that the relationship between exchange rates and inflation may not be perfect. Foreign capital inflows enabled Brazil to maintain a 32 percent per year rate of inflation between 1972 and 1978, while the exchange rate was devalued by only 26 percent per year. Improvement in the terms of trade as coffee prices increased enabled Colombia to hold the exchange rate virtually constant in 1977, even though inflation ran at almost 30 percent.

Even if prices in general increase at the same speed as the exchange rate depreciates, it is almost certain that the particular prices relevant to an individual project will not change at the same rate. It is the changes in these prices that must be predicted and, along with changes in the exchange rate, incorporated into the cost–benefit analysis.

In order to take explicit account of differences in the rates at which exchange rates and product and input prices change, explicit projections of prices and exchange rates should be made. Using these projections, all benefits and costs are projected and denominated in (possibly different) currencies. If an American firm is doing the analysis, costs and benefits in foreign currencies then would be converted to dollars using the projected exchange rates. The results would be a project net benefit stream expressed in current dollars. This stream then would be discounted to determine net-present-dollar value of the project. Since revenues and costs are expressed in terms of current dollars, care should be taken to adjust the firm's cost of capital for the dollar inflation rate. For example, if the firm's real cost of capital is 5 percent and the rate of inflation in the United States is expected to be 5 percent, the discount rate should be about 10 percent.

The cost–benefit analysis of a plant to produce purified terephthalic acid (PTA) in Mexico will illustrate what is required. PTA is the main raw material in the production of polyester fiber and is produced in turn from paraxylene, a petrochemical derived ultimately from the refining of crude oil. A company known as TEMEX was formed in Mexico as a joint venture to produce PTA. The main shareholders of TEMEX are Celanese Mexicana (CELMEX) (a Mexican textile producer that is itself a joint venture between Celanese Corporation and Mexican interests), two Mexican Government financial institutions (Nacional Financiera (NAFINSA) and SOMEX), and Amoco Chemicals Corporation of the United States. Amoco is one of the largest producers of PTA worldwide and is the technical partner in the project.

The project will produce 135,000 tons of PTA from paraxylene, to be purchased from Petroleos Mexicanos (PEMEX) and supplied by pipeline from a giant new PEMEX petrochemical complex located on the southeast Gulf coast of Mexico. The TEMEX plant was designed at a scale large enough to take advantage of economies of scale. Consequently, in the first years of operation, TEMEX will have to export a significant part of its output in order to utilize its capacity.

The total cost of the project is expected to be about $100 million, of which half is for machinery and equipment. Engineering and technical assistance are capitalized and constitute another important element of capital costs. Well over half of total costs, including much of the equipment and its erection, are expected to be incurred in Mexico and paid in pesos. Other equipment and technical assistance will be purchased in the United States in dollars.

In order to assess the financial viability of this project, it is necessary to project the following items:

1. Investment costs:
   a. Equipment costs in the United States.
   b. Equipment costs in Mexico.
   c. Construction costs in Mexico.
2. Sales:
   a. Prices of PTA in Mexico.
   b. Prices of PTA in the world market.
3. Operating costs:
   a. Prices of paraxylene from PEMEX.
   b. Prices of other raw materials.
   c. Wage rates.

The critical elements in the evaluation of the project are the projections of the future prices of PTA in Mexico and abroad, relative to prices for equipment and raw materials. In 1978, when the project was being appraised, petrochemical prices on the world market were depressed in relation to both costs of raw materials and construction costs. Of course, by restricting imports, the Mexican Government could enable TEMEX to charge prices above the level on world markets. The profitability of the project also could be enhanced if the raw materials prices were held below world market levels by PEMEX.

The relationship between Mexican inflation and the exchange rate of the peso will be a critical factor determining profitability of the project for foreign investors, but also for domestic investors. If prices of PTA and paraxylene in Mexico increase as rapidly as the rate of inflation, profits on domestic sales will increase at the same rate. If, at the same time, the exchange rate depreciates at a rate equal to the difference between the Mexican and U.S. inflation rates, profits on domestic sales expressed in terms of dollars will grow at the dollar inflation rate; that is, profits will be constant in real terms, and inflation with devaluation will have no effect on real profits. The same will be true of profits on export sales if prices of exports are increasing at the same rate as general inflation in the United States.

A long string of assumptions have to be valid, however, for the real value of dollar profits to be unaffected by inflation and devaluation in Mexico. What happens if there is 15 percent inflation in Mexico and 5 percent inflation in the United States, but the exchange rate depreciates by only 5 percent? Operating profits on domestic sales of TEMEX expressed in pesos then would increase by 15 percent (assuming domestic prices of paraxylene and PTA also increase by 15 percent). When converted to dollars, these profits would increase by about 10 percent, which is faster than the rate of dollar inflation, so that there would be an increase in the real dollar value of profits on domestic sales.

There is a different story with regard to export sales. Assuming export prices increase at the dollar inflation rate of 5 percent, operating profit of these sales still would decline in real dollar terms because the cost of raw material, which is purchased with pesos, would increase by 10 percent (i.e., 15 percent peso inflation minus 5 percent depreciation).

The net effect of these divergent influences depends on the relative importance of export and domestic sales and the importance of local costs in relation to sales prices. In a heavily export-oriented project, the reduced real-dollar profits on export sales would outweigh the gains on local sales, particularly where local costs are high relative to sales. In the example, however, export sales are relatively small, so that devaluation at a slower rate than would be indicated by the relative rate of inflation would increase the real value of profits when translated to dollars. This project thus would present favorable opportunities for foreign investors, under the assumed circumstances.

The assumption of relatively slow devaluation may be quite valid in Mexico in the coming years. With the recent petroleum discoveries, an increase is expected in exports of petroleum and petroleum products. The increasing share of petroleum exports will improve the terms of trade for Mexico so that the value of the peso will not need to reflect completely the relative inflation rates. If inflation were higher in Mexico than in the United States, for example, the peso would not have to depreciate as rapidly as otherwise would have been necessary to maintain balance-of-payments equilibrium. In that case, the example shows that production for the local Mexican market would be more profitable for foreign (and local) investors than would production for export. If, on the other hand, depreciation of the exchange rate were more rapid than indicated by relative inflation rates, production for export would be favored.

It is clear from the example that several factors beyond the control of the investors will determine, at least in part, the outcome of the investment. Unpredictable movements of exchange rates in relation to price levels, in particular, contribute substantially to the risk of foreign projects. Methods for taking risk explicitly into account will be discussed later in this chapter.

The business judgments incorporated in projections of prices and exchange rates are the essence of project appraisal and are much more important in themselves than the mechanical technique of incorporating them in cost–benefit analysis. They involve judgments that ultimately can be made only by decision makers. Will copper prices recover in real terms sufficiently to justify investment in a new copper mine? Will petrochemical prices increase relative to capital costs? Will aluminum prices remain high in relation to bauxite and conversion costs? Will the Mexican peso appreciate in real terms? These are the crucial types of questions that must be answered as part of an effective foreign project appraisal.

Once the price and exchange-rate projections have been made, incorporating inflation and changes in exchange rates in cost–benefit analysis involves only a few technical issues. First, inflation itself will require increases over time in working capital investments in a project. As inflation proceeds, accounts payable, accounts receivable, and inventories will have to increase in nominal terms, and additional investments will have to be made to finance the increased current assets. These additional investments are costs of the project and have to be counted as such in the cost–benefit analysis. They may offset, wholly or in part, any gains due to inflation and slower depreciation of the exchange rate, if that is indeed what happens.

The additions to working capital required by a project may be completely different from the accounting losses that may arise from the

application of standard accounting principles to a situation involving inflation and devaluation. The accounting approach requires the calculations of
"losses" of working capital that are due to devaluation. Those losses equal
the difference in working capital (current assets minus current liabilities)
converted to dollars at the old and new exchange rates. Such accounting
losses, of course, do not necessarily equal the additional input of resources
needed to maintain working capital at a level needed to conduct business.

The differences between the two approaches reflect the fact that
accountants are concerned with the liquidation value of an enterprise, while
cost–benefit analysis attempts to measure the accumulated operating value
of an enterprise over its life; thus, the accountant calculates how much
liquidation value would be lost due to depreciation of the currency, while
in the cost–benefit analysis an estimate is made of the additional investment
needed to maintain operations in the face of an inflating price level. As long
as the rate of inflation and the rate of currency depreciation are different,
the "losses" calculated by the two methods will be different.

Government Intervention and Relative Prices

Government intervention in business certainly is not unknown, even in the
home countries of firms engaged in international business. All kinds of
restrictions are put on business operations in the United States, for example,
including those relating to the environment and prices. There even have
been examples of expropriation for public use and necessity in many home
countries.

In the case of foreign operations, however, the character of government
intervention is often different, because it is directed specifically at the
foreign firms. Governments are concerned about the impact of foreign firms
on the people of the country; therefore, they interpose themselves more
often between foreigners and local citizens. Governments are concerned
about the total benefits from a project and the distribution of those benefits
between local and foreign citizens. For this reason, treatment of foreign
firms is likely to be different from treatment of local firms.

There are many ways in which governments intervene in the business
of foreign firms, not all of which will be discussed in detail in this chapter.

- They influence relative prices of inputs and outputs through tariffs,
  quotas, taxes, and subsidies.
- They provide direct subsidies and grants (to be discussed in Chapter
  13 on financing of foreign investment).
- They intervene in foreign exchange markets.

- They impose performance requirements relating to such things as exports and employment of local citizens.
- They regulate ownership of local firms by foreign firms, restricting the extent of foreign ownership, sometimes forcing divestment of foreign ownership, and, at the extreme, expropriating the operation.

The effect of changes in relative prices due to such things as tariffs is easy to incorporate in a cost–benefit analysis, to the extent that they can be predicted. Tariffs on imported inputs increase costs and thus reduce net benefits. A tariff on the finished product may have several effects. It permits the investing firm to raise its price and hence, to experience increased revenues, should everything else remain the same. Other things may not remain the same, however. A higher price probably would reduce the quantity that could be sold. The final effect that higher prices may have on revenue, therefore, depends on the relationship between price and quantity sold. If the quantity sold is very sensitive to price, net revenue may fall if the price is increased. In that situation the firm would not wish to raise its prices, despite the imposition of a protective tariff. This, however, usually is not the case; instead, the tariff, under most circumstances, allows the firm to capture monopolistic profits.

Governments sometimes restrict the amount of profits a foreign firm can repatriate to reduce pressure on the balance of payments of the host country, and to increase the country's benefits from foreign investments. A large number of different restrictions have been used over the years. Most of them can be classified into the following three general types:

1. Taxes on dividends.
2. Repatriation at a less favorable exchange rate.
3. Specific limitations on the amount of dividends that can be repatriated.

All of these restrictions tend to reduce the value of an investment to the foreign investor. Taxes directly reduce the amount of earnings that can be repatriated; however, the same effect can be obtained by forcing the foreign firm to convert dividends at a less favorable exchange rate. Suppose, for example, that the subsidiary of a U.S. firm operating in South America has earned 100,000 pesos. At an exchange rate of 4 pesos per dollar, and a dividend tax of 20 percent, the net repatriation would be $20,000 [i.e., (100,000) (¼) (80 percent)]. The same result can be achieved by forcing the firm to convert the 100,000 pesos at an exchange rate of 5 pesos per dollar, while all other transactions are allowed to use a rate of 4 pesos to the dollar.

Quantitative limitations on the amount of dividends to be repatriated have effects that are more difficult to evaluate. When the firm cannot repatriate profits, it either must accumulate idle balances or must reinvest retained earnings in the host country, whether it wants to or not. The effect of this limitation then depends on the rate of return that can be earned on these unrepatriated and reinvested funds.

One type of quantitative restriction often employed is that of limiting the repatriation of profits to a percentage of net worth. The earnings that cannot be repatriated are reinvested and contribute to increased earnings in the future, while adding to net worth and thus expanding the base on which future calculations of allowable repatriations are based. The effect of these restrictions, therefore, is to force reinvestment. The net present value of the project to the foreign firm will be reduced if the rate of return on this forced reinvestment is lower than the return on the original project.

Governments also impose specific performance requirements on foreign firms, which may take several forms:

- Domestic content requirements.
- Export requirements.
- Employment requirements.

Many countries require foreign investors in the automobile industry to acquire or produce a certain proportion of the finished value of the product in the local economy. In the case of Spain, for example, the local content required is 90 percent. It is lower in the Andean Common Market (about 65 percent), in recognition that the market is smaller and unable to support efficient plants for such operations as metal stampings. Ford Motor Company negotiated an arrangement with Spain in 1976 that permitted Ford to have less than 90 percent local content, but in return Ford agreed to limit sales in the local market in any year to 10 percent of automobile registrations in the previous year. As a result, Ford agreed to export a substantial portion of the output of its Spanish plant.

These types of requirements, if they have any effect, force firms to do things they otherwise would not do. The export requirements, for example, could force firms like Ford to export at prices that do not cover full costs. Ford may be willing to submit to these types of requirements, of course, because it is getting other types of benefits from the project, including specific incentives. The incentives may be in the form of a protected domestic market, financing on favorable terms, or inputs at favorable prices. Foreign firms also may be willing to submit to these performance requirements to make the project more attractive to the host country in comparison to projects proposed by other firms. In an era of competition among foreign investors (see Chapter 8), host countries will be able to improve the terms on which projects are implemented. Methods used by host countries to evaluate projects are discussed in the last section of this chapter.

The effects of performance requirements are incorporated easily into the cost–benefit analysis of the project. If exports are required, they are valued at the export price that can be obtained. If local labor has to be substituted for expatriates, the effect may be felt in higher training costs and lower output (of course, it is often the case that local labor, even in managerial posts, is fully as productive as expatriates, and the performance requirements are needed only to help foreign firms to overcome irrational preferences). Performance requirements thus may result in either reduced benefits or increased costs to the firm, perhaps offset by other incentives.

The final type of government intervention into projects sponsored by foreign firms includes all of the various ways in which governments regulate the ownership status of an investment. Government intervention can, at the minimum, force the foreign firm to put its money in earlier than it would have liked. This will tend to reduce the net present value of the project to the foreign firm by increasing the period between the investment and the completion of the project, when the benefits begin. Governments also intervene to force divestment of ownership after some period in the life of the project. Foreign investments in the Andean Common Market must divest at least 51 percent of total equity to citizens of the member countries within 15 to 20 years after the project is initiated. The divestment may be possible only at a price of shares that is below the value of expected future earnings. In that case, the effect of divestment is to reduce the total net present value of the project.

The ultimate intervention by governments in ownership, of course, is expropriation. Governments have the right, in international law, to take private property for beneficial purposes. They have an obligation, at the same time, to compensate the foreign investor for the loss; however, not all governments fully accept that obligation and hence the actual loss from expropriation is determined by the amount of compensation provided.

There have been a large number of expropriations since 1960, as may be seen in Table 12–1. Many of them occurred in former British colonies after independence, when foreign-owned banks and insurance companies were nationalized. Almost half of the U.S. firms expropriated were in Latin America, and the extent to which compensation was paid in these expropriations is not known.

Host countries expropriate foreign-owned property for a variety of economic and political reasons. One noted economist, Martin Bronfenbren-

Table 12–1 Number of Expropriations between 1960 and 1976

		Sector of Expropriated Firm					
	Total	Mining	Petroleum	Agriculture	Manufacturing	Banking/ Insurance	Other
Number	1,369	80	220	272	221	349	121

	Home Country of Expropriated Firm				
	Total	U.S.	U.K.	France	Other
Number	1,447[a]	342	521	146	438

[a] Greater than 1369 because in some cases the parent company had more than one nationality.
Source: U.N., *Transnational Corporations in World Development*, March 1978, Annex Tables 111–29 and 111–30.

ner,[1] has written that there is always an economic incentive for countries to expropriate without paying compensation for the taken property. The country avoids paying interest and dividends on the confiscated foreign capital and simultaneously retains use of the assets. Consequently, the net benefits available to the taking country, from the firm's assets, are increased by confiscation.

If valid, Bronfenbrenner's conclusions would spell the end of private foreign direct investment, since any firm foolish enough to make an investment would have it taken away immediately. Fortunately, there are other factors to be put on the scales when host countries weigh the economic costs and benefits of expropriation. First, expropriation will discourage other foreign firms from making private investments in the country. If such investment would produce any benefits for the country, its loss would involve a real economic loss that would have to be weighed against the gains from expropriation. In addition, the expropriated firm may provide a real service to the host country that it cannot provide for itself. For example, the firm may have access to export markets not otherwise open to the host country. The foreign firm also may supply technical know-how or managerial talent not available to the host country from other sources; that is, the firm has unique capabilities. If the country were to expropriate investments of this kind, the advantages it obtained from the foreign firm's unique contributions would be lost. These losses have to be counted against any gains from expropriation.

[1]Martin Bronfenbrenner, "The Appeal of Confiscation in Economic Development," *Economic Development and Cultural Change*, 3:3, 1955, pp. 201–218.

Differences in the special services provided by foreign firms may tend to explain why expropriation takes place in some industries but not in others. For example, copper mines have been a tempting target for expropriation because foreign copper companies have few special skills or resources to contribute that the host countries cannot provide themselves. Many copper-producing countries, such as Chile and Peru, have developed their own technical and managerial expertise for the mining industry. Marketing, likewise, presents no special problems because there are many relatively small buyers of copper, and a well-developed institutional market mechanism exists in the London Metals Exchange through which the product can be sold. It is not surprising, therefore, that even with the overthrow of the Allende Government in Chile the copper mines were not returned to their former owners.

The situation is quite different in the case of bauxite and aluminum. Markets are controlled by a few aluminum refiners, and bauxite is available widely throughout the world. A government that expropriates a bauxite mine would have a hard time selling the output, even if it could operate the mines. In these circumstances, the cost of expropriation to the host government could be quite high, and it is not surprising that there have been few instances of expropriations in the aluminum industry.

Expropriation is a frightening prospect to foreign investors. Its actual effect, however, on the net present value of an investment depends on two factors: (1) the timing of its occurrence in the life of the investment, and (2) the amount of compensation paid by the expropriating country. Within the capital budgeting framework developed earlier, the effect of expropriation is to cut off both benefits and costs. If this event were to occur early in the life of the project, the loss would be substantial, since there would be little time to generate enough cash flow to offset the project's large initial capital costs. On the other hand, if the expropriation occurred after the project had been in operation for some time, its effect would be less important because some cash inflows would have been realized to offset the initial capital costs. Moreover, if paid compensation does reflect expected future earnings beyond the date of expropriation, the effect of the expropriation on net present value would be reduced to the vanishing point.

An example can be used to demonstrate both the effect of expropriation timing and the amount of compensation on a project's net present value. Table 12–2 gives the net benefits of a project to produce nitrogen fertilizer in Brazil, plus the present value of net benefits in each year, assuming a 5 percent real cost of capital. The net benefits are negative in the early years, reflecting the high capital expenditure, and then increase as production begins to increase toward full capacity in the eighth year.

Each entry in Table 12–3 then, is calculated by summing annual net

Table 12-2   Net Present Value of a Fertilizer Project in Millions of Dollars at 5 Percent Cost of Capital

Year	Net Benefits (1)	Discount Factors (2)	Present Values (3)
1973	−35.0	1.00	−35.0
1974	−36.0	1.05	−34.3
1975	1.8	1.10	1.6
1976	4.4	1.16	3.8
1977	9.6	1.22	7.9
1978	12.3	1.28	9.6
1979	14.8	1.34	11.0
1980	20.0	1.41	14.3
1981	20.0	1.48	13.6
1982	20.0	1.55	12.9
1983	20.0	1.63	12.3
1984	20.0	1.71	11.7
1985	20.0	1.80	11.1
1986	20.0	1.89	10.6
1987	20.0	1.98	10.1
1988	20.0	2.08	9.6
1989	27.0	2.19	12.3
Net present value			83.0

Table 12-3   Net Present Value under Various Assumptions of Expropriation and Compensation

Expropriation at the End of Year	Percentage of Remaining NPV Paid as Compensation				
	0	25	50	75	100
5	−56.0	−21.2	13.6	48.4	83.1
10	5.4	24.8	44.2	63.6	83.1
15	61.2	66.7	72.2	77.7	83.1
Never	83.1	83.1	83.1	83.1	83.1

present values in Table 12–2, up to the year of expropriation, and then adding the appropriate percentage of remaining net present value that is paid as compensation. Clearly, in this case, expropriation is disastrous only if it occurs early in the life of the project and if compensation is at most 25 percent. Otherwise, net present value is positive, although less than it would have been had the expropriation not occurred.

This example does not imply that a foreign investor always will escape from expropriation with a positive net present value. While expropriation can be a catastrophe, it usually does not occur until the investment has been in place for a while. Also, some compensation usually is paid. Only in situations where there has been a social revolution is expropriation likely to be unaccompanied by compensation of some sort. Chile paid some compensation to most expropriated U.S. firms and, with the normalization of relations, China also paid some compensation for expropriated property. While expropriation is sometimes a threat, it is not always ruinous.

RISK ADJUSTMENT METHODS USED BY MULTINATIONAL FIRMS

Considering the possibility of expropriation and all the other variables that affect the outcome of foreign projects, it is not surprising that most observers regard foreign projects as being more risky than domestic projects. There are more things that can go wrong. There are more variables that can affect the outcome of the project. The net present value of the project will be at one level if tariff protection is granted by the host country, but will be much lower if it is not, and will be somewhere in between the two extremes if protection is given only for part of the project's life. The expropriation example in the preceding section gives another set of alternative outcomes, depending on action essentially beyond the control of the firm.

Risk, of course, is undesirable. Businessmen would prefer less risky projects to more-risky ones, other things being equal. Other things may not be equal, but it still is necessary to incorporate measures of risk in the appraisal of international projects. While there may be more risk factors in international business, the techniques of incorporating risk in the appraisal of international projects are no different from those used to analyze domestic projects. Basically, the approach is to work with the cash flow to determine how changes in the various variables affect the net present value (NPV). Instead of having just a single net present value, the decision maker will be confronted with a number of alternative NPVs from which to choose in making a decision about the desirability of a project.

Judgment necessarily plays an important part in project analysis in risky environments. Many firms select what they think are the most likely values for the crucial variables and use these to calculate the NPV of the project. Then the firms might do a sensitivity analysis to determine how the NPV would change if one or more of the key variables changed. The decision makers then have to make a judgment as to whether the range of outcome is acceptable.

Expected Net Present Value

Other firms attempt to incorporate the alternative outcomes of a project and information about the probabilities of the alternatives into a decision framework by calculating the *expected* value of the project's NPV. This approach may be illustrated using the alternative outcomes from expropriation and compensation discussed in the preceding section. If expropriation and alternative levels of compensation were the only source of risk, there would be 20 alternative outcomes of the project due to different possible timings of the expropriation and different levels of compensation. Some possible probabilities of these alternatives are given in Table 12–4.

The expected value of the project is calculated in Table 12–5 by multiplying each element in Table 12–3 by its probability in Table 12–4. The expected NPV of the project is positive, which means that, if a lot of similar projects were implemented subject to the same risks, the average NPV obtained would be approximately equal to the expected NPV.

Difficulties with the Expected-Value Method

The decision ordinarily would be to accept a project with a positive expected net present value. The expected value, however, still does not tell the decision maker very much about the risk of the project—about the variability of outcomes around the expected value. The difficulties in using expected NPV as a basis for deciding about the desirability of a project are illustrated in Table 12–6. The two alternative projects illustrated in the

Table 12–4   Probabilities of Expropriation and Compensation

		Probability of Compensation at				
		0%	25%	50%	75%	100%
Probability of				*Equals*		
Expropriation		*0.1*	*0.2*	*0.4*	*0.2*	*0.1*
At the end of 5 years	0.2	0.02	0.04	0.08	0.04	0.02
At the end of 10 years	0.2	0.02	0.04	0.08	0.04	0.02
At the end of 15 years	0.4	0.04	0.08	0.16	0.08	0.04
Never	0.2	0.02	0.04	0.08	0.04	0.02

Table 12–5   Expected Net Present Values (product of Tables 3 and 4)

Expropriation at the End of Year	Percentage of Remaining Net Present Value Received					
	0	25	50	75	100	Sum
5	−1.12	−0.85	1.09	1.94	1.66	2.72
10	0.11	0.99	3.54	2.54	1.66	8.84
15	2.45	5.34	11.55	6.22	3.32	28.88
Never	1.66	3.32	6.64	3.32	1.66	16.60
						57.04

table have the same expected net present value if their capital costs are equal. Clearly, however, the first project is less risky than the second because the largest and the smallest cash flows are less likely to occur.

The expected-value method fails to take into account such differences in the probabilities. Instead, the expected-value method assumes that the utility of a gain to the investing firm is the same as the disutility of an equal loss, and that the average utility of a large loss or gain equals that of a small loss or gain. With these assumptions, differences in probabilities of gains and losses, as in Table 12–6, do not matter to the decision maker, and the decision can be based on the expected value. These assumptions, however, may not be valid, particularly in the case of losses. A small loss may be acceptable and have disutility that equals the utility of an equally small gain. A large loss, on the other hand, may be catastrophic because it would result in bankruptcy. Executives of an investing firm will want to avoid projects that have any possibility of a large loss.

Table 12–6   Expected Annual Cash Flows of Two Alternative Projects

Project 1			Project 2		
Alternative Annual Cash Flows (millions U.S. $) (1)	Probability (2)	Product [(1) × (2)] (3)	Alternative Annual Cash Flows (millions U.S. $) (1)	Probability (2)	Product [(1) × (2)] (3)
30	.05	1.5	30	.10	3.0
25	.20	5.0	25	.20	5.0
20	.50	10.0	20	.40	8.0
15	.20	3.0	15	.20	3.0
10	.05	0.5	10	.10	1.0
Expected value of annual cash flows:		20.0			20.0

Different utilities of losses and gains may be incorporated explicitly into expected-value analysis. Large expected losses may be inflated to account for their disutility, while large expected gains may be deflated. A risk-adjusted net present value then may be calculated.

There are few, if any, firms that explicitly adjust expected cash flow for their utilities; however, many firms often do something that is equivalent: they increase their cost of capital to account for risk. The discount factor is increased, and the present value of benefits and costs that occur in the future are discounted much more heavily than those that occur early in the project's life. Since the heaviest costs usually occur early, while the major benefits are not obtained until later, this process is equivalent to deflating benefits relative to costs. The risk-adjustment that is made to the cost of capital is more or less arbitrary. In some instances, the adjustment is based solely on the subjective feelings of the firm's executives. In others, a more elaborate procedure is used: risks are listed and classified, and adjustments to the cost of capital are made for each type of risk present. The amount of each adjustment still is arbitrary, however.

Ultimately, there is no substitute for judgment in evaluating the risk of foreign projects. In making these judgments, however, executives must keep basic objectives clearly in mind. The basic objective of any project, foreign or domestic, is to improve the welfare of the stockholders of the firm. In evaluating the risk of a project, therefore, it is the risk, as viewed by the security markets, that is important. The problem of project evaluation is to identify and to measure those project risks that would affect the firm's stock price.

Investors in the equity of a firm are not concerned about all sources of variability in the cash flow of the project that arise from such factors as changes in exchange rates and tariff protection. In the first place, any project will affect stockholders indirectly, so that other operations of the firm may compensate for losses on one project. Foreign exchange losses in one country may be offset by foreign exchange gains elsewhere. More importantly, an investor in the equity of a firm investing in a foreign country can diversify his portfolio over a wide variety of assets. Reduction in the return from one security may be offset by increases from others.

In the final analysis, an investor will be concerned only about those aspects of variability in the cash flow from a foreign project that cannot be compensated for or avoided by means of diversification. Such undiversifiable risk is the systematic risk of the project, and it is the aspect of the project risk that would cause an investor to discount the expected net present value. A project that has no systematic risk in this sense would add the full expected net present value of the project to the market value of the firm's equity. The full expected net present value of a project with systematic risk would not be added to the market value of the firm.

The critical risk of a foreign project, therefore, involves only those aspects of the variability of the cash flow from the project that an investor cannot offset by means of diversification of his security portfolio; thus, the facts that exchange rates change, inflation occurs at variable rates, and tariff protection is granted or withdrawn, contribute to risk only to the extent that these factors cannot be offset through diversification. The executive, therefore, can focus on judging the risk of a project solely on the elements of risk in the project that may contribute to the variability in the return on a diversified portfolio.

There is no substitute for the judgment of the decision maker in identifying the risk of a foreign project and determining how that risk will affect the value that securities markets will place on the project. The main point of this discussion is that ultimately it is the securities markets that determine the value of foreign projects and their risks. The decision maker needs to have some idea what factors the markets will take into account when making this determination.

GOVERNMENT EVALUATION OF PROJECTS

Private firms and their stockholders are not the only ones concerned about the impact of foreign projects. An increasing number of governments are reviewing and evaluating the projects of foreign firms to be sure that they are beneficial to the host country. The nature and extent of these reviews vary. In some cases they may be a perfunctory check to determine if the proposed project meets general priorities of the government. In other cases, a detailed analysis is done to determine whether the benefits to the country expected from the project exceed the costs. Depending on the outcome, the project may be accepted or rejected, or suggestions may be made for changes that would increase its attractiveness to the host country.

In most cases the host country wants to know whether local resources invested in the project will be used efficiently and whether the country will get a fair share of the benefits from the project. A project can be profitable to foreign investors and still not represent an efficient use of resources, if profitability is due to subsidies of various kinds provided directly or indirectly by the host country. Even if the project is efficient, it may not be beneficial to the country because of an unfavorable division of benefits. Governments, therefore, are concerned with getting a true picture of the benefits they receive from a project and with determining whether the benefits are adequate in relation to the true costs incurred by the country.

In order to do that, they first must strip subsidies and taxes from the financial flows of a project in order to identify its true opportunity costs and benefits.

Adjusting for Taxes, Subsidies, and Other Market Distortions

Protection of the local market with tariff and quotas has been perhaps the most important source of subsidies for projects in which foreign firms (and local firms for that matter) have been involved, particularly in developing countries. Tariffs and quotas enable firms producing within a country to charge a price that is higher than the delivered price of imports; yet, the price of imports, including cost, insurance, and freight (c.i.f.), represents the real opportunity value of domestic production to the local economy, because that is what the country would have had to pay in order get the product, were it not produced in the country.

Subsidies also are provided to exports and to the inputs used in production. Export subsidies have become increasingly common in recent years as countries realize that there are benefits of expanding the scale of production beyond what is possible in the local market alone. Subsidies on energy inputs (power, fuel) are common, sometimes reflected in charges for transport that are below full costs. Other raw materials may be subsidized, particularly if they are supplied by a state enterprise that does not have to cover its full costs of production. Subsidies also are provided by many countries for agricultural products that are used as raw material. Greece, for example, subsidized the growing of tomatoes, which were canned and exported by a subsidiary of a U.S. company.

In some cases the subsidies are offset partially or wholly by taxes and other factors that increase the cost of inputs and lower the value of output. Taxes are imposed on exports, particularly of minerals such as petroleum, copper, nickel, and the like. Tariffs and quotas may raise the price of raw materials and equipment above the c.i.f. price of imports. Inputs that are not tradeable, such as labor and some raw materials, may cost more than they should in light of their alternative uses. For example, it usually is thought that the wage rate for unskilled labor in developing countries, where there is often large-scale unemployment, is above the opportunity cost of labor. A supplier of a raw material who has a monopoly also may be able to raise the price of the material above its opportunity cost.

In evaluating the impact of a project on the host country, all subsidies and taxes have to be removed from the financial costs and benefits of the project so that they may reflect the true benefits and costs to the economy as a whole. All tradeable goods produced or used by the project should be valued at border prices; that is, output that substitutes for imports, and inputs that will be—or could be—imported, should be valued at the c.i.f. price of imports. Output that will be exported, and inputs used by the project but that otherwise would be exported, should be valued at the free-on-board (f.o.b.) price of exports. Output should be valued at the f.o.b. price, if the effect of the project is to increase net exports of the country, even though the specific production of the project is sold on the local market.

Inputs and outputs that cannot be traded because of high transport costs and other reasons must be valued in terms of the true economic cost to the economy. Nontradeable outputs would be valued at the market price at which they could be sold, because the market price reflects what users are willing to pay and there are no other alternative sources of supply. Nontradeable inputs are valued at the economic cost of production or the opportunity value in other uses. Electric power, for example, is a very important input in aluminum smelting and should be valued at a price sufficient to cover the costs of building and operating power-generating facilities (usually hydroelectric). Unskilled labor, on the other hand, should be valued at its opportunity cost, which in some countries may be only a subsistence wage.

All inputs and outputs must be expressed in terms of the same currency when the host country is evaluating a project, as when it is being evaluated by a private investor. Where the projections of financial costs and benefits in different currencies are converted at the actual exchange rate, however, the costs and benefits to the country should be converted at the opportunity cost of foreign exchange. The opportunity cost of foreign exchange is the number of units of domestic currency that must be spent to generate one unit of foreign currency, either by increasing exports from the country or by increasing local production to substitute for imports.

There are two main reasons why the opportunity cost of foreign exchange may be different from the actual exchange rate. (1) A country can maintain an overvalued exchange rate for some time by drawing down reserves and through foreign borrowing. Mexico maintained the exchange rate of the peso at 12.5 pesos per dollar in the early 1970s by foreign borrowing, until devaluation was forced in the fall of 1976 and the exchange rate went to over 20 pesos per dollar. Countries also can maintain an undervalued exchange rate, as Germany and Japan did in the 1970s, by accumulating reserves. (2) Even if reserves are not being drawn down or accumulated, however, the actual exchange rate will differ from the opportunity cost of foreign exchange because of tariffs and other restrictions on trade. If tariffs and quotas on imports, and taxes and subsidies on exports, were removed, the equilibrium exchange rate would be different (higher *or* lower). If Mexico had a 10 percent tariff on all imports and a 10 percent subsidy on all exports, the opportunity cost of foreign exchange would be approximately 10 percent above the exchange rate; thus, if the exchange rate is 20 pesos per dollar, the opportunity cost of foreign exchange would be 22 pesos per dollar. The additional 2 pesos would pay the export subsidy needed to generate an additional dollar of exports, or pay the higher local costs of inputs for local production needed to substitute for a dollar of imports. The opportunity cost of foreign exchange, sometimes known as the shadow exchange rate, should be used by Mexico to convert local currency costs and benefits to foreign currency for the purpose of project evaluation.

External Benefits and Costs

The evaluation of a project by a country will include benefits and costs not considered by the private investors in the project. For example, the Intercontinental Hotel in Jakarta, Indonesia has trained about 4000 workers, many of whom have gone to work for other hotels. This training is an external benefit of the project. The value of this benefit to Indonesia is the cost of providing equivalent training in other ways. Other examples of external benefits include (1) reduced costs in other industries due to the increased volume of production made possible by the project being evaluated, (2) infrastructure (ports, roads, and so on) that can be used by others, and (3) reduced inventories in other industries made possible by local production. Production of special steels in Turkey, for example, would enable automobile and tractor producers to reduce their inventories of material imported from Germany, because order time would be reduced, defective products could be returned, and smaller lots could be ordered.

A project may produce external costs as well as benefits for the host country, of course. Some of the sales of the project may be diverted from existing producers, for example. The value of these sales to the country is only the costs avoided by the other producer. The project also may produce pollution or congestion, which will entail costs for others in the country. A new hotel in Acapulco, for example, may divert customers from existing hotels, and any additional customers generated may produce pollution and congestion on the beach. When these factors are taken into account, the value of the hotel to the economy may be considerably below its value to the private investors in the project.

The net present value of a project to the host country can be calculated after all inputs and outputs are valued at opportunity costs and external benefits and costs are identified and measured. The total benefits and costs of the project would be discounted at the opportunity cost of capital to the host country. If the NPV is positive, the project represents an efficient use of resources.

Even with a positive NPV, a project is not necessarily beneficial to the host country. The cost of foreign capital invested in the project may be so high that most of the benefits accrue to the foreign investors, leaving little for the host country. The final stage of the analysis, therefore, involves an assessment of the division of benefits among the host country and foreign investors.

Division of Benefits

The benefits remaining to the host country equal the total net benefits, to which foreign capital inflows must be added and from which the cost of servicing foreign capital (interest, principal, dividends) must be subtracted. The cost of servicing foreign capital will be raised by subsidies (tariff protection, low-cost financing, subsidized imports) given to the project. The subsidies do not affect the net benefits, which are valued at opportunity cost; but they do increase profits, which will accrue to foreign owners. The financial profits available to foreign owners are available for repatriation, and are a cost of the project to the host country. It is possible that projects with high shares of foreign ownership and large subsidies may not be beneficial to the country, even when they are efficient.

Some of these ideas are illustrated in the appendix to this chapter, where the cash flows arising from investment in a cement plant are shown. In the example, benefits to the country from cement production are less than the local market price, because tariffs raise the local market price of cement above the c.i.f. cost of importing cement into the country. The financial value of operating costs also is below the opportunity cost, because fuel, an important input in cement production, is subsidized. The project has a positive NPV when both input and output are valued at opportunity costs and discounted at the opportunity cost of capital (10 percent). The project has no net value to the country, however, because net benefits remaining in the country after foreign capital flows and their servicing are taken into account have virtually a zero NPV. The costs of servicing foreign capital are raised by the subsidies provided by higher local market prices and low-cost fuel, which raise profits, and thus dividends, flowing to foreign owners.

The reader may be excused for wondering, at this point, why countries enact such measures as protection and fuel subsidies, when they produce such an undesirable result. The answer, to the extent that there is a rational reason, is that these measures were designed with domestic investors in mind. One of the purposes of a project appraisal done by a country is to identify and prohibit or alter those projects that take advantage of such measures to the detriment of the country.

Summary

A wide range of material has been introduced in this chapter, beginning with cost–benefit analysis by the firm and ending with cost–benefit analysis by host governments. In between, an attempt has been made to acquaint readers with the wide variety of factors that influence the outcome of a foreign investment, and to outline some conceptual approaches to the assessment of project risk. In the end, it has been emphasized that judgment ultimately plays a major role in project analysis—judgment about relative prices, about risk, and about attitude of host governments. It is only through experience that the capacity to make informed judgments can be acquired, but that capacity can be aided by a correct formulation of the analytical problem in the terms outlined in the chapter.

Selected Readings

Baranson, Jack, *Automotive Industries in Developing Countries,* World Bank Staff Occasional Papers, Number 8 (Washington, D.C.: World Bank, 1969).

Behrman, Jack, *The Role of International Companies in Latin American Integration* (Lexington, Mass.: D.C. Heath, 1972).

Bronfenbrenner, Martin, "The Appeal of Confiscation in Economic Development," *Economic Development and Cultural Change,* 3:3, 1955, pp. 201–218.

Cohn, Richard, & John J. Pringle, "Imperfections in International Financial Markets: Implications for Risk Premia and the Cost of Capital to Firms," *Journal of Finance,* 28:1, 1973, pp. 59–66.

Hamada, Robert, "Portfolio Analysis, Market Equilibrium and Corporation Finance," *Journal of Finance,* 24:1, 1969, pp. 3–31.

Lessard, Donald, "World, National and Industry Factors in Equity Returns," *Journal of Finance,* 29:2, 1974, pp. 379–391.

Little, Ian, & James Mirrlees, *Appraisal and Planning for Developing Countries* (New York: Basic Books, 1974).

Quirin, G. David, *The Capital Expenditure Decision* (Homewood, Ill.: Richard D. Irwin, 1967).

Rodriguez, Rita, & Eugene Carter, *International Financial Management,* 2nd Edition (Englewood Cliffs, N.J.: Prentice-Hall, 1979), Chapters 10 & 13.

Sharpe, William, *Portfolio Theory and Capital Markets* (New York: McGraw-Hill, 1970), Chapter 5.

Stevens, Guy v.g., "On the Impact of Uncertainty on the Value and Investment of the Neoclassical Firm," *American Economic Review,* 64:3, 1974, pp. 319–336.

Zenoff, David, & Jack Zwick, *International Financial Management* (Englewood Cliffs, N.J.: Prentice-Hall, 1969).

Appendix: Costs and Benefits of a Cement Plant

The plant has a designed production capacity of about 850,000 tons of cement per year. Total project costs, including escalation, contingencies, interest during construction, and working capital, amount to $160 million. The project is in a remote location, so investment costs also include expenditure on infrastructure (port, roads), which have other uses as well. The project is financed in the following way:

Equity		$ 58 million
Foreign	$44 million	
Local	14 million	
Debt (all foreign)		$102 million
Total		$160 million

Thus, foreign investors put up over 90 percent of total project financing.

The cash flows from the project, valued at local market prices and at opportunity cost, are shown in Table 12–7. The financial costs and benefits of the project to the sponsors are the flows valued at market prices, whereas the flows valued at opportunity costs indicate the value of the benefits and costs to the country where the project is located. Differences in the value of the flows arise for many reasons.

Investment Costs. Investment costs to the sponsor ("at market prices") are higher than costs to the country ("at opportunity cost") because infrastructure investments made in the project also will have other uses. It would have been possible to include the value of these other uses as a benefit to the project. Instead of doing that, the costs were reduced slightly to reflect the portion of the infrastructure that could be allocated to these other uses.

Output Value. Cement can be imported into the country at $70 per ton, but because of tariffs and other protection against imports, the local market price is higher than $70 per ton; thus, the sponsors get a subsidy over and above the true value of the cement to the country.

Operating Costs. Operating costs at market prices are lower than the opportunity costs because fuel-oil prices are subsidized. Fuel oil is an important input in the production of cement.

The project is efficient, in the sense that it has a positive net present

Table 12–7 Cement Project: Cash Flows (millions constant U.S. $)

Year	Investment Costs — At Market Prices	Investment Costs — At Opportunity Cost	Output Value — At Market Prices	Output Value — At c.i.f. Value	Operating Costs — At Market Prices	Operating Costs — At Opportunity Costs	Net Benefits — At Market Prices $(1 + 3 - 5)$	Net Benefits — At Opportunity Values $(2 + 4 - 6)$
	1	*2*	*3*	*4*	*5*	*6*	*7*	*8*
1	(27.3)	(26.8)					(27.3)	(26.8)
2	(61.5)	(60.2)					(61.5)	(60.2)
3	(52.5)	(51.8)					(52.5)	(51.8)
4	(1.5)	(1.6)	33.4	32.9	13.4	18.1	18.4	13.1
5	(0.6)	(0.7)	45.9	44.9	16.2	22.3	28.6	21.8
6	(0.6)	(0.6)	55.1	53.5	16.1	25.6	35.2	27.3
7	(0.2)	(0.2)	61.6	59.5	19.9	27.8	40.3	31.6
8			62.4	59.5	19.6	27.6	40.7	32.0
9			63.2	59.5	19.5	27.4	40.9	32.1
10			63.2	59.5	19.4	27.4	41.0	32.2
11–14			63.2	59.5	19.4	27.4	41.0	32.2
15			63.2	59.5	19.4	27.4	61.3	53.1
Present Value	20.3	21.0						33.9

302

Table 12–7 Cement Project: Cash Flows (millions constant U.S. $), continued

Year	9 Inflow Equity	10 Inflow of Loans	11 Repayment of Loans	12 Interest	13 Dividends	14 Net Benefits to Equity (9 + 13)	15 Net Benefits of Foreign Capital (9 + 10 + 11 + 12 + 13)	16 Net Benefits to Local Economy (8 − 15)
1	(6.5)	(15.1)				(6.5)	(21.6)	(5.2)
2	(17.4)	(40.4)				(17.4)	(57.8)	(2.4)
3	(20.1)	(46.5)				(20.1)	(66.6)	14.8
4			3.0	10.3	5.1	5.1	18.4	(5.3)
5			10.3	10.1	7.0	7.0	27.4	(5.6)
6			15.0	8.3	10.0	10.0	33.3	(6.0)
7			15.0	6.8	14.9	14.9	36.7	(5.1)
8			15.0	5.3	16.9	16.9	37.2	(5.2)
9			10.6	3.7	22.0	22.0	36.3	(4.2)
10			10.6	2.9	13.7	13.7	27.2	5.0
11			10.6	1.8	14.6	14.6	27.0	5.2
12			7.6	0.9	17.4	17.4	25.9	6.3
13			3.8	0.3	21.1	21.1	25.2	7.0
14					24.0	24.0	24.0	8.2
15					39.3	39.3	39.3	13.8
Present Value							33.7	0.2

value, even when both outputs and inputs are valued at opportunity costs; however, the project ultimately has no net benefit for the country. The NPV of the investment to foreign investors is equal to the overall value of the project; thus, the foreign investors extract virtually all of the net benefits. They are able to do so because of all the subsidies that are given. Higher cement prices and lower fuel costs increase profits, which accrue mainly to foreign investors. The return to foreign equity investors in the project, therefore, is very high.

13

Financing Foreign Investments

INTRODUCTION

Multinational corporations can tap a wide variety of alternative sources of funds to finance their subsidiaries, some of which will be described in the first section of this chapter. The choice among these alternatives is relatively straightforward when financial markets are functioning efficiently, as will be discussed in the second part of the chapter. There are still many impediments to the efficient functioning of capital markets, however, despite the emergence of Eurocurrency markets in recent years. Some of the more important impediments, particularly those due to policies of governments, will be discussed in the third section. Methods of identifying a good financial plan will be outlined in the fourth section.

Most of the discussion in this chapter is in the context of a wholly-owned subsidiary; however, foreign investments increasingly are being made as joint ventures between two or more firms. Such ventures are becoming almost mandatory in many developing countries, but there are many reasons why they might be desirable even when not required. Some of the financial issues associated with joint ventures, therefore, will be described in the fifth section.

SOURCES OF FINANCE

Funds from the Home Country

The parent firm usually provides a substantial proportion of the funds needed in its foreign operations. The parent must provide sufficient equity financing to its overseas subsidiaries to maintain ownership and control, but it also can provide loans to foreign subsidiaries.[1] The parent can provide its equity contribution to foreign operations in any of several forms, including liquid capital transferred to the subsidiary through the exchange markets. In addition, however, the parent can provide equipment, raw materials, or finished products. Patents, processes, and management services also might be capitalized as the parent's contribution to the subsidiary's capital.

An equity investment of liquid capital can be financed in a number of ways. The usual procedure is to raise the capital either from the retained earnings of the parent, or by selling securities (stocks or bonds) in capital markets of the home country. Another possibility, however, would be for the parent to borrow on international capital markets or to transfer funds from another foreign subsidiary.

There are other ways for the subsidiary to obtain home-country financing, other than funds from the parent. Among these possibilities are direct borrowing by the subsidiary from financial intermediaries in the home country, as well as the sale of bonds on the capital market of the home country. Borrowing by a subsidiary in the home country is unlikely without a guarantee by the parent company. A more likely prospect is for the subsidiary to obtain export credit financing on material and equipment purchased in the home country. The United States Export–Import Bank, for example, is a government-sponsored institution in the business of making loans directly to finance exports or of guaranteeing loans made by U.S. commercial banks to importers in foreign countries. As a result of these loans, the exporting firm gets its money immediately, while the importer (in this case the subsidiary) makes payment for the equipment over an extended period.

There are other government institutions in industrial countries that under some circumstances may supply funds to foreign subsidiaries of national firms, particularly those located in developing countries. Many

---

[1] Loans may reduce taxes and avoid restrictions on dividend repatriations. Interest is deductible from profits when taxes are computed in most countries, unlike dividends. Moreover, when foreign exchange is scarce and the host country imposes restrictions on its use, payment of interest usually is given priority over the repatriation of profit.

industrial countries have government-supported institutions whose objective is to encourage direct investment in developing countries. In the United States, the Overseas Private Investment Corporation (OPIC) has a small amount of funds that can be loaned to subsidiaries of U.S. firms investing in developing countries. Likewise, in Germany, Deutsche Entwicklungesellshaft (DEG) acts as a partner in investments involving German firms in developing countries. DEG can provide both loans and equity investments to the subsidiaries of German firms. The interest rates on loans from such government institutions often are subsidized to some extent, being below the rates on equivalent commercial loans.

Funds from the Host Country

To the extent that the need of a subsidiary for capital is not satisfied by the parent and other sources in the home country, the subsidiary may be able to obtain equity capital, borrow from banks and other financial intermediaries, and sell bonds on the securities markets of the host country. It is possible, even probable, however, that the range of financing alternatives open to a firm in the United States will not be available in most other countries. Capital markets, for example, generally are undeveloped in less-developed countries, and many financial intermediaries simply do not exist. Commercial banks exist and can be tapped for short-term capital, but primary and secondary markets for securities also are undeveloped. Thus, it usually is difficult to raise capital by selling bonds or stock.

To help meet the problems of longer-term financing in these countries, public and private development banks have been established. These banks are financed by the national government or by foreign governments and international institutions like the World Bank. They provide medium- and long-term loans, often at subsidized interest rates, to private firms and public agencies engaged in high-priority activities.

Underdeveloped capital markets, of course, are not limited to less-developed countries. Many European countries also do not have the full range of financial institutions and markets available in the United States, the United Kingdom, or Japan. Table 13–1 shows that total financial assets in the United States, Canada, and Japan, relative to gross national product, are substantially larger than in France and Germany. These figures suggest that external sources of funds probably would be more readily available to subsidiaries of foreign firms in the former group of countries.

Even where capital markets are relatively well developed, differences exist in the various types of finance that may be available to subsidiaries of foreign firms (or to local firms for that matter). In some countries, including Germany, banks dominate the financing system. As seen in Table 13–1,

Table 13–1   Selected Financial Ratios for Seven Countries (percentages)

		Germany	Netherlands	France	Japan	Canada	United States
1.	Commercial bank assets/GNP	70	79	60	84	79	70
2.	Total deposit bank assets/GNP	120	121	84	120	88	97
3.	Securities/GNP	54		34	92	128	120
	a Bonds/GNP	42		22	55	75	65
	b Shares/GNP	12	20	12	33	42	45
4.	Total financial assets broadly defined (2 + 3)/GNP	174		118	212	216	217

Source: David Gill, "Banks and Securities Markets: Some Thoughts on Evaluating Financial System Depth and Efficiency," First International Conference on the Financial Development of Latin America and the Caribbean, Garaballeda LaGuara, Venezuela, February 26–28, 1979.

banks hold a large portion of financial assets in Germany, whereas securities market are a much more important source of finance in the United States and Canada.

Even where securities markets exist, they can be dominated by deposit banks, as in Germany and France. In Japan, on the other hand, bank and security functions are almost completely separated. A high degree of separation between banking and security-market functions is found in Canada and the United States as well, although not to tbe same extent as in Japan. Some countries stand between these polar extremes. In the Netherlands, banks and securities markets are not separated formally. Initially, market forces resulted in a significant degree of functional specialization by class of institution, but this specialization has diminished in recent decades.

Banks dominate all aspects of the financial market in Germany. There are no laws or regulations that segregate banking and other financial market functions, and banks in this legal and regulatory environment have come to dominate all securities-market functions. There are a great many different types of banking institutions in Germany, however, and only the large commercial banks and private banks engage in securities-market activities as underwriters, brokers, and managers of securities portfolios. These banks also own large positions in the equity securities of major firms, intervene in the management of these firms, and actively vote the shares of the trust accounts that they manage. As is apparent from Table 13–1, the German banking system is very deep by international standards. By contrast, the German securities market is far less developed compared with many other developed countries. The share market is shallow, and the level of secondary market activity is especially low.

By way of contrast, commercial banks in Japan are confined largely to short-term banking and, by law or regulation, are not allowed to engage in securities-market functions. Securities regulations prohibit commercial banks from acting as underwriters, except for federal and local government and government-guaranteed bonds. Broker–dealers conduct all other primary and all secondary market securities distribution. The management of mutual funds and investment trusts is conducted by still another class of separate institutions. Even with these restrictions, the Japanese banking system is very well developed in the sense that the ratio of total deposit bank assets to GNP is as high as any of the other developed countries covered in Table 13–1. The securities market also is well developed in that the securities/GNP ratio is greater than all countries in the sample except Canada and the United States.

It is widely believed that Japan has relied to an extraordinary degree on its banking system for long-term finance. This often is understood to mean that, not only is the banking system very large and the securities market not as large, but the banking system engages in a high degree of maturity imbalance that allows it to substitute for a bond market. To some degree this was true in the early postwar period, when Japanese authorities allowed the banking system to lend long in order to finance reconstruction; however, Japanese regulations and legislation tend to favor the development of the securities market, and in recent years the securities market has become quite important.

These differences in the financial systems of various countries are reflected in differences in the ways in which nonfinancial corporations are financed. As is depicted in Table 13–2, U.S. corporations rely heavily on equity financing and long-term bonds sold in security markets. Japanese corporations, on the other hand, rely on short-term borrowings from banks and on trade credit for about two-thirds of their financing. French and German firms also use substantial amounts of short-term borrowings and trade credit, but to a lesser extent than Japanese firms. As would be expected, French and German firms get a small proportion of their total financing from securities markets, but the same can be said of Japanese nonfinancial corporations, even though Japanese securities markets are somewhat better developed than those in France and Germany.

These observations suggest that foreign subsidiaries investing in Japan and the United States may have greater access to local sources of finance than would be the case in Germany and, particularly, France. Subsidiaries in Germany will be more heavily dependent on banks for local finance, while there will be greater possibility of selling securities in the United States and Japan. Of course, there may be constraints on the types and amounts of local financing available to subsidiaries of foreign firms, particularly in less-developed countries. Consequently, it may be necessary for both the parent and the subsidiary to explore international sources of funds.

Table 13–2   Sources of Capital of Nonfinancial Corporations (all figures are percentages)

	Germany		France		U.S.		Japan	
	1970	1976	1970	1976	1970	1977	1970	1976
Equity	37	37	34	27	55	58	15	13
4.1 Share capital	20	17	19	12	—	—	7	5
4.2 Reserves	8	8	15	14	—	—	8	8
4.3 Provisions	9	13	—	—	—	—	—	—
Short-term liability	41	41	47	54	22	18	65	62
5.1 Bills and bonds	—	—	—	—	1	1	0	0
5.2 Borrowed funds	—	—	20	23	7	7	25	25
5.3 Trade credit	—	—	27	31	13	9	28	26
5.4 Other payable	—	—	—	—	1	1	12	12
Long-term liability	19	20	19	19	24	24	20	25
6.1 Staff retirement	—	—	—	—	—	—	1	1
6.2 Long-term bonds	—	—	3	2	13	13	2	2
6.3 Other	—	—	17	17	10	11	17	22
6.3.1 Affiliates	—	—	—	—	1	1	—	—
6.3.2 Banks	—	—	—	—	2	2	14	17
6.3.3 Other	3	2	—	—	7	8	3	5
TOTAL	100	100	100	100	100	100	100	100

Source: OECD, *Financial Statistics, 1978* Bulletin 12, Tome 1, (Paris: OECD October 1978), Tables A 211/01, A 211/08, A 211/07, A 211/21.

International Sources of Funds

Funds supplied by investors or through institutions in countries other than the home or host country can be regarded as international. There are two major sources of these funds: (1) through selling securities or borrowing in the capital markets of third countries and (2) through borrowing in the international capital markets.

Export credit is one easy method of borrowing from third countries. Most developed countries have institutions similar to the United States Export–Import Bank to finance exports. Even some developing countries now provide long-term financing for the exports of their emerging capital goods industries. Foreign subsidiaries can obtain such medium- and long-term financing when buying machinery and equipment from a third country.

In addition to export credit, it sometimes is possible for a subsidiary to sell bonds in third-country capital markets. For example, the subsidiary of a U.S. firm that is domiciled in France may be able to sell bonds in the Swiss capital market. These bonds would be denominated in Swiss francs, so that the subsidiary, whose revenues are probably in French francs, would have to bear the risk of the French franc being devalued relative to the Swiss franc. If such a devaluation should occur, the subsidiary would need more French francs to repay the loan than it initially obtained from it. Perhaps because of this exchange risk, and because most countries limit the access of foreigners to their domestic capital markets, sale of bonds in third countries has not been an important method of financing foreign operations. The total magnitude of foreign borrowing in the capital markets of major countries was over $20 billion in 1978. About $3 billion of that total was borrowed by private, nonfinancial enterprises, only a small portion of which was due to borrowing by subsidiaries of multinational enterprises.

The development of a truly international capital market was described in Chapter 6. These are markets in which funds are obtained either from financial intermediaries (the credit market) or through the sales of bonds (the bond market). The funds are provided in currencies other than that of the country where the financial intermediary is located or the bond is sold.

These international capital markets have become an important source of funds for multinational corporations. The international bond market, for example, provided substantial financing for U.S. multinational corporations when restrictions were placed on capital outflows from the United States in 1968. International bond financing by U.S. firms reached $2.1 billion in 1968, or 60 percent of the total of $3.5 billion in bonds sold that year. After 1968, the share of Eurobond sales by U.S. corporations attempting to finance their foreign operations fluctuated but never again reached the level attained in 1968. In 1974, the year in which direct investment controls were dropped, international bond sales by U.S. corporations fell to only $105 million, out of total international bond sales in that year of $4.5 billion.

International credit markets by now have probably surpassed international bond markets as a source of funds for the financing of subsidiaries of multinational enterprises. Although the largest borrowers in these markets have been governments and state-owned enterprises, international commercial banks have become increasingly interested in lending to private projects, particularly those sponsored by multinational corporations. Table 13–3 shows that commercial-bank lenders provided private, nonfinancial enterprises with over $13 billion in credit in both 1978 and 1979. Not all, or even most, of these funds went to subsidiaries of foreign firms. At the same time, it should be remembered that *publicized* international currency credits are substantially less than total lending by commercial banks (see Tables 6–2 and 6–3). It is probable that a large portion of unpublicized international credits go to private firms, including subsidiaries of multinational firms. Some of the publicized credits that went to subsidiaries of foreign firms during the first half of 1979 are shown in Table 13–4.

An additional source of financing for foreign subsidiaries operating in developing countries is provided by the International Finance Corporation (IFC), which is a member of the World Bank Group. IFC is an international organization established by 113 governments to provide financing for private

Table 13-3 Categories of Borrowers of International Credit (millions U.S. $)

	1976	1977	1978	1979
Central government	5,882.3	10,041.8	21,162.4	11,669.2
State or local government	887.0	1,501.5	1,640.2	1,813.3
Public nonfinancial enterprises	8,471.6	9,107.1	21,962.8	22,466.4
Private nonfinancial enterprises	5,932.4	4,803.6	13,680.5	13,523.9
Deposit money banks	636.8	1,061.4	2,027.9	6,720.1
Central monetary institutions	2,352.0	1,126.0	2,928.3	2,171.5
Other public financial institutions	3,612.4	6,085.1	9,298.0	8,742.5
Other private financial institutions	485.8	261.8	804.7	1,454.3
International organizations	377.0	197.0	181.7	310.0
Others	66.0	——	37.0	——

Source: World Bank, *Borrowing in International Capital Markets*, various issues.

projects in developing member countries. IFC finances both projects that are wholly-owned by entrepreneurs in the developing countries and joint ventures between foreign and local investors. The Volvo project in Brazil, which secured loan financing from a Bank of America syndicate shown in Table 13-4, also secured a loan from IFC. Both loan and equity investments can be made by IFC but it will not take more than 25 percent of total equity and will not, in any event, participate in management. IFC will provide at most 25 to 30 percent of total project cost.

It should be clear by now that there is a wide variety of sources available to finance the subsidiaries of multinational corporations. In fact, the alternatives are so numerous and diverse that a problem of choice is presented. This problem will be addressed in the following section.

Table 13-4 Selected Credits to Subsidiaries of Foreign Firms: 1979

Country	Firm	Parent	Amount (Millions U.S. $)	Term (Years)	Lender (Lead Manager)
Brazil	Alcan-Alumino do Brazil	Alcan Aluminum	80.0	12	Orion Bank
Brazil	Volvo do Brazil	Volvo	50.0	N.A.	Bank of America
Mexico	Celanese Mexicana	Celanese	39.0	N.A.	Banco Nacional de Mexico
Spain	ERTISA	Rio Tinto ICI	20.0	10	Lloyds Bank
Spain	Tarragona Quimica	Rio Tinto Hoechst	25.0	8	Continental Illinois

N.A. - Not available.
Source: World Bank, *Borrowing in International Capital Market* (Washington, D.C.: World Bank, 1979).

FINANCIAL THEORY

There are two major questions that multinational firms must answer concerning the financing of foreign subsidiaries. First, how is the total financing of the subsidiary to be divided among the various alternative sources of funds outlined in the preceding section? Second, what effects will the financing decision have on the value of the project to the investing firm? Will the present value of the investment be increased by the use of low-cost debt, or alternatively, if national restrictions on international capital flows prevent use of low-cost loans, will the net present value be reduced?

In a classic study, Franco Modigliani & Merton Miller have provided a framework that can be used to help answer these questions, when international capital markets operate efficiently. Efficiency in this context means that financial transactions by individuals or firms are not impeded in any way. International capital markets are not, in fact, efficient in this sense; yet it is still worthwhile to examine the Modigliani–Miller model because it can be used to identify market imperfections that critically affect optimal financing decisions and the desirability of projects. The theory, in effect, provides a framework that can be used to structure the complexities of the real world.

Modigliani & Miller have shown that when capital markets are operating efficiently, the value of a project to the investing firm's stockholders does not depend on the exact methods used to finance the project. In a perfect capital market the risk and return of a stockholder's portfolio is independent of financing decisions made by firms. For example, a firm may decide to finance an investment in France partially by borrowing in the French capital market. This decision releases resources for payment of dividends to stockholders, but at the same time increases the riskiness of the stock because of the financial leverage added by the bond financing. If the stockholder does not want to bear the additional risk, the additional dividends can be used to buy some of the debt issued by the French subsidiary. In this way, the same earnings and risk are achieved that would have been achieved if the subsidiary had been financed with retained earnings. On the other hand, if the subsidiary had been financed with retained earnings, the stockholder could have wanted the prospect of greater return and greater risk that is achieved by financial leverage. This leverage can be created by borrowing to finance some of the stockholdings. Then the prospective return and the portfolio risk would be the same as they would have been had the subsidiary been financed partially with debt.

When these alternatives are open to a firm's stockholders, the market value of the firm (i.e., the sum of the market value of outstanding stocks and bonds) does not depend on the proportion of debt in its capital structure. In order to suggest the reasons for this conclusion, suppose two firms are identical in every respect except that their capital structures differ. Investors can obtain the same earnings stream and risk by purchasing, say, 10 percent of the unlevered firm's stock, or 10 percent of both the levered firm's stock and bonds. But if earnings and risk are identical, then the market values of the two alternative investments must be equal. Otherwise, the investor can obtain a higher return on his investment in the firm whose market value is lower. Clearly, in a perfect capital market, every investor would want to invest in the lower-valued firm and disinvest in the higher-valued firm, so that the price of one would be driven up, while the price of the other would be driven down. This process would end when the market value of the unlevered firm (which is the value of its shares) equals the market value of the levered firm (shares plus bonds outstanding).

By the same reasoning process, it can be shown that the value of a project is independent of its financing. The value of a project is the resulting addition to the investing firm's market value. If the project is financed wholly from retained earnings, its value will show up as an addition to the value of outstanding common stock. If it is financed with retained earnings and new debt, its value is the resulting change in the value of common stock plus the market value of the new bonds.

If the value of a project is independent of its financing, it does not matter to the investing firm's current stockholders how it is financed. The value and risk of their portfolio will be exactly the same regardless of the financing method chosen. If some debt financing is used, for example, an equivalent amount of the firm's resources is released for dividends to stockholders. These dividends can be used to buy some of the bonds that have been issued to finance the project. Since the market value of the project is invariant with the method of financing, the stockholder in this way can achieve exactly the same risk and return as would have been achieved if the project had been financed from retained earnings.

As an example of this process, consider again the Brazilian fertilizer project described in Table 12–2. The net present value of the project is $83.0 million. If the project is financed from retained earnings of the parent, the value of outstanding common stock will increase by $83.0 million. The holdings of a stockholder who owns 10 percent of the outstanding common stock will increase in value by $8.3 million. Now suppose that the project is financed partially by selling $30 million worth of bonds by the subsidiary. This releases $30 million of the parent firm's resources to be distributed as dividends. The 10 percent stockholder will receive an additional $3.0 million. If the $3.0 million are used to purchase bonds issued by the subsidiary, the stockholder still will own 10 percent of the subsidiary's earnings.[2] Moreover, the value of his holdings will have increased by $8.3 million. His holdings of bonds will have increased by $3.0 million, while his holdings of stock will have increased by $5.3 million because the total value of the project is $83 million and $30 million in bonds were issued, leaving $53 million as the addition to outstanding common stock.

Stockholders in the investing firm need not care whether bonds are issued in the home country or in the subsidiary's host country, providing there are no restrictions on international capital movements. When international capital markets are functioning perfectly, the value of the project remains the same to stockholders regardless of which alternative source of finance is chosen. Of course, the interest rate may be higher in the foreign country. Offsetting this, however, is the fact that foreign financing reduces the exchange risk of the project's cash flow. The reduction in risk just offsets the effect of higher interest rates when there are no restrictions on international capital movements. If this were not true, stockholders in the parent firm could increase their wealth by purchasing the subsidiary's foreign currency bonds with the increased dividends made possible by the debt financing. These purchases would drive up the bond price and would lower the interest rate on the bonds. The interest rate would fall to the point where the additional interest on foreign currency financing is exactly offset by the reduction in risk made possible by that financing.

This result depends on the assumption that international capital markets function perfectly. A perfectly functioning international capital market means, in particular, that (1) information is available freely to everyone, and there are no restrictions or costs of transactions and (2) any financial arrangement available to firms is available to individuals. The first assumption is necessary, for example, to assure that individual stockholders can purchase the securities issued by subsidiaries at prices determined only by the project's earnings and exchange-rate risk. The second assumption rules out the possibility that the firm can increase the stockholders' wealth by taking advantage of a source of capital not available to individuals.

None of these assumptions implies that interest rates have to be the same in all countries. Interest rates may differ because of foreign exchange risk. If interest rates differ because of outside interference with international capital flows, however, the results of the Modigliani–Miller theory do not hold; therefore, in the next section, international capital markets are examined for evidence of the following:

1. Restrictions on international capital flows.
2. Discrimination in the price of capital to different users.

[2]This assumes that the stockholder pays no income taxes.

INTERNATIONAL CAPITAL-MARKET IMPERFECTIONS

The search for imperfections in world capital markets need not be very thorough to uncover countless examples. Governments, as well as powerful individuals, always have regulated the flow of capital to achieve special objectives. In addition, governments in all parts of the world provide subsidized capital to favored investments. Any list of these restrictions to capital flows and subsidies soon would be out of date. All that can be done, therefore, is to describe some of the more important and permanent characteristics of current capital-market imperfections.

Government Restrictions on International Capital Movements

If anything about the international economy is permanent, it is government restrictions on international capital movements. Specific restrictions come and go but an international businessman always can count on governments interfering with movements of capital in some way. Not all governments restrict capital movements, nor do many countries interefere with all types of international capital flows. Most countries, however, attempt to control some types of capital movement into and out of their areas.

Governments do not restrict international capital flows simply to make life difficult for international business managers. The restrictions usually are designed to achieve specific policy objectives. Perhaps the most important are: (1) to reduce balance-of-payments pressures at fixed exchange rates, (2) to reduce the cost of capital to domestic business, (3) to boost domestic employment, and (4) to limit foreign control of the domestic economy.

Balance-of-payments pressures, for example, led the United States in the 1960s to abandon its traditional practice of allowing free movements of capital into and out of the country. Restrictions on capital outflows were begun in 1963 with the interest-equalization tax on foreign portfolio investments. Federal Reserve restrictions on U.S. bank lending abroad were added a little later. Finally, mandatory restrictions on direct investment were imposed in 1968. All of these restrictions were continued until January 1974.

European countries and Japan, likewise, have at one time or another instituted and still maintain restrictions on the access of foreigners to their local capital markets. Until recently, the United Kingdom restricted direct-investment capital outflows by means of exchange restrictions. Sweden has controlled direct-investment capital outflows since the late 1970s to protect employment at home.

The effect of these restrictions on capital flows is to lower the cost of acquiring capital to firms in capital-exporting countries, while raising the cost to firms in capital-importing countries. In the terminology of recent capital-market theory, the restrictions lower both the risk-free rate of interest and the market price of risk in capital-exporting countries, while raising both parameters in capital-importing countries. The effect of the U.S. restrictions on capital exports, for example, were seen in Figure 6–1. While the restrictions were in effect, the deposit rate in U.S. commercial banks was substantially below the six-month Eurodollar deposit rate. The differential narrowed after the restrictions were removed in 1974.

In fact, the differentials between U.S. and Eurocurrency interest rates began to narrow before the restrictions on U.S. capital outflows were lifted, as investors and business executives helped to develop international credit and bond markets as a way around various national restrictions on capital flows. Firms and other borrowers unable to obtain funds in the United States because of U.S. attempts to restrict foreign investment were able to borrow in the international capital markets. For example, municipalities excluded from the U.S. capital market by the interest-equalization tax borrowed in the Eurobond market. United States firms not able to export capital to Europe also used the Euromarkets to finance their direct investments.

While governments restrict some types of international capital flows, they subsidize others in order to achieve certain national objectives. Export credits are one important form of international capital flow that most governments, at least in the industrial countries, have subsidized. Subsidized export credit is a way of increasing exports, particularly of machinery and equipment. The subsidies are provided by the government of the exporting country and usually take the form of lower interest rates and longer maturities and grace periods than would be available in the capital markets. These subsidies are available only to firms purchasing capital equipment and thus constitute an important capital-market imperfection that must be taken into account in the financing of foreign operations.

Discrimination by Domestic Financial Institutions

Other sources of subsidized capital will be available in the countries where subsidiaries are located. Financial institutions in these countries may provide capital to some borrowers at favorable rates, providing that these institutions have some monopoly power or providing that they do not depend on their own earnings for survival. When either of these conditions are met, some firms may be able to acquire capital at lower rates of interest than others; accordingly some can and do acquire capital for less than it costs individuals.

Financial monopolies are particularly prevalent in less-developed countries where capital markets are undeveloped. A few banks often dominate the financial system and hold considerable economic power, which can be used to discriminate among borrowers. Subsidiaries of foreign firms are sometimes the beneficiaries of this discrimination because they have alternative sources of funds not available to domestic firms. A more important source of discrimination comes from financial institutions owned or subsidized by governments. These institutions often are established to accomplish a specific purpose. For example, their mission may be to encourage industry in an underdeveloped region of the country, and to do so they make loans on subsidized terms to firms willing to meet their objectives.

Most European countries provide such subsidized loans, as do individual states in the United States. These subsidies range from outright grants to interest rates on loans that are below market rates. The State of Pennsylvania provided Volkswagen with low-interest loans to induce the company to locate its U.S. assembly plant at New Stanton, Pennsylvania. The Canadian government gave Ford Motor Company a grant to locate a new engine plant in Ontario rather than in Ohio. The British Government in September 1977 gave Ford a package of incentives estimated to be worth 40 percent of the investment amount to locate a $315-million engine plant in South Wales.

The European Community is undertaking to limit the extent of the subsidies that the member countries can give to lure new investment. The Community has established rules that require incentives to be made in readily identifiable and quantifiable forms. It also has placed limits on the amounts of incentives, allowing greater incentives in less-developed regions, such as Ireland and Southern Italy.

Less-developed countries also have established means of providing subsidized financing to preferred investments and to investments in preferred locations. Brazil, for example, has a scheme that enables taxpayers to invest some portion of their owed taxes in financial institutions, which in turn use the funds to provide low-cost funds to projects in less-developed regions, such as the northeast and the Amazon. Any return on these funds would be pure gain to the taxpayers, who otherwise would have lost them to the tax authorities; therefore, these funds are made available to borrowers at very low cost.

Another source of imperfection in capital markets stems from inflation and its attendant exchange controls. Very often in the inflationary economies real interest rates are low or negative because the rate of price inflation exceeds the nominal rate of interest. Naturally, lenders do not want to make loans at negative interest rates; however, they have difficulty forecasting the rate of inflation, particularly when inflation is accelerating.

As a consequence, the purchasing power of the currency lent may be greater than that repaid, even after allowance is made for interest payments. Borrowers in the country, including subsidiaries of foreign firms, can take advantage of these low real rates of interest; however, the parent firms and foreign individuals cannot borrow at such low rates, either because there are laws prohibiting loans to foreigners or because exchange controls prevent the foreign borrower from exchanging the proceeds of the loan for domestic currency. As a result, the subsidiary can obtain capital on better terms than stockholders of the parent firm, and the wealth of stockholders can be increased if the subsidiary takes advantage of these opportunities.

FINANCING DECISIONS

We can conclude from the preceding section that the assumptions underlying Modigliani & Miller's analysis usually are not satisfied in fact. Individuals cannot make all the financial arrangements open to firms. The cost of capital from different sources does not differ solely because of differences in risk. Some sources of capital are available at subsidized rates, while other sources are taxed.

Managers of multinational corporations, therefore, cannot assume that the value of a project to stockholders is independent of the way in which it is financed, as is true when there are perfect capital markets. They therefore should choose explicitly the optimal sources of finance for each project and should determine how their choice affects the value of the project to stockholders.

Actually, when some sources of capital are subsidized while others are taxed, the choice among them is a rather simple matter. The firm should use as much of the subsidized capital as is available. Sources of capital with the largest subsidies should be used first. When these are exhausted, sources with lower subsidies should be used, and so on until financing of the project is completed. Of course, it is unlikely that the entire project can be financed with subsidized capital, since capital of this kind always is rationed; therefore, some high-cost sources will have to be used, and the mix will depend on the circumstances.

The use of subsidized sources of capital to create value for stockholders is demonstrated by an investment in a copper mine made by Freeport Minerals Company in Indonesia between 1969 and 1973.[3] When the overall project was evaluated the expected net present value at a 15 percent

---

[3]This example is taken from William E. Fruhan Jr., *Financial Strategy: Studies in the Creation, Transfer and Destruction of Shareholder Value* (Homewood, Ill.: R. D. Irwin, 1979), Chapter 5.

discount rate was negative. Assuming that the average cost of capital to Freeport was 15 percent, this means that in a perfect capital market it would not have been profitable for Freeport to undertake the project. No matter what mix of debt and equity Freeport would have used to finance the project, the average cost of the capital would have been 15 percent and the net present value of the project would have been negative. Even if it had been possible to raise loan financing for the project without a Freeport guarantee, if the terms of the loan were no better than could have been obtained by Freeport itself, investing in the project would not have improved the welfare of Freeport shareholders.[4]

Freeport, however, obtained substantial subsidized loans to help finance the project. The total financing required by the Indonesian project was $120 million. Of this total, Freeport put up only $20 million as equity, securing loans for the remaining $100 million. The loans were made to the project without recourse to Freeport and probably at better terms than Freeport could have obtained borrowing on its own credit. A $20-million subordinated loan was provided by a consortium of Japanese copper smelters and guaranteed by the Japanese Export–Import Bank at an interest rate of 8.4 percent. The guaranteed loan was made in return for an agreement by Freeport to sell two-thirds of the mine output to the Japanese smelters. Likewise, a $22-million loan was obtained from a German bank at 7 percent, guaranteed by the Federal Republic of Germany, in return for a commitment to sell one-third of the output to a German smelter. Both Germany and Japan were willing to provide the guarantees in order to assure a supply of copper concentrate for domestic smelters. Another $18 million was provided by U.S. banks and guaranteed by the U.S. Export–Import Bank to finance purchases of equipment in the United States. The interest rate was one-half of a percentage point over the U.S. prime rate. Finally, $40 million was obtained from five U.S. insurance companies at 9 1/4 percent interest. This loan was guaranteed by the Overseas Private Investment Corporation (OPIC) for a fee of 1 3/4 percent per year. The OPIC guarantee was made available in order to promote the investment in a developing country of particular interest to the United States.

---

[4]The reason for this last conclusion may be seen by referring to the previous analysis. If the loans for the project were not raised through Freeport, but were raised on the same terms as loans raised by Freeport, the shareholders could be in the same position as when Freeport provided all of the project financing. The Freeport shareholder could buy the bonds issued by the project and thus have the same claim to revenue and the same risk as if the project had been financed by Freeport. Thus, if the project were not desirable in the latter case, it also would not be desirable in the former.

Freeport thus was able to leverage its investment at relatively low interest rates, considering the inherent risk of the project, without any guarantees by the parent company. In a perfect capital market, less debt would have been possible, and only at higher rates. The value of the guarantees made available to Freeport is the difference between the net present value of the actual loans obtained and the present value of loans that could have been obtained without the various guarantees.

An example of the net subsidy is calculated in Table 13–5 by assuming that the best Freeport could have done without the guarantees would have been an interest rate one-half of a percent higher than that actually obtained from the U.S. insurance companies (i.e., 11 1/2 percent, counting the guarantee fee as a cost of the loan). The NPV of the loans actually obtained, discounted at 15 percent, was $19.1 million. The NPV of loans that could have been obtained without the guarantees would have been $11.6 million at the assumed terms. The guarantees were thus worth $7.5 million and made the project a viable investment for Freeport.

Table 13–5 Subsidy from Favorable Loan Terms (millions U.S. $)

Year	Loans Obtained[a]		Alternative without Guarantees (11½% interest)	
	Principal	Interest Net	Principal	Interest Net
1970	18.5	—	18.5	—
1971	38.5	−1.69	38.5	−2.13
1972	43.0	−5.22	43.0	−5.70
1973	—	−9.13	—	−8.70
1974	−7.9	−9.13	−7.9	−7.56
1975	−12.0	−8.50	−12.0	−6.05
1976	−12.0	−7.44	−12.0	−4.58
1977	−12.5	−6.43	−12.5	−3.38
1978	−12.5	−5.23	−12.5	−2.40
1979	−12.5	−4.04	−12.5	−1.62
1980	−12.5	−2.90	−12.5	−1.00
1981	−9.1	−1.74	−9.1	−0.51
1982	−9.0	−0.86	−9.0	−0.22
Net Present Value				
(at 15%)		19.14		11.62
Subsidy due to guarantees		7.52		

[a] From Fruhan, *op. cit.*, Table 5.6, p. 137.

OTHER SOURCES OF EQUITY

The preceding analysis of financing alternatives has assumed that the parent firm would provide 100 percent of the equity for a foreign subsidiary. Increasingly, though, multinational firms are opening their foreign operations to other equity investors. These can include other foreign firms, a local firm, or even small local investors who do not intend to participate in management of the subsidiary. There are many reasons why firms investing in a foreign country may seek, or at least tolerate, other investors in the equity of the subsidiary. Another firm may bring complementary skills and resources to a project, which will increase its profitability. A local firm, moreover, may bring knowledge of the local market or control of a raw-material source to the venture. Each partner may bring complementary technical skills to the venture, or the foreign firm may have access to foreign markets and a marketing organization, while a local firm may have production know-how.

Another important reason for joint ventures is that they may be required by the host government. Joint ventures are particularly popular among governments of developing countries, which feel that they reduce the control of the economy by foreigners. Governments also view joint ventures as a vehicle for transfering management and technical skills to local firms and as a way by which the local economy can participate in monopoly profits of foreign firms. It should be remembered from Chapter 10 that foreign investors usually have some monopoly advantage that they are trying to exploit by means of their foreign investment, and the joint venture is one way in which local investors can share in the profits from that advantage.

In purely financial terms, it is worthwhile to have equity investments from other sources if the outside equity can be obtained at a cost that is less than the average cost of capital of the parent firm. Cheap equity capital normally would not be available in a perfect international capital market, since all equity investors would face the same opportunities, would perceive risks of a particular project in a similar way, and therefore would require the same return to justify an investment. In the real world of capital subsidies, restrictions on the use of capital and various other market imperfections may make it possible for a parent firm to find lower-cost capital from other equity investors. Anything that reduces the alternatives open to other investors might reduce the return they would require to justify investment in a subsidiary. For example, the direct-investment controls imposed by the United States until 1974, or the exchange control of the United Kingdom in effect until mid-1979, could have lowered the return horizons of investors (including firms) for investments in those countries. Foreign firms investing in those countries could take advantage of such opportunities to increase the return on their own equity. They could do so by means of many devices, including selling shares to the other equity investors at a higher price than they themselves effectively paid.

A parent firm might be in the less happy situation of having to accept higher-cost equity from other sources simply to finance a project. Very large investments with highly variable cash flows often require large amounts of equity in their financial structures. The large equity base is needed to provide adequate assurance to lenders that the loans will be serviced in the event of price declines or other unfavorable events. A large mining project may require a total investment of $500 million to $1 billion and equity of $300 million to $400 million. Equity of that magnitude is almost certainly more than one firm, no matter how large, is willing or able to provide. A group of equity investors may be needed, some of whom may require higher returns than others.

Obviously, it will only be possible to put together a group of equity investors if the overall return to equity is adequate to meet their varying requirements. There must be some "fat" in the project to enable the parent to accept higher-cost equity from other sources and still meet its own return targets. The surplus return available to equity investors may be the result either of the general profitability of the project or of subsidies provided by low-cost debt, as was the case with the Freeport Minerals project described earlier.

Coordination of the partners and formulation of financial policy will present a continuing challenge when the equity investors have different required returns. Those seeking higher returns, for example, probably will want higher dividend payouts. They also will want to apply different standards to new investments. In all, management will be more difficult when equity investors with differing objectives and perspectives provide the equity financing of an enterprise.

Summary

This chapter discusses another complicating element facing firms when they "go international": the bewildering array of possible sources of financing of corporate investments. The typical firm doing business only in a single country raises funds, as a general rule, within that country's borders. Even so, the choice among the various sources of financing is a complex one. For the truly multinational company, operating subsidiaries in many nations, the available sources of funds are far more numerous and the decision is much more difficult. Financing still might be done predominantly at home, especially if the parent were located in a capital-abundant country, but other attractive sources may be available both from within various host countries and sometimes from international agencies.

If international capital markets were perfect, the choice among sources of financing would be simple and the value of a particular project would not depend on the financing decision; however, the world is replete with examples of capital restrictions and other market imperfections. Because of these imperfections some sources of funds will be considerably cheaper to a firm than others. Under these circumstances, companies must evaluate several alternative financing plans to determine the effects of each plan on a project's cash flows.

The way in which subsidiaries actually have been financed has changed substantially as circumstances have changed. In 1968, for example, controls were placed on the outflows of funds from the United States so subsidiaries of U.S. firms substituted funds borrowed outside of U.S. for funds from the U.S. New equity funds from parents fell from 24 percent to only 3.3 percent of total sources. As a substitute for funds from the parent, subsidiaries increased their reliance on short-term debt owed to foreigners, particularly trade credit.

It may be somewhat surprising that trade credit was such an important part of the response by multinational firms to the U.S. Government's mandatory restrictions on direct investment; however, this response demonstrates that financial managers of multinational firms are perhaps the most sophisticated and resourceful in the world.

This resourcefulness has been demonstrated under changing conditions in the 1970s. After controls were repealed in 1974, U.S. multinational corporations again had free access to funds from the United States. By that time, however, financial managers could take advantage of the development of both national and international capital markets. As a result, they probably obtained a larger share of funds from financial intermediaries outside the United States. At the same time, multinational firms had to respond to greater pressures (and opportunities) to accept outside investors in their foreign ventures, so that outside equity also probably has become more important as a source of finance for subsidiaries.[5]

It is certain that the future will bring new challenges for multinational financial managers, whatever the accomplishments of the past. International capital markets are in a continual state of flux. New restrictions on capital flows are being imposed by governments as others are lifted. New sources

[5]The share of minority-owned subsidiaries in the total number of subsidiaries established by U.S. multinational enterprises in developing countries increased substantially in the first half of the 1970s. See U.N., Commission on Transnational Corporations, *Transnational Corporations in World Development* (U.N., 1978), Table 111–25, page 229.

of subsidized capital are being developed as others are phased out. In this changing environment, financial managers of multinational firms can survive only by basing decisions on fundamental analysis of opportunities as outlined in this chapter.

SELECTED READINGS

Business International Corporation, *Financing Foreign Operations* (New York: Business International, current issues).

Fama, Eugene, & Merton Miller, *The Theory of Finance* (New York: Holt, Rhinehart and Winston, 1972), Chapters 1–4.

de Faro, Cloris, & James Jucker, "The Impact of Inflation and Devaluation on the Selection of an International Borrowing Source," *Journal of International Business Studies,* Vol. 4, #2, Fall 1973, p. 97 ff.

Fruhan, William, *Financial Strategy: Studies in the Creation, Transfer and Destruction of Shareholder Value* (Homewood, Ill.: R. D. Irwin, 1978), Chapter 5.

Goldsmith, Raymond, *Financial Structure and Development* (New Haven, Conn.: Yale University Press, 1969), Chapter 1.

McKinnon, Ronald, *Money and Capital in Economic Development* (Washington, D.C.: Brookings Institution, 1973).

Modigliani, Franco, & Merton Miller, "The Cost of Capital, Corporation Finance, and the Theory of Investment," *American Economic Review,* Vol. 48, #3, June 1958, pp. 261–297.

Robbins, Sidney, & Robert Stobaugh, *Money in the Multinational Enterprise* (New York: Basic Books, 1973), Chapters 2, 4, 7, & 9.

Rodriguez, Rita, & Eugene Carter, *International Financial Management,* 2nd Ed. (Englewood Cliffs, N.J.: Prentice-Hall,) Chapters 14–16.

Shapiro, Alan, "Financial Structure and Cost of Capital in the Multinational Corporation," *Journal of Financial and Quantitative Analysis,* Vol. 13, #2, June 1978, pp. 211–226.

Simonson, Mario, "Inflation in the Money and Capital Markets of Brazil," in Howard Ellis (ed.), *The Economy of Brazil* (Berkeley: University of California Press, 1969), pp. 133–161.

World Bank, *Borrowing in International Capital Markets* (Washington, D.C.: World Bank, published quarterly).

CHAPTER 14

International
Financial
Management

INTRODUCTION

The key element differentiating financial management of internationally-involved enterprises from that of purely domestic operations is the possibility of incurring gains and losses through foreign exchange-rate changes. To be sure, there are other differences that already have been discussed in Chapters 12 and 13, but these relate mostly to the long-term acquisition and investment of funds in an on-going multinational firm. Global corporations do confront both problems and opportunities that would be quite unfamiliar to firms dealing only within the domestic economy; yet, even these differences basically are keyed to possible impacts on the firm of some future alteration in exchange rates. In managing the corporation's resources, executives must be continually cognizant of the cash-flow implications of such alterations.

This chapter will survey major aspects of financial management problems flowing from internationalization. Discussion will deal mostly with multinational corporate management, but in some cases the problems also apply to managers in firms with only trade relationships abroad. The first section will treat the concept of foreign exchange exposure and especially the problems of deriving meaningful ways to measure exposure. The chapter then will discuss methods for corporations to deal with exposure. Two final sections will introduce trade financing techniques and briefly describe the rapidly growing field of international banking.

FOREIGN EXCHANGE EXPOSURE

It is readily apparent that when a firm invests in plant and equipment overseas, the anticipated revenues and expenses from the investment generally will be denominated in a foreign currency. In fact, the assets and liabilities of the subsidiary itself technically are those of a foreign corporation and therefore also are carried in the host country's currency terms. On the other hand, parent-company executives are interested in the value of foreign cash flows (and the value of assets and liabilities held abroad) in the investing country's currency. Their shareholders, after all, usually are residents of that country and think of their wealth position in terms of its monetary units. As long as exchange rates remain stable, converting money measures from one currency to another presents little difficulty. Where exchange-rate instability occurs, however, then the difficult task of translating performance or balance-sheet figures from one currency to another inevitably arises. Under these circumstances, the parent firm may show either gains or losses strictly as a consequence of the exchange-rate movement. This possibility is the essence of foreign exchange exposure.

A brief example or two will serve to illustrate the problem. Table 14–1 depicts the balance sheet of A. R. Waters Cookie Company, Ltd., a wholly-owned British subsidiary of the U. S. corporation, Fantastic Bakeries, Inc.

Table 14–1   A. R. Waters Cookie Company, Ltd.

	Balance Sheet February 29, 1980		
	£	Exchange Rate	$
Cash	400	$2.28/	912
Accounts receivable	600		1,368
Inventory	700		1,596
Net plant and equipment	1,000		2,280
Total assets	£ 2,700		$6,156
Accounts payable	700		1,596
Long-term loans	400		912
Common stock	1,000		2,280
Retained earnings	600		1,368
Total liabilities and equity	£ 2,700		$6,156

As the table indicates, it is a simple matter for Fantastic to consolidate Waters' figures with its own through the established exchange rate, but suppose the rate were to change, say, to $2.00 prior to the end of the next accounting period. Would all accounts simply be translated at the new exchange rate? Or, would only some accounts be so translated? And what about any change in dollar value that results? These are the types of questions that arise in exposure considerations, and we shall be returning to them in the next section.

Changes in exchange rates, of course, affect not only balance-sheet items but also cash-flow transactions, which might be denominated in a currency other than that of the parent corporation. Suppose, for example, that an American importer purchased Mercedes-Benz trucks from West Germany in a transaction billed in marks for payment in 30 days. Clearly, an upward revaluation of the mark by, say, 20 percent relative to the dollar within the 30-day period would have an immediate and distressing impact upon the importer. The payment now would require approximately 20 percent more dollars than had been planned at the time the purchase was made. This type of exposure obviously is one inevitably encountered by some party in an international transaction whenever time elapses between the real goods transfer and its matching financial payment. It is also one, as we shall see later, for which avoidance mechanisms are an integral part of the world financial system.

Types of Exposure

Assuming that the objective of a corporation's management is maximization of stockholder welfare, the only meaningful type of exposure is one relating possible exchange-rate changes to effects on future cash flows. That is, managerial decisions regarding the appropriate actions to take either in anticipation of, or in response to, exchange-rate movements should concentrate on maximizing the present value of the firm's cash flows as measured in the parent company's currency. This type of exposure concept is markedly different from those usually measured, and it has been termed "economic" exposure. Its advantage is it forces managements to think about the future and decisions affecting it; its disadvantage is its inherent subjectivity and the difficulty of carrying out the necessary analysis.

Other exposure concepts typically deal with existing accounting information and, as such, may or may not be appropriate as a decision guide. One type, "translation" exposure, is intended to assist managements in interpreting balance-sheet figures when these figures are expressed nominally in a foreign currency changing in value relative to the parent company's currency. Translation exposure is supposed to indicate something about the possible change in liquidation value of the firm's overseas subsidiaries consequent to an exchange-rate movement. The major problem in such a measurement concept is that the exchange-rate fluctuations both cause, and are caused by, a host of other economic variables in the system; therefore, to ascertain the ultimate effects of an exchange-rate change alone is problematical, at best. Measures derived tend to use rather arbitrary rules to modify the accounting data, and the outcomes are heavily dependent upon the particular rules selected. Some of these and their impacts will be discussed later.

The other major exposure measure is called "transaction exposure." It is related more closely to economic exposure in that it does focus on the valuation of known future cash flows. Transaction exposure deals with the possibility of gain or loss stemming from the completion of a transaction occurring after an exchange rate has changed. Our example of the liability resulting from the importation of Mercedes-Benz trucks is a case of transaction exposure. When a firm's outstanding claims exceed its liabilities in a foreign currency, the company is said to be *positively* exposed. A foreign currency devaluation affecting a positively exposed firm would result in smaller-than-anticipated cash flows in the home currency. Other variations are derived easily.

Measuring transaction exposure is relatively straightforward, but, for other types of exposure, measurement causes real problems. Even in the conceptually simpler case, that of translation exposure, measurement is anything but obvious. To gain some feeling for the difficulties, consider again the balance sheet of A. R. Waters Company, Ltd., given in Table 14–1. Under rules adopted by the Financial Accounting Standards Board (FASB), translation of accounts at the new exchange rate would be based essentially on a monetary/nonmonetary division, sometimes called the *temporal method* when taken from an American accounting perspective. Using this convention, all monetary assets and liabilities would be translated at the new exchange rate; other accounts still would be converted at the exchange rate at which they were recorded originally.

The import of this translation schema can be seen using the Waters Company example. Table 14–2 depicts the method now required for the British subsidiary to be consolidated with the American parent after a 20-percent devaluation of the pound. The $46 exchange gain shown is clearly a direct consequence of the fact that the sum of monetary assets (£ 400 + £ 600) is smaller than the sum of monetary liabilities (£ 700 + £ 400). Thus, a pound devaluation reduces liabilities, measured in dollars, more than assets are lowered. Had the relevant grouping of assets been larger than liabilities (or had a pound revaluation upward taken place), an exchange loss would have been recorded. Such gains or losses, under the FASB convention, must be reported in each quarterly operations statement.

Two questions arise: (1) would alternative accounting conventions

Table 14–2   A. R. Waters Cookie Company, Ltd.

Balance Sheet
(After hypothetical change in exchange rate from $2.28/£ to $1.82/£)

	$ Old ($2.28/£)	$ New ($1.82/£)
Cash	912	728[a]
Accounts receivable	1,368	1,092[a]
Inventory	1,596	1,596
Net plant and equipment	2,280	2,280
Total	$6,156	$5,696
Accounts payable	1,596	1,274[a]
Long-term loans	912	728[a]
Common stock	2,280	2,280
Retained earnings	1,368	1,368
Exchange (loss) or gain	——	46
Total	$6,156	$5,696

[a]Accounts translated at new rate.

result in different gains and losses? and (2) what are the financial implications, if any, of the requirement to report foreign exchange gains and losses currently?

On the first question, the answer clearly is yes, as a quick glance at the figures will demonstrate. One among several alternative accounting methods, perfectly acceptable prior to the FASB pronouncement, is called the "current/noncurrent" translation. Under this method, current assets and liabilities would be translated at the new (or current) exchange rate, while noncurrent items would be converted at the previous rate. In the Waters Company case, for example, the current/noncurrent translation method would result in a $460 gain in the period, as compared with the $46 gain reported under the temporal method. It should be stressed that only the translation method has changed here; nothing in the "real world" differs between the two cases shown. For reasons unnecessary to elaborate here, the FASB has mandated that all American-based multinational corporations must be consistent in their use of the temporal method. Still, it should be remembered that this method is an arbitrarily selected convention that should, in principle, have little bearing on operational decision making.

If this conclusion is correct, then the second question, regarding the financial implications of reported gains and losses, would seem a strange one. Who, if not managers, is affected by the reported figures? Many executives, even some who agree that translation gains and losses should not be a guide to decision making, claim that the reported figures are, in fact, relevant. The reason, these managers assert, is that such figures are used to gauge performance and therefore to set managerial remuneration. One ignores reported net income only at one's peril, in this view.

Even if managers were not so evaluated, there might be yet another reason to be concerned about foreign exchange gains and losses being reported period by period in the corporate income statement. Before the current FASB rules were authorized, the effects of exchange variation could be smoothed through a reserve account. Disallowing use of sucb accounts has increased the variability of reported earnings, leading, some claim, to a higher level of perceived risk for shareholders. Higher risk, in turn, tends to lower the market value of a multinational company's share; therefore, the argument goes, executives must take steps to reduce foreign exchange translation gains and losses in order to preserve their shareholders' wealth positions. Unfortunately, as we shall see soon, offsetting profit variations from balance-sheet translation generally is not costless. Thus, reducing reported income fluctuations can have the side effect of lowering overall profitability.

In any case, the arguments supporting policies that hedge balance-sheet positions in foreign currencies are faulty on other grounds. If, for example, executive performance is measured primarily by "the bottom line," it should be a simple matter to adjust the figures to correct for translation variations. There is no evidence, moreover, that increased variability in reported income has any impact upon stock prices. It is difficult, therefore, to make a case for hedging based upon some presumed deleterious effect on shareholders. Evidence that does exist would suggest the opposite conclusion; that is, foreign exchange gains and losses stemming from balance-sheet translation have little or no effects on stockholders.

Economic exposure, although most relevant in principle to decision-making also is exceedingly difficult to measure. The reason, of course, is that changes in future cash flows resulting from an exchange-rate movement are highly conjectural. One must be concerned with estimating exchange-rate impacts on such operating variables as sales revenue and volume, manufacturing costs, and imput prices. For example, currency devaluations often are accompanied by price inflation, which might allow a foreign subsidiary to raise its sales prices without materially affecting volume. Cash flows, measured in the parent-company currency, would be unaffected by the devaluation under these circumstances. On the other hand, higher domestic currency prices, to the subsidiary, of imported materials would have the opposite effect.

The point is that measurement of a subsidiary's economic exposure entails a detailed analysis of the range of variables affecting future cash flows. This analysis, in turn, assumes knowledge of a variety of other aspects of the company's business environment. Minimally, the estimation would require information on demand elasticities, likely competitive reactions to both the exchange-rate change and the firm's prospective strategies, and data on manufacturing alternatives. Economic exposure analysis, therefore, must be part of a company's overall strategic planning activities.

Dealing with Exposure

Should managements wish to reduce foreign exposure, there is a variety of methods available. Increasingly, however, managers of large multinational corporations are choosing to leave some types of exposure uncovered. Their reason partly is that reducing one type of exposure can increase another type. (We will illustrate such cases later.) In addition, relatively efficient international capital markets make remedying some types of exposure more costly than the anticipated losses from the exposure itself. Where this occurs, executives more and more are accepting the possible exposure losses as another cost of doing business. This topic, too, will be discussed after further elaboration of exposure is given.

Translation and Transaction Exposure. We have stated previously that positive translation exposure exists when relevant exposed assets exceed liabilities on the foreign subsidiary's balance sheet. Relevancy, of course, depends upon the particular exposure measure chosen. The most obvious way to eliminate translation exposure involves restructuring the assets and liabilities in such a way that the measured exposure disappears. Returning to the Waters Cookie Company example, translation exposure, measured in British pounds, is negative (£ 100, see Table 14–1). To correct for this exposure, a manager might either increase monetary assets, reduce monetary liabilities, or both. In this case, that would entail enlarging either cash or accounts receivable, as one set of alternatives, or reducing accounts payable, or, less likely, taking out long-term loans.

It should be readily apparent that such moves might make little sense from a operational point of view, even though potential book losses from an exchange-rate change would be eliminated. Should the cash account be expanded solely for exposure reasons if additional working capital cannot be justified on operational grounds? Should payments on the subsidiary's liabilities be accelerated? If the response to such questions is negative, then quite conceivably correcting for the translation exposure could increase economic exposure. Stated differently, altering the balance-sheet accounts to avoid translation losses can reduce future cash flows, whether or not the exchange rate ultimately changes.

Translation and, especially, transaction exposures can be offset by hedges, and two major types of hedges are common: forward exchange market and money market. Both inovlve establishing offsetting transactions to eliminate possible foreign exchange gains and losses. Forward exchange contracts and their use in removing foreign exchange risk should be familiar from our discussion in Chapter 4. Generally, forward sale contracts are utilized to offset future receipts in a foreign currency; that is, by entering a contract to deliver the foreign currency at the date of obtaining the expected transaction revenues, the firm eliminates any possible gain or loss from an exchange-rate change. Conversely, forward purchase contracts for the appropriate term are utilized to cancel exchange positions involving foreign currency liabilities. In each case, forward contracts usually are self-liquidating when transaction exposures are hedged.

As in the forward market hedge, money market hedges involve creating a foreign currency asset (liability) to compensate for an upcoming debt (receipt). To hedge a forthcoming foreign currency debt, for example, a firm would convert parent-country funds to the currency of the liability. Once converted, the funds simply would be invested in that country until needed to meet the expected liability. On the other hand, a future foreign currency receipt would be hedged by borrowing that currency, entering the spot exchange market to obtain an equivalent amount of the home currency, then investing the funds in some type of earning asset there. Because of the need to convert from one currency to another in a money market hedge, it should be clear that countering a short-term transaction abroad can have the effect of modifying the firm's translation exposure; that is, cancelling a transaction exposure might add to a company's translation exposure.

The costs of entering hedges of the two types just discussed are, in well-developed money markets, generally equivalent. Exchange market hedges have costs (or possibly gains) that are related to the difference between the forward exchange rate and the spot rate, in addition to modest transactions charges. Similarly, costs of money market hedges are tied to the difference between the interest rates of the two countries involved in the hedge. For example, funds might be borrowed at interest abroad, converted, and reinvested at home. The fact that the two hedging methods are equivalent in principle can be understood easily by recalling the mechanism that determines the spread between spot and forward exchange rates. Interest arbitrage assures that the forward premium (discount) for currency will be related closely to the amount by which the foreign short-term interest rate is less (greater) than that at home.

A quick example might serve to make this point more clearly. Imagine yourself as an American importer of West German motorcycles, with payment for a recent shipment worth 100,000 DM due in 90 days. The hedging possibilities are:

1. Buy 90-day forward DMs.
2. Buy spot DMs, invest for 90 days in West Germany.

What are the hedging costs? In the first option, if forward DMs are selling at a premium, the cost would be the difference between the spot and forward rates. Suppose these rates were $.557 and $.551, respectively. The cost of entering the forward contract would be: 100,000 (.571−.557) = $1,400 or about 10 percent on an annualized basis. As we have seen in Chapter 4, however, the existence of a 10 percent forward premium implies that interest rates in West Germany would be approximately 10 percent lower than in the United States. The opportunity cost of choosing the second option thus would be the difference between the interest rate at which funds would have been invested (U.S.) and the rate in the country of short-term funds use (Germany). In both options, of course, the charge by the German exporter for deferred payment also would be a cost. We have assumed this charge to be part of the 100,000 DM owed.

Noting the high cost of hedging your liability, you could choose simply to accelerate payment, thereby avoiding the need to hedge at all. This type of strategy sometimes is used with respect to currencies that are expected to rise in value compared to the debtor's currency. In the opposite case, where the other currency is anticipated to devalue, one might lag payment as long as possible, in hopes of minimizing payment in the home currency. Such strategies have been termed "leads and lags," for obvious reasons.

It should be noted that if international capital market participants are correct in their collective assessment of the future, a leads-and-lags strategy will yield no gains or losses from a foreign exchange point of view. Our earlier example can be used to demonstrate why this should be so. Suppose that German and U.S. interest rates were, respectively, 5 and 15 percent (annual rates), which would be consistent with the observed spot and forward exchange rates. The implicit cost of paying early is the foregone interest on the short-term dollar investments from which the funds would be withdrawn, or 15 percent. If market indications were accurate, on the other hand, the mark should increase in value relative to the dollar by 2½ percent (10 percent, annualized) over the 90-day period. This amount represents the anticipated foreign exchange cost of delaying payment. In addition, interest charges would bave to be paid on the DM bill of exchange, which, given German interest rates, would approximate 5 percent again. The expected total cost would be 15 percent on an annualized basis.

Note that the condition, "if international capital market participants are correct,'' does contain the word ''if.'' In fact, market participants could be wrong in their collective judgement about the future exchange rate. If, for example, the mark appreciated by 3 percent instead of 2 ½, then the annualized cost of delaying payment would be 17 percent. Accelerating payment, viewed retrospectively, would then appear to have been the right decision. Had the actual exchange rate movement been less than 2½ percent, however, the cost of advanced payment would have exceeded the cost of delaying remittal, again in retrospect. In brief, the *realized* cost of accelerating payment is entirely a function of the actual change in the exchange rate over the period.

Of course, business executives accelerate payments or enter hedging arrangements expressly to avoid having to worry about future movements in foreign exchange rates. They typically prefer to deal with situations characterized by certainty rather than uncertainty, especially since, during these rather chaotic times, exchange-rate movements are a decidedly uncertain aspect of the international financial scene. Not infrequently, business managers willingly incur higher costs in order to escape the possibility of adverse movements in currency values, even where such movements would, in fact, have resulted in no foreign exchange losses.

It should be mentioned in concluding our discussion of translation and transaction exposure hedging that many multinational executives are having second thoughts about subjecting their companies to the extra costs of uncertainity avoidance. The reasons are not difficult to comprehend. With their normal transactions in a multiplicity of currencies, multinational firms have such diverse exposure that they can take advantage of the statistical regularities characterizing foreign exchange markets. While single exposures might be hedged reasonably, a firm experiencing over a period of time 100 such exposures would find a policy of no hedging to be appealing. With that many exposures, foreign exchange gains might be expected to just about offset losses over time. For such firms, persistent hedging simply increases operating costs by the amount of the transaction expenses.

There are other reasons to expect that this conclusion might be true. Several studies have shown that capital markets of most industrial nations are sufficiently integrated with each other that exchange rates are a good indication of future expectations. Thus, in statistical terms, the forward exchange rate is an unbiased estimator of the future spot rate for several currencies vis-a-vis the dollar. So also is the relative price-inflation rate between two countries an indication of future expectations regarding their exchange rates. In situations where such linkages generally hold, costs of hedging (aside from transactions costs) on average will equal foreign exchange losses for a firm engaged in large numbers of transactions. Large multinational corporations can minimize costs, therefore, by remaining unhedged for many of their transactions in developed parts of the world, thus eliminating expenses incurred in entering and closing hedges.

Economic Exposure. By its very nature, dealing with economic exposure is more complicated then either translation or transaction exposure. As stated previously, concern about a corporation's future cash flows is the basic subject matter of strategic planning and therefore cannot be separated from that activity. Fluctuating exchange rates are only one element of a constantly shifting international economic environment that a firm must factor into the strategic decision-making apparatus; therefore, it should be remembered in the following brief discussion that concentrating here only on corporate adjustments to exchange-rate movements is tantamount to observing only the visible portion of an iceberg.

Discussion of economic exposure strategies can be most easily accomplished through a case example. Consider a Japanese manufacturer of color television sets, of which a substantial proportion are exported to the United States. The yen has been rising in value relative to the dollar, and the likelihood of further increases appears to be high. Part of the reason for the rising yen value is the persistent rate of U.S. price inflation as compared with Japan. The pertinent economic exposure question is: how, if at all, does the manufacturer adapt operations to assure the highest possible yen cash flows over time?

One can imagine a variety of possible reactions, depending upon the economic impacts of the continued dollar deterioration on the firm's business. It is possible, for example, that the relatively higher U.S. inflation rate is not reflected in prices for television sets here. If so, then the Japanese firm can look forward to increased price competition, the prospect of being unable to adjust dollar prices to compensate for exchange-rate changes, and, as a result, diminished yen operating margins. Clearly, the distressing outlook calls for some kind of shift in the strategic position of the manufacturer with respect to at least the American market.

One possibility is to concentrate sales and promotion efforts in the United States on models less sensitive to higher prices. Stressing higher quality might be a strategy that consciously abandons the mass market, but it also might be the only plan that would reasonably assure continued cash flows. Alternatively, the Japanese manufacturer might consider other manufacturing locations, including the United States itself. If the exchange-rate movement, together with prevailing trends in manufacturing technology, indicates a shifting pattern of comparative advantage, as it seems to in our hypothesized example, then diversifying production facilities may be the only viable long-term strategic move. In the shorter term, the company could consider methods to reduce effective prices by altering credit terms or by holding local inventories in the United States. Such means lower overall costs to American distributors and retailers, enabling them to maintain competitive prices in the marketplace.

One can imagine easily other strategies that like those outlined previously, actually have been followed by Japanese television manufacturers. These would include production, financial, and marketing options. We hope that the point has been made: economic exposure analysis is, in reality, equivalent to long-term strategic planning that considers exchange-rate movements along with a multitude of other variables. Moreover, it should be emphasized that economic exposure is not a problem restricted only to firms doing business internationally; purely local firms can be exposed as well. Certainly, shifting exchange rates have precipitated much increased competition for German textile producers, as American companies find newly attractive market opportunities in Europe. The Germans have not been major exporters, and yet their local market position has been eroded as a consequence of the rising value of marks in terms of dollars. This, too, is a case of economic exposure.

Other Measures. In our necessarily brief discussion of ways to deal with exposure, we have focused on only a few common methods employed by companies. There are, of course, other possibilities that will not be covered at any length here. For example, a variety of so-called swap arrangements can be utilized, especially in countries with restricted capital markets. Under one such arrangement, companies obtain needed funds abroad in cooperation with a company or bank needing dollar loans here or elsewhere. In fact, our major emphasis in this section has been on hedging in industrial countries, where financing can take place quite freely across national boundaries. For U.S. businesses, transactions in these countries represent by far the majority of cases exposed to exchange risk. When capital markets are less free, problems of handling risk are more complex. Readers desiring to learn more about such situations are referred to the selection of international business finance books listed at the end of the chapter.

TRADE FINANCING

By far the largest international requirement for financing is derived from exporters and importers. Without adaptable financing procedures, the amount of trade conducted surely would not have expanded as rapidly as has been experienced, especially since the advent of relatively flexible exchange rates. Because time inevitably is required in the production–export sequence, foreign exchange risk is an inescapable aspect of trade financing. Someone in the trading relationship must experience exposure, and, to be effective, the financial procedures and instruments must be available to allow the parties to avoid exchange risk. In the paragraphs to follow, a few of the more commonly used trade documents are described.

Financial Instruments Used in International Trade

Letters of Credit.   Generally, a letter of credit is a commerical-bank document issued at the request of an importer. In effect, the bank, through a letter of credit, substitutes its better-known credit for that of its client importer. The bank agrees to honor an exporter's claim for a clearly specified shipment. Needless to say, the bank's willingness to act as a financial intermediary is contingent upon the importer's credit standing and ability to repay the bank. The letter can be sent directly to the exporter or to the exporter's bank.

There are numerous variations on the standard letter, but its ultimate value is that it authorizes the exporter, under prescribed conditions, to draw drafts (described later) on tbe issuing bank and to receive payment without worrying about the importer's credit worthiness.

Export Drafts.   With or without the security of a commercial bank's letter of credit, an exporter can issue a draft to finance a transaction. An export draft is similar to a personal check, except that it is initiated by the party ultimately to receive the funds, usually the exporter or its bank. The draft is a written order instructing the importer (or the importer's bank) to pay a particular amount at a specified time to a designated individual or, in some cases, to the bearer of the document. Draft amounts may be due on sight or may specify that payment is to be made at a particular future date.

Banker's Acceptance.   A time export draft drawn on an importer's bank, when expressly acknowledged by the bank, becomes a banker's acceptance. The bank's guarantee makes an acceptance a highly marketable financial instrument that can be sold to any interested investor. This feature gives the exporter considerably more flexibility in obtaining funds immediately or at any time prior to the acceptances' maturity, simply by selling at a discount. The importance of acceptances in U.S. foreign trade can be gauged by the almost $30 billion in acceptances outstanding on banks in this country.

Other Aspects of Trade Financing

Most international trade transactions involve a parallel financial interchange in the foreign exchange market. Because of this aspect of trade, exports and imports are probably the single largest source of transaction exposure. Almost inevitably, someone in an international sales arrangement assumes a position with exchange risk. Frequently, therefore, trade financing involves not only an instrument of the type described previously but also an additional transaction intended for hedging purposes. The hedge normally is carried out in the forward market in a manner discussed earlier.

It should be noted that not all trade results in a foreign exchange transaction. On some occasions, exporters or importers might be willing to conduct business in a currency other than their own and might, for this reason, maintain deposits in that currency. The most obvious example is trade financed through the Eurodollar market, in which foreigners maintain continuous deposits. Needless to say, a Eurodollar deposit, if left unhedged, exposes the holder to the foreign exchange risk of that currency, but the exposure is not a direct consequence of the international trade transaction itself.

INTERNATIONAL BANKING

Conventional wisdom holds that the expansion of American banks abroad has been a response to the needs of their large corporate clients. As the corporations became multinational, it was necessary for banks wishing to retain their client borrowers to follow along. In addition to this natural desire, some observers also would cite U.S. capital controls of the later 1960s as a stimulus for bank internationalization. These controls made it very difficult for corporations to raise funds in the United States for use in financing most overseas operations. Instead, the companies were forced to borrow abroad, and if New York banks wanted to retain this business, they were obliged to establish their own international branches.

It is true that the international interests of American banks expanded rapidly in the decade of the 1960s. During that time, the number of banks with branches in foreign countries grew from 8 to more than 100; and the assets of these branches expanded 10-fold, from $3.5 billion to $37.6 billion. It thus it easy to verify that the follow-the-client motivation was a strong one for bank managers.

In more recent years, however, the persuasiveness of that view would be difficult to maintain. The number of banks abroad has changed little since 1970, but by the end of 1977 their branch assets had increased to an incredible $195 billion.[1] During this time, the contribution of multinational corporate borrowing overseas has been quite small. In fact, for the regional

---

[1]Federal Reserve Bank of Chicago, *International Letter,* No. 372, June 23, 1978.

banks entering world markets for the first time in the early 1970s, multinationals represent a very small percentage of the banks' international portfolio.[2] On the contrary, growth today is due to new lending opportunities abroad, ones more attractive to the banks than an expansion of loans at home. Moreover, the rate of growth of foreign lending in recent years has been higbest in the less-developed countries which have been hard hit by rising energy prices.

International Bank Functions

Today's sophisticated international bank can offer services to both traders and large manufacturing corporations that cannot be matched by purely local institutions serving the same customers. To be sure, smaller banks attempt to provide similar services through correspondent relationships with banks abroad, but for the frequent customer the level of service tends to be inferior. This can be seen by reference to typical functions undertaken in international banking.

As a rule, the foreign branches of American banks attempt to provide approximately the same services for corporate clients that local banks in those countries offer. These would include trade financing, short- and medium-term lending (including lending through syndication), deposit services, and financial advice. With local branch offices, however, international banks can provide a continuity service for corporate customers that is essentially an extension of the home-country operation. The bank's personnel know and understand customers' problems through long familiarity. Smaller banks have attempted to compete through their overseas correspondent branches and were quite successful in earlier days because of the correspondent's greater familiarity with the local environment. Over time, however, this advantage has been eroded as the branch banks themselves develop more and more local contacts and knowledge.

In addition to continuity of service, international banks have other valuable strengths. Probably most important from the viewpoint of a multinational corporation is the global network of branch offices maintained by the large banks. Not only does this network permit the corporation to obtain familiar banking services wherever it has business, but the network's existence allows the bank to develop other services. Primary among tbese is the international bank's world-wide information system, permitting virtually instantaneous transfer of funds. Large banks today can reduce costs

---

[2]David Ramsour, "An Inquiry into the Meaning of and Policy Response to Country Risk in Bank Credit," unpublished Ph.D. dissertation, The University of Texas at Dallas, October 1979.

greatly for the multinational corporation by assisting its managers in their global cash-management tasks.

Organization of International Banking

United States international banking activities frequently are organized in rather complex ways; however, the major structural characteristics of the organizations can be described by two somewhat distinct patterns: branch banking and Edge Act subsidiaries. Most of the banking offices abroad are, in fact, branch banks of an American parent. These branches are legal extensions of the parent U.S. bank in the sense that their assets and liabilities are considered part of the respective parents. For example, deposits are legal obligations of the parent banks, a fact that lends considerably more security to the branches' activities.

Possibly of more interest here are Edge Act subsidiaries of American banks. These subsidiaries are authorized under a law passed over 60 years ago, but their popularity has increased immensely in recent times. The Edge Act authorizes banks to establish wholly- or partially-owned subsidiaries to conduct international financial operations, including banking. Unlike their parents, Edge Act corporations can invest in equity securities of manufacturing and other types of companies. In addition, they are allowed to own foreign banking subsidiaries or to participate in joint ventures with foreign financial institutions. These provisions of tbe law have enabled U.S. banks to take part in a variety of activities otherwise not possible. A large bank today is likely to have numerous Edge Act subsidiaries, and tbese subsidiaries in turn will have other subsidiaries and joint venture/consortia operations throughout the world.

Summary

This chapter has served as an introduction to international financial management, a topic far more extensive than can be covered adequately here. In particular, the chapter concentrated on the various definitions of foreign exchange exposure and on methods available to managers for dealing with that exposure. Economic exposure, which stresses the impact of foreign exchange-rate movements on the firm's cash flows, was regarded here as most pertinent to a company's strategic plans. At the same time, this type of exposure was shown to be both subjective and difficult to measure. Other types of exposure measures, in particular translation and transaction, have been derived from accounting information. Sometimes such measures are consistent with economic exposure calculations, as when a rate change affects the value of an account receivable. In other cases, the measures can conflict, as when a firm lowers working capital below its optimal level to reduce a translation exposure.

Hedges have been derived for most exposures. Normally, these hedges take the form of transactions in forward exchange or money markets; however, companies can avoid translation exposures by adjusting the structure of the firms' foreign assets and liabilities. The chapter concluded with a brief discussion of the topics of trade financing methods and of the rapidly expanding field of international banking.

SELECTED READINGS

Aggarwal, Raj, *Financial Policies for the Multinational Company: The Management of Foreign Exchange* (New York: Praeger, 1976).

Aliber, R.Z., & C.P. Stickney, "Accounting Measures of Foreign Exchange Risk: The Long and Short of H," *Accounting Review,* January 1975, pp. 44–57.

Eiteman, David, & Arthur Stonehill, *Multinational Business Finance,* Second Edition (Reading, Mass.: Addison-Wesley, 1979).

Giddy, Ian, "Exchange Risk: Whose View?" *Financial Management,* Summer 1977, pp. 23–33.

Giddy, Ian, "An Integrated Theory of Exchange Rate Equilibrium," *Journal of Financial and Quantitative Analysis,* December 1976, pp. 883–892.

Heckerman, D., "The Exchange Risks of Foreign Operations," *Journal of Business,* January 1972, pp. 42–48.

Henning, Charles, William Pigott, & R.H. Scott, *International Financial Management* (New York: McGraw-Hill, 1978).

Logue, D., & G. Oldfield, "Managing Foreign Assets When Foreign Exchange Markets Are Efficient," *Financial Management,* Summer 1977, pp. 16–22.

Ricks, David, *International Dimensions of Corporate Finance* (Englewood Cliffs, N.J.: Prentice-Hall, 1978).

Robbins, Sidney, & Robert Stobaugh, *Money in the Multinational Enterprise: A Study of Financial Policy* (New York: Basic Books, 1973).

Rodriguez, Rita, & E. Carter, *International Financial Management,* Second Edition (Englewood Cliffs, N.J.: Prentice-Hall, 1979).

Shapiro, Alan, "Defining Exchange Risk," *The Journal of Business,* January 1977, pp. 37–39.

Weston, J.F., & B.W. Sorge, *Guide to International Financial Management* (New York: McGraw-Hill, 1977).

CHAPTER

15

Organizing for International Production

INTRODUCTION

A new set of problems emerges once the decision to invest abroad has been made. The multinational enterprise has to incorporate the new investment into its world-wide production, marketing, financing, and research plans. An organizational structure must be devised so that foreign investments make a maximum contribution to the profits of the multinational firm. This organizational structure is an aggregate of several components. On the one hand, it is a legal description of the firm and its subunits that determines the rights and obligations the firm has with the governments concerned. On the other hand, the organization is a structure to be used to establish objectives, identify problems, process information, and reach decisions. Such a decision-making structure specifies certain reporting and authority relationships, information flow networks, and the location of decision-making authority within the firm.

The complexity of the organizational problems facing large, multinational corporations can be illustrated by reference to a specific example. The Charles Pfizer Corporation, a large pharmaceutical firm, produces finished pharmaceuticals, bulk pharmaceuticals, veterinary medicines, fine chemicals, and cosmetics. Bulk pharmaceuticals are manufactured in about eight countries around the world, which include the United States, the United Kingdom, Argentina, India, and Spain. These bulk pharmaceuticals then are either processed into finished drugs and veterinary medicines or sold to other drug manufacturers. For the most part, drug-processing and veterinary-medicine plants are smaller than the bulk-pharmaceutical plants sold to other drug manufacturers. For the most part, drug-processing and veterinary-medicine plants are smaller than the bulk-pharmaceutical plants and are located in many countries. Production of both chemicals and cosmetics is independent of pharmaceutical production. Chemicals are produced in Australia, Belgium, Argentina, France, the United Kingdom, and Canada. Cosmetics are produced outside the United States in several countries, including France, Mexico, Chile, and Italy.

Pfizer does not produce an unusual number of products; indeed, it does not operate in an unusual number of countries when compared with other multinational corporations. Yet, obviously the company must be organized to make a large number of decisions. It must decide which markets to serve and the prices to be charged for each product. In addition, it must decide which plant or plants will supply each market. Finally, with pharmaceuticals and veterinary products, it must decide how the output of each bulk pharmaceutical plant is to be divided among the various pharmaceutical and veterinary processing plants as opposed to external markets. This last problem is complicated by the fact that there are many types of bulk pharmaceuticals, each of which must be allocated among several users.

How then can the company organize itself to make these decisions? Clearly there are too many decisions to be made by one person. Some sort of decentralization is required, but how far should it be carried? Should each plant make its own price, output, and input decisions? Should decisions be centralized for each product? These are the kinds of questions that will be addressed in this chapter.

LEGAL ORGANIZATION

The legal form taken by a corporation operating in many countries will depend on the laws of the countries, and particularly on the laws of the "home" country.[1] Firms located in the United States may organize foreign operations as either branches or as legally independent subsidiaries. A branch is an integral part of the parent in the sense that its accounts are consolidated automatically with those of the parent and hence its earnings are taxed immediately by the United States. If the foreign operation is organized as a subsidiary, its earnings usually are not taxed until they are repatriated as dividends. A subsidiary's accounts may or may not be consolidated with those of the parent.

The choice between organizing a foreign operation as a branch or as a subsidiary usually will be determined by the tax laws of the home country.

---

[1]The home country is the country from which foreign investments are made and usually is the country where a majority of stockholders resides.

In the case of U.S. corporations investing overseas, organizing a foreign operation as a branch of the parent is desirable when consolidation of accounts is advantageous. Consolidation is advantageous either when the foreign operation produces at a loss so that the taxable income of the parent can be reduced, or in extractive industries so that a depletion allowance can be calculated on the revenues of the foreign operation.

Consolidation, for tax purposes, of the foreign operation with those of the U.S. parent is automatic if the foreign operation is organized as a branch. Firms in oil and mining industries, therefore, usually organize their foreign extractive operations as branches. Firms in other industries also may organize their foreign operations as branches in their early, unprofitable years. When the operation becomes profitable, it then can be acquired as a wholly-owned subsidiary of the parent so that the benefits of tax deferral are obtained.

Besides the legal choice between organizing foreign operations as branches or subsidiaries, taxes have other influences on the organizational structure of multinational enterprises. The desire to defer taxes leads corporations to establish subsidiaries in countries with low tax rates. The function of these "tax-haven" subsidiaries is to "collect" profits and thus to reduce the corporation's total tax liability. For example, Pittsburgh Plate Glass Company (PPG) set up a Swiss subsidiary and sold glass to it. The subsidiary then resold most of the products to two PPG subsidiaries in Canada. These, in turn, used the glass to make automobile windows and other products. The Swiss subsidiary never handled the glass, which was shipped directly from the United States to Canada; however, through the use of transfer prices, PPG's Swiss subsidiary recorded a substantial profit that otherwise would have been earned by its Canadian or U.S. subsidiaries. Since tax rates on corporate profits are lower in Switzerland than in the United States or Canada, the use of the Swiss subsidiary enabled PPG to reduce its total tax bill.[2]

Use of tax-haven subsidiaries such as PPG's Swiss subsidiary has been curtailed by the tax reform act of 1962. That act made profits of foreign subsidiaries, earned on purchases from or sales to other controlled subsidiaries, subject to immediate U.S. income taxation. Thus, the profits of PPG's Swiss subsidiary, if it did nothing else but buy glass from the U.S. parent and sell it to the Canadian subsidiary, would be taxed by the United States. If, however, the Swiss subsidiary earns less than 30 percent of its profits from the buying and selling transactions, its profits are not taxed by the United States. As the proportion of profits from intrafirm transactions

[2]William Carley, "Lands of Opportunity; International Concerns Use a Variety of Means to Cut U.S. Tax Bills," *Wall Street Journal,* 53:1, October 18, 1972, page 1.

increases above 30 percent, the proportion subject to immediate U.S. taxation also increases; hence, when 80 percent of profits are earned from such transactions, all profits are taxed at the full rate by the United States. It would appear, then, that the tax reform act has left some remaining scope for the operation of tax havens.

CENTRALIZATION OR DECENTRALIZATION OF DECISIONS

The legal form adopted by a multinational firm has little bearing on the organization for decision making. The major part of this chapter deals with the more important issues of centralization or decentralization of decisions. This issue is critical because most other choices with respect to organizational form are influenced strongly by the extent to which decisions are or can be decentralized. A firm's information network, for example, must be tailored to the locus of decision-making authority.

Centralization versus decentralization is not a black-and-white matter. There are degrees of decentralization. Some types of decisions may be decentralized while others are necessarily centralized. The main organizational problem is that of determining which decisions should be decentralized and the *extent* to which they should or must be decentralized.

Because of differing needs, individual multinational corporations have dealt with the issue of decentralization in different ways. Some, including Pfizer, give their subsidiaries a great deal of autonomy. Others, including the international oil companies, maintain tight central control over most aspects of production, finance, and marketing. These differences in organizational philosophy and practice are not the result of mere whims on the part of the managements involved; rather, they reflect real differences in the characteristics of the firms and the circumstances they confront in the international marketplace. Specifically, organizational choice reflects the extent to which a firm's international operations are interdependent. Centralization of decisions is attractive when international operations are interdependent, that is, when the actions of one subsidiary affect the results of one or more of the others. Decentralized decisions, in a situation of interdependence, may not take into account the effects of the decisions on other parts of the firm. Consequently, decisions may be made that are not optimal for the firm as a whole, even though the individual subsidiary may be optimizing its own operations through these same decisions. Centralization is imposed to avoid such suboptimal decisions and to coordinate activities where interdependence is important.

Obvious examples of interdependence are found in the areas of production; however, interdependence in marketing and finance are equally important. Production interdependence may be due to the technical characteristics of the production process, or to input–output relations among subsidiaries. Production processes are technically interdependent if a by-product is produced at one stage of production and can be used at a later stage. For example, carbon dioxide gas is a by-product in the production of ammonia. It is then used with ammonia to produce urea, a basic nitrogenous fertilizer.

Production processes are interdependent in another sense when one subsidiary supplies inputs to other subsidiaries. For example, Charles Pfizer's bulk pharmaceutical subsidiaries are interrelated with the veterinary medicine and finished pharmaceutical plants because the latter two use bulk pharmaceuticals as inputs. Nevertheless, interdependence is not complete because bulk pharmaceuticals also can be bought and sold on the world market, even though a portion of them are being transferred between subsidiaries.

Interdependence in the marketing activities of the multinational firm is less clear-cut; however, it is no less important than production interdependence. Marketing activities of subsidiaries may be competitive, especially when two or more subsidiaries produce the same or similar products and compete with each other in export markets. The converse also is true. Marketing activities may be complementary. This is the case when common marketing channels are used for different products of the same firm, or when advertising in one area of the world spills over into other areas and influences the sales of other subsidiaries. In either situation the subsidiaries are interdependent because decisions made by one affect the performance of one or more of the others.

Financial interdependence among subsidiaries of multinational corporations is probably more pervasive than either production or marketing interdependence. Financing decisions are interdependent if the financing of one subsidiary influences the amount, terms, and availability of capital to another. This interdependence exists if the amount of capital the parent firm can obtain is limited; this is especially true if the terms of finance are determined by the corporation's overall capital structure. Of course, as indicated in Chapter 13, if international capital markets function efficiently, the cost and availability of capital to a particular investment project would be independent of the corporation's other activities; that is, a perfect capital market would judge a project on its own merits. Unfortunately, international capital markets are far from perfect, and financial interdependence is a fact of life in most multinational corporations.

Interdependence in production, marketing, or finance increases the attractiveness of centralized decisions because it cannot be assumed that decentralized decisions will take the interests of the entire corporation into account. Suppose, for example, that Pfizer's pharmaceutical and veterinary medicine subsidiaries were allowed to decide the amount and source of their bulk pharmaceutical inputs. It is entirely possible that they would decide to purchase on the open market, even when the company's own bulk plants were operating at less than capacity. Similarly, each subsidiary might decide to undertake too little advertising or too much investment because they did not take into account the effects of their own individual actions on the sales or capital costs of other subsidiaries. In all of these cases there is an incentive for the parent firm to centralize these decisions so that the corporate point of view will prevail.

Centralization of decisions is not without its costs. For example, centralization of the important decisions does little or nothing to improve the motivation of subsidiary managers. Most managers are motivated by a need for concrete achievement. One indication of their achievement is the performance of the units under their control. In a business-oriented society, performance usually is measured by profitability; however, if important decisions are centralized, the profitability of a subsidiary is determined largely by influences beyond local management's control, so there may be little incentive for local managers to perform effectively in areas that remain within their control.

In addition to motivation problems, centralization of decision making also requires extensive communication that is both costly and time consuming. While monetary costs of international communication have been reduced in recent years through jet air travel, communications satellites, computers, and other electronic devices, the costs of communication nevertheless involve more than the monetary expenditures required to send information between subsidiary and parent. Noise and distortion inevitably are introduced into the communications process, with the result that bad decisions sometimes are made, and good decisions may fail to be implemented adequately. Added to these problems are the costs of delays resulting from centralization. Delay may cause opportunities to be missed or costs to be incurred that could have been avoided if greater flexibility in decision making had been possible.

The costs of delay are greatest where markets and the competitive environment change rapidly. Swift decisions are essential in such situations, either to take advantage of opportunities or to avoid threats and disasters. Some of the efficiency of centralized decisions may have to be sacrificed, therefore, to achieve the benefits of flexible response to changes in local conditions.

The ability of a firm to centralize decisions, of course, depends on the form its foreign operations take. As was seen earlier, the firm has less control over the decisions of licensees than of a wholly-owned subsidiary. Some of the organizational issues presented by different forms of foreign operations are discussed in a later section of this chapter.

In summary, there are advantages both to centralization and to decentralization of decisions in a multinational enterprise. The problem facing an international business manager is that of devising an organizational structure that decentralizes decisions as much as possible, in order to encourage motivation and flexibility, while it retains sufficient centralization to exploit fully the cost or other savings brought about by interdependence. Appropriate structures will be different in every case, because the nature of interdependence and the requirements for flexibility are different in every firm. Nevertheless, some broad alternative structures are considered in the following sections.

DECENTRALIZATION BY MEANS OF TRANSFER PRICES

The bulk pharmaceutical plants of Charles Pfizer Company are interdependent with finished-pharmaceuticals and veterinary-medicine plants because bulk pharmaceuticals are used to make finished medicines for both humans and animals. While production of the various plants could be coordinated by centralizing production decisions, many firms attempt to coordinate production decisions in such circumstances by setting appropriate transfer prices on intrafirm transfers. Each subsidiary then is told to maximize its own profits, with the hope that the transfer price will lead all of the subsidiaries to make production and sales decisions in the best interests of the firm as a whole. Production decisions thus are coordinated even though they have been decentralized.

The problem of coordinating production decisions among interrelated subsidiaries is no different from the problem of coordinating decisions within an entire economy. There are interrelations among various firms in an economy, just as there are interrelations among the subsidiaries of one firm. The objective of the entire economy is to use its resources efficiently, just as the objective of an individual firm is to produce what is demanded by consumers at the lowest possible cost.

Prices serve to coordinate production decisions among firms in an interrelated economy, by telling producers what products are demanded and indicating consumer preferences for current and future consumption. Prices also indicate costs of production. Prices, therefore, provide the information that is necessary for decentralizing decisions. If the economy is competitive, decentralized decisions based on market prices can result in an efficient use of the economy's resources.

If prices make possible efficient decentralized decisions in an entire economy, can they perform the same function for subsidiaries of a single firm? To answer this question, consider one of Charles Pfizer's bulk pharmaceutical subsidiaries and an associated pharmaceutical processing subsidiary. Can a price be set for bulk pharmaceuticals that would allow both subsidiaries to make decentralized decisions that maximize their individual profits and simultaneously maximize profits of the firm? If so, what is the price with these magical qualities, and who should set it?

Establishing a Transfer Price That Will Achieve Decentralization

The answer to these questions depends on the circumstances. Complete decentralization of Pfizer's production decisions can be achieved if there is a competitive world market for bulk pharmaceuticals. Should that be the case, the bulk product should be transferred between the subsidiaries at the world market price, and each subsidiary could be allowed freedom in making production and sales decisions. Under these circumstances, if each subsidiary attempts to maximize its own profit, together they simultaneously will maximize the firm's profits.

When the world market for bulk pharmaceuticals is not competitive, the situation is more complicated. It then is not possible to allow the subsidiaries complete freedom in their decision making. Some central direction is required if the firm's profits are to be maximized.

The nature of the central direction that is needed may be demonstrated by assuming that the supplying subsidiary has a world monopoly in the production of certain bulk pharmaceuticals. World market demand for these bulk pharmaceuticals is given by the curve DD_m in Figure 15–1. Since we are assuming a monopoly, it also is true that this curve is the demand curve facing the division producing the bulk pharmaceuticals. This obviously is not a situation of perfect competition; hence, there is need for a transfer-pricing decision. The demand curve indicates the average price that can be obtained for all units at each level of sales. Marginal revenue, MR_m in the figure, indicates the additional revenue obtained from the sale of one more unit of bulk pharmaceuticals in the market. Marginal revenue is below the demand curve because an additional unit can be sold only by lowering the price on all other units.

The supplying subsidiary can sell to a processing subsidiary in another country, as well as on the open market. The processing subsidiary processes the bulk pharmaceuticals into finished drugs and sells them to produce the net marginal revenue to the firm of NMR_p in Figure 15–1. Net marginal revenue from processing is marginal revenue from selling finished drugs less the marginal cost of processing.

Marginal revenue from world market sales and from sales to the processing subsidiary each may be denominated in different currencies; however, it is assumed that exchange rates are fixed and all marginal revenues may be expressed in the same currency and summed to produce the total marginal revenue (TMR) available to the firm for the production

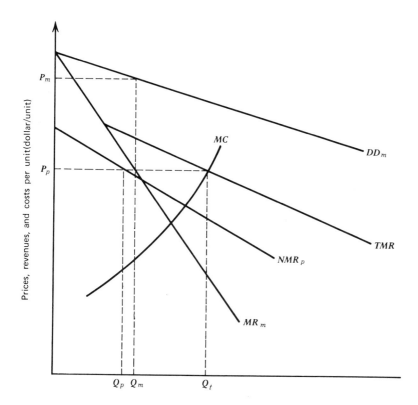

Figure 15–1. Quantity of bulk pharmaceuticals.

of bulk pharmaceuticals. Total marginal revenue is the maximum additional net revenue available to the firm from the production and sale (either on the open market or to the processing subsidiary) of one more unit of bulk pharmaceuticals. Clearly, the additional net revenue that can be obtained from the sale of an additional unit of bulk pharmaceuticals falls as the number of units already being sold increases.

The profits of the drug firm are maximized if the marginal cost (MC) of producing bulk pharmaceuticals equals the marginal net revenue from its sale or further processing. Optimum output is Q_t in Figure 15–1, at the point where *TMR* equals *MC*. This total is allocated optimally between sale and further processing when the marginal revenue obtained from each use is equal (otherwise reallocation between uses would be profitable). Consequently, Q_t should be divided so that Q_m is sold on the world market (at a price of P_m), while Q_p is transferred to the processing subsidiary at a price of P_p.

A processing subsidiary free to maximize its own profits would buy Q_p

only if the transfer price were set at P_p, the marginal cost of producing Q_t. The processing subsidiary maximizes its profits by equating its net marginal revenue from processing to the transfer price (which is its marginal cost of acquiring the bulk pharmaceutical). The processing subsidiary would not find it profitable to process as much as Q_p if the transfer price were higher than P_p. Processing and selling an amount less than Q_p, however, would reduce the drug company's total profits, since the additional revenue that could be obtained from processing additional amounts of bulk pharmaceuticals would exceed the cost of producing the additional units. The transfer price therefore must be set at P_p to induce the profit-maximizing processing subsidiary to purchase an optimum amount of bulk pharmaceuticals.

A supplying subsidiary would not set the transfer price at P_p if it were free to maximize its own profits. Instead, it would regard the NMR_p curve in Figure 15–1 as the processing subsidiary's demand curve. In turn, it would calculate its marginal revenue from that curve. As with external sales, marginal revenue from sales to the processing division then would be less than the selling price; therefore, if the supplying division equated total marginal revenue to marginal cost, it would sell less than Q_p to the processing division and would charge a price that was higher than P_p. Clearly, such behavior would reduce the profits of the firm as a whole. The marginal revenue that the firm obtained from an additional unit of processed bulk pharmaceuticals (as is indicated by NMR_p) would exceed the marginal cost of producing the additional bulk; hence, the firm's profits would be increased by increasing the production and processing of bulk pharmaceuticals.

Charles Pfizer, therefore, cannot tell the two subsidiaries just to maximize profits, as it could if there were a competitive market for bulk pharmaceuticals. It must calculate centrally the marginal cost of production at the optimum output, Q_t. Then it must set the transfer price at P_p equal to the marginal cost, and must instruct the supplying subsidiary to transfer as much of the bulk pharmaceutical as the processing division demands at that price.

Of course, the management of the supplying subsidiary will not be happy about transferring bulk pharmaceuticals to the processing subsidiary at a price of P_p, when the world market price is P_m. If the inevitable conflicts concerning the transfer price can be contained, however, the advantages of decentralized decision making can be obtained with only minimal central interference.

Transfer pricing makes it possible to coordinate production decisions even when there is interdependence. Other types of interdependence require other organizational responses. Some of the organizational forms used by multinational firms to achieve decentralization of decisions, along with the necessary coordination, are outlined in the following section.

ORGANIZING FOR DECENTRALIZATION

A business organization is built by dividing the firm's activities into several separate groups or divisions. Decision-making authority is delegated to each division, which, in turn, coordinates the activities under its jurisdiction. This jurisdiction is determined either by top management or by a process of negotiation between division-level management and top or corporate-level management. The extent of centralization of decision making will determine the scope of each jurisdiction. Within each division, activities and decision-making authority may be subdivided further, so that the organization becomes a pyramidal structure.

A firm's world-wide activities may be grouped together in many ways; however, most firms organize along either functional, product, or area lines. A functional organization combines activities by type: production, finance, marketing, and the like. Decision-making authority is delegated to each division, which, in turn, coordinates the firm's world-wide production, marketing, or financial decisions.

A product organization, on the other hand, combines production, marketing, and financing activities for a product or group of related products into separate divisions. Each product division then coordinates most of the decisions affecting its product. In turn, it operates more or less independently of other product divisions.

An area organization subdivides the firm's activities and the responsibility for coordination into geographic area divisions. Use of an international division is one crude form of decentralization by area. The international division handles all, or most, decisions relating to business outside the home country, while the main corporate structure deals with business within the home country. Of course, area decentralization may be carried further than a simple distinction between domestic and foreign operations. The firm's activities, for example, may be grouped by continent, with one management center for North America, another for Europe, a third for Latin America, and so forth. Alternatively, countries may be grouped by type, with one management center for industrial countries, for example, and others for developing countries at different stages of development.

Whichever basic structure is adopted, further decentralization may be possible. For example, a firm adopting a basic product structure may decentralize each product division along area lines. Alternatively, one product division may be decentralized by function. The result may be an organization like that shown in Figure 15–2.

Factors Affecting the Choice of Organization

As was pointed out earlier, the multinational corporation should choose an organizational structure that maximizes decentralization while still providing for the coordination of activities that are interdependent with one another. Following this principle, very few multinational corporations adopt a functional organization for their international business. Stopford & Wells studied the organizational structure of 170 multinational corporations and found that by 1968 virtually none of them used a functional organization.[3]

There are several good reasons why firms avoid functional organizations, but perhaps the most important is that a functional organization involves too much centralization in a multiproduct, multinational business. Interdependence among functional decisions rarely extends to all products and areas; therefore, decentralization by product or area usually is possible without sacrificing too much in the way of capacity to coordinate interdependent activities. In fact, the use of a product or area organization may improve the firm's capacity to coordinate production, finance, and marketing decisions relating to a particular product or area. A functional structure makes coordination of functional decisions more difficult.

The functional organization may be appropriate for some firms. Control Data Corporation, for example, used a functional organization until the end of 1972. By that time Control Data's product line and international business

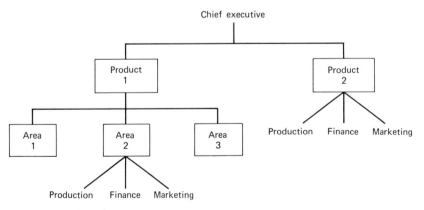

Figure 15–2.

[3]John Stopford & Louis Wells, *Managing the Multinational Enterprise* (New York: Basic Books, 1972), Figure 2–3, p. 28.

had expanded to the point where it needed an organization that would permit more decentralized decision making and less involvement by top corporate officers in day-to-day operations. Consequently, Control Data adopted a product organization with separate operating divisions for computers, peripheral equipment, and commercial credit.

Functional organizations still are maintained by many firms in extractive industries. These firms are integrated vertically from extraction to sales, and each stage in the production process is organized as a separate division. Most petroleum firms, for example, are organized into functional divisions for exploration, crude production, transportation, refining, and marketing. These functional operations sometimes are coordinated on an area basis.

Functional organizations still are maintained by many firms in extractive industries. These firms are integrated vertically from extraction to sales, and each stage in the production process is organized as a separate division. Most petroleum firms, for example, are organized into functional divisions for exploration, crude production, transportation, refining, and marketing. These functional operations sometimes are coordinated on an area basis.

Once a miltinational firm decides that a functional organization is no longer adequate for its needs, its choice between product and area organizations will depend mainly on the diversity of its product line. Stopford & Wells found that 101 of 125 firms with low product diversity chose an area organization.[4] In diversified firms, on the other hand, products that require different technologies and have different end uses usually are grouped into separate divisions, which then operate more or less independently in the world market.

As stated earlier, Charles Pfizer produces a relatively narrow line of related products, consisting mainly of pharmaceuticals, fine chemicals, and agricultural chemicals. It is not surprising, therefore, that Pfizer chose to organize mainly by area, as diagrammed in Figure 15–3. With this organization it is possible to coordinate within areas the interrelationships described earlier between bulk pharmaceuticals, finished pharmaceuticals, and veterinary medicines.[5] In general, firms adopting an area organization tend to have a more mature product line. Because of the maturity of the product line, there is great emphasis on both lowering manufacturing costs

---

[4]*Ibid.*, Table 3–3, p. 41. An international division was classified as an area organization in interpreting Stopford & Wells' statistics.

[5]Even Pfizer has several international product divisions (not shown in Figure 15–3) to produce and market orthopedic, hospital, and dental supplies (Howmedica); cosmetics (Coty); and refractories (Quigley).

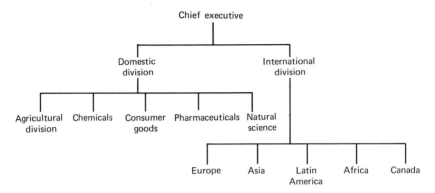

Figure 15–3. Charles Pfizer's organization.

by specializing production in large plants and on marketing techniques that achieve product differentiation.[6] Industries with these characteristics include food, beverage, containers, automotive, farm equipment, pharmaceuticals, and cosmetics.

The choice of organization structures ultimately must be decided by factors specific to each firm. Consequently, the structures of firms in the same industry may be quite different. In the computer industry, Control Data has used a functional organization until recently. IBM has relied on a modified area organization, with most international operations under the control of an international division: IBM World Trade Corporation. Sperry Rand, in contrast to the other two firms, uses the world-wide product organization that is shown in Figure 15–4, reflecting its diversified product line.

As circumstances have changed, these firms have begun to adopt different organizational structures to meet the new situations or even to find better solutions to old problems. For example, IBM recently moved

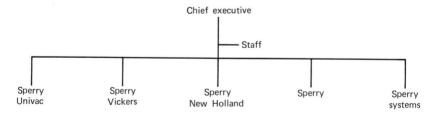

Figure 15–4. Sperry Rand's Organization.

[6]Stanley M. Davis, *Managing and Organizing Multinational Corporations* (New York: Pergamon, 1979), p. 206.

away somewhat from its area organization to set up a separate, world-wide product organization for its office products. Any organization choice involves trade-offs, such as giving up some geographic coordination to obtain some more product coordination, or giving up some functional coordination to obtain area coordination. Firms are trying continually to find better ways to decentralize while still coordinating interdependent activities. Some of the new organizational approaches that have been developed to achieve these dual objectives are discussed in the following.

Complex Organizations

The organization structures described thus far provide for coordination of activities in only one dimension. An area organization coordinates all activities within each area, but there is no reason to expect that all interdependence is confined to the area. The production of a product in one area, for example, may be interrelated with production in other areas. Financial decisions in one area may affect financial alternatives elsewhere.

An organizational structure providing for coordination in only one dimension is not adequate to cope with such multidimensional interdependence. For this reason, several firms have been searching for structures that provide for simultaneous world-wide coordination on product, area, and even functional lines, while still permitting some decentralization of decisions.

Massey-Ferguson, a large multinational manufacturer of farm machinery, is one of the firms that has been searching for a new organizational structure to deal with interdependence. This company was organized geographically prior to 1966. Production and marketing decisions were decentralized to regions and countries, although financial and engineering decisions were centralized.

Massey–Ferguson began branching out of the farm-machinery business, however. It had acquired the Perkins Engine Company in 1958 and also began production of industrial and construction machinery. Interdependence within product lines seemed to be more important than interdependence existing within regions, so Massey began to move toward a world-wide product organization in 1966.

The firm found, however, that interdependence within geographic areas was still important; so important, in fact, that they moved back to a regional organization in 1973. The new organization, however, differed in important respects from the one abandoned in 1966. Its most interesting feature was that product vice-presidents were retained in the structure with regional vice-presidents. The product vice-presidents have responsibility for product design and coordination throughout the world; the position was described in the annual report as follows:

> The product vice presidents will maintain control of their respective product lines world-wide. The regions will represent the needs of their particular markets and make strategic product proposals. However, the responsibility for specifying and developing the optimum product line lies with the product vice president.[7]

Massey–Ferguson thus created a grid-type or matrix organization in which an individual plant manager may be subject to two masters (product and area vice-presidents). The organization is complicated further by the fact that the Perkins Engine division is operated as a separate entity, even though its output is used in the production of both industrial and farm machinery. The resulting organization is depicted in Figure 15–5, although an organization chart cannot do justice to the complex interrelationships involved.

Other multinational firms have tried similar structures as they have recognized the multidimensional interdependence that, in fact, exists in their businesses. Dow Chemical Company, like Massey–Ferguson, developed an organization with both area divisions and product managers. The area divisions had prime responsibility for all the products in their territories, whereas the corporate product departments took a long-term view of product planning, capital investment, and the meeting of production schedules for the world-wide markets for each product line. Westinghouse

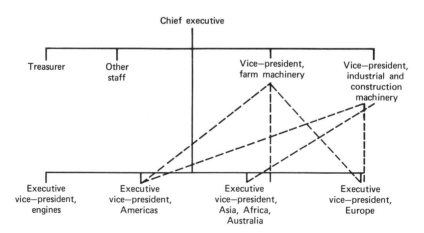

Figure 15–5. Massey–Ferguson organization.

[7]Massey–Ferguson, *1972 Annual Report*, p. 40.

Electric established a matrix organization in 1979 by superimposing country and area divisions on its existing product organization. The purpose of the area organization is to coordinate the activities of the product divisions in each region and to centralize and thus avoid duplication of staff functions (accounting, finance) at a regional level.[8]

Financial institutions, as well as industrial multinational corporations, use matrix-type organizations. The international operations of Citibank are organized both by area and by type of business, with multinational corporation accounts being handled by a separate division. The World Bank is organized along both geographic and sectoral lines, with the regional departments being responsible for the development of over-all country programs, while the sectoral project departments (agriculture, power, and so forth) are responsible for developing the specific projects that make up a program.

Such matrix organizations violate one of the sacred principles of management: unity of command. For this reason, they require a continuing commitment by top management if they are to function well and serve the purposes for which they are designed. Even with that commitment, the Dow Chemical grid organization has tended to revert to an area organization.[9] Nevertheless, other matrix organizations continue to function and meet a need to deal with the real complexities of international business. Those complexities have been increased in recent years as the wholly- or majority-owned subsidiary has been replaced, to some extent, by other forms of involvement by multinational firms in particular countries. Some of the issues raised by these new forms for organization will be discussed in the following section.

ORGANIZATION AND OWNERSHIP STRUCTURE

In recent years, multinational firms have been participating increasingly in ventures in which they do not control the equity. They have participated in joint ventures as minority partners. They have licensed products and production processes and have taken management contracts in ventures that they don't otherwise control. How should such operations be incorporated in the world-wide organizational structure of the multinational firm?

Where these new-style operations are not interdependent with other operations of the firm, there is no problem: they can be allowed to function independently without being incorporated into the formal organizational

---

[8]Hugh O. Menzies, "Westinghouse Takes Aim at the World," *Fortune:* January 14, 1980, p. 48.

[9]Davis, *op. cit.,* p. 245.

structure. This would be the case, for example, when the enterprise produces only for the local market without exporting and without imports from other parts of the firm. Moreover, even when there is potential interdependence, it sometimes is possible for the multinational firm to control an enterprise in which it does not own a majority of the equity. Control can be exercised even as a minority partner if the remainder of the equity is effectively disbursed to small investors. Effective control also may be maintained for a time by means of a management contract. Hilton International, for example, maintains a highly interdependent organization by means of management contracts to operate hotels in which it has at most a minority equity interest.

Even when the operation is expected to import from or export to other parts of the organization, it may be possible to let it operate as an independent unit if an effective transfer pricing system can be set up. Such a system will be difficult to establish, however, because the multinational firm will have definite preferences as to where it wants profits to be located. Transfer pricing is a solution to the organizational problem only if a competitive market exists for the products traded by the parent organization with the minority subsidiary. In these cases the market makes the subsidiary effectively independent.

As a diversion, it is interesting to note that the changing ownership structure of subsidiaries of multinational firms can help to create competitive markets where none existed before. The most interesting example of this phenomenon may be found in the oil industry. Before national oil companies in oil-producing countries gained control of crude-oil production, there was little sale of oil through the spot market. Most oil was transferred internally within the integrated oil companies or was sold through long-term contracts. As the international oil companies have lost control of crude production, however, an increasing share of world crude-oil production has been sold on the spot market.

The most difficult organizational problem exists, of course, when the activities of a minority subsidiary cannot be viewed as being independent of the organization; for example, when it exports in competition with other (possibly wholly-owned) subsidiaries or imports raw materials or subassemblies. In these cases all that the parent can do is to try to control the actions of the independent minority subsidiary by means of legal agreements. When there is a license involved, the parent may try to restrict when and where the licensee can export products produced from the license. It also may include tying agreements in a license, requiring the purchase of raw material, intermediate products and subassemblies, and even capital equipment through the parent.

Such agreements, of course, will not be popular with countries in which minority subsidiaries are located. Developing countries, in particular, have reacted against such agreements, viewing them as a means of reducing their benefits from industrial development and as a way of maintaining their subservience to foreign enterprises. As a result, the developing countries have sought to negotiate a "Code of Conduct" on technology transfer through UNCTAD (United Nations Conference of Trade and Development) that would restrict or eliminate many of the very agreements that foreign firms may attempt to use to control the actions of foreign operations in which they are involved but which they do not control. As of this writing, the status of the Code of Conduct on Technology Transfer is not yet determined, but it seems possible that some type of voluntary code will emerge from the negotiation process, with monitoring of actual technological agreements to be done by the UNCTAD secretariat.

Summary

Problems for governments begin when pricing, investment, financing, production, and other decisions that affect foreign subsidiaries are centralized by the parent firm. When this occurs, factors beyond control of the government enter into decisions affecting the welfare of host countries. The geographical horizon over which decisions are made in the multinational firm extends beyond the confines of individual countries. These decisions can benefit one country but may become detrimental to another. The decision to centralize the organization, therefore, almost inevitably creates conflict with host governments. These conflicts will be discussed in more detail in Chapter 18. Perhaps the main point to be made here is that these conflicts must be taken into account when the choice of organizational structure is made. Certainly, firms will attempt to remove interdependencies among operating units in order to increase efficiency. This usually involves some form of centralization, but centralization removes certain decisions from the subsidiary level and hence from the purview of the host government. This creates tensions and even struggles for power between the firm and the host government. The potential for a clash of goals always is present.

SELECTED READINGS

Brooke, Michael, & H. Lee Remmers, *The Strategy of Multinational Enterprise* (London: Longmans, 1970).

Davis, Stanley, *Managing and Organizing Multinational Corporations* (New York: Pergamon, 1979).

Duerr, Michael, & John Roach, *Organization and Control of International Operations* (New York: The Conference Board, 1973).

Franko, Laurence, "The Move Toward a Multidivisional Structure in European Organizations," *Administrative Science Quarterly,* 20:4, 1975, pp. 493–506.

Friedmann, Wolfgang, & George Kalmanoff (eds.), *Joint International Business Ventures* (New York: Columbia University Press, 1961).

Greene, James, & Michael Duerr, *Intercompany Transactions in the Multinational Firm,* Managing International Business, Report No. 6, (New York: National Industrial Conference Board, 1970).

Hirschleifer, Jack, "On the Economics of Transfer Pricing," *Journal of Business,* 29:3, July 1956, pp. 172–184.

Menzies, Hugh, "Westinghouse Takes Aim at the World," *Fortune,* January 14, 1980, pp. 48–53.

Neufeld, E. P., *A Global Corporation* (Toronto: University of Toronto Press, 1969).

Stopford, John, & Louis Wells, *Managing the Multinational Enterprise* (New York: Basic Books, 1972).

Vaitsos, Constantine, *Intercountry Income Distribution and Transnational Enterprises* (London: Oxford University Press, 1974).

16

Staffing and Managing the Multinational Enterprise

INTRODUCTION

This chapter deals specifically with the subject of staffing and managing international enterprises. It deals primarily with the enterprise that has numerous investments abroad. The focus is upon the subsidiaries of such corporations operating in foreign countries.

Not every aspect of the manager's job in a multinational enterprise is different simply because the enterprise operates abroad. Culture, however, does matter, and it is essential to understand those aspects of the manager's job that are heavily affected by cultural differences. The firm investing abroad can react in various ways in terms of how it either accommodates to the culture on the one hand or attempts to adapt that culture to its own needs on the other. Indeed, it is suggested here that one of the unique characteristics of a multinational firm is its desire and ability to bring about a homogenization of the international economy. International firms are attempting to make various economies more and more alike. They accomplish this through their transfers of technology, products, marketing techniques, financing methods, and managerial practices. By making individual national economies more and more similar to one another, the multinational firm improves its own ability to survive and function effectively on its own terms.

We address several questions in this chapter. First, we raise the question as to whether management is culture bound. Is the practice of management something that is unique to individual cultures and cannot be transferred readily to other cultures? A second question arises as to the extent of being culture bound. If management cannot be transferred intact, what kinds of adaptations do firms seem able to make in accommodating to different cultures? A third question is: To what extent is the firm forced to adapt its methods in order to operate successfully in the foreign culture?

For example, some countries force certain cultural attitudes or policies upon the multinational enterprise. On the other hand, multinationals have certain unique characteristics that cannot be adapted to local conditions. We shall discuss some of these by comparing multinational and local firms wherever we have information suitable for such comparisons. Multinational firms from different cultures also differ from one another in their practices. In this context, it may well be that different managerial systems are equally effective in third cultures. For example, Japanese management practices are known to differ from American practices; yet, when the performances of Japanese and American multinationals operating in third countries are compared in terms of enterprise profitability and other measures, they seem to be equally effective.

We also shall explore questions regarding how managing the multinational firm differs from managing a strictly national firm. Finally, we shall explore the degree to which parent or headquarters companies at home become involved in the operations of subsidiaries located abroad. There are varying degrees of autonomy that can be granted to a subsidiary, and it appears that the nationality of the parent company has a great deal to do with the degree of involvement occurring between parent and subsidiary.

MANAGEMENT AND CULTURE

Numerous authors have asked, "Is management culture bound?" There is no definitive answer to this question, but it would appear that management practices, at least in part, can be transferred from one culture to another. Some features of a managerial system, however, are transferred more easily than others. For example, the technological (physical capital) aspects usually are transferred more easily than are such subjective aspects as marketing and industrial relations.

We see considerable adaptation in some aspects of management practice when international firms move from their home culture to a foreign one. At the same time, other aspects of managerial practice may display little in the way of adaptation when we examine the operations of the firm in two different cultures. What might determine which aspects of management practice are adapted and which are not? Largely, this seems to be a function of the degree to which the operating subsidiary must engage the local culture in which it resides. For example, some subsidiaries produce primarily for export, as do the American and Japanese electronics firms operating in Taiwan and Malaysia. While they are owned by U.S.-based or Japanese-based multinational firms, their technology and managerial practices differ very little from those followed by parent companies in the home country. Why might this be? One first must understand the nature of these operating entities. They are primarily assembly operations in which most of the raw materials and other critical material inputs are imported from the parent company, processed and assembled in the subsidiary, and shipped back to the parent or to a sister subsidiary for further assembly or final sale. The technology is nearly identical to that used throughout the parent organization, as are the mangerial practices. Moreover, the assembly operations are relatively simple and uncomplicated. Unskilled workers can be trained to be proficient assemblers. Under these circumstances there is little need for the subsidiary to become intimately involved within the culture in which it resides. The enterprise hires workers, trains them to do simple assembly operations, provides all of the operating procedures, and trains a rudimentary managerial group to monitor the standards implicit in the procedures. The consequence is that very little in the way of managerial methods or technology actually is transferred.

Even when a multinational firm must deal intimately with the culture where the subsidiary resides, there often is little in the way of adaptation of the organization's procedures to accommodate the culture. Indeed, it appears that multinational firms do their utmost to adapt the environment to their own unique requirements. They do this by hiring the best-educated nationals available. They prefer to hire those who have been educated abroad, most especially those educated in the parent organization's home country. Multinational firms also would prefer to hire a national who has been educated in the specialty in which the enterprise is most interested; again, the preference is for the national to have received that education in the home country of the parent. For example, the subsidiary of a U.S.-based firm, seeking to employ a mechanical engineer, would prefer to hire a national trained in mechanical engineering at a reputable institution in the United States. Moreover, wherever feasible, the multinational firm employs nationals who speak the language of the parent firm's home country. For example, in Brazil, a U.S.-based firm would attempt to employ managers or other high-level personnel who are of Brazilian extraction but also are fluent in English. On the other hand, a Japanese firm operating in Brazil would attempt to employ Japanese-speaking Brazilians.

The job of the manager is value laden, and these values are an outgrowth of the culture that nurtured the managerial system; thus, insofar as there are differences among cultures, we also should expect there to be differences in managerial systems or at least in the premises underlying the decision-making apparatus and attitudes embedded in these systems. What is important in one culture may be relatively unimportant in another. Anglo-Saxon preoccupation with schedules and being on time finds its direct counterpart in Latin societies where being ''a bit late'' is considered quite acceptable and being early is almost inexcusable.

Management is composed of both art and science. Some aspects of the manager's role can be quantified scientifically and taught to most anyone. These are the aspects of management that are transferred most easily between cultures; however, these seemingly culture-free truths can be accepted, rejected, or just ignored. Which fate they receive still depends on underlying attitudes. If those attitudes place little importance upon planning, quantification, and completion of tasks on schedule, then good teaching about scientific management will do little to improve managerial practice. Often, the manager operating in a foreign culture finds the greatest challenge to be achieving local acceptance for corporate managerial values and philosophy. Incentive systems that work at home may fail to work in a new setting, and many managerial beliefs commonly accepted at home may fall flat in another society.

Business practice also differs. Today, many American firms complain that they are losing business to European, Japanese, and Korean firms in the Middle East because Americans no longer can engage in bribery (or, euphemistically, ''use foreign sales agents''). Here is an instance in which the U.S. government has attempted to impose its cultural values upon the conduct of business in foreign lands. The consequence may be that American firms will be penalized when they attempt to compete against firms of other nationalities—nationalities that do not share the same value system as that generally accepted in the United States.

ADAPTATION OF MANAGEMENT METHODS TO LOCAL CONDITIONS

Lest we leave the impression that multinational firms do not adapt to the local environment, we should point out that certain aspects of management and the operations of multinational corporations are adapted to the local culture. These tend to be those most intimately involved in dealing with people in the local culture: marketing, public relations, and personnel and labor relations. Indeed an examination of the staffing patterns in multinational firms indicates that the directorial positions in marketing, public relations, and personnel and labor relations are more often than not staffed by nationals. On the other hand, certain managerial positions are staffed almost exclusively by expatriates.[1] Positions usually held by expatriates from the home country are those of chief executive, chief financial officer, and chief technical officer.

How does the multinational firm adapt? It essentially adapts to the changed institutional framework and institutional setting available in the local culture. It often must adapt to a lower level of educational attainment, on the part of members of the work force, than that at home, as well as to a more rudimentary distribution system, to a less well-developed media system, and to a labor market that does not provide all the skills required by the multinational firm's technologies. To state it briefly, adaptation is made in marketing methods, public relations techniques, recruiting and training methods, and, to some extent, in the application of technology to the production of products and services.

The multinational firm attempts to bring about change within the local culture so that the firm will not have to adapt. We might say that the multinational firm attempts to adapt the culture to its own needs rather than adapting itself to the culture's needs. To some observers, this aspect of the multinational firm's behavior is offensive; however, when we understand that the multinational firm is attempting to develop an international set of standards for products, processes, and raw materials and labor, it becomes clear why it goes to such major efforts to press the local culture ever more closely into a mold of its own making. By so doing, it reduces the variance across countries and the cost of doing business on an international scale. The multinational firm brings with it a set of technologies and managerial methods and procedures. To support this, it hires the best-educated people, especially those who have been educated abroad, to staff many of its managerial and high-level technical positions. In addition, it trains workers and others within the organization in its own methods. It tends to pay workers higher wages than local firms do, so it is in a position to select the very best workers. In most of its manufacturing operations, workers are hired not so much on the basis of existing skills as on the basis of proficiency on vocational tests and the learning curve. Those workers who cannot achieve these standards are released from employment. Since the multinational firm pays higher wages and generally has better fringe benefits, it is able ultimately to develop a superior work force. This sometimes is resented by local firms and others within the larger society.

---

[1]An expatriate is a person who is not a citizen of the country in which he resides. When we say "an expatriate from the home country" when referring to a person in a U.S. multinational firm, we mean an American citizen.

Indeed, multinational firms are accused by local firms of hiring away the best-educated and best-trained workers. This accusation, however, seldom can be supported by the facts. The multinational firm does more in the way of training and development of personnel than does the average local enterprise.

Multinational firms bring about adaptation in the local culture in other ways. They tend to work very closely with local suppliers of parts and raw materials. Quality and quality control are extremely important to multinational firms. In order to maintain their quality standards it usually is necessary to work with local suppliers to develop procedures to meet those quality standards. It is not sufficient merely to supply local vendors (suppliers) with a set of blueprints, drawings, product or part descriptions, and specifications. It also is necessary, if one is to achieve the quality standards desired, to supply the managerial and technical software or knowledge of processes to the vendor. Indeed, it is quite often the case that multinational firms will place one of their own engineers or other technicians within the vendor's organization for a period of time, extending to several months in some cases, to assure that the vendor can achieve the quality standards desired. Achieving these standards is quite important. The multinational firm is attempting to serve an international market, and it must achieve consistently a set of quality standards that will allow the sale of its products in international markets in competition with other firms. It is often the case in some countries, however, that international quality standards are not really necessary. In this respect, the multinational firm brings with it a certain degree of waste. It could satisfy many local market needs via its local production without always achieving the quality standards required of the international marketplace. At least in the short run, the multinational firm might be able to produce at somewhat lower cost by accepting a lower quality standard for the local market. In the longer run, however, the country itself wishes to acquire the technology and know-how of the multinational firm and to perform to international quality standards in manufacturing the products produced locally. This is so that export markets can be developed eventually.

We conclude that management practice is to a large degree culture bound and that multinational firms do not make major adaptations to their technological and managerial processes. Instead, through training and skillful recruiting within the local environment, they manage to adapt the environment to their own specialized needs and requirements. The major adaptations they do make tend to be in areas such as marketing, industrial and labor relations, and public relations, where cultural content is by necessity rather high.

COMPARISONS OF MULTINATIONAL CORPORATIONS WITH
LOCAL FIRMS

One way to illustrate the points made previously is to compare multinational corporations with local firms. The behavior and characteristics of multinational firms tend to be considerably different from those of local firms. There are, however, some local firms that, although not multinationals themselves, nevertheless behave somewhat like them. These tend to be the more prominent local firms that compete directly with multinationals, primarily in the host country's national market. It is interesting to note that, with the exception of a few prominent local firms, the large majority of locally owned firms does not compete directly with multinational firms. Largely, the two groups tend to complement one another. Particularly in developing countries, local firms usually do not have the technology and managerial systems required to produce the types of products and services that multinational firms produce. Local firms instead produce the more traditional products and/or act as suppliers of inputs to the multinationals.

Local firms tend to use less capital per worker, even when they produce the same products as those produced by multinationals. Staffing patterns of locally owned firms require less in the way of managerial and high-level technical personnel and require more skilled blue-collar workers and what we might call professionals: accountants, lawyers, and vocationally trained technicians. The local firm's management system is likely to be much less formal than that of the multinational. Moreover, the local firm is apt to be owned by a single family or a very small group of stockholders. By definition, the ownership of a multinational enterprise's subsidiaries is in the hands of a parent organization in a foreign country, even though the stock of the parent company may be held widely both in the home country and internationally. From this point of view, the local firm may have an ownership structure that is much more highly concentrated; however, it is less likely to be resented than is the multinational one, simply because ownership is in the hands of nationals rather than a foreign entity.

Perhaps it is a function of large size and the complexity of the multinational enterprise, but we see some additional differences in how multinationals organize activities when compared with local firms. There are more formalized procedures in accounting, finance, corporate planning, evaluation of managerial performance, quality control, and the like. Communication in this formalized system tends to be much more on the basis of written reports, rather than on the basis of interpersonal communication. In the local firm, just the opposite is likely to be true, with much less formalization and a great deal more interpersonal communication. To accommodate its more formalized system and to adapt the local environment to its needs, the multinational firm also tends to spend more money, time, and effort on personnel training at every level of the organization. Once an individual is trained, the multinational firm tends to pay that person a higher wage and provide better fringe benefits than do even the most prominent local firms. The consequence is that multinational firms tend to have lower rates of personnel turnover and absenteeism when compared with their local counterparts.

A COMPARISON OF MULTINATIONAL CORPORATIONS FROM DIFFERENT CULTURES

Multinational corporations from different cultures tend to be different from one another. For example, there are major differences in how multinational corporations headquartered in Japan are managed when compared with those headquartered in the United States. Multinational corporations from Europe tend to fall somewhere between the polar extremes of American and Japanese multinationals in terms of management. To simplify, we make some distinctions between American and Japanese firms and indicate how European firms might differ from these types.

In a recent study by Brandt & Hulbert in Brazil, a comparison was made of American, Japanese and European companies.[2] Brandt & Hulbert concluded that

> "American subsidiaries reported to their home offices in far greater variety and with greater frequency than their Japanese or European rivals. Industrial goods companies reported more often than makers of consumer products; otherwise, the major influence on reporting (apart from nationality) was the company's control philosophy . . . "[3]

In more detail, the Brandt & Hulbert study discloses that American firms use personal visits, both from the home office to the subsidiary and vice versa, much more than do either European or Japanese firms. Also, there are tighter budgetary limits on the American and Japanese firms than on the European firms. It appears that European subsidiaries in Brazil have a great deal more autonomy and freedom of action than do American and Japanese companies.[4]

[2]William K. Brandt & James M. Hulbert, "Communications and Control of the Multinational Enterprise," in Warren J. Keegan & Charles S. Mayer (eds.), *Multinational Product Management,* American Marketing Association, Proceedings Series, 1977, pp. 119–146.

[3]*Ibid.,* p. 122.

[4]*Ibid.,* Tables 1 and 2, pp. 126 & 135.

The Brandt & Hulbert study seems to indicate that American firms use much more in the way of formalized methods than do the Japanese- and European-based firms; however, such a conclusion, as they point out, can be misleading. American-based multinational enterprises simply are, on the average, much larger and geographically much more diversified than are Japanese and European companies. The consequence is that they have a much larger number of subsidiaries to manage and integrate into a functioning whole. It may be necessary, then, to have considerably more in the way of formalized control procedures in order to integrate a more complex system made up of a larger number of subsidiaries.

Other studies have borne out the notion that Japanese management is indeed different from American and European types. Ouchi & Jaeger have attempted to typify the American and Japanese models of management.[5] In their study, the American firm was typified as emphasizing short-term employment, individual decision making, individual responsibility, rapid evaluation and promotion, explicit and formalized control, specialized career paths, and segmented concern. The Japanese type of enterprise was typified by lifetime employment, consensual decision making, collective responsibility, slow evaluation and promotion, implicit and informal control, nonspecialized career paths, and holistic concerns. These are stereotypical listings of the characteristics of the two types of organizations; however, what Ouchi & Jaeger attempted to display is simply the point that there are major differences between American and Japanese types of enterprise. It is difficult for a Westerner to understand and appreciate fully what goes on in a Japanese enterprise. If one asks to see "the boss" in a Japanese enterprise, one is likely to be asking an inappropriate question. Who is the boss in a Japanese enterprise depends very much upon the situation being discussed. It is not uncommon for an individual in a Japanese enterprise to have been in a position of decision-making authority in one situation and to appear to be "the boss." In another situation, however, he or she may be under the decision-making authority of another individual who, in the previous situation, had been part of a group of subordinates. So-called lines of authority in a Japanese enterprise are not as well defined as in American or European enterprises.

Other studies, some published and others not, have noted differences in Japanese methods. One major difference noted in the literature is that Japanese enterprises abroad use many more expatriates from Japan. Communication in the decision-making process in Japanese enterprises is both vertical and horizontal. This horizontal, or lateral, communication appears

[5]William G. Ouchi & Alfred M. Jaeger, "Type Z Organizations: Stability in the Midst of Instability," *Academy of Management Review,* 3:2, 1978, pp. 305–314.

to be much more important to the Japanese enterprise than to American or European ones. There is much more personal communication, either in written form or by telephone and to some extent by personal visits, at lower levels in the hierarchy of the Japanese subsidiary in its dealings with its parent company. It appears that the large number of expatriates in Japanese subsidiaries are there for purposes of communication and control. This, in part, may explain the more informal methods of control used by the Japanese enterprises. Control involves considerably more interpersonal communication at lower levels in the organization than in an American or European company, where communication tends to take place between high-level managers in the subsidiary's interactions with its parent company at home.

We might say the following: Japanese overseas subsidiaries tend to staff more deeply into the organization with expatriates than do either U.S.- or European-based enterprises. Moreover, the expatriates in a Japanese enterprise are removed from foreign subsidiaries much later in the life of the subsidiary than is true for firms of other nationalities. This might be attributed to two things. The first is that American and European firms have had longer experience in international operations. Accordingly, these two groups have developed more extensive management and technical training programs. Given the hierarchical form of management systems in U.S. and European firms, where authority/responsibility relationships are well spelled out and where financial planning and control are well developed, there is a broader range of opportunity to train locally recruited personnel for managerial positions. This follows from the more tightly defined person-nel relationships and job content in the American and European management systems.

The second barrier to participation of nationals in management among Japanese subsidiaries is the *ringi* system of decision making.[6] *Ringi* is not well understood outside the Japanese culture. It has some similarities to "participative management" in American firms, but it is much more complex. It is a process of consultation and compromise that attempts to accommodate everyone's interests and needs. Much bargaining and trading take place in any decision; even very junior managers are consulted. By American standards, the process might seem agonizing and overly lengthy, but the ultimate decision is understood by everyone concerned and is embraced with a total organizational commitment. The nationals in most other countries, however, have been acculturated in a hierarchically ordered society where authority/responsibility relationships usually are well spelled

[6]For a description of the *ringi* system, see Michael Y. Yoshino, *Japan's Multinational Enterprises* (Cambridge, Mass.: Harvard University Press, 1976), pp. 162–171.

out. To them, *ringi* must seem a total mystery. Most nationals probably are incredulous when confronted with *ringi* and would consider as insincere suggestions that their opinion matters. Moreover, in a managerial position in a Japanese firm, they would find it difficult to confer intensively and at length with their subordinates about decisions. So far, it does not appear that Japanese firms have been successful in training nationals to appreciate and become a part of the Japanese managerial system. This may account for the much higher proportion of Japanese expatriates in key management and technical positions in Japanese subsidiaries, as compared with either American or European firms.

Some observers have concluded that the extensive use of expatriates in Japanese subsidiaries is a matter of communication problems. Japanese is a very difficult language to learn. Japanese enterprises do not expect that nationals in a foreign country will ever learn Japanese well enough to communicate with the headquarters in Japan; thus, it is necessary to have native Japanese present, trained in the local language and/or English. These Japanese are used as a communication link between nationals and the parent company back in Japan. Japanese expatriates do tend to learn the local language; however, it is notable that in some countries the Japanese communicate with nationals only in English. In any case, Japanese expatriates in Japanese subsidiaries operating abroad are there primarily to work as a communication and control device between nationals and Japanese managers and technicians in the parent company in Japan.[7]

These features of the Japanese managerial system do raise questions, because most developing countries are pressing multinational firms to decrease the numbers and/or proportion of expatriates in high-level managerial and technical positions. When asked why they do not reduce the number of expatriates, Japanese managers often suggest that there are few qualified nationals. Some also indicate they plan to provide skills training in management, accounting, and the like, but few have actually integrated nationals into their operation in any of the key managerial or technical positions.[8] Those nationals actually occupying management positions usually occupy very junior posts in personnel, accounting, quality control, and production scheduling. It is extremely difficult, although perhaps not impossible, to integrate nationals effectively into the *ringi* system. Perhaps

---

[7]Michael Yoshino, *op. cit.*, pp. 173–175.

[8]This information is preliminary and is based on research conducted by R. Hal Mason on over 30 foreign subsidiaries of Japanese firms. See R. Hal Mason, "Technology Transfers: A Comparison of American and Japanese Practices in Developing Countries," working paper, prepared for the Japan Society's Business Educational Workshop, May 30–June 4, 1978, Graduate School of Management, University of California, Los Angeles.

the Japanese system of management can be adapted to a non-Japanese culture, but only with great difficulty; since this is the case, it is necessary to adapt nationals to that system. That process, in turn, is also difficult and time consuming.

Planning in the Japanese firm is a very informal process. This is not to say there are not some rituals. Subsidiaries do have a system of periodic reporting, but whereas American subsidiaries report at least quarterly and sometimes as often as monthly, Japanese subsidiaries may report no more than twice per year, and that report is likely to be delivered personally within a group meeting at headquarters.

In the preparation of plans, it appears that more of the initiative resides in the subsidiaries of American firms than is true for Japanese firms. Again, this gets back to *ringi,* on the one hand, and the notion of responsibility and authority relationships, on the other. In the American subsidiary, it is the responsibility of subsidiary managers to initiate decisions and make requests via plans for financial resources. Once resources are committed, the subsidiary manager has the authority to allocate resources and implement the plan without intervention from headquarters, unless there is a request for assistance of some kind. Also, performance measures are formalized and become a part of the plan. Japanese firms, on the other hand, see decision making as a joint responsibility between the parent and the subsidiary. Indeed, in contrast to American firms, it appears to be much more likely in a Japanese firm that initiatives for new directions for individual subsidiaries, including expansions, will be initiated at headquarters level, but there will be considerable discussion back and forth. Technical experts and others, including junior managers, will participate, and there probably will be consultations among all of those conceivably affected by any major decision that might be taken.

Among some Japanese firms, depending upon the importance of the subsidiary, the managing director of the subsidiary may be a member of the managing board of the parent firm. This would be an unusual practice in an American firm. Japanese boards are much larger and are heavily dominated by "insiders" when compared with American boards of directors. Meetings of Japanese boards (or actually the highest levels of management) bring together managers of major operating units. Much of the long-range planning for the firm, including subsidiary plans, takes place at these meetings. In contrast, American firms use the board to set policy, while long-range plans are developed within an entirely different context. The American board, other than setting board policy guidelines, plays only a minor role in the actual development of the formal long-range plan prepared by professional staff personnel and operating managers.

DEGREE OF INVOLVEMENT OF PARENT

The degree of involvement of the parent in the affairs of its overseas subsidiaries depends on things other than the culture of the parent. It was noted earlier that the degree of the subsidiary's control seems to depend on the national origin of the parent, but this may have more to do with the size of the subsidiary, number of overseas subsidiaries the parent has, type of product being produced, and complexity of the subsidiary's operations.

The study by Brandt & Hulbert suggests that the larger a subsidiary, the more autonomy it is likely to have, simply because it can serve many of its own needs efficiently.[9] It is also true that small subsidiaries have a great deal of autonomy. It is just too costly, relative to what could be gained, to establish elaborate control procedures for small subsidiaries. Thus, it is the medium-sized subsidiary that is subjected to the greatest amount of control, with the parent becoming more involved in its affairs than is true for large or small subsidiaries. As the number of subsidiaries operating abroad increases, we find from Brandt & Hulbert's work that the degree of control by the parent tends to escalate. It becomes increasingly essential, as the number of subsidiaries increases, to have a more formal system of communication and more frequent reporting so that the parent can determine where variances from plan may arise.

A third critical variable seems to be the type of product produced. Subsidiaries producing industrial goods or capital-intensive products tend to be monitored and controlled more closely by the parent firm than do those producing labor-intensive products. This seems reasonable, since capital-intensive products require larger expenditures on fixed capital in their production. Moreover, in a capital-intensive product, because there are fewer variable costs to be monitored, it is easier to establish a financial control system. In labor-intensive production, on the other hand, the subsidiary is likely to be in a much better position to evaluate what is going on than is the parent. Stated differently, the parent organization has less expertise in dealing with the local labor market situation than it does in dealing with capital-intensive production in which many of the machines may have been supplied by the parent itself. In this instance, familiarity gives the parent more leverage in the establishment of a control system.

Finally, complexity of the subsidiary's operations leads to greater control efforts on the part of the parent. It is likely that the parent, through its control system, is attempting to understand the more complex operations

---

[9]William K. Brandt and James M. Hulbert, "Headquarters Guidance in Marketing Strategy in the Multinational Subsidiary," *Columbia Journal of World Business*, 13:4, 1978, pp. 7–14. See especially page 11.

of the subsidiary that has numerous product lines or divisions. When there are more products being produced, or more organizational units being supervised, the occasion for making errors increases. Again, the gains to be made by a well-developed control system are greater the more complex the subsidiary becomes.

At any rate, there is need for considerably more research into the relationships between parent firms and foreign subsidiaries, to determine whether the nationality of the parent is as important as some researchers suggest. It may be, instead, that it is the nature of the subsidiary that determines the degree of involvement with the parent, rather than the nationality of the parent.

MANAGING THE MULTINATIONAL CORPORATION: DOES IT DIFFER FROM MANAGING A NATIONAL CORPORATION?

It has been noted previously that multinational corporations from different cultures differ in their behavior and methods of management. Thus, what we say in this section, in a general way, should be tempered in the reader's mind by concepts introduced earlier. Much of this section is based upon research into the methods being used by American firms. There has not been nearly as much research done on European and Japanese enterprises. These comments, therefore, must be interpreted in light of the fact that what is said applies primarily to American enterprises. Much may be generalized to European and Japanese enterprises, however.

Managing the multinational firm differs more in degree than in kind when compared with strictly national firms. While differences in methods are recognizable, it is also true that differences emerge in application of these methods. As we have noted already, it is in those aspects of the multinational enterprise that deal directly with the local culture that the major differences appear. For example, marketing, industrial and labor relations, and public relations are much different when comparing the multinational with the national firm, as opposed to finance, production management, and operational planning. Marketing, industrial and labor relations, and public relations are less subject to routinization than are finance, budgeting, production, quality control, and operational planning. When we use the term routinization, we mean that well-developed written procedures for data collection and processing have been, or can be, provided. Because cultures and languages differ, the functions of marketing, industrial and labor relations, and public relations may require considerably more deviation from standards and norms than the more numerically oriented functions. It should be noted, however, that in a field such as accounting, where accounting rules and taxation laws differ, and where there are different attitudes toward the use of numerical information, the function of accounting also will be subject to major differences across national boundaries.

Even though a multinational firm might produce and market the same product abroad as at home, it nevertheless encounters major needs to adapt to the local culture. This adaptation comes in marketing in the sense that the institutional framework supporting the distribution system may be much different in the foreign country from that at home. For example, one of the reasons given for the poor performance of American multinationals operating in Japan is the very complicated wholesaling and retailing system in the Japanese economy. Direct marketing such as we know in the United States is virtually unheard of in many countries, including Japan. Thus, multinational firms' subsidiaries each must cope with a different institutional system insofar as the marketing of products is concerned. It is interesting to note in this connection that marketing is one function that often is staffed by nationals rather than by expatriates. National managers, meaning a national in the management position, have a much better understanding of the local culture, distribution system, and advertising media needed to market various products.

Much the same can be said for industrial and labor relations. The habits, attitudes, and beliefs of the local workforce generally can be dealt with much more effectively by a national than by a foreigner. Thus, in such things as labor negotiations, workers' grievances, and the like, the superior approach usually is to have a national rather than a foreigner dealing with these problems. It is usually true that the industrial relations framework in a developing country will be much more rudimentary than is true for advanced countries. In fact, labor negotiations may be the exception rather than the rule. In many countries, labor unions do not exist, and in those where they do exist, they often are passive rather than active. Strikes may be outlawed by governmental decree, but even where strikes are allowed, they usually are short-lived and may be more symbolic than real in terms of their use as a bargaining tool.

In production management, major differences occur when comparing an American firm operating at home and abroad. Differences appear in the volume of production, the degree of specialization, and the amount of inspection and quality control required to achieve standards. Production plants in the United States usually are much larger than those abroad. Accordingly, production can be organized differently in the United States than elsewhere. The consequence is that multinational firms must deal with two types of systems: an American system and a foreign system. The plants of multinational firms in the United States are much more specialized than those operating abroad. Plants in the United States are more specialized, not only in terms of the product they produce but in the degree to which they are integrated across functional areas. To illustrate, an automobile assembly plant in the United States might assemble two or three different products and will produce a thousand units per day. A plant in non-European countries would assemble perhaps four, five, or six different products and would produce no more than four or five hundred units per day, usually considerably less. This means that workers on these latter assembly lines must know how to assemble more different models of automobiles. Secondly, they must know more different jobs on the assembly line simply because there are fewer units per day being assembled. They must, therefore, undertake two or three different jobs. In the United States, an assembler would have only a single operation to perform. The consequence is that the worker in the American plant is more skilled in that one job, but is less skilled in a general way to undertake two or three other operations along the assembly line. This need in foreign plants complicates the problem of training for skills, particularly in the developing countries. Not only is the multinational firm having to work with people who are somewhat less educated and perhaps less skilled to begin with, but it has to train those individuals for a wider spectrum of skills if they are to function effectively on the assembly line. In this sense, workers in the subsidiaries of multinational firms are less specialized than workers in the home country performing similar work.

Quality control tends to be more of a problem in overseas operations because of the less-specialized nature of the work. Because individual workers must perform more separate operations on the average, and because individual workers tend to be less well-educated and trained, there is greater opportunity for mistakes and bad batches of product. To avoid or ameliorate this problem, firms include a much larger number of inspectors and quality-control personnel in the production process than is true in the United States. Inspection is integrated into the production line to a much greater degree so that quality can be checked after each and every operation. There is a tendency to try to catch mistakes prior to the final inspection. Stated differently, one cannot afford to wait until final inspection to identify mistakes. It is just too costly.

Another major difference between a strictly national and a multinational firm appears in the financial function. The multinational firm can source capital from many different markets. It can tap the local market, the Eurocurrency market, or its own home financial market. The purely national firm is less likely to undertake these kinds of banking and financial connections. It is much more likely to rely on one or a few banks in its own home country.

The foreign subsidiaries of a multinational firm tend to have a great deal more freedom in their financial dealings than do subsidiaries at home.

Even a very large subsidiary in the home country may be under the direct control of the parent or headquarters organization. It may have very little latitude in terms of the amount of capital expenditures it can make in any single decision, whereas the foreign subsidiary may. Partly, this is a matter of proximity. The foreign subsidiary must have the flexibility to make decisions without having to be in touch with the parent corporation on every single matter. For example, in several countries, the availability of capital is quite constrained. The banking system is much more closely under the control of the government, and funds may be made available only for borrowing at certain times for certain types of capital expenditures. Only those firms that can move quickly and have well-developed banking connections within the local market will have an opportunity to borrow these funds. Thus, it is necessary for the foreign subsidiary to have greater flexibility in obtaining financing from various sources.

Financial and accounting reporting requirements also may be different in the foreign subsidiary. Often the foreign subsidiary does not have readily available to it the same kinds of resources available to a subsidiary at home. For example, the home-country subsidiary can be tied in directly to a central system and obtain financial and accounting data almost instantaneously. While it is true that, with satellite communications, a foreign subsidiary may have access to that same capability, this is the exception rather than the rule. Most foreign subsidiaries do not have the same capability in terms of accounting and financial control systems as that of the home-country subsidiary.

All of these aspects of managing foreign subsidiaries make strategic and operational planning somewhat more complicated. One cannot always use the same identical methods for assessing markets, industrial and labor relations, and public relations as are used in the home country. Moreover, financial and accounting data may be more difficult to generate, and the timing of financial and accounting reports thereby often does not meet the schedules of the parent company. Parents often complain that subsidiaries abroad cannot get their reports in on schedule. On the other hand, subsidiaries complain of too much paper work and red tape and accuse the parent company of not understanding their problems. These problems, more likely than not, are connected to the lower level of skills available and the more rudimentary business support systems available.

Summary

It has been noted in this chapter on several occasions that management practice is a function of culture. When multinational firms move abroad, they transfer their management practices and, while they do make some adaptations in those practices, the tendency is for these firms to attempt to adapt the culture to their own needs. This is done by hiring those who have been educated in the multinational firm's home country or in a country similar to it. In addition, workers and others in the organization are trained in the methods of the multinational firm. The firm brings with it a set of technologies and procedures, into which the local workers and managers become indoctrinated. A multinational firm also works with local suppliers to help them to meet the product, service, and quality specifications set by the parent company. These are international standards, rather than local standards. Ultimately, the recipient country wishes to produce to these standards, and it is through methods acquired from the multinational firms that these standards can be achieved.

Each culture has its own distinct set of attitudes toward work and leisure, thriftiness, superior/subordinate relationships, security of employment, promptness, agreements and contracts, and so forth. Differing sets of attitudes make life for the multinational corporation different from that of a purely national corporation. Multinationals, when compared with local firms, tend to pay higher wages, spend more money and effort on training, hire the best-trained workers, and use more formalized organizational procedures, especially in accounting, finance, corporate planning, evaluation of management performance, quality control, and the like. Multinational firms do differ from one another, however, because they originate in different cultures. Japanese-based multinationals tend to use more expatriate personnel, and they are more willing to accept different methods of operation. For example, they are more willing to use joint ventures. There are other differences that appear to be the result of Japanese cultural differences, such as the decision-making system based on consensus. We also see differences between multinationals in terms of the degree of involvement on the part of the parent. It appears that this degree of involvement is higher with American firms, followed by Japanese firms and then European firms. Whether this is a result of cultural differences is as yet undetermined. For example, American subsidiaries tend to be larger, more numerous, more capital intensive, and often have more complex product lines than multinationals from Europe or Japan. These differences seem to be related to the degree of involvement of the parent company. Yet the degree of involvement may depend more on the total system of subsidiaries and its complexity rather than the nationality of the parent. At a functional level, we find major differences between managing a multinational corporation and managing a strictly national corporation. There are differences in how marketing, industrial relations, public relations, finance and accounting, production management and quality control, and strategic and operating planning are handled. These dimensions make a multinational corporation a more complex managerial problem, but this is what one would expect.

SELECTED READINGS

Brandt, William K., "Determinants and Effects of Structural Design in the Multinational Organization," research paper no. 136A, Graduate School of Business, Columbia University, New York, N.Y., 1978.

Brandt, William K., James M. Hulbert, & Raimar Richers, "Coordinating Planning in Multinational Corporations: A Comparative Perspective," working paper, Graduate School of Business, Columbia University, New York, N.Y. (no date).

Brandt, William K., & James M. Hulbert, "Patterns of Communications in the Multinational Corporation: An Empirical Study," *Journal of International Business Studies,* Spring 1976, pp. 57–64.

Brandt, William K., & James M. Hulbert, "Headquarters Guidance in Marketing Strategy in the Multinational Subsidiary," *Columbia Journal of World Business,* Winter 1977, pp. 7–14.

Brandt, William K., & James M. Hulbert, "Communication and Control in the Multinational Enterprise," in Warren J. Keegan & Charles S. Mayer (eds.), *Multinational Product Management* (American Marketing Association, Proceedings Series, 1977), pp. 119–146.

Dunn, S. Watson, "Effect of National Identity on Multinational Promotion Strategy in Europe," *Journal of Marketing,* 40:4, 1976, pp. 50–57.

Franko, Lawrence G., *The European Multinationals* (Stamford, Conn.: Greylock Publishers, 1976).

Granick, David, *Managerial Comparisons of Four Developed Countries: France, Britain, United States, and Russia* (Cambridge, Mass.: M.I.T. Press, 1972).

Harbison, Frederick, & Charles A. Meyers, *Education Manpower and Economic Growth* (New York: McGraw-Hill, 1964).

Lorange, Peter, "A Framework for Strategic Planning in Multinational Corporations," *Long Range Planning,* 9:3, 1976, pp. 30–37.

Okochi, Kazuo, Bernard Karsh, & Solomon B. Levine, *Workers and Employers in Japan: The Japanese Employment Relations System* (Princeton, N.J.: Princeton University Press, 1974).

Ouchi, William G., & Alfred M. Jaeger, "Type Z Organization: Stability in the Midst of Mobility," *Academy of Management Review,* 3:2, 1978, pp. 305–314.

Ringbakk, Kjell-Arne, "Strategic Planning in a Turbulent International Environment," *Long Range Planning,* 9:3, 1976, pp. 2–11.

Robinson, Richard D., *International Business Management: A Guide to Decision Making,* 2nd ed. (Hinsdale, Ill.: The Dryden Press, 1978).

Stopford, John R., "Organizing the Multinational Firm: Can the Americans Learn from the Europeans?" in Michael Brooke & H. Lee Remmers (eds.), *The Multinational Company in Europe* (Ann Arbor: University of Michigan Press, 1972), pp. 77–92.

Stopford, John R., & Louis T. Wells, Jr., *Managing the Multinational Enterprise* (New York: Basic Books, 1972).

Tsurumi, Yoshi, *The Japanese are Coming* (Cambridge, Mass.: Ballinger Publishing, 1976).

Yoshino, Michael Y., *Japan's Managerial System: Tradition and Innovation* (Cambridge, Mass.: M.I.T. Press, 1968).

Yoshino, Michael Y., *Japan's Multinational Enterprises* (Cambridge, Mass.: Harvard University Press, 1976).

Three

RELATIONS BETWEEN HOST COUNTRIES AND INTERNATIONAL FIRMS

Now that some understanding has been developed about why and how corporations function internationally, we can turn briefly to another set of questions. We will be concerned in Part III with host-country reactions to the multinational firm, particularly reactions by less-developed nations, where issues are drawn most sharply. Multinational corporations have not been received uniformly with enthusiasm. In fact, host-country responses to private investment from abroad have been decidedly ambivalent, even schizophrenic. Chapter 17 will review these reactions and outline reasons why they are sometimes quite hostile.

Partly because of these responses, the future of corporate multinationality is uncertain. The closing years of the twentieth century undoubtedly will be ones of considerable change in international economic relationships, and resultant impacts on the private sectors of all countries surely will be substantial. Chapter 18 will close the book with brief speculation about the future of the multinational enterprise.

CHAPTER 17

Conflicts between Host Countries and the International Enterprise

INTRODUCTION

In earlier chapters the broad macroenvironment has been examined. It is here that firms must operate when they become internationally engaged. This environment includes international trade, the balance of payments, foreign exchange markets, and international financing arrangements. It also includes the wide variety of national policies, both at home and abroad, that are used to influence trade, investment, and finance. All of these topics were considered in Part I. Now, within this macroeconomic milieu, it is largely privately owned firms that make the everyday decisions with respect to trade, investment, and finance.

Many of the issues alluded to earlier will be discussed now, those issues that tend to bring international firms into conflict with sovereign states, especially ones acting as hosts to firms involved in direct foreign investment.

In this context, it hardly is necessary to point out that one need only read the daily newspaper or weekly news periodicals for a few weeks to realize that all is not well in the field of international business relations. Whether benign or pathological, most, but not all, host-country policies toward multinational firms represent a form of nationalism. Some policies are designed to serve the objectives of equity or economic efficiency, or both. The purpose of this chapter is to examine some of the more critical issues surrounding the involvement of foreign-based firms in the economies of host countries. We will focus mainly on direct foreign investment that involves foreign ownership of assets located within the borders of host countries.

ATTITUDES TOWARD DIRECT FOREIGN INVESTMENT

Countries differ in attitudes toward the foreign presence. As both Raymond Vernon and Jack Behrman point out,[1] foreign-controlled investments create tensions. Countries differ in the degree of tension they display. Comparatively, and on the average, developing countries would tend to rank higher than advanced nations in the degree of tension. Moreover, the underlying risk of direct control, expropriation, or nationalization generally would be greater among the developing countries. Although we might agree that countries differ in attitudes toward the foreign presence, we frequently have little understanding of the conflicts that arise. While there is some commonality among countries as to the demands and accusations being made, differences appear in the strength of certain convictions and in the measures taken in pursuit of those convictions. Countries also vary in the degree of ambivalence with which they approach these issues.

Many of the studies conducted on the benefits of foreign investment agree that the foreign presence is highly beneficial in an economic sense. Foreign firms bring in new techniques, help develop financial connections and export markets, elevate the level of competition and efficiency, and break down old agreements that constrain competition. Politicians and others often suggest, however, that the growth of foreign interests should be constrained in various ways, even to the point of reserving certain sectors to be exploited only by locally controlled capital.[2] Decisions of this kind are motivated by political or nationalistic, rather than economic, considerations. While they may be rooted in a distrust of foreign firms, because these firms answer to the government of another nation, perhaps more important is the fact that every nation has within it groups that wield political power and represent vested interests. It is these vested-interest

---

[1]Raymond Vernon, *Sovereignty at Bay: The Multinational Spread of U.S. Enterprises* (New York: Basic Books, 1971). Jack N. Behrman, *National Interests and the Multinational Enterprise: Tensions Among the North Atlantic Countries* (Englewood Cliffs, N.J.: Prentice-Hall, 1970).

[2]There is also the fear of dependence on foreign firms. For a review of these issues, see Thomas W. Allen, "Industrial Development Strategies and Foreign Investment Policies of Southeast Asian and South Pacific Developing Countries," in R. Hal Mason (ed.) *International Business in the Pacific Basin* (Lexington, Mass.: Lexington Books, D. C. Heath, 1978), pp. 51–92.

groups that see opportunities for economic gain by constraining the multinational firm. The end result, however, may be that society as a whole will be made worse off than it would be if constraints were not put into place. This chapter will examine some forms of conflict, recognizing that most are an outgrowth of nationalism and/or political pandering to vested interests.[3] The presentation will be weighted toward the developing countries because conflicts there are more critical and more sharply focused. Although most of the detailed discussion will concern these conflicts, it should be recognized that many of the same problems exist in advanced countries, albeit hidden behind a heavier veil.

ATTRACTING FOREIGN INVESTMENT THROUGH IMPORT-SUBSTITUTION PROGRAMS

Most countries have looked to industrialization as the means of reallocating resources, improving productivity, and achieving more rapid economic growth. To get the process of resource reallocation and more rapid growth started, governments have offered incentives to firms operating in high-priority industries. These incentives have taken several forms, but the more common ones are tariff protection, preferential treatment on imports of capital equipment or key ingredients, tax holidays or forgiveness of income and property tax, subsidized land purchases, accelerated depreciation, and subsidization of building purchases and rentals. These incentives were not intended to apply only to foreign investment; yet, in many instances, this has been the result simply because local firms did not possess, nor were they equipped with the knowledge to obtain, the factors of production required to succeed in the favored industries.

One of the favorite industrialization strategies adopted has been that of import-substitution programs. While there are other variations, let us use as an example consumer durables, such as washing machines, automobiles, and refrigerators, to describe the import-substitution process.

The market initially is served from abroad by importation of these items. As the market grows, it becomes large enough to support one or more small plants; however, import substitution through investment does not take place until a tariff is levied against imports. The tariff (or other incentive such as a subsidy with a quota or other exclusionary device against foreign production) must be sufficiently high (or the subsidy sufficiently great) that the price of home production to consumers is lower than the price that foreign producers can offer. If a tariff is used, the costs of

---

[3]We also should recognize that multinational firms are not beyond "greasing a palm" now and then. They, too, can and do become a part of vested-interest groups.

foreign goods are raised. If a subsidy is used, the cost to local producers is lowered. In either case, cost conditions must be so altered that it becomes attractive for producers to establish a plant within the consuming country to serve that market. Given that foreign firms are technologically better endowed and already have developed the market, it is most likely that the induced investment will be foreign controlled. Prices to consumers will be much higher, perhaps two or three times as high as those for the goods formerly imported.[4] Although there is forced expenditure-switching away from foreign-produced to locally produced goods, there is also an elevation of profits for home investment. The stimulates home investment, which may be either locally or foreign-controlled; however, one, two, or perhaps three firms can supply the entire domestic market easily, even with the smallest technically feasible plant. This creates an oligopolistically competitive situation or, perhaps, even a complete monopoly. Moreover, the key parts and supplies needed in the production of these consumer's goods must be imported because there is little or no indigenous capacity to produce them. In the process, resources are bid away from export industries. If the country lacks skills and the ability to transform,[5] exports may fall and, with the inclusion of monopolistic profits and repatriation of foreign capital, the rate of growth and the overall balance-of-payments position may be improved little if at all.

The next step in the cycle is born of frustration. Economic growth slows and the balance of payments fails to respond; hence, more of the same medicine is applied. As the initial import-substituting sector grows, demand for parts and other supplies becomes large enough to justify (in a technical sense) another import-substituting sector.[6] Tariffs are levied against parts and other intermediate goods. Backward linkages into the economy begin to form. There arises a small set of industries that supplies parts and components to the consumer-goods sector. The government, in addition to tariff protection, may impose local content requirements;[7] but again the investment is induced by tariff protection or subsidies or both.

---

[4]This includes the indirect cost of the subsidy where a subsidy is used as an incentive rather than a tariff.

[5]Resources are not readily available from the traditional sector because of low skill levels and lack of mobility.

[6]This is to say that enough demand exists to support the output of the smallest technically feasible plant, but usually not a plant having the lowest cost of production.

[7]Local content requirements are regulations stipulating that a certain percentage of the product being produced must be of local origin, that is, contain local materials, labor, and the like.

Ultimately, the market at each level of production becomes saturated, and the quest for industrialization and balance-of-payments relief through import substitution comes to an end. It is then that countries establish policies that pressure firms to develop products for export or to design programs that allow trade-offs between exported products and the imports needed in the production process. For example, in the Mexican and Brazilian automobile industries, which are foreign dominated, firms are allowed to import many components for assembly into automoblies if they also can develop export markets for locally produced parts or components. Despite the fact that much of the exported product could be produced more cheaply elsewhere, firms engage in these practices because the imported items they need can be produced even more cheaply abroad than in Mexico or Brazil.

Perhaps an example can be used to demonstrate the problem of import-substitution programs. Among the Association of Southeast Asian Nations (ASEAN) the largest market for automobiles is Thailand, with sales of about 90,000 units per year including personal automobiles, commercial vehicles, and trucks. Half of the total units are imported as completely built units. These are mainly commercial vehicles and trucks. The remaining half is of the completely knocked-down (CKD) variety, which undergoes final assembly in Thailand. The industry is protected by tariffs, and there are some 16 assembly plants that assemble these 45,000 units, or an average of less than 3,000 units per year per plant. This is equivalent to a three-day run for an optimum-sized assembly plant in the United States or Europe. This is just the beginning, however; virtually every country in the region has imposed local content requirements and most have achieved a level of 25 percent to 50 percent. Items that make up the local content are glass, radiators, starters, generators, tires, batteries, seats and upholstery, paint, springs, hoses, mufflers and tailpipes, external trim, steering linkages, metal bracings and fasteners, fuel tanks, brake components, and several other parts. Some of the jigs and hand tools used in the assembly process also are supplied locally. Wheels and a few other items sometimes are acquired locally; however, with approximately 100 different models being assembled in Thailand (and in other countries, too) there are few opportunities to exploit economies of scale, either in the assembly phase or in the local production of parts. The result is a vehicle that costs the consumer two to three times as much as the equivalent, fully-assembled vehicle imported from Japan or Europe. The story is much the same in many other developing countries.

The next step being taken is to force establishment of stamping plants, engine plants, and axle and transmission plants. These are by far the most capital-intensive aspects of automobile production, where economies of scale are extremely important.[8] Whereas assembly itself is relatively labor intensive and can be undertaken efficiently at almost any volume, other aspects of automobile production cannot. Within an assembly plant composed of body assembly, painting, and final assembly of components, it is the paint shop that sets the lower limit on optimum size. An optimum painting line requires on the order of 25,000 units per year. One progresses upward from there, in terms of the smallest economic module, as follows:

stamping plant	75,000 units/year
axle plant	130,000 units/year
transmission plant	130,000 units/year
engine plant	130,000 units/year

From this, we can see that one totally integrated plant requires a market of 130,000 units per year to achieve full efficiency and should involve the production of models that use approximately the same components.

To deal with this problem, the ASEAN countries are attempting to develop complementation programs in automobiles, home appliances, farm machinery, and several other product groups. Industry clubs have been formed with heavy reliance on the private sector in order to attempt greater specialization, with each country specializing on one or a few aspects of component production, yet each having its own final assembly plants. There would be cross-hauling of those components involving economies of scale, for example, stampings, engines, axles, transmissions, and wheels. Successful achievement of the full economies, however, undoubtedly would mean a reduction in the number of models produced and probably the number of firms involved. The countries essentially are attempting to deal with the problem of an inappropriate product mix and historical acquisition of inappropriate technologies, which have resulted in high-cost final products.

The ASEAN complementation program is a second-best solution aimed at correcting serious distortions resulting from indiscriminately applied import-substitution programs. It is a partial rejection of import substitution and a partial adherence to the notion of comparative advantage. It is evident that the entire ASEAN market of about 350,000 units per year (cars, trucks,

---

[8]In a study conducted by Mason, it was found that capital per worker in assembly averaged about $12,000 at 1978 prices. In stamping, the capital-per-worker ratio was about three times that for assembly; and in engines, axles, and transmission production, it was even more. See R. Hal Mason, "Technology Transfers: A Comparison of American and Japanese Practice in Developing Countries," working paper, Graudate School of Management, UCLA, 1978.

and commercial vehicles in total) cannot sustain an integration of production for all the firms involved, including General Motors, Ford Motor, Chrysler, Nissan Motors, Isuzu Motors, Mercedes Benz, Fiat, and others. Even if one firm were given a monopoly, efficient integration of production across countries would imply no more than three or four models of vehicles.

As just noted, the foreign firm is often better able than local firms to take advantage of the incentives offered by host governments. This appears particularly true in developing countries, although it is not confined to them. Import-substituting industrialization strategies have attracted foreign firms to invest; in many instances, these firms in turn have become dominant in their respective sectors. This is a situation that generates conflicts between the foreign firms and host governments.

CRITICISMS OF DIRECT FOREIGN INVESTMENT

The criticisms of foreign investment are numerous and often are linked to the type of investment involved. Moreover, policy measures taken vary with the type of investment and the dominance and visibility of the foreign firm.

At one time, because they lacked government infrastructure, technology, marketing skills, and management know-how, the developing countries were in a poor bargaining position vis-a-vis foreign firms. The situation has changed dramatically over time, however. The countries now recognize the value of the resources they possess. Not only have they become more skilled in the bargaining process, but they are more ready to exert their sovereignty. The outcome is what one would expect in a bilateral monopoly where one bargainer becomes increasingly well-informed and much of the foreign technology and know-how has been transferred. Whereas initially the countries were highly dependent, it is now the companies who are dependent. Under these circumstances, the countries can and have increased their share of the profits, particularly in the extractive industries. During the past two decades, host-country governments have increased their share of the earnings stream through increased taxation, profit sharing and even direct ownership.

Most countries, moreover, now screen investment proposals to see whether or not any new investment meets certain criteria, such as its

1. Contribution to employment.
2. Location.
3. Contribution to training.

4.   Contribution to perceived national needs for new technology.
5.   Development of managerial and high-level technical skills.[9]

Despite the changing conditions, foreign firms continue to be accused of being exploitative; the implication of many arguments is that foreign firms somehow take unfair advantage. Morever, they are seen as a threat to national sovereignty. The list of complaints is lengthy. Some of those most often voiced are that international firms

1.   Restrict or allocate markets among subsidiaries and do not allow manufacturing subsidiaries to develop export markets.
2.   Extract excessive profits and fees based on monopolistic advantage.
3.   Enter the market by "taking over" existing local firms rather than developing new productive investments.
4.   Finance their entry mainly through local debt and maintain a majority or even 100 percent of the equity with the parent.
5.   Divert local savings away from productive investment by nationals. (Much the same is said for other resources, that is, they hire away the most talented personnel and the like.)
6.   Restrict access to modern technology by centralizing research facilities in the home country and by licensing subsidiaries and others to use only existing or even outmoded technologies.
7.   Restrict the "learning-by-doing" process by staffing key technical and managerial positions with expatriates.
8.   Fail to do enough in the way of training and development of personnel.
9.   Behave badly with respect to social customs or the objectives of the national plan.
10. Distort undesirably the income distribution.
11. Stimulate consumer demand for frivolous and sometimes undesirable luxury goods.
12. Contribute to price inflation,
13. Dominate key industrial sectors.
14. Answer to a foreign government.

[9]For a review of several countries' screening programs, see: R. Hal Mason, "Technology Transfer Control Systems: The Case of East and Southeast Asian Developing Countries," in *Proceedings of the International Conference on Technology Transfer Control Systems,* University of Washington, Seattle, 1979. See also Richard D. Robinson, *National Control of Foreign Business Entry* (New York: Praeger, 1976).

This list is not exhaustive, but it identifies the key criticisms that in turn are the result of underlying conflict.[10]

SOURCES OF CONFLICT

We ask: What are the causes of conflict? Conflict arises from an asymmetry of goals or objectives, such as between host country and investing firm. Host countries have certain goals, which may or may not be explicitly stated. Frequently, multinational firms do not serve these goals as nearly optimally as host-country governments believe they should. Thus, the major source of conflict comes from a divergence of the country's and the firm's goals. This divergence need not be of the firm's making, because the country's goals may change over time and, indeed, opposing goals sometimes exist simultaneously within a single country. Conflict also may occur when the country's emphasis shifts from one goal to another: the firm may become the focal point for animosity or frustration if it is unable or refuses to adapt readily. If the goal is nationalism (local ownership or control of the means of production), there is no way in which the foreign firm can adapt, short of divesting itself of a majority, or perhaps the entirety, of its capital in the subsidiary.

The process of economic development and the policies surrounding it can and do affect the structure of goals and the relative emphasis each is to receive. Foreign direct investment may at one point in time serve the perceived goals and at another point in time may not. Under circumstances in which the country is short on know-how in particular sectors and the potential for improved productivity and growth are great, foreign direct investment is likely to be welcomed and embraced. Once the know-how is largely transferred and the potential for further gains in productivity and growth are not so great, however, the foreign presence may seem burdensome. Under the appropriate circumstances, it indeed can be; that is, it can extract excessive profits based not on its productive contributions but rather on either its monopolistic position or the continuing receipt of subsidies that were provided initially to attract its entry and accumulated know-how.

The complaints listed in the preceding section are but the external signs of the underlying difficulty. Most of the policy measures being taken by host countries, however, often are designed to deal one-by-one with

[10]For an extensive review, see C. Fred Bergsten, Thomas Horst, & Theodore H. Moran, *American Multinationals and American Interests* (Washington, D.C.: Brookings Institution, 1978), Chapter 10.

these symptoms, rather than directly with the true sources of conflict. There are a few exceptions to this statement, and, most particularly, one of the exceptions tends to be national ownership (public or private) as a policy goal. Where this is the case, the source of conflict often is dealt with directly through forced divestiture of a part or all of its equity capital by the foreign firm.

A Clash of Goals

What are the goals of most countries? What is there about direct foreign investment that makes it desirable or undesirable in relation to these goals? These questions demand answers. Some of the major goals toward which countries direct their policies are:

1. Economic growth.
2. Reasonably full employment of the trained work force.
3. Reduction of unemployment or underemployment among the less skilled.
4. Reasonably stable prices.
5. Balance-of-payments equilibrium.
6. Reasonably equitable distribution of national income.
7. Control over the pattern of economic development and use of technology.

In addition to these goals, there may be the objective, either stated or unstated, of nationalizing the ownership in certain sectors. Insofar as foreign-owned firms participate in these sectors, they become a subject of conflict.

Not discussed here are a nation's broad fiscal, monetary, and exchange-rate policies and how they are or should be directed to these ends. Instead, the focus is on the role of international investors in assisting or retarding countries in achieving these ends. At the same time, it should be recognized that firms, too, have goals. The international firm hopes to:

1. Obtain a satisfactory return on its invested capital.
2. Allocate production, marketing, financing, and research resources among its subsidiaries, based on economic efficiency or other performance criteria.
3. Maintain its technological and other proprietary advantages.
4. Keep financial risks within tolerable limits.

Because they have many alternatives and great flexibility for reallocatiion of resources, international firms will respond differently than will purely national firms to host-countries' policies. This, too, becomes a point of frustation for host countries.

It is not entirely clear from a simple statement of country and firm goals that there can be and are incongruencies between the two sets. In terms of country goals, direct foreign investment, under appropriate circumstances, offers certain advantages not obtainable from locally controlled investment. Generally speaking, however, foreign investment is not specifically invited in. It comes in response to profit opportunities that may be the result of government policies and incentives toward investments, including those made by nationals. Indeed, foreign investment may be an unintended consequence of protective policies.

We can state the sources of conflict in relation to goals in terms of benefits and costs. First, the main benefit the host country hopes to obtain from foreign investment is an augmentation of national resources and improved allocation of existing resources. These are essential in the pursuit of the economic-growth goal. The country also hopes that, in the longer run, the foreign firm's skill will be transferred to nationals through training programs and work experience. The firm, however, has invested in research to develop its technological superiority; thus, it does not want to transfer completely all of its know-how. If it did, it would be unable to maintain its competitive advantages over local firms. As a result, the host country continues to be technologically dependent on the foreign firm. This constitutes one basis for conflict.

A second national goal often is the conservation of foreign exchange, which may result in firms being evaluated on the basis of their contributions to the balance of payments. The country may hope that the foreign firm will produce for export; however, if the installation is in a protected industry, its costs may be higher than those of other of the firm's subsidiaries located in other countries. The firm chooses to supply markets from low-cost rather than high-cost sources. The country, however, takes this as not being its interests when it believes there is a need to stimulate exports.

Countries are concerned about economic growth (the intertemporal allocation of resources), on the one hand, and equity (distribution of economic gains from growth), on the other. They desire the gains to be obtained from foreign capital, technology, and managerial know-how but at a cost they consider to be tolerable. Conflicts arise when the costs are considered intolerable in relation to the benefits received, and the costs need not be economic ones. They may be sociopolitical instead; and, indeed, they may be imagined rather than real. Although foreign participants either do for the country something it cannot do alone, or do more effectively what already is being done, countries nevertheless wish to develop their own form of industrialization. This is difficult to do if a large proportion of the capital in key sectors is controlled by outsiders.

This leads us to a discussion of the conflicts arising from the multinational firm, the perceived threat of imperialism, and the economic effects of direct foreign investment.

The Multinational Firm as a Source of Conflict

Multinational firms are unaccountable in many senses. They answer to a multiplicity of government jurisdictions, each of which has only partial information on the total operation of the enterprise. Any single nation has control only over that portion of the firm residing within its borders. While its government may be able to influence the decisions taken in other countries, that influence is at best remote and at worst nonexistent. The multinational firm has the advantage of well-developed intelligence regarding sources of supply, market conditions, and the like; and it bases its decisions on this information. It can expand or withdraw. It can dictate to its subsidiaries what the role of each is to be. It can reallocate from one subsidiary to another, based on relative rates of profitability and risk. Unlike a purely national firm, it can resist the pressures of any single government by threatening to withdraw or by curtailing activities. With some exceptions, the purely national firm is not so well equipped with information on alternatives elsewhere. As a consequence, it is much more likely to accommodate government pressures. This distinctive characteristic of the multinational firm rankles host governments that may be attempting to shape the destiny of particular industries, and the firms therein, through an economic plan. The multinational firm may not fulfill neatly the role assigned to it. This is not to say that multinational firms are above sovereignty, but they are in a position of greater flexibility vis-à-vis national firms when dealing with the governments concerned.

A second point of rancor is the fact that no matter how multinational a firm becomes, it nevertheless does have a home country where it is headquartered. For some host governments this is cause for apprehension. Private foreign investors, including the multinational firm, can be caught up in big-power politics such that their behavior and decisions at times may be based on home-country pressures. Moreover, in its application of antitrust laws, the U.S. government, for example, has not been averse to invoking extraterritorial rights.

The Perceived Threat of Imperialism

Developing countries also voice the fear that they may be relegated, so to speak, to "second-class citizenship" by multnational firms—doomed to the role of supplying raw materials and cheap labor but never becoming an integral part of the production and marketing process that relies heavily on new technology and know-how. Moreover, any investment that could provide technological capacity and, ultimately, the ability to participate more fully in the world economic community may not be forthcoming. Manufacturing investments are designed almost exclusively to serve the local market and in many instances are so constrained by the multinational parent. The serving of industrial export markets is reserved to the parent or to one of its advanced-country subsidiaries; thus, developing countries envision a potentially bleak future for themselves should "free investment" be allowed to go unchecked by the government.

Of course, it also can be argued that if the developing countries had not squandered their capital and most highly skilled personnel on inefficient import-substituting programs, they might have been able more effectively to mount an export-promotion program. This might be countered by some to the effect that, "No matter, even if we had, the advanced countries would never have opened their markets to our exports." The question is: Why was Japan able to penetrate advanced-country markets, especially that of the U.S., despite the fact that it did not have large natural resources and faced the same tariff barriers? One answer is that Japan, unlike the developing countries, was never a colony, nor was its industrial sector ever dominated by foreign firms. Colonialism in many instances throttled the incipient industrialization of these countries. The mother country made allocative decisions that built up domestic industry while insisting on specialization among the colonies on production of primary commodities and simple intermediate goods. Developing countries see a close analogy between the "mother country" and the "mother corporation." There is the feeling that, should allocative decisions be left entirely to the "mother company," the developing-country subsidiary will be left to accomplish merely menial tasks that contribute only modestly toward the goals of economic development.

Even when a subsidiary could be considered to be a good corporate citizen and brings in valuable know-how, there will be distrust. Because the mother company "giveth," suspicions are that the mother company also "taketh away." It is this being "above and beyond" the sovereignty of the state that is nettlesome.

Economic Effects of Foreign Investment

Every investment has distributional, allocative, balance-of-payments, and dynamic growth effects. The dynamic growth effects are what most countries are seeking when they invite foreign investors in. Perhaps this is done without sufficient recognition that there also will be distributional effects on national output. The particular recipients of total gains will be affected especially by distributional differences between local capital and foreign capital. In addition to the dynamic growth effects, countries hope that foreign investment will help bring about a reallocation of resources; however, with reallocation, there are always gainers and losers. Even though gains to society as a whole may far outweigh the losses, if the losers are politically potent, there may be great resistance to change. The foreign firm becomes the likely scapegoat on which to place the blame for the losses of a few. If there is a strong nationalistic bent, even those who gain from the foreign presence may be propagandized into believing that they too are somehow worse off because "foreigners" are using "their" resources.

This should not be construed to mean that foreign investment is always beneficial. Foreign firms can be just as guilty of misallocating resources and of constraining competition as can locally controlled firms. Factor markets often are distorted by import-substitution policies that favor tariff protection and import controls. Consequent high rates of return attract the foreign investor. This, coupled with permitting several firms into the market, may result in small, uneconomic plants. Overvalued currencies, rapid rates of inflation, and pegged interest rates also favor capital misallocation (plants that are relatively too capital intensive). There also will be income redistribution within the economy. Little notice is taken so long as the redistribution is from one group of nationals to another; however, when the foreign investor participates in this redistribution (i.e., he shares in the subsidy), the redistribution is from nationals to foreigners. It is then that foreign firms are accused of being exploitative. It seldom is recognized that it is the industrialization policies, rather than the foreign firm, that are at fault for the misallocation of resources and redistribution of real wealth away from nationals to foreigners. It also is true that once an import-substitution program is embarked upon, reversal of the process is difficult because local investors and certain local labor groups also share in the subsidies. Thus, governments may choose to place controls over foreign capital rather than to remove the source of the distortions that result in redistributive effects.

Redistributive Effects of Foreign Investment. Whether or not the foreign presence brings a net benefit to the host country depends on the gains in productivity and growth as compared with the costs of the subsidies received. If foreign firms are dominant in preferred sectors and the incentives are large, the redistribution of income away from nationals to foreign residents can outweigh the gains from resource reallocation and growth. Also, with tariff protection, we must consider as a cost the diminished gains from international trade resulting from protected domestic production. As

Mundell[11] has demonstrated, use of protective tariffs to attract foreign capital can be beneficial only if there are external economies (learning by doing, for instance). That is to say, the foreign firms would have to stimulate productivity by more than enough to cover the profits captured by their capital investment if the country is to be made better off by the foreign investment. If the country overconceded in its initial attempts at industrialization, and if competition did not emerge sufficiently to drive down the profit rate, then the foreign firm would receive a windfall gain: a rate of return to its capital in excess of that which would have induced its entry. Under these circumstances, the host government would have a legitmate reason for changing its behavior toward the foreign firm. The obvious solution would be to lower the tariff protection, if this were the initial inducement. By so doing, imports would be encouraged and the profit rate would be driven down by competitive forces. Balance-of-payments considerations, however, may preclude such a move. In a static sense, it may be more costly in foreign exchange to pay for the imports than to service the repatriation of the foreign firm's earnings.

Host governments may seek other means to redistribute a part of the surplus away from foreigners back into the hands of nationals. These efforts may be accompanied by the overtones of nationalism, yet there are instances where the objectives of efficiency, growth, and equity are served. Whether they are depends on the prevailing conditions; but, regardless of whether these objectives are served, we can expect that international firms will confront a growing multiplicity of direct controls as the future unfolds. Conditions of entry and conditions for remaining are likely to become more, rather than less, restrictive.

Another aspect of the redistributive effects of foreign investment has to do with the distribution of income among various domestic groups as industrialization proceeds. It is sometimes the case that the rich do get much richer while the poor are standing still or barely improving their lot. It also is true that the income distribution has become more egalitarian in several developing countries as industrialization has proceeded. Multinational firms often are blamed for skewing the income distribution to favor the rich; however, firms seldom get the credit for making the income distribution more egalitarian. The facts appear to be that there is little relationship between the degree to which multinationals are present and the type of income distribution a country actually has.[12] Much more hinges upon the tax structure and the degree to which specific governments are

[11]Robert A. Mundell, "International Trade and Factor Mobility," *American Economic Review,* 47: 3, 1975, pp. 321–335.

[12]See Bergsten, Horst, & Moran, *op. cit.,* pp. 361–364.

committed to a more egalitarian income distribution. The effect, if any, of foreign investment on income distribution is still a controversial and underexplored field.

Balance-of-Payments Effects of Direct Foreign Investment. Foreign investment is desired not only for its potential ability to bring about resource reallocation and improved productivity. Balance-of-payments reasons also figure in country strategies, often as a primary consideration. Foreign exchange is a scarce resource for many countries, especially the developing ones. It provides command over the complementary factors needed to foster an industrialization program. As we have noted, one way to attracting these factors is through import substitution. We may ask: If foreign exchange is a scarce resource, why not obtain it through export expansion rather than through development of import competing industries? The answer, or answers, are complex. Philosophically as well as mechanically, it is easier to identify home markets than it is to identify and penetrate foreign markets. Moreover, the infant-industry or learning-by-doing arguments are persuasive. It is argued that since the country does not possess the needed complementary factors, it is not in a position to export. This is mainly true; however, to attract resources to serve the local market through import substitution can be no more justified on economic grounds than is attracting them into export expansion, except that an import-substitution program is more easily implemented. There also is always the supposition that subsidized infant industries eventually will grow up to become competitive and able to export.

It is appealing to believe that the subsidy paid to import-competing industries is captured at home while the same subsidy paid to exporters is captured abroad; that is, that the redistribution of income under import substitution is from one group of nationals to another (from consumers to producers) while the subsidy to export expansion is from nationals to foreigners (nationals *in toto* to foreign consumers). Nothing could be further from the truth, so long as the needed complementary factors are owned by foreigners. This reality is one of the key sources of conflict.

Direct foreign investment does have an effect on a country's balance of payments; however, the effect changes with the passage of time. Initially, the foreign firm brings in capital in the form of machinery, materials, labor, and the like. Payment of these ordinarily must be made in foreign currency. Indeed, some countries insist that foreign investors cover the initial foreign exchange costs of new investments. If there is no such requirement, however, and if there is a well-developed local capital market, a large part of the total financing may be raised locally. If local savers are not induced to increase the proportion of their income saved, then someone (if not the firm) must borrow abroad. Thus, new investment, if it cannot be financed by increased local savings, must be financed abroad, either directly by the investing firm or by a financial intermediary. The result is a capital inflow, that is, the savings of foreigners are brought in.

Once an investment has been put into place (its gestation period over) and the plant is made operational, there is a second effect on the balance of payments. If the investment is import competing, there will be expenditure-switching away from foreign-produced goods to goods now produced at home. The balance of payments is affected positively in an indirect manner. If the investment produces goods for export, the balance of payments is affected directly in the positive direction. Indeed, when investments are enticed in for balance-of-payments reasons, it is this effect that countries seek. In the longer run, however, there is a third effect as firms begin to repatriate their capital, providing, of course, that the investment is profitable. If it is profitable, then the foreign owners wish to be rewarded for having risked their capital initially. It is the promise of reward that induces firms to invest in the first place. To conserve on foreign exchange, however, a likely target for control is the profits of foreign firms. Several countries have placed ceilings on the amount of profits that can be repatriated each year. Through exchange control, they also may discriminate against profit repatriation by offering a less favorable rate of exchange than that offered for other purposes.

Policies that restrict the level of profit repatriation are in conflict with the desire to avoid external domination. Countries cannot have it both ways. If the firm cannot repatriate, it has little choice but to plow its earnings into further investment or to engage in deceptive means of profit repatriation. If it plows its earnings back, it must grow. Indeed, it is through this mechanism that some foreign-owned subsidiaries have become large and even dominant in their chosen economic activities. Not in all cases did this occur merely because the firm could not repatriate its profits. Usually, plowing back retained earnings occurs because profits are high and there are lucrative opportunities yet to be exploited.

The placement of ceilings on the amount of profits, licensing fees, and royalties that can be repatriated has encouraged various forms of deception. One is the use of intracorporate transfer prices as a means of repatriating profits.

Ultimately, the net effect of a direct foreign investment upon the balance of payments depends upon the efficiency of the investment. If it is located in a small country, is protected behind a tariff wall, is unnecessarily small, and is unable to compete in the international market, its net effect on the balance of payments is most likely to be negative. Whether or not it is negative depends upon the initial conditions present before the investment came in. Only under rare circumstances would such an invest-ment be an improvement over internationally competitive imported goods. Externalities would have to be large indeed. Regardless of the efficiency qualities of foreign investment, however, it is likely to be singled out for special treatment on balance-of-payments grounds, insofar as profit repa-triation is concerned, during balance-of-payments crises.

HOST-COUNTRY RESPONSES TO FOREIGN INVESTMENT

Developing Countries' Concerns

Host-country responses to foreign investment vary. Much depends upon the perceived degree of dependence on the foreign presence, the relative dominance of foreign firms in certain sectors, and the degree to which the operations of foreign firms are subsidized by the host government. Various policy stances are taken.

Some policies are designed to redress the balance with respect to the distribution of income between nationals and foreigners. Other policies are motivated purely and simply by overt nationalism. Nationalistic policies are designed to reduce the influence of, and even dependence on, external forces. They are politically motivated. An example is the reservation of certain sectors for locally owned firms. Such a policy does not have economic efficiency or even economic equity as its objective. Even if a foreign firm obviously were much more efficient than locally controlled firms, it would not be allowed to invest in the restricted sector. Thus, the products or services forthcoming would be more costly than necessary. Even national-defense arguments for foreclosing foreign investment from certain sectors are rather weak. The fact that foreigners own the resources does not mean they cannot be used for national purposes. Subsidiaries of foreign corporations are chartered in the host country and ultimately must answer to its laws, just as do corporations owned by nationals. Foreign-owned firms do not exist in a vacuum that cannot be touched by host governments. If national survival were threatened by foreign firms, the host government could use the ultimate among its prerogatives: it could confis-cate or nationalize the property. Foreclosing foreign firms from participation in selected sectors merely denies the country access to its skills and operating knowledge.

Although most policies have nationalistic overtones, they are not always inefficient. Whether they are depends on the initial conditions. If foreign firms are subsidized heavily, and if local firms also share in the subsidy, it may be difficult politically to remove the subsidy. Other policy measures then are taken and are directed at the foreign firm. The object often is to reduce the cost of the subsidy paid to foreign firms while leaving the subsidy paid to local firms intact. The purpose is to obtain a distribution of income more favorable to nationals and, on occasion, to conserve on foreign exchange. Some of the policies adopted toward foreign firms are:

1. Require that foreign firms share ownership with nationals.
2. Require that a specified proportion of key positions in executive ranks and on boards of directors be held by nationals.
3. Remove foreign participation from technologically stagnant industries.
4. Place ceiling rates on royalties and fees paid for technology (and in some instances disallow foreign firms from collecting licensing fees from subsidiaries).
5. Renegotiate concessions contracts in extractive industries to be more favorable to local interests.
6. Insist that foreign firms raise more of their debt financing outside of local capital markets and use the local market to raise equity capital. (This not only assures participation by nationals but also contributes to the development of local financial institutions and markets.)
7. Pressure foreign firms to engage in wider scaled and more intensive training programs.
8. Continually increase local content requirements.
9. Pressure foreign firms to develop export markets.

It is hoped that such measures not only will achieve redistributive effects favoring nationals but also will internalize more quickly the foreign firms' technological and managerial know-how within the country and improve the country's foreign exchange position. Such policies serve the objectives of income redistribution and lowered dependency on the foreign presence.

Policy may shift from being very permissive at one point to being progressively restrictive. In priority sectors, policy will be permissive and will be accompanied by incentives to induce entry. As the know-how and skills become inculcated among nationals, there will be ever greater pressure to reduce the foreign presence.[13] Thus, technology-rich foreign investors likely will share in the incentive schemes, whereas foreign investors in mature industries likely will be pressured to share ownership with nationals or to sell out to local interests entirely. Perhaps as time passes and

---

[13]See R. Hal Mason, "Technology Acquisition in the Pacific Basin: Direct Foreign Investment versus Unpackaged Technology," in R. Hal Mason (ed.), *International Business in the Pacific Basin* (Lexington, Mass.: Lexington Books, D. C. Heath, 1978), pp. 117–129.

developing countries become more developed economically, we shall see some relaxation of controls.

There is virtually no empirical evidence regarding the effects that measures like those listed previously may have on economic welfare within the countries using them. There are arguments pro and con. Some feel that forcing foreign firms to share ownership will, in fact, stimulate domestic savings. The reasoning is that if nationals have the opportunity to invest in the operations of a well-known international firm, then they will, where those operations are visible and can be evaluated; whereas, if these opportunities are lacking, the funds would go, instead, into either consumption or speculative investments such as real estate. On the other hand, it is argued that these measures reduce the rate of return to foreign investment and therefore curtail the flow of new capital and technology coming in. Both, perhaps, are correct; yet it is almost impossible to evaluate the net benefits or costs of these measures.

Multinational firms use a counterargument that is almost patently empty. They argue that if nationals wish to share more fully in the gains made by foreign capital, nationals should buy stock in the parent organization. If, however, General Motors-Holden in Australia is reaping a 25 percent return on capital, whereas General Motors Corporation as a whole reaps but 18 percent, Australians investing in the parent company would not obtain as much on their investment as they could by investing in the local subsidiary. Of course, it works both ways; but, generally speaking, the returns on investment among the foreign subsidiaries of multinational firms tend to exceed the returns they obtain on home investment.

A more persuasive arguement for ownership participation in the subsidiary rather than the parent is that nationals, in this way, will have some say in the operations of the subsidiary. In contrast, if they invest in the stock of a gigantic multinational firm, they shall have little or no say in the operations of either the parent or the subsidiary.

All of the policy measures we have noted do tend to redistribute income from foreigners to nationals. While some of them may induce greater local savings and foster dynamic growth effects, they also reduce the rate of return to foreign capital. Taken in isolation, these conditions would suggest that the flow of foreign investment would be constrained; however, some argue that so long as foreign investment yields a risk-discounted rate of return greater than that obtainable on home investment, multinational firms neither will be driven away nor necessarily reduce their investments. Most important, here, is the consistency and fairness of policies.

These issues remain open questions. The country using restrictive policy measures may very well obtain a redistribution of income favoring nationals, an internalization of know-how through greater participation by nationals, and an increase in productive local savings by the investment in foreign-controlled firms. It also may experience a lower level of foreign participation and total capital investment than would have been the case otherwise. There is no precise method of evaluating the outcome. Perhaps more important than almost any other variables are the relative levels of economic activity and the rate of growth. If a country is growing rapidly and is not plagued by serious cyclical disturbances, foreign investors will continue to invest despite highly restrictive policies—if those policies are applied consistently and fairly. Instability and uncertainty are the bane of an investor's existence. If these can be dampened, perhaps foreign investors will be willing to live within a highly constrained but predictable environment and, in the course of events, to accept a somewhat lower rate of return than they have become accustomed to under highly variable circumstances.

Another criticism of foreign investors is that they finance their investments in such a way that they hold the equity but nationals hold the debt. Nationals reason that if the mix of local financing could be shifted so that a greater share of equity and a smaller share of debt were held locally, there would be a smaller drain on the balance of payments, because profits to the foreign firm would be reduced. There is some truth to this; however, the conclusion is based on partial equilibrium analysis. Whether the balance of payments is improved depends on whether or not nationals reinvest their now-larger share of the earnings. If they reinvest more than the foreign firm would have, the possibility exists that the balance of payments will be improved. This depends on whether the new investment is as productive as one that would have been undertaken by the foreign firm. Sharing of ownership certainly will not necessarily lead to an improvement in the balance of payments. The balance of payments can be worsened if:

1. Foreign firms reduce their planned investments because the debt-to-equity relationship is altered and the return to foreign equity is thereby reduced.
2. Nationals cannot find investment opportunities that are as productive as those open to foreign firms.
3. Nationals consume the increased dividend income instead of reinvesting it.
4. Nationals invest abroad rather than at home. (The fact that nationals now receive a larger share of the profits need not mean they will invest at home rather than abroad.)

Balance-of-payments difficulties also figure in policies of local content requirements, export expansion programs, and the employment of nationals.

With few exceptions, however, it is difficult to make the case. Import substitution and local content requirements result in high-cost local production. If there are external economies (learning by doing) and import-competing industries become efficient, the balance of payments will be improved in the long run as these industries begin to export; however, it appears that this seldom occurs. Pressures on multinational firms to export may improve the balance of payments but may reduce the overall efficiency of the firm. Use of nationals may or may not improve the balance of payments. If nationals are equally as productive as the expatriates they replace and if they are not bid away from equally productive enterprises, the balance of payments will be improved. Sharing of ownership also may or may not influence the balance of payments in the positive direction. As noted, whether it does depends on underlying conditions.

Developing countries have argued, sometimes vehemently, that multinational firms are exploitative; that is, they take advantage and are able to extract monopolistic profits. If one examines rates of return to direct investments, though, there appear to be only modest differences in average rates around the world. Rates of return in Latin America do not seem greatly out of line with those in Europe.

It can be suggested that comparing rate-of-return data is a useless exercise. International firms can distort the data through their transfer-pricing practices; that is, they can hide their true profits by pricing goods that they transfer between operating units at other than market value. Transfer pricing as a mechanism for repatriating profits however, is probably much less widespread than is thought. Host governments have taken more stringent efforts to police transfer-pricing practices. Certainly in the extractive industries this has been true. Transfer prices are negotiated, as is the share of profits the firms are to receive. In the manufacturing sector there is, perhaps, even less latitude for firms to exploit the transfer-pricing mechanism, simply because little in the way of goods and services is transferred between developing-country subsidiaries and units operating elsewhere. This is changing, however, as the developing-country foreign subsidiaries in manufacturing have begun to export an increasing share of their total output.

The flow of licensing royalties and other fees is also a target. Much, if not most, of the flow of fees from international licensing involves relationships between parent firms and their international subsidiaries. Subsidiaries are licensed to use the parents and trademarks of the parent firm. This is often distasteful to host governments, which argue that multinational firms already have been given preferential treatment through protective measures. These firms, consequently, extract monopolistic profits and hence should not require their subsidiaries also to pay licensing royalties. The counterargument is that the subsidiary has at its disposal all of the accumulated experience of the parent firm, including its research discoveries, and should therefore share in the cost of technological advancement. Whether or not the developing countries are paying inflated prices for the know-how that they, in fact, receive is very much an open question; however, it would appear that it is not the licensing arrangements that are so much at fault as it is the industrialization policies of the developing countries. In the absence of high levels of protection, investments would be more competitive and could participate in international markets. Moreover, competition would eliminate monopoly profits and the high cost of imported and sometimes alien technologies.

Discussion of Developing-Country Reactions

The notion that a larger say by nationals in the affairs of foreign-owned firms will lead to changed behavior on the part of the the firm may have some validity, but it is not evident that any consequent alteration of corporate behavior necessarily will lead to an improvement in national welfare. The forms that changed behavior take are all-important. For example, there appears to be some evidence to indicate that the multinational enterprise as a partner in foreign–local joint ventures is much more likely to prefer a plowing back of earnings, whereas local partners tend to prefer higher dividends.[14] If the multinational partner accedes to the higher dividend payout, the country may be made worse off. Whether it is depends on what the dividends are used for. If they merely support luxury consumption rather than investment, economic growth may be lower than if there were no local sharing in ownership. Local investors may be more nationalistic, but they may not be more patriotic. Little evidence exists that nationals, simply because they are nationals, will behave in a way that increases the national gains from operating enterprises.

A second argument against local sharing, especially as applied to developing countries, is that those nationals who are sufficiently well endowed with capital to enter joint ventures are the ruling elite. They already are in political control. Sharing of control then compounds the problems of monopolization and cartelization of local industry. For example, in a study of Japanese joint ventures, it was found that 89 percent of total Japanese investment in the Philippines involved 77 ventures in which 46 prominent Filipino families held equity in one or more of these ventures.

---

[14]Karen Kraus Bivens and Enid Baird Lovell, *Joint Ventures with Foreign Partners: International Survey of Business Opinion and Experience,* (New York: National Industrial Conference Board, 1966) pp. 48–49.

The Philippine government also figured importantly as an equity owner in some of these ventures.[15] What is notable is that these joint ventures did little to disperse ownership and may even have concentrated if further as compared to what the outcome might have been using wholly-owned, foreign subsidiaries. In such cases, the foreign entrant merely becomes a party to such arrangements.

Of course, there is always a partner of last resort: the host government. While the foreign firm–host government joint venture may avoid the previous problem, it causes others. There is no longer an arm's-length bargaining between firm and government. Moreover, political considerations may frustrate the decision-making process. For example, the government partner may wish to sell certain outputs at or below cost, in order to subsidize producers in selected sectors of the economy. This is directly in conflict with the private investor's desire to maximize profit. This is not to say that joint ventures of this kind cannot succeed; however, it is perhaps with good reason that foreign firms harbor a healthy distrust of such arrangements and, if given a choice, will seldom become a participant. If they cannot control, they prefer to attain their ends by using other vehicles, such as licenses, technical-aid agreements, and management contracts.

Countries are concerned that they have operating within their borders enterprises that may not have as their first priority the needs of the local populace. These enterprises answer to a parent firm headquartered elsewhere a firm that ultimately answers to the nation or state in which it is incorporated. The resources committed by the firm also can be taken away if the opportunity for profit is brighter elsewhere. There is the feeling that these resources would be committed more tightly to national priorities if they were controlled by nationals or, at least, if nationals had a substantial voice in their development. Host countries somehow feel threatened; that is, they feel they cannot exercise their sovereignty adequately in confrontation with large multinational firms. Yet, in many ways, this is an empty threat, since the firms doing business within any host-country's borders are chartered locally. Perhaps the fear needs to be restated. It is not a threat to sovereignty so much as it is a threat to national welfare. If the state exercises its sovereignty against the multinational firm in the same way it might against a locally owned firm, the multinational firm has the option of withdrawing or curtailing its activities. It is this greater freedom to act that poses a problem for host governments. They desire the benefits to be gained from the multinational firm's presence but are uneasy about accepting the uncertainty connected with obtaining the benefits.

It is still an open question whether or not behavior can be altered

[15]See Mamoru Tsuda, *A Preliminary Study of Japanese–Filipino Joint Ventures,* (Quezon City, Philippines: Foundation for Nationalist Studies, 1978).

beneficially by having local equity share in firms controlled by foreign capital. For the future, we might expect increasing pressure for local participation, regardless of the fact that most arguments by the proponents are at best misleading. There is no evidence that nationals are more influential in management among joint ventures as compared with wholly-owned subsidiaries. There has been a continuing effort on the part of foreign firms to prepare nationals for positions of managerial responsibility. While it is true that the positions of chief executive officer, chief financial officer, and chief engineer or scientist often are reserved for expatriates, there are many exceptions. Even among joint ventures where the foreign firm is a minority holder, these jobs may be held by expatriates under a management and technical-aid contract. Local sharing in ownership cannot erase the realities of skills shortages in these high-level classifications. It would seem that nationals are as likely to internalize the know-how if employed by wholly foreign-owned subsidiaries as they would in a joint venture.

The balance-of-payments issue is even more dubious. As we noted previously, where capital is subsidized, foreigners share in the subsidy and there is a transfer of real wealth from nationals to foreigners. Repatriation of monopolistic or excessive profits can be critical. Additional exports must be generated or imports must be curtailed if returns to foreign ownership are to be serviced. If the burden is considered too great, there are several mechanisms that can be used to reduce the burden, but forcing local sharing in ownership would not appear to be one of the more effective. If it is attractive for foreign owners to take dividends instead of reinvesting the earnings stream, it may be just as attractive for nationals to do the same. It also may be just as attractive for nationals to transfer their dividends to another country. Where this is true, local ownership has the same balance-of-payments effect as foreign ownership.

There may be peculiar reasons as to why a foreign firm has monopolistic advantages not afforded to local capital. If this is the case, the host government is faced with a dilemma. Should it invite in more foreign firms in hopes of increasing competition and driving down the rate-of-return to capital, or should it attempt to regulate the foreign firm as it would a utility? Certainly, if there are economies of scale, inviting more firms in may result only in small, uneconomic plants. While the rate of return to foreigners and their profit repatriation are reduced, this is accomplished by increasing the cost of output.

Summary on Developing-Country Responses

The requirements that there be nationals on the board of directors, that the managing director be a national, that nationals be included in the executive suite, and that nationals share in ownership are myriad. Presumably, it is expected that these requirements will induce local participation to be greater than if there were no requirements. We have virtually no evidence on this score, but the hoped-for effect is twofold: that the firm can be induced to become a better "national" citizen, and that its technology and know-how can be internalized more readily or made indigenous to the country. Perhaps these demands can have some effect, yet they may be but window dressing producing little real change in behavior or the acquisition of know-how. Local participation has an element of the learning-by-doing argument, and in the long run perhaps it does augment the supply of skills. In the short run, however, such requirements merely may constrain the supply of high-level skills by forcing the use of nationals rather than expatriates. Because of this artificial constraint on skills, the types of technology that can be transferred also may be constrained. While countries may become somewhat less technologically dependent in the process, they also may not receive the technology that is most efficient.

ADVANCED COUNTRIES' CONCERNS

The concern of advanced countries, generally, are not as overtly evident as those in developing countries. The industrial sectors of advanced countries are, on the average, much larger and more highly developed; thus, foreign firms in advanced countries, with a few exceptions, are less visible and have a proportionately smaller impact than is true in developing countries. This fact, however, does not insulate foreign investment from substantial criticism and, at times, antipathy in advanced economies.

Although some advanced countries share some of the same concerns as developing countries, the degree of control exerted is much lower. Generally, foreign firms are given the same treatment afforded to locally controlled firms. Like the developing countries, however, some advanced countries tend to reserve certain sectors[16] for nationals only, but usually this is in the form of public rather than private ownership.

In many instances, it has become a matter of national pride. To those having strong nationalistic sentiments, it is demeaning that the high-technology sectors have become so heavily dependent on the actions of a few multinational firms, regardless of national origin. With the exception of the possibility that foreign firms obtain an inordinate share of the subsidy offered by protective tariffs, there seem to be few really sound aruguments

[16]Railroads, communications, electric utilities, and banking are the main sectors that are reserved in some countries; however, in the Japanese case, there are very few lines of economic activity in which foreigners are allowed majority control.

for restricting foreign investment. Dunning's[17] research indicates that U.S. investors have contributed mightily to European growth and improved productivity in relation to the total European capital stock under their control. Safarian,[18] in his study of foreign-owned firms in Canada, concluded that the performance of foreign firms was, on the average, as good as or better than that of Canadian-owned counterpart firms facing similar industry characteristics. It is notable that U.S. investors have sought out not only the most rapidly growing sectors but also the most rapidly growing countries in Europe. It is there that they have focused their efforts, which indicates that they operate where profit potential is greatest while leaving the less-interesting possibilities to be exploited by local firms.

With the exception of Japan, advanced countries tend to treat foreign owners as though they were nationals; that is, they have no specific policy measures that either favor or penalize foreign investors in relation to local investors. Whatever actions are taken are more on the order of ad hoc decisions than they are of standing policy. Various types of pressures are brought to bear to influence firm behavior, but they often are ineffective. There is an implied threat that if conditions do not change there will be regulation; however, as yet, little has been done to control foreign investors on the basis that they are foreign. Even in Canada and Australia, where emotions and attitudes are quite sensitive toward foreign investment, there continues to be an even-handed treatment of foreign investors. Will this continue to be true, or will we see a proliferation of measures similar to those adopted by some developing countries? There is no ready answer to this question, but it is unlikely that the advanced countries will move as far as have some developing countries toward the detailed control of foreign investment. One might expect, however, that investment will be scrutinized more closely and that entry by takeover of local firms increasingly will be denied.

In many respects the arguments of advanced countries against direct foreign investment are more nationalistic than those of developing countries. Developing countries, because of their small markets and low level of skills, often are unable to take advantage fully of the advanced technology harbored in international firms. Moreover, the tariff protection offered often benefits only the foreign investor because local firms do not have the technical capabilities to participate on a major scale in the favored industries. Although these same conditions do occur in advanced countries, they

[17]John H. Dunning, *American Investment in British Manufacturing Industry,* (London: George Allen and Union, 1958).

[18]A. E. Safarian, *The Performance of Foreign-Owned Firms in Canada* (Washington, D.C.: Canadian–American Committee, National Planning Association, 1969).

are not nearly so pervasive there, yet the complaints are often much the same: that somehow advanced countries are victimized by foreign investment. It is difficult to make the case. By and large, foreign investors in advanced countries do have local competition, either from locally controlled firms or from other international firms. Generally, international firms have a keenly competitive spirit; they set the tone of economic activity. In Europe, where cartels and gentlemen's agreements had long held sway, international firms tended to "rock the boat" and were berated for behaving badly, not observing the well-developed traditions of doing business. What this means is that local firms may, for the first time, be confronted with the need to compete if they are to survive. It is always disappointing to learn that the "quiet life" is over and that one must work vigorously to assure survival.

"Takeover" has become a particularly odious term in advanced countries. Many international firms prefer to buy their way into a market instead of building from scratch. Because they have the capacity to make an operation more productive, they usually can offer attractive terms to local firms, who, in turn, sell out. Much of the expansion of foreign investment in Europe has been of this nature. The same phenomenon is observed in the United States, as European, Canadian, and Japanese firms find it increasingly attractive to serve the U.S. market through local production rather than imports.

It should be noted that the recent devaluations of the U.S. dollar vis-à-vis certain European currencies and the Japanese yen have altered the situation. It has become much more attractive for European and Japanese firms to invest in the United States. We are seeing a growing wave of takeovers of U.S. firms by foreign investors. Now that the "shoe is on the other foot," so to speak, it will be interesting to observe attitudes in the United States toward foreign firms. There are some who already advocate discriminatory legislation against foreign firms investing in the stocks of U.S. firms, presumably to thwart the acquisition of a controlling interest by foreign investors.

Examination of advanced-country attitudes toward foreign investment has been much less extensive than that offered on the developing countries; however, many of the complaints are the same and most arguments are rooted in nationalistic sentiments.

Summary

Host countries differ in the degree of tension they display toward direct foreign investment and hence toward the multinational firm. The larger and more visible the firm, the greater the tension is likely to be. There are also sectoral differences. Investments in primary production and utilities are viewed differently than those in manufacturing and trade.

Countries have growth aspirations and look heavily to the industrial sectors as a source of growth and economic transformation. But investments have allocative, distributive, and balance-of-payments effects. Out of these, conflicts often arise. When they do, governments will treat foreign-controlled investments differently from the way they treat locally controlled ones. Often, foreign investors become dominant in high-priority sectors where incentives to invest are offered. Large foreign firms are most able to capture the incentives because they have the appropriate endowment of technical and managerial know-how. The resulting reallocation of resources redistributes income, away from nationals and toward foreign residents. Efforts may be taken to redress the imbalance.

Initially, the treatment of foreign capital may be highly favorable, as an inducement to establish and/or expand high-priority sectors. As import substitution proceeds, local content requirements and exchange control also may emerge. Firms may be pressured to develop export markets if they wish to obtain the foreign exchange for needed imports and/or profit repatriation.

Nationalism plays an overriding role in the shaping of attitudes toward the large multinational firm, because it has great flexibility to change its patterns of production, marketing, research, and financing around the world. It also makes allocative decisions on the basis of efficiency and, in so doing, defines the role each subsidiary is to play in a centrally orchestrated corporate plan. The particular assignments may be in conflict with national needs as perceived by host governments. It is out of this set of conditions that conflicts will continue to emerge over how the nation's resources are to be used, who will control their use, and how the gains are to be shared between capital and labor and between local and foreign residents. Whether conflicts are sufficiently serious for foreign firms to be treated differently from local firms will depend on how society, through the political process, defines its welfare function and on the response of foreign firms to this societal definition.

SELECTED READINGS

Behrman, Jack N., *National Interests and the Multinational Enterprise: Tensions Among the North Atlantic Countries* (Englewood Cliffs, N.J.: Prentice-Hall, 1970), Chapters 3 to 5.

Bergsten, C. Fred, Thomas Horst, & Theodore H. Moran, *American Multinationals and American Interests* (Washington, D.C.: Brookings Institution, 1978).

Brash, Donald T., *American Investment in Australian Industry* (Cambridge, Mass.: Harvard University Press, 1966), Chapter XI.

Diaz-Alejandro, Carlos F., "Direct Foreign Investment in Latin America," in Charles P. Kinkleberger (ed.), *The International Corporation* (Cambridge, Mass.: M.I.T. Press, 1970), Chapter 13.

Doz, Yves L., *Government Control and Multinational Strategic Management: Power Systems and Telecommunication Equipment* (New York: Praeger, 1979).

Dunning, John H., *American Investment in British Manufacturing Industry* (London: George Allen and Unwin, 1958).

Dunning, John H, "Multinational Enterprises and Nation States," in A. Kapoor & Phillip D. Grubb (eds.), *The Multinational Enterprise in Transition* (Princeton, N.J.: Darwin Press, 1972), Chapter 28.

Grubel, Herbert G., *International Economics* (Homewood, Ill.: Irwin, 1977), Chapters 25 & 26.

Hawkins, Robert G. (ed.), *The Economic Effects of Multinational Corporations: Vol. 1* (New York: Jai Press, 1979).

Johnson, Harry G., "A Theoretical Model of Economic Nationalism in New and Developing States," *Political Science Quarterly*, 80, June 1965, pp. 169–185.

Johnson, Harry G., "The Efficiency and Welfare Implication of the International Corporation," in Charles P. Kindleberger (ed.), *The International Corporation* (Cambridge, Mass: M.I.T. Press, 1970), Chapter 2.

Kindleberger, Charles P., *American Business Abroad* (New Haven, Conn.: Yale University Press, 1969).

Kindleberger Charles P., & Peter H. Lindert, *International Economics,* 6th ed. (Homewood, Ill.: Irwin, 1978), Chapters 25 & 26.

Safarian, A. E., *The Performance of Foreign-Owned Firms in Canada* (Washington, D.C.: Canadian–American Committee, National Planning Association, 1969).

Streeten, Paul, "Costs and Benefits of Multinational Enterprises in Less-Developed Countries," in John H. Dunning (ed.), *The Multinational Enterprise* (London: George Allen and Unwin, 1971), Chapter 9.

Sunkel, Osvaldo, "Big Business and 'Dependencia': A Latin American View," *Foreign Affairs Quarterly,* April 1972, pp. 517–531.

Vaitsos, Constantine V., "Income Distribution and Welfare Considerations," in John H. Dunning (ed.), *Economic Analysis and the Multinational Enterprise* (New York: Praeger, 1974), Chapter 12.

Vernon, Raymond, *Sovereignty at Bay: The Multinational Spread of U.S. Enterprise* (New York: Basic Books, 1971), Chapters 5 to 8.

Vernon Raymond, *Storm Over the Multinationals* (Cambridge, Mass.: Harvard University Press, 1977), Chapters 6, 7, & 8 in particular.

Chapter 18

Epilogue

The purpose of this book is to introduce would-be decision makers to the world of international business. For those with experience in the international business field, the analysis offered also has aimed at sharpening perceptions and providing an analytical framework through which business decision-making processes can be aided and improved. Most of the discussion has been based on an economic interpretation of observed behavior. In this endeavor we are much indebted to many of our predecessors and contemporaries for their efforts in making comprehensible the events of a complex and interdependent world. We have drawn heavily on their contributions.

The field of international business has been the subject of rather detailed study for nearly two centuries. It has not been possible to review all of these many contributions; thus, we have been selective in our attempts to distill out of the literature the ideas that are of greatest use to business managers.

We have focused more on the external behavior of the firm than on the internal processes through which decisions are made. For the most part, managers have been viewed as rational economic agents. There is, however, another side to management, which, while not contrary to the view of the manager as an economic agent, is of a different character and should be discussed in a book of this kind.

Managers must plan and coordinate their decisions and decision-making units within the total enterprise. Most of our efforts have been directed toward these dimensions of the manager's job. In Part I, we examined the economic environment confronting international business firms. In Part II, we examined the economic aspects of decision making as though there were few problems internal to the firm in its international decision-making actions; however, the social and political aspects of the total environment and the internal processes of the firm are equally important. We cannot hope to examine all of the characteristics of the enterprises that are so heavily influenced by social and political factors. What we do wish to recognize is that international business takes place in a multicultural world. This, in itself, expands the number of variables managers must take into account when they enter the international arena. The result is that managerial behavior, staffing practices, training programs, marketing efforts, and so on must be altered to reflect different realities in different locations. Indeed, when one compares the practices of multinational firms in the United States with those of their subsidiaries located abroad, discernible differences emerge. Although the same general system may be applied in both settings, evidence indicates that there is substantial alteration of those systems to accommodate the local environment. It is also true, however, that there are discernible differences between the subsidiaries of multinational firms and locally owned and controlled firms. In terms of their practices, subsidiaries fall on a scale somewhere between home-country parents and locally owned competitors. They do adapt parent-firm methods and procedures, but they do not adopt totally the methods used by local firms. Many observers would agree that adaptation is a direct outgrowth of environmental factors. Certainly some, such as adaptation of production, are due to economic forces. Others, which may be far more important to the overall success of the firm, are triggered by culturally determined variables.

It is noteworthy that staffing practices often reflect the differing realities of different cultures. Those positions of employment that are not dependent directly on face-to-face relations, and are not dependent heavily on a sound knowledge of the culture, often are staffed by home-country expatriates rather than nationals of the host country. Jobs having a high cultural content tend to be staffed by nationals. The positions of chief executive, chief financial officer, and chief scientist or engineer may tend to be the preserves of expatriates. These positions often are insulated from direct negotiation with the environment. Even the chief executive officer may interact as much or more with expatriates than with nationals, because the banking connections of the subsidiary, suppliers, and the like often are composed of firms headquartered in the home, rather than host, country. Those positions that are more dependent on a knowledge of the cultural environment, including production manager, marketing manager, director of personnel and public relations, and legal services, are quite likely to be staffed by nationals. Of course, these are only general tendencies, with numerous exceptions.

In any case, the use of expatriates by foreign investors is not extensive, probably being less than one-half of one percent of total employment in U.S. subsidiaries abroad. Most of those are employed in managerial, technical, and professional capacities. In fact, the major reason expatriates are used as much as they are is that needed high-level skills are in short supply, particularly in developing areas. On the other hand, in Europe, where managerial and technical talent is more readily available, the use of expatriates is much more limited. The percentage of managerial and technical positions filled by expatriates in the developing areas undoubtedly will decline rapidly as economic development proceeds and the supply of locally available skills expands. This, of course, is the direction considered most acceptable by the developing countries themselves.

It will be interesting to see the extent to which multinational firms truly become international in their executive recruitment, staffing, and labor policies. To date, the internal processes of the firm, such as uniform reporting and evaluation procedures, labor and staffing plans, and the like, have tended to dominate in the positioning of personnel. Expatriates have been used extensively because they have been acculturated to the firm's mode of operation, but as a growing group of nationals acquires familiarity with the international methods and policies, and as cultural variables become more important, less concern for the maintenance of "homegrown" dominance in staffing decisions should be observed.

In that event, will management of subsidiaries become a preserve for nationals only? There appears to be a tendency in that direction, rooted not in the desires of multinational firms but in the nationalistic bent of many nations. The culmination of such a tendency would be hurtful to multinational firms. It would defeat their attempts to recruit, staff, and promote on the basis of merit. It also would reduce greatly their flexibility to shift talent to the geographic locations where it is most needed.

Staffing constraints, however, are only part of a larger issue. Multinational firms are attempting to integrate and to rationalize production internationally while they also meet the demand of nation-states for a larger voice in the decisions taken by these firms. Thus, while the multinational firm wishes to push the international environment toward greater homogeneity in order to simplify and rationalize its own operations, countries seem to be emphasizing the preservation of cultural identity and economic independence; therefore, the strengths that supported the multinational firm during a period of nearly unbridled expansion may not be the strengths most suited to the future, given worldwide inflation, energy shortages, and consequent nationalism and regionalism. Moreover, as was pointed out in Chapter 17, the countries themselves have become more knowledgeable and perhaps less trusting of the role of multinational enterprises in the process of industrialization.

In fact, the multinational enterprise grew up in a period of unprecedented liberalism and growth in the world economy. Since the Second World War, government restrictions on international trade and investment have been reduced progressively, leading to rapid expansion in both areas. This has been an ideal environment for the multinational corporation to develop and flourish in. The greatest strength of the multinational corporation, as has been noted many times in this book, is its ability to marshal resources efficiently, apply technology, develop markets, and organize its activities on a global scale. In order to exploit its inherent advantages, it must be able to move goods, people, and money freely among the countries of the world.

The liberal world in which the multinational corporation grew and prospered now is threatened by many adverse factors, perhaps most importantly by the fundamental disequilibrium introduced into the world economy by the enormous increase in oil prices that has taken place since 1973. The resulting structural balance-of-payments deficits of oil-importing countries has led to an enormous increase in debt and has raised the threat that imports might have to be restricted if continued balance-of-payments financing is not forthcoming. All oil-importing countries are searching for ways to control their deficits and ultimately may resort to restrictions on trade and investments. In fact, trade protectionism is increasing already. Without considerable discipline and wisdom on the part of all concerned, the international framework needed by the multinational enterprise may disintegrate.

In such an environment, the multinational firm may become a target vehicle through which countries may attempt to achieve ends not normally considered within the purview of the foreign investor. Particularly, it is likely that the multinational firm will be pressured in many ways to act as an agent for solving balance-of-payments problems and for securing the redistribution of world wealth and income.

If this happens, the position of the multinational firm will become increasingly untenable. It has grown and flourished because it has helped to provide benefits to all parties, both home and host countries. In the strained international environment that currently prevails, however, any movement by one country to secure benefits at the expense of others will call into question the fundamental value of the multinational corporations.

This, in fact, already may be happening, as many countries attempt to use foreign investors to help solve balance-of-payments problems by requiring certain levels of exports in return for incentives, such as the right to operate in a protected local market. These policies are viewed by many home countries as being similar to the beggar-thy-neighbor trade policies of the 1930s.[1] Increasingly, therefore, international investment by multinational firms is no longer regarded as a positive game in which all participants benefit.

The multinational corporation, as a central participant in the game, may end up being the major loser. Indeed, there are some who believe that the day of the multinational firm's ascendancy is coming to an end; instead of continued growth and integration of the world economy, we may be entering an age of disintegration and stagnation, given the existing structural imbalances and growing demands on limited resources.

Although we do not share fully this pessimistic view, it is one that cannot be ignored. Throughout this book we have described a system that has functioned reasonably well in meeting the material demands of an expanding world population. We close on the caveat that this system, should it endure, will be subjected to very serious stresses during the last years of the twentieth century. It shall be interesting indeed, to observe how well the multinational firm, a central character on the modern scene, will fare.

SELECTED READINGS

Bergsten, C. Fred, "Coming Investment Wars?" *Foreign Affairs* 53:1 1974, pp. 135–152.

Bergsten, C. Fred, Thomas Horst, & Theodore Moran, *American Multinationals and American Interests* (Washington, D.C.: Brookings Institution, 1978).

Vernon, Raymond, *Storm Over the Multinationals* (Cambridge, Mass.: Harvard University Press, 1977).

Wells, Louis, "The Internationalization of Firms from Developing Countries," in Agmon & Kindleberger (eds.) *Multinationals from Small Countries* (Cambridge, Mass.: M.I.T. Press, 1977).

World Bank, *World Development Report, 1979* (Washington, D.C.: World Bank, 1979).

[1]"Beggar-thy-neighbor" is a term coined by British economist Joan Robinson. It refers to policies that benefit one country only by subtracting benefits from another.

Name Index

Subject Index